The Baby Name Countdown

Meanings and Popularity Ratings for Over 50,000 Names

....Janet Schwegel....

PARAGON HOUSE
New York

DEDICATION

To my number cruncher and constant support, Bryan Larocque.

Published in the United States by

Paragon House
90 Fifth Avenue
New York, NY 10011

Manufactured in the United States of America

Canadian Cataloguing in Publication Data
Schwegel, Janet, 1959- The baby name countdown : popularity and meanings of today's baby names
ISBN 0-921377-02-9 1. Names, Personal — Canada. 2. Names, Personal — United States.
I. Title.CS2375.C2S25 1988 929.4'4 C88-091320-7
10 9 8 7 6 5 4

Please note: All governments and government branches who have supplied data for this book specifically disclaim responsibility for any analyses, interpretations or conclusions. As well, the publisher and author disclaim responsibility for any analyses, interpretations or conclusions, and for any typos or spelling errors.

Contents

What Is Special About This Book

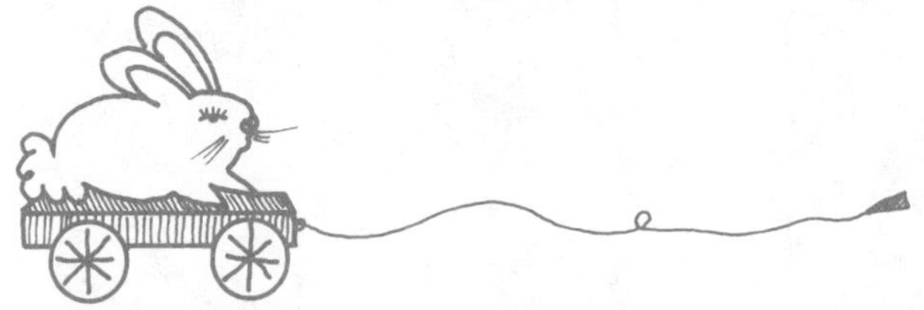

The Baby Name Countdown is an inspirational list of tens of thousands of first names given recently to North American babies. In addition to a vast list of unusual names and a complete list of popular names, you'll find ratings indicating the current popularity of the names, as well as the meanings and origins of the popular ones. While the meanings and origins of names don't change, the popularity of them does. That's why *The Baby Name Countdown* is vital in ensuring that you find the kind of name you want for your baby.

As you look through this book, you'll probably be surprised at the popularity of many names. Many of the names favored for children when today's parents were children are no longer the ones most frequently used; other names rarely used then are now topping the lists.

The terms popular and unusual are used in this book in a very specific sense: Names which were given to a minimum number of boys and girls in the data are called popular; names which were given to fewer than that minimum number are called unusual. In terms of the popularity ratings, names with a rating of .02 or greater are "popular"; those with a rating of .01 or less are "unusual."

All the popularity information in *The Baby Name Countdown* is based on actual records of births in Canada and the United States—almost 2 million children from every region of these countries. From the data on these births, the popularity of each name is given as a number per thousand. For instance, in the chart, the 100 most popular Boy names in North America, the number 32.4 beside Michael means that over all the data, of every thousand boys born, 32.4 were named Michael. In this section you'll see that, overall, Michael is the most popular name for boys these days, but when you check the tops sections for individual areas, you'll see that in a few regions, the name Christopher is more popular than Michael, followed closely by Matthew.

How to Use This Book

Start by browsing through it, just to familiarize yourself with its organization and to satisfy your curiosity about the popularity of your own name, your relatives' names, your friends' names, the names you've been considering for your baby . . . you've probably already done this. If you have, you've seen that the book is divided into three sections: The most popular girls' and boys' names (overall and by region), popular names with meanings, and unusual names.

Popularity ratings

The 100 most popular name lists and the popular names with meanings include popularity ratings. To understand the popularity ratings is to view them as relative rankings: **the higher the number, the more popular the name.** (The ratings for all the "unusual" names is .01 or less.)

The next thing you can count on is that the ratings are not simply rankings but can be multiplied or added: A name with a rating of 2 is twice as popular as one with a rating of 1. This means that you could add up the ratings for all the variant spellings of Christopher in the popular name section to find out whether it is actually more popular than the name Michael.

The ratings give popularity per thousand boys or girls, but by moving the decimal places in the population and the popularity rating to the right or left, you can quickly calculate other statistical frequencies.

For example, my own name, Janet, has a popularity of

.26 per 1,000

which is equivalent to

.026 per 100
2.6 per 10,000
26 per 100,000
and 260 per 1,000,000.

These figures are simply multiplications or divisions by 10, 100, and 1,000.

Advanced Arithmetic

If you enjoy arithmetic acrobatics, you can go further with the data in *The Baby Name Countdown* and estimate roughly how many children in any geographical location will receive a certain name.

Start with this fact:

The average birth rate in the United States and Canada is approximately 15 per thousand, meaning that for every thousand people, 15 children are born each year.

To calculate the approximate number of children that will be born in any geographical location, multiply that location's population by .015 (15 divided by 1000):

(1) $b = g \times .015$

where b is the number of births, and g is the population of some geographical location. Once you know the number of children born in a year in a community, you can estimate how many will be called a certain name using formula (2):

(2) $n = b \times p/1000$

where n is the number of children who will receive a particular name, and p is the popularity rating of that name.

For example, the city I live in has a population of about 600,000. To estimate how many children will be named Janet this year in this city, first I calculate the approximate number of children that will be born here:

(1) $b = g \times .015$

$b = 600{,}000 \times .015$

$b = 9000$

The popularity rating for the name Janet is .26. So to estimate how many children will be named Janet, use formula (2):

(2) $n = b \times p/1000$

$n = 9000 \times .26/1000$

$n = 2.34$

Based on current trends, this equation states that roughly two children born in this city this year will be named Janet.

You could also estimate the frequency of use of a name among other populations, using the following formula:

(3) $n = s \times p/1000$

where s is the number of children in the sample.

For example, if I'm curious how many children might have the name Michael in a kindergarten class of 30 children in 4 or 5 years, I can plug values into formula (3) thus:

$s = 30$ [the number of children in the class]

$p = 32.37$ [the popularity rating for Michael]

$n = s \times p/1000$

$n = 30 \times 32.37/1000$

$n = .9711$

In other words, I estimate roughly that almost all kindergarten classes will have one boy named Michael in four or five years.

The point of all these examples is that you can play with the popularity ratings to estimate statistical likelihoods of a certain number of children with a particular name in a particular place. (The term statistical is used to remind you that any calculations based on the data do not give you actual frequencies of use of names, but estimated—or statistical—probabilities based on all of the data collected being summed together. Further, due to rounding, these estimated probabilities are rough approximations.)

Finally, since all the unusual names have a popularity rating of .01 or less, if you use the rating .01 as p in the formulas above, you will get a very rough probability for an unusual name. For most of the unusual names, the frequency will be lower than that calculated using a p of .01.

Section I

Popular Names

The Most Popular Names in the United States in 1960 (in Order of Popularity)

GIRLS	BOYS
Mary	Michael
Deborah	David
Karen	Robert
Susan	James
Linda	John
Patricia	Mark
Kimberly	Steven
Catherine	Thomas
Cynthia	William
Lori	Joseph
Kathleen	Kevin
Sandra	Richard
Nancy	Kenneth
Cheryl	Jeffrey
Denise	Timothy
Pamela	Daniel
Donna	Brian
Carol(e)	Paul
Lisa	Ronald
Michelle	Gregory
Diane	Anthony
Sharon	Donald
Barbara	Charles
Laura	Christopher
Theresa	Keith

The 100 Most Popular Names in North America Today

• • • • GIRLS • • • •

27.7	Jessica
26.5	Ashley
21.6	Amanda
19.8	Jennifer
15.7	Sarah
12.4	Stephanie
11.8	Nicole
10.9	Brittany
10.3	Heather
10.2	Melissa
9.6	Megan
9.2	Elizabeth
8.8	Amber
8.1	Lauren
8.0	Danielle
7.7	Michelle
7.4	Christina
6.8	Crystal
6.2	Laura
5.9	Kimberly
5.7	Rachel
5.7	Amy
5.7	Tiffany
5.6	Samantha
5.1	Emily
5.0	Rebecca
4.7	Vanessa
4.4	Erin
4.2	Sara
4.2	Kelly
3.9	Jamie
3.8	Whitney
3.8	Katherine
3.8	Courtney
3.7	Angela
3.6	Andrea
3.5	Mary
3.4	Lisa
3.4	Lindsay
3.4	Lindsey
3.4	Erica
3.3	Shannon
3.2	Katie
3.1	Maria
3.0	Kristen
2.8	Allison
2.7	Alicia
2.6	Jenna
2.5	Kathryn
2.5	Christine
2.3	Victoria
2.3	April
2.2	Holly
2.2	Anna
2.2	Kristin
2.2	Tara
2.2	Natalie
2.2	Kayla
2.1	Julie
2.0	Natasha
1.9	Brittney
1.8	Cassandra
1.6	Krystal
1.6	Kathleen
1.6	Meghan
1.6	Catherine
1.5	Jacqueline
1.5	Melanie
1.4	Kristina
1.4	Brandy
1.4	Brandi
1.4	Alexandra
1.4	Caitlin
1.4	Monica
1.4	Chelsea
1.3	Patricia
1.3	Mallory
1.2	Leah
1.2	Krista
1.2	Hannah
1.2	Marie
1.2	Leslie
1.2	Candice
1.2	Stacey
1.2	Candace
1.2	Casey
1.2	Julia
1.1	Alison
1.1	Kendra
1.1	Margaret
1.1	Felicia
1.1	Dana
1.1	Katrina
1.0	Karen
1.0	Bethany
1.0	Brooke
1.0	Stacy
1.0	Jasmine
1.0	Valerie
1.0	Jillian

• • • • BOYS • • • •

32.4	Michael
28.9	Christopher
24.1	Matthew
19.7	David
19.4	Daniel
18.9	Joshua
17.9	Andrew
17.2	James
16.1	Robert
15.0	Ryan
14.4	John
14.1	Joseph
12.1	Brandon
11.9	Jason
11.3	Justin
11.3	Jonathan
11.0	Nicholas
10.4	Anthony
9.8	William
9.7	Eric
9.6	Steven
8.3	Adam
8.3	Kyle
7.7	Kevin
7.3	Brian
6.5	Thomas
6.4	Jeremy
6.4	Timothy
5.6	Tyler
5.5	Jeffrey
5.4	Mark
5.3	Richard
5.2	Benjamin
5.0	Stephen
4.5	Charles
4.5	Dustin
4.5	Patrick
4.4	Jacob
4.4	Aaron
4.3	Scott
4.3	Sean
4.2	Zachary
4.1	Nathan
4.0	Alexander
4.0	Jose
3.7	Bradley
3.7	Paul
3.7	Gregory
3.6	Jordan
3.4	Travis
3.4	Jesse
3.1	Shawn
3.0	Kenneth
2.9	Bryan
2.9	Cody
2.9	Derek
2.6	Corey
2.6	Samuel
2.5	Chad
2.2	Shane
2.1	Jared
2.1	Peter
2.1	Cory
1.9	Brett
1.9	Jonathon
1.8	Edward
1.7	Donald
1.7	Keith
1.7	Marcus
1.6	Ian
1.6	Phillip
1.5	Trevor
1.5	Ronald
1.5	Craig
1.5	George
1.4	Joel
1.4	Gary
1.3	Evan
1.3	Curtis
1.3	Douglas
1.3	Alex
1.3	Philip
1.3	Antonio
1.3	Casey
1.3	Jeffery
1.2	Nathaniel
1.2	Wesley
1.2	Derrick
1.2	Brent
1.2	Raymond
1.0	Mitchell
1.0	Terry
1.0	Blake
1.0	Luke
1.0	Colin
0.9	Austin
0.9	Seth
0.9	Mathew
0.9	Larry
0.9	Randy

The 100 Most Popular Names by Region

Northeastern United States

• • • • GIRLS • • • •

29.8	Jessica	5.5	Lisa	2.6	Colleen
27.8	Ashley	5.3	Allison	2.6	Julia
25.5	Amanda	5.1	Angela	2.6	Alison
21.1	Jennifer	5.0	Shannon	2.4	Leah
18.3	Nicole	5.0	Caitlin	2.4	Krista
17.7	Sarah	4.9	Katie	2.3	Victoria
13.7	Stephanie	4.9	Crystal	2.3	Margaret
13.7	Lauren	4.7	Mary	2.2	Bethany
12.2	Elizabeth	4.5	Alicia	2.2	Kara
11.6	Melissa	4.5	Lindsay	2.2	Casey
11.0	Heather	4.5	Kathryn	2.1	Marissa
10.6	Megan	4.4	Jenna	1.9	Stacey
10.5	Danielle	4.3	Andrea	1.9	Dana
10.0	Laura	4.2	Meghan	1.9	Patricia
8.9	Samantha	4.0	Lindsey	1.9	Gina
8.8	Kelly	4.0	Kristin	1.9	Natalie
8.8	Emily	3.7	Kathleen	1.8	Monica
8.7	Brittany	3.7	Tara	1.8	Melanie
8.7	Rachel	3.7	Julie	1.7	Rachael
8.5	Amy	3.2	Vanessa	1.7	Hannah
8.2	Rebecca	3.2	Jillian	1.6	Kayla
8.1	Christina	3.2	Baby	1.5	April
8.1	Michelle	3.2	Catherine	1.5	Mallory
7.5	Erin	3.1	Alexandra	1.5	Renee
7.0	Sara	2.9	Katelyn	1.3	Nichole
6.9	Amber	2.8	Holly	1.3	Kimberly
6.6	Kimberly	2.8	Kristina	1.3	Jacquelin
6.6	Kristen	2.7	Cassandra	1.2	Kaitlyn
6.3	Christine	2.7	Whitney	1.2	Kaitlin
6.2	Katherine	2.7	Alyssa	1.1	Valerie
6.2	Tiffany	2.7	Natasha	1.1	Krystal
5.9	Jamie	2.7	Maria	1.0	Caroline
5.7	Erica	2.7	Anna		
5.6	Courtney	2.6	Jacqueline		

• • • • BOYS • • • •

46.9	Michael	7.3	Alexander	2.7	Dustin
33.2	Matthew	7.3	Jonathan	2.7	Philip
26.5	Christopher	7.2	Zachary	2.7	Brett
23.6	Daniel	6.9	Jonathon	2.6	Donald
22.4	David	6.8	Jeremy	2.6	Douglas
21.7	Andrew	6.6	Paul	2.5	Ronald
20.3	John	6.0	Nathan	2.3	Bradley
20.2	Joseph	5.8	Charles	2.3	Alex
19.7	Ryan	5.6	Peter	2.3	Raymond
19.6	Robert	5.5	Shawn	2.2	Brendan
19.3	James	5.2	Aaron	2.2	Nathaniel
18.1	Joshua	5.1	Christophe	2.1	Cory
15.7	Brian	5.1	Bryan	2.1	Joel
14.7	William	5.0	Richard	2.0	Vincent
14.3	Justin	4.9	Tyler	1.9	Kyele
14.1	Kevin	4.5	Edward	1.9	Seth
13.8	Nicholas	4.5	Richard	1.9	Frank
13.7	Jason	4.4	Jacob	1.8	Christian
12.9	Anthony	4.2	Jesse	1.8	Dennis
12.9	Thomas	4.2	Kenneth	1.8	Marc
12.4	Timothy	4.0	Samuel	1.7	Luke
11.9	Eric	3.9	Derek	1.7	Erik
11.6	Adam	3.9	Keith	1.6	Phillip
10.4	Steven	3.8	Shane	1.6	Jose
10.3	Stephen	3.7	Jared	1.6	Gary
10.2	Brandon	3.6	Baby	1.5	Cody
10.0	Jeffrey	3.5	Corey	1.5	Francis
9.8	Mark	3.2	Ian	1.4	Todd
9.7	Sean	3.2	Jordan	1.1	Luis
8.8	Patrick	3.2	Travis	1.0	Marcus
8.6	Kyle	3.1	Craig	0.9	Colin
7.6	Benjamin	2.9	George	0.9	Brent
7.5	Gregory	2.9	Chad		
7.3	Scott	2.9	Evan		

The 100 Most Popular Names by Region

Southeastern United States

• • • • GIRLS • • • •

25.8	Ashley
25.2	Jessica
18.7	Amanda
18.4	Tamara
15.3	Jennifer
14.8	Tabitha
14.0	Robin
14.0	Brittany
9.7	Heather
9.7	Sarah
9.5	Tiffany
8.8	Stephanie
8.3	Amber
8.1	Lauren
7.8	Kimberly
7.1	Elizabeth
6.8	Megan
6.8	Crystal
6.4	Melissa
6.4	Courtney
6.3	Cynthia
6.2	Christina
6.0	Amy
6.0	Nicole
5.9	Rachel
5.9	Danielle
5.6	Jena
5.6	Samantha
5.5	Sara
5.1	Mary
5.0	Laura
4.9	Rebecca
4.6	Erica
4.6	Michelle
4.6	Vanessa
4.6	Emily
4.3	Katherine
4.3	Meredith
4.3	Jamie
4.2	Lindsey
4.2	Kelly
3.8	Whitney
3.7	Kristen
3.7	April
3.7	Brittney
3.7	Erin
3.6	Shannon
3.4	Angela
3.4	Alisha
3.4	Christine
3.3	Brooke
3.3	Katie
3.3	Latoya
3.2	Andrea
3.2	Lindsay
3.1	Alicia
3.0	Victoria
2.9	Cassandra
2.9	Allison
2.8	Patricia
2.8	Anna
2.7	Natalie
2.7	Kathryn
2.7	Krystal
2.7	Maria
2.6	Kristin
2.6	Brandy
2.6	Brandi
2.5	Kayla
2.5	Julia
2.5	Dana
2.5	Lisa
2.5	Candace
2.4	Alexandra
2.4	Haley
2.4	Kristina
2.3	Holly
2.2	Erika
2.2	Monica
2.2	Britney
2.1	Casey
2.1	Morgan
2.1	Jenna
2.1	Tara
2.0	Alexis
2.0	Hannah
1.9	Mallory
1.9	Dominique
1.9	Jasmine
1.9	Catherine
1.8	Natasha
1.8	Leslie
1.8	Julie
1.7	Candice
1.7	Kendra
1.7	Cristina
1.7	Kathleen
1.7	Kelli
1.7	Monique
1.7	Bethany

• • • • BOYS • • • •

34.1	Christopher	6.6	Dustin	3.2	Shawn
30.1	Michael	6.2	Benjamin	3.2	Donald
23.6	Rodney	5.6	Patrick	3.1	Chad
22.8	Joshua	5.5	Kenneth	3.0	Jared
22.4	James	5.4	Brandon	2.9	Carlos
21.0	Matthew	5.4	Jeffrey	2.8	Frank
18.7	Blake	5.3	Jacob	2.8	Derek
17.5	John	5.2	Mark	2.8	Lance
17.4	David	4.8	Gregory	2.8	Edward
17.3	William	4.6	Travis	2.7	Shane
17.2	Robert	4.6	Aaron	2.7	Ronald
16.3	Johnathan	4.6	Sean	2.6	Derrick
16.2	Justin	4.5	Bobby	2.6	Craig
15.3	Daniel	4.3	Wesley	2.6	Cory
14.3	Joseph	4.2	Marcus	2.6	Keith
14.1	Jonathan	4.2	Corey	2.5	George
12.6	Andrew	4.2	Bryan	2.5	Juan
10.7	Jeremy	4.1	Alexander	2.5	Casey
10.3	Jason	3.8	Paul	2.4	Jeffery
9.8	Anthony	3.8	Samuel	2.3	Brett
9.5	Charles	3.8	Jesse	2.3	Christian
9.4	Kevin	3.7	Cody	2.3	Terry
8.9	Brian	3.7	Zachary	2.3	Gary
8.8	Timothy	3.6	Bradley	2.2	Jorge
8.7	Nicholas	3.6	Tyler	2.2	Luis
8.6	Steven	3.6	Jose	2.2	Micheal
8.6	Thomas	3.5	Antonio	2.1	Devin
8.4	Eric	3.5	Nathan	2.1	Peter
7.9	Richard	3.4	Jordan	2.1	Ricky
7.4	Adam	3.4	Alex	2.0	Carl
6.9	Kyle	3.3	Raymond	2.0	Chase
6.9	Seth	3.3	Scott	2.0	Dana
6.7	Ryan	3.2	Phillip		
6.6	Stephen	3.2	Nathan		

The 100 Most Popular Names by Region

Midwestern United States

• • • • GIRLS • • • •

34.9 Ashley
31.0 Jessica
29.1 Amanda
20.9 Sarah
20.3 Jennifer
15.0 Megan
13.6 Stephanie
13.6 Heather
13.0 Brittany
12.5 Amber
12.1 Elizabeth
11.8 Nicole
10.6 Emily
10.6 Rachel
10.3 Melissa
9.7 Samantha
9.6 Amy
9.2 Laura
8.9 Kimberly
8.7 Rebecca
8.4 Danielle
8.2 Sara
7.8 Whitney
7.7 Lauren
7.6 Michelle
7.1 Katie
7.1 Angela
7.0 Katherine
7.0 Kelly
6.9 Erin
6.7 Jamie
6.6 Tiffany
6.5 Crystal
6.2 Christina
6.0 Lindsey
5.9 Andrea
5.7 Mary
5.2 Courtney
5.2 Kelsey
4.9 Erica
4.6 Lindsay
4.6 Lisa
4.4 Kayla
4.4 Alicia
4.2 Allison
4.1 Kristen
4.1 Tara
4.1 Shannon
4.0 Kathryn
4.0 Cassandra
4.0 April
3.9 Kristin
3.9 Anna
3.7 Jenna
3.5 Holly
3.5 Molly
3.3 Christine
3.2 Julie
3.2 Natalie
3.2 Casey
3.1 Tabitha
3.1 Brittney
3.1 Brandy
3.0 Brandi
2.9 Michaela
2.8 Leslie
2.8 Abby
2.8 Krystal
2.7 Mallory
2.7 Alyssa
2.6 Felicia
2.5 Kathleen
2.5 Savannah
2.5 Bethany
2.4 Kara
2.4 Hannah
2.4 Catherine
2.4 Kendra
2.4 Lacey
2.3 Heidi
2.3 Jordan
2.3 Victoria
2.3 Margaret
2.3 Robin
2.3 Meghan
2.3 Stacy
2.2 Stacey
2.2 Carrie
2.1 Chelsea
2.1 Candace
2.1 Kristina
2.1 Nichole
2.1 Vanessa
2.1 Brooke
2.0 Monica
2.0 Jill
2.0 Kylie
2.0 Misty
2.0 Susan
2.0 Leah

• • • • BOYS • • • •

31.9	Michael	7.1	Zachary	2.1	Luke
29.4	Christopher	6.4	Travis	2.0	Lucas
28.6	Matthew	6.3	Bradley	2.0	Jonathon
26.6	Joshua	6.2	Patrick	2.0	Kenneth
23.0	Andrew	6.0	Richard	2.0	Dylan
19.4	James	5.9	Scott	1.9	Billy
18.8	Ryan	5.9	Jordan	1.9	Terry
18.2	Daniel	5.3	Alexander	1.9	Bryce
18.1	Brandon	5.2	Derek	1.9	Jay
17.6	David	5.1	Paul	1.8	Todd
17.4	Justin	5.1	Jesse	1.8	Clayton
16.1	Joseph	4.5	Chad	1.8	Lance
15.7	Nicholas	4.4	Samuel	1.8	Randy
15.5	John	3.8	Charles	1.8	Carl
15.1	Kyle	3.3	Peter	1.8	Jerry
14.9	Robert	3.1	Gary	1.8	Roger
14.2	Adam	3.0	Bobby	1.8	Jeremiah
12.7	William	2.8	Mitchell	1.7	Bryan
12.4	Jason	2.6	Ronald	1.7	Gregory
12.3	Jacob	2.5	Cole	1.7	Randall
12.1	Eric	2.4	Johnathan	1.7	Shawn
12.0	Brian	2.4	Joel	1.7	Philip
11.0	Jonathan	2.3	Stephen	1.7	Ian
10.6	Anthony	2.3	Drew	1.7	Levi
10.5	Jeremy	2.3	Larry	1.6	Raymond
10.5	Tyler	2.3	Derrick	1.6	Alan
10.2	Benjamin	2.2	Edward	1.6	Vincent
10.1	Kevin	2.2	Chase	1.5	Devin
9.4	Dustin	2.2	Jimmy	1.5	Danny
9.0	Aaron	2.2	Ricky	1.4	Trevor
8.5	Nathan	2.1	Grant	1.4	Corey
8.0	Timothy	2.1	Logan	1.4	Sean
7.8	Jeffrey	2.1	Caleb		
7.1	Mark	2.1	George		

The 100 Most Popular Names by Region

Northwestern United States

• • • • GIRLS • • • •

25.3 Jessica
22.7 Amanda
18.6 Ashley
18.3 Sarah
15.1 Jennifer
11.9 Stephanie
11.0 Danielle
11.0 Nicole
10.0 Amber
9.4 Megan
9.1 Samantha
9.0 Heather
8.7 Brittany
8.5 Elizabeth
8.3 Melissa
8.1 Rachel
8.0 Jamie
7.9 Rebecca
7.1 Emily
7.1 Katie
7.0 Laura
6.9 Sara
6.6 Michelle
6.6 Tiffany
6.5 Kimberly
6.2 Crystal
5.9 Erin
5.9 Amy
5.5 Katherine
5.1 Courtney
5.1 Christina
5.0 Chelsea
4.9 Courtney
4.8 Lisa
4.7 Andrea
4.7 Mary
4.7 Courtney
4.6 Lindsey
4.6 Anna
4.6 Kelsey
4.4 Kelly
4.2 Kayla
4.1 Angela
4.0 Kristin
4.0 Lindsay
4.0 Erica
3.9 Vanessa
3.7 Kendra
3.7 Misty
3.7 Jenna
3.7 Christine
3.7 Katrina
3.6 Alicia
3.5 Allison
3.5 Hannah
3.5 Shannon
3.3 Krista
3.3 Lauren
3.3 Holly
3.2 Tara
3.1 Kathleen
3.1 Kathryn
3.1 Krystal
3.1 Patricia
3.0 Leah
2.8 Whitney
2.8 Brittney
2.8 Cassandra
2.8 Kristen
2.6 Victoria
2.4 Alexis
2.4 Brianna
2.4 Caitlin
2.4 Catherine
2.4 Heidi
2.4 Julia
2.4 Julie
2.4 Kristina
2.4 Meghan
2.4 Molly
2.4 Nichole
2.3 Desiree
2.3 Erika
2.3 Maria
2.3 Natasha
2.3 Robin
2.1 Alexandra
2.1 Bethany
2.1 Cynthia
2.1 Jenny
2.1 Jordan
2.1 Monica
2.1 Morgan
2.1 Natalie
2.1 Rebekah
2.1 Shawna
1.9 Casey
1.9 Jacqueline
1.9 Mallory
1.7 April

• • • • BOYS • • • •

27.4 Michael
25.2 Christopher
21.7 Matthew
19.7 Joshua
19.2 Ryan
17.3 Daniel
15.9 John
15.7 Andrew
15.5 David
15.4 James
15.4 Robert
13.8 Justin
13.5 Kyle
13.5 William
13.3 Tyler
12.4 Joseph
12.3 Nicholas
11.5 Brandon
11.2 Brian
11.2 Jacob
10.1 Benjamin
9.7 Jason
9.3 Jesse
9.1 Dustin
8.5 Cody
8.5 Thomas
8.4 Aaron
8.1 Eric
8.1 Jonathan
8.1 Kevin
8.1 Timothy
7.8 Anthony
7.5 Steven
7.3 Patrick
7.2 Jeremy
7.2 Sean
7.1 Alexander
6.9 Nathan
6.7 Richard
6.6 Jeffrey
6.6 Adam
6.3 Scott
6.0 Samuel
6.0 Travis
5.9 Paul
5.7 Jordan
5.7 Kenneth
5.4 Charles
5.2 Mark
5.2 Stephen
5.0 Jared
5.0 Peter
4.9 Shane
4.7 Derek
4.5 Gregory
4.5 Shawn
4.2 Casey
4.2 Chad
3.6 Bryan
3.6 Luke
3.4 Cory
3.4 Donald
3.4 Garrett
3.4 Zachary
3.2 Edward
3.2 George
3.1 Alex
3.1 Brett
3.1 Ian
3.1 Nathaniel
2.9 Cameron
2.9 Curtis
2.8 Douglas
2.8 Frank
2.8 Joel
2.8 Phillip
2.8 Ronald
2.6 Corey
2.6 Erik
2.5 Stephen
2.4 Bradley
2.4 Dennis
2.4 Kristopher
2.4 Taylor
2.4 Theodore
2.3 Carl
2.3 Gary
2.3 Jeffery
2.3 Seth
2.3 Troy
2.1 Gabriel
2.1 Keth
1.9 Clayton
1.9 Craig
1.9 Jeremiah
1.9 Jerry
1.9 Marcus
1.9 Trevor
1.8 Dylan
1.8 Johnathan

The 100 Most Popular Names by Region

Southwestern United States

• • • • GIRLS • • • •

25.8 Jessica
19.4 Ashley
18.6 Jennifer
16.5 Amanda
13.5 Sarah
11.8 Stephanie
11.7 Nicole
10.4 Melissa
9.9 Elizabeth
9.4 Christina
8.8 Emily
8.5 Brittany
8.3 Michelle
8.3 Amy
8.3 Rachel
8.2 Megan
8.2 Heather
8.2 Vanessa
8.1 Whitney
7.8 Amber
7.3 Kimberly
7.3 Erin
7.3 Lauren
7.1 Danielle
7.1 Crystal
7.0 Laura
6.9 Sara
6.8 Tiffany
6.7 Samantha
6.7 Rebecca
6.5 Katie
6.3 Maria
6.3 Andrea
6.0 Jamie
5.9 Katherine
5.8 Lindsey
5.7 Angela
5.2 Lindsay
5.2 Kelly
4.8 Lisa
4.7 Heidi
4.6 Natalie
4.5 Kathryn
4.5 Chelsea
4.3 Victoria
4.2 Erica
4.2 Shannon
4.1 Allison
4.0 Courtney
3.9 Kristen
3.8 Hannah
3.8 Alicia
3.7 Ashlee
3.7 Alexandra
3.6 Cassandra
3.6 Kristin
3.5 Anna
3.5 Brooke
3.5 Mary
3.5 Monica
3.3 Melanie
3.2 Brittney
3.2 Holly
3.1 Julie
3.1 Tara
2.8 April
2.7 Krystal
2.7 Jenna
2.6 Catherine
2.6 Erika
2.6 Natasha
2.5 Mallory
2.5 Valerie
2.5 Camille
2.5 Cassie
2.5 Kayla
2.5 Nichole
2.5 Kathleen
2.4 Caitlin
2.4 Julia
2.4 Kendra
2.4 Molly
2.3 Jacqueline
2.3 Meghan
2.2 Lacey
2.2 Katrina
2.2 Kelsey
2.1 Kristina
2.1 Kirsta
2.1 Brandi
2.1 Jordan
2.1 Leah
2.1 Patricia
2.1 Alyssa
2.0 Margaret
2.0 Veronica
2.0 Stacy
2.0 Morgan
1.9 Alisha
1.9 Kara

• • • • BOYS • • • •

30.3 Michael
27.3 Christopher
21.8 Daniel
21.5 David
19.8 Matthew
16.7 Andrew
15.7 Joshua
14.1 Tyler
13.2 James
12.7 Joseph
12.3 Anthony
12.0 Justin
12.0 John
11.8 Nicholas
11.7 Kyle
11.6 Jose
11.5 Jonathan
11.3 Jason
11.0 Brandon
10.6 Jacob
10.2 Eric
10.2 Adam
10.0 Brian
9.9 Benjamin
9.5 Steven
9.2 William
9.1 Kevin
9.1 Nathan
8.3 Jeremy
8.2 Jeffrey
7.6 Cody
7.4 Scott
7.4 Thomas
6.8 Sean
6.8 Tyson
6.8 Timothy
6.7 Aaron
6.7 Travis
6.6 Dustin
6.6 Mark
6.6 Richard
6.4 Alexander
6.1 Cameron
6.1 Stephen
6.1 Jesse
5.9 Spencer
5.7 Derek
5.6 Patrick
5.5 Paul
5.5 Jordan
4.9 Jared
4.9 Cerek
4.8 Bryan
4.4 Charles
4.4 Zachary
4.4 Brady
4.1 Austin
4.1 Chad
4.1 Samuel
4.1 Trevor
4.0 Gregory
4.0 Kenneth
3.8 Alex
3.7 Shawn
3.7 Chase
3.6 Bryce
3.4 Casey
3.3 Evan
3.2 Luke
3.2 Colby
3.1 Shane
3.1 Brett
3.0 Ian
2.9 Blake
2.9 Todd
2.9 Cory
2.7 Peter
2.6 Taylor
2.6 Marcus
2.6 Seth
2.6 Lance
2.5 Lucas
2.5 Landon
2.4 Mitchell
2.3 Brent
2.3 Skyler
2.3 Keith
2.3 Raymond
2.2 Christian
2.2 Colton
2.2 Devin
2.2 Preston
2.2 Curtis
2.2 Joel
2.1 Russell
2.1 Alan
2.1 Jake
2.1 Edward
2.1 Erik
2.1 Corey

The 100 Most Popular Names by Region

Western Canada

• • • • GIRLS • • • •

23.6 Amanda
22.0 Ashley
22.0 Jennifer
17.7 Jessica
17.2 Nicole
17.2 Sarah
14.7 Stephanie
13.5 Melissa
11.3 Megan
9.8 Michelle
9.7 Danielle
9.2 Laura
8.6 Amy
8.2 Lindsay
8.0 Brittany
7.6 Kimberly
7.6 Erin
7.4 Heather
7.0 Amber
7.0 Lisa
6.9 Samantha
6.4 Andrea
6.3 Crystal
6.2 Jenna
6.0 Rebecca
5.9 Christina
5.8 Angela
5.8 Chelsea
5.7 Vanessa
5.7 Christine
5.2 Katherine
5.0 Sara
4.8 Emily
4.8 Shannon
4.7 Jamie
4.4 Courtney
4.4 Rachel
4.4 Natasha
4.3 Elizabeth
4.3 Kelsey
4.3 Tara
4.2 Kristen
3.9 Kathleen
3.9 Lindsey
3.8 Kelly
3.6 Meghan
3.5 Lauren
3.5 Whitney
3.5 Krista
3.5 Tiffany
3.4 Sheena
3.4 Anna
3.4 Kendra
3.4 Allison
3.4 Melanie
3.3 Victoria
3.3 Leah
3.3 Tanya
3.2 Alicia
3.2 Chelsey
3.2 Tamara
3.2 Kathryn
3.1 Jacqueline
3.0 Natalie
3.0 Meagan
3.0 Stacey
3.0 Julie
2.9 Janelle
2.9 Caitlin
2.9 Kristin
2.9 Chantel
2.9 Rachelle
2.8 Cassandra
2.8 Carly
2.8 Kayla
2.8 Katrina
2.7 Krystal
2.7 Robyn
2.7 Katie
2.7 Karen
2.7 Kimberley
2.6 Kara
2.6 Mallory
2.5 Kristina
2.5 Hayley
2.5 Pamela
2.5 Cheryl
2.4 Catherine
2.4 Alexandra
2.4 Erica
2.4 Lacey
2.4 Tracy
2.4 Alison
2.3 Brandi
2.3 Brittney
2.3 Jocelyn
2.3 Chantelle
2.3 Emma
2.3 Holly
2.3 Jillian

• • • • BOYS • • • •

27.1 Michael
25.4 Christopher
24.6 Matthew
22.8 Ryan
20.1 Daniel
20.0 Kyle
19.1 David
17.2 Andrew
14.8 Tyler
14.0 Justin
13.4 Jason
13.2 Robert
12.8 James
12.5 Joshua
12.2 Adam
12.1 Kevin
10.2 Steven
10.1 Jonathan
10.1 Scott
10.0 Jeffrey
9.8 Mark
9.8 Cody
9.5 Jordan
9.1 Brandon
8.7 Dustin
8.1 Sean
7.8 Nicholas
7.8 John
7.5 Bradley
7.4 Aaron
7.3 Jesse
7.1 Richard
7.0 Nathan
6.8 Stephen
6.7 Joseph
6.5 Alexander
6.5 Derek
6.5 Travis
6.5 Eric
6.5 Thomas
6.5 William
6.2 Jeremy
6.2 Brian
5.9 Trevor
5.7 Shawn
5.6 Benjamin
5.4 Anthony
5.3 Timothy
5.2 Curtis
5.2 Paul
5.0 Shane
5.0 Patrick
4.7 Cory
4.7 Gregory
4.6 Chad
4.6 Colin
4.4 Brett
4.4 Joel
4.2 Peter
4.2 Ian
4.1 Corey
3.9 Evan
3.7 Bryan
3.7 Cameron
3.7 Jared
3.7 Craig
3.7 Riley
3.4 Brennan
3.4 Dallas
3.3 Darren
3.3 Brent
3.2 Mathew
3.2 Mitchell
3.2 Kenneth
3.0 Raymond
3.0 Kristopher
3.0 Dylan
2.8 Samuel
2.8 Todd
2.6 Devin
2.6 Shaun
2.6 Jacob
2.5 Darcy
2.5 Micheal
2.4 Douglas
2.3 Brendan
2.3 Bryce
2.3 Landon
2.3 Jamie
2.3 Keith
2.3 Graham
2.3 Geoffrey
2.2 Troy
2.2 Blair
2.2 Wade
2.2 Clayton
2.2 Cole
2.1 Devon
2.1 Adrian
2.1 Philip

The 100 Most Popular Names by Region

Central Canada

• • • • GIRLS • • • •

26.9	Ashley	5.5	Jenna	2.7	Erica
26.8	Amanda	5.5	Courtney	2.7	Candice
25.8	Sarah	5.3	Kelly	2.7	Kayla
25.3	Jessica	5.3	Natalie	2.6	Karen
25.3	Jennifer	5.0	Julie	2.5	Lindsey
19.1	Stephanie	4.7	Crystal	2.5	Patricia
16.7	Melissa	4.7	Angela	2.5	Kristina
16.0	Nicole	4.5	Kimberly	2.4	Katelyn
15.0	Laura	4.4	Natasha	2.4	Leah
11.8	Michelle	4.3	Alexandra	2.3	Katrina
10.5	Danielle	4.3	Kathleen	2.3	Emma
9.2	Samantha	4.2	Amber	2.3	Maria
8.7	Lindsay	4.0	Alicia	2.3	Anna
8.5	Marie	4.0	Meghan	2.3	Chantal
8.3	Lisa	3.9	Tiffany	2.3	Sabrina
8.2	Heather	3.8	Jacqueline	2.3	Diana
7.9	Megan	3.8	Katie	2.2	Valerie
7.8	Rebecca	3.8	Allison	2.2	Meaghan
7.5	Shannon	3.8	Holly	2.2	Robyn
7.5	Erin	3.7	Tanya	2.2	Jillian
7.3	Brittany	3.6	Kristen	2.1	Renee
7.1	Amy	3.5	Kathryn	2.0	Mallory
7.1	Elizabeth	3.5	Tara	2.0	Kristin
7.0	Andrea	3.4	Caitlin	1.9	Monica
6.9	Christina	3.2	Catherine	1.9	April
6.9	Christine	3.1	Stacey	1.9	Kimberley
6.9	Emily	3.0	Whitney	1.8	Meagan
6.5	Katherine	3.0	Mary	1.8	Pamela
6.1	Victoria	3.0	Krista	1.8	Sandra
6.1	Lauren	3.0	Jamie	1.8	Kaitlin
6.1	Rachel	3.0	Julia	1.7	Chelsea
6.0	Sara	3.0	Alison	1.7	Joanna
5.6	Vanessa	3.0	Krystal		
5.6	Melanie	2.8	Cassandra		

• • • • BOYS • • • •

38.6	Michael
33.8	Matthew
31.0	Christopher
29.1	Andrew
22.9	Daniel
22.5	David
22.1	Ryan
19.7	Kyle
18.8	Adam
16.6	Robert
16.3	Jason
16.3	James
15.6	Joseph
14.2	Justin
14.1	Jonathan
13.9	Joshua
12.7	Kevin
11.4	John
11.3	Jeffrey
11.1	Tyler
11.0	Mark
10.7	Nicholas
10.6	Steven
9.9	Alexander
9.6	Eric
9.4	Brandon
9.1	Scott
9.1	William
7.8	Bradley
7.7	Sean
7.7	Brian
7.7	Paul
7.7	Thomas
7.5	Shawn
7.4	Stephen
7.3	Jordan
6.9	Anthony
6.8	Richard
6.7	Patrick
6.5	Benjamin
6.3	Aaron
6.3	Gregory
6.3	Jesse
5.8	Peter
5.7	Timothy
5.6	Jeremy
5.5	Derek
5.2	Nathan
5.1	Ian
5.0	Corey
5.0	Shane
4.6	Trevor
4.1	Bryan
3.9	Cory
3.7	Joel
3.4	Craig
3.2	Jacob
3.2	Colin
3.1	Marc
3.1	Philip
3.0	Mathew
2.9	Brent
2.8	Brett
2.8	Kenneth
2.8	Zachary
2.8	Charles
2.7	Jamie
2.6	Evan
2.6	Adrian
2.6	Cody
2.4	Cameron
2.4	Dustin
2.4	Chad
2.3	Curtis
2.3	Brendan
2.2	Travis
2.2	Darren
2.1	Samuel
2.0	Simon
2.0	Mitchell
2.0	Luke
2.0	Micheal
2.0	Douglas
1.9	Graham
1.9	Andre
1.9	Edward
1.8	Donald
1.8	Keith
1.8	Geoffrey
1.7	Christian
1.7	Raymond
1.6	Dylan
1.6	Erik
1.6	George
1.6	Jeffery
1.5	Neil
1.5	Taylor
1.5	Shaun
1.5	Phillip
1.5	Kristopher

The 100 Most Popular Names by Region

Eastern Canada

• • • • GIRLS • • • •

31.8	Jennifer	5.4	Shannon	2.8	Lori
24.6	Amanda	5.3	Natalie	2.7	Candace
23.6	Melissa	5.2	Cindy	2.7	Cynthia
22.1	Ashley	5.0	Brittany	2.6	Courtney
19.3	Jessica	4.9	Andrea	2.6	Julia
17.9	Sarah	4.9	Kelly	2.6	Stéphanie
15.6	Stephanie	4.9	Lindsay	2.5	Joanne
14.2	Nicole	4.5	Christina	2.5	Karen
12.7	Crystal	4.5	Jillian	2.5	Tracy
12.2	Heather	4.5	Kimberly	2.4	Alicia
10.2	Julie	4.5	Renee	2.4	Charlene
10.1	Michelle	4.5	Samantha	2.4	Dawn
9.7	Amy	4.5	Tara	2.4	Isabelle
9.7	Laura	4.4	Elizabeth	2.4	Jenna
9.6	Lisa	4.4	Emily	2.4	Katie
9.3	Krista	4.2	Katherine	2.3	Caroline
8.7	Holly	4.1	Mary	2.3	Mélissa
8.6	Kayla	4.1	Victoria	2.3	Sylvie
8.5	Natasha	3.9	Meghan	2.3	Terri
8.2	Megan	3.8	Erica	2.1	Christa
7.7	Melanie	3.4	Nadine	2.1	Josée
7.6	Angela	3.4	Tiffany	2.1	Nathalie
7.4	Jamie	3.3	Susan	2.0	Mallory
7.2	Marie	3.2	Chantal	2.0	Sophie
7.0	Erin	3.2	Robyn	1.9	Kathleen
6.2	Rebecca	3.1	Joel	1.9	Lesley
6.1	April	3.1	Krystal	1.9	Leslie
6.1	Danielle	3.0	Karine	1.9	Rhonda
6.1	Sara	3.0	Sheena	1.8	Cheryl
5.9	Allison	3.0	Vanessa	1.8	Kathryn
5.9	Christine	2.9	Rachel	1.8	Patricia
5.5	Catherine	2.9	Tanya	1.7	Monica
5.5	Mélanie	2.8	Annie		
5.5	Pamela	2.8	Kristen		

• • • • BOYS • • • •

39.2	Christopher
33.7	Matthew
31.6	Michael
22.4	Jonathan
21.8	David
21.4	Adam
21.3	Andrew
20.0	Justin
19.5	Ryan
17.4	Stephen
16.9	Jason
16.3	Robert
14.8	Joshua
14.0	Joseph
13.5	Daniel
13.5	Mark
13.4	James
13.3	Bradley
11.4	John
11.4	Nicholas
11.0	Jeremy
10.5	Patrick
10.1	Scott
9.9	William
9.8	Kevin
9.4	Steven
8.9	Jeffrey
8.4	Gregory
8.2	Brian
8.2	Kyle
8.0	Paul
6.9	Richard
6.9	Timothy
6.6	Eric
6.3	Tyler
6.1	Shawn
6.1	Thomas
5.9	Corey
5.8	Jordan
5.8	Mathieu
5.4	Aaron
5.4	Peter
5.0	Travis
4.9	Chad
4.7	Kenneth
4.7	Marc
4.7	Trevor
4.6	Cory
4.5	Colin
4.2	Alexander
4.2	Sean
4.1	Brandon
3.9	Charles
3.9	Denis
3.8	Craig
3.8	Shane
3.7	Curtis
3.7	Ian
3.7	Nathan
3.6	Mitchell
3.5	Anthony
3.4	Luc
3.3	Martin
3.1	Benjamin
3.1	Bryan
3.0	Pierre
2.9	Julien
2.9	Marc-André
2.7	Dustin
2.7	Keith
2.7	Robin
2.7	Sébastien
2.5	Douglas
2.3	Christian
2.3	Jesse
2.3	Kristopher
2.3	Wayne
2.2	André
2.2	Michel
2.2	Neil
2.2	Randy
2.1	Gary
2.1	Rémi
2.0	Donald
2.0	Edward
2.0	Philippe
1.9	Derek
1.8	Evan
1.8	Nicolas
1.8	Samuel
1.8	Todd
1.7	Alain
1.7	Blair
1.7	Joey
1.7	Roger
1.7	Sheldon
1.7	Sylvain
1.6	Darren
1.6	Geoffrey
1.6	Guillaume

Section II

Popularity Ratings and Meanings of Names

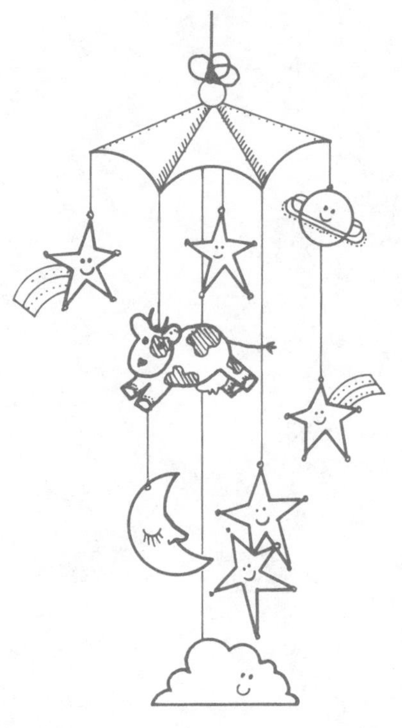

Popular Girls Names

RATING	NAME	ORIGIN AND MEANING
	A	
0.02	**Aaron**	*Hebrew* to sing, to shine, to teach, enlightened; *Arabic* a messenger
0.08	**Abbey**	*Hebrew* father of joy
0.08	**Abbie**	*Hebrew* father of joy
0.33	**Abby**	*Hebrew* father of joy
0.55	**Abigail**	*Hebrew* father of joy
0.04	**Ada**	*English* prosperous, happy; *Hebrew* an ornament
0.02	**Addie**	*German* noble, kind (Adele)
0.04	**Adele**	*German* noble, kind
0.02	**Adeline**	*German* noble, kind
0.02	**Adina**	*German* noble, kind; *Hebrew* sensuous, voluptuous
0.02	**Adria**	*Latin* dark one; rich
0.07	**Adrian**	*Latin* dark one; rich
0.12	**Adriana**	*Latin* dark one; rich
0.03	**Adriane**	*Latin* dark one; rich
0.04	**Adrianna**	*Latin* dark one; rich
0.08	**Adrianne**	*Latin* dark one; rich
0.49	**Adrienne**	*Latin* dark one; rich
0.04	**Afton**	*Arabic* warrior; *British* place name and surname
0.02	**Agatha**	*Greek* good woman
0.02	**Agnes**	*Greek* pure, chaste; *Latin* lamb
0.07	**Aileen**	*Irish* form of Helen; *Gaelic* light bearer
0.02	**Aime**	*French* from *Latin* beloved
0.51	**Aimee**	*French* from *Latin* beloved
0.03	**Ainsley**	*Scottish* from one's own meadow
0.08	**Aisha**	*African* life
0.04	**Aja**	*Hindu* goat (Capricorn in the Zodiac)
0.17	**Alaina**	*Irish* fair, beautiful

0.33	**Alana**	*Irish* fair, beautiful
0.17	**Alanna**	*Irish* fair, beautiful
0.02	**Alayna**	*Irish* fair, beautiful
0.02	**Alea**	*Arabic* high, exalted; *Persian* God's being
0.02	**Aleah**	*Arabic* high, exalted; *Persian* God's being
0.10	**Alecia**	*German* noble; *Greek* truthful
0.02	**Aleesha**	*German* noble; *Greek* truthful
0.03	**Aleisha**	*German* noble; *Greek* truthful
0.03	**Alejandra**	*Greek* defender of mankind
0.03	**Alena**	*Greek* a torch, light
0.07	**Alesha**	*German* noble; *Greek* truthful
0.02	**Aleshia**	*German* noble; *Greek* truthful
0.02	**Alesia**	*German* noble; *Greek* truthful
0.03	**Alessandra**	*Greek* defender of mankind
0.03	**Alex**	*Greek* defender of mankind
0.14	**Alexa**	*Greek* defender of mankind
1.39	**Alexandra**	*Greek* defender of mankind
0.02	**Alexandrea**	*Greek* defender of mankind
0.27	**Alexandria**	*Greek* defender of mankind
0.04	**Alexia**	*Greek* defender of mankind
0.72	**Alexis**	*Greek* defender of mankind
0.09	**Ali**	contemporary American form of Alice or Alison
0.04	**Alia**	*Arabic* high, exalted; *Persian* God's being
0.23	**Alice**	*German* noble; *Greek* truthful
2.73	**Alicia**	*German* noble; *Greek* truthful
0.02	**Alida**	*Latin* little winged one
0.05	**Alina**	*Polish* and *Russian* bright, beautiful
0.02	**Aline**	*Polish* and *Russian* bright, beautiful
0.12	**Alisa**	*German* noble; *Greek* truthful
0.02	**Alise**	*German* noble; *Greek* truthful
0.81	**Alisha**	*German* noble; *Greek* truthful
0.03	**Alishia**	*German* noble; *Greek* truthful
0.02	**Alisia**	*German* noble; *Greek* truthful
1.15	**Alison**	*German* noble; *Greek* truthful
0.20	**Alissa**	*German* noble; *Greek* truthful
0.03	**Alix**	*Greek* defender of mankind
0.02	**Aliya**	*Hebrew* to ascend, to go up
0.02	**Aliza**	*German* noble; *Greek* truthful

0.05	**Allie**	*Greek* defender of mankind; *German* noble *Greek* truth
2.81	**Allison**	*German* noble; *Greek* truthful
0.28	**Allyson**	*German* noble; *Greek* truthful
0.05	**Alma**	*Arabic* learned; *Italian* soul
0.02	**Alyce**	*German* noble; *Greek* truthful
0.08	**Alycia**	*German* noble; *Greek* truthful
0.03	**Alysa**	*German* noble; *Greek* truthful
0.07	**Alyse**	*German* noble; *Greek* truthful
0.09	**Alysha**	*German* noble; *Greek* truthful
0.02	**Alyshia**	*German* noble; *Greek* truthful
0.07	**Alysia**	*German* noble; *Greek* truthful
0.21	**Alyson**	*German* noble; *Greek* truthful
0.91	**Alyssa**	*Greek* logical one
0.02	**Alysse**	*German* noble; *Greek* truthful
21:58	**Amanda**	*Latin* worthy of love
0.03	**Amandeep**	*Punjabi* light of peace
0.02	**Amaris**	*Hebrew* what God has promised
8.78	**Amber**	*French* amber
0.07	**Amberly**	*French* amber
0.32	**Amelia**	*Latin* work
0.02	**Amelie**	*Latin* work
0.04	**Ami**	*Latin* beloved
0.16	**Amie**	*Latin* beloved
0.03	**Amina**	*Arabic* security
5.71	**Amy**	*Latin* beloved
0.20	**Ana**	Greek resurrection
0.02	**Anais**	*Hebrew* one of grace, gracious (Anna)
0.02	**Anastacia**	*Greek* resurrection
0.12	**Anastasia**	*Greek* resurrection
0.02	**Andra**	*Greek* valiant, strong, courageous; *Latin* womanly
3.64	**Andrea**	*Greek* valiant, strong, courageous; *Latin* womanly
0.02	**Andree**	*Greek* valiant, strong, courageous; *Latin* womanly
0.05	**Andria**	*Greek* valiant, strong, courageous; *Latin* womanly
0.55	**Angel**	*Latin* angelic

3.70	**Angela**	*Latin* angelic
0.03	**Angele**	*Latin* angelic
0.02	**Angelia**	*Latin* angelic
0.02	**Angelic**	*Latin* angelic
0.34	**Angelica**	*Latin* angelic
0.16	**Angelina**	*Latin* angelic
0.05	**Angeline**	*Latin* angelic
0.08	**Angelique**	*Latin* angelic
0.04	**Angelle**	*Latin* angelic
0.10	**Angie**	*Latin* angelic
0.03	**Anika**	*Hebrew* gracious
0.02	**Anisha**	*Hebrew* gracious
0.27	**Anita**	*Hebrew* gracious
0.02	**Anjelica**	*Latin* angelic
0.36	**Ann**	*Hebrew* gracious
2.23	**Anna**	*Italian, German, Russian* forms of *Hebrew* one of grace, gracious
0.02	**Annamarie**	Anna + Mary
0.60	**Anne**	*Hebrew* gracious
0.04	**Anne-Marie**	Anna + Mary
0.02	**Annemarie**	Anna + Mary
0.13	**Annette**	*Hebrew* gracious
0.26	**Annie**	*Hebrew* gracious
0.02	**Annik**	*Hebrew* gracious
0.02	**Annika**	*Hebrew* gracious
0.03	**Annmarie**	Anna + Mary
0.02	**Antionette**	*Latin* priceless
0.02	**Antoinet**	*Latin* priceless
0.19	**Antoinette**	*Latin* priceless
0.02	**Antonella**	*Latin* priceless
0.06	**Antonia**	*Latin* priceless
0.02	**Antonella**	*Latin* priceless
0.02	**Anya**	*Hebrew* gracious
2.26	**April**	*Latin* open
0.02	**Apryl**	*Latin* open
0.05	**Ariana**	*Greek* most holy
0.03	**Ariane**	*Greek* most holy
0.02	**Arianna**	*Greek* most holy
0.03	**Arianne**	*Greek* most holy

0.15	**Ariel**	*Hebrew* likeness of God
0.09	**Arielle**	*Hebrew* likeness of God
0.02	**Arin**	*Hebrew* to sing, to shine, to teach, enlightened; *Arabic* a messenger
0.07	**Arlene**	*Irish* pledge
0.05	**Asha**	*Hindi* hope; *Arabic* sunset; living, prosperous; wife of Muhammed
0.05	**Ashely**	*English* from the ash tree meadow
0.05	**Ashlea**	*English* from the ash tree meadow
0.71	**Ashlee**	*English* from the ash tree meadow
0.02	**Ashlei**	*English* from the ash tree meadow
0.47	**Ashleigh**	*English* from the ash tree meadow
26.49	**Ashley**	*English* from the ash tree meadow
0.06	**Ashli**	*English* from the ash tree meadow
0.13	**Ashlie**	*English* from the ash tree meadow
0.13	**Ashly**	*English* from the ash tree meadow
0.04	**Ashlyn**	*English* from the ash tree pool
0.02	**Ashlynn**	*English* from the ash tree pool
0.02	**Ashtin**	*English* from the ash tree farm
0.37	**Ashton**	*English* from the ash tree farm
0.08	**Asia**	*Greek* resurrection
0.02	**Aspen**	*English* aspen
0.06	**Athena**	*Greek* wisdom
0.04	**Aubree**	*French* blond ruler; elf ruler
0.20	**Aubrey**	*French* blond ruler; elf ruler
0.03	**Aubrie**	*French* blond ruler; elf ruler
0.12	**Audra**	*English* noble strength
0.41	**Audrey**	*English* noble strength
0.04	**Aurora**	*Latin* daybreak
0.02	**Austin**	*Latin* queenly one
0.35	**Autumn**	*Latin* autumn
0.03	**Ava**	*Latin* birdlike
0.04	**Avery**	*French* blond ruler; elf ruler
0.02	**Ayanna**	*Hindi* innocent being
0.02	**Ayesha**	*Muslim* one of Muhammed's wives
0.04	**Ayla**	*Hebrew* oak tree

B

0.20	**Bailey**	*English* fortification
0.04	**Bandi**	*Punjabi* prisoner
0.55	**Barbara**	*Latin* stranger
0.04	**Beatrice**	*Latin* she who makes others happy
0.02	**Beatriz**	*Latin* she who makes others happy
0.12	**Becky**	*Hebrew* to tie, to bind
0.11	**Belinda**	*Spanish* beautiful
0.02	**Benita**	*Latin* blessed
0.07	**Bernadette**	*French* brave warrior
0.02	**Bertha**	*German* brilliant, glorious one
0.35	**Beth**	*Hebrew* house of God; short form of names containing "beth"
0.02	**Bethanie**	*Greek* and *Latin* house of figs
1.00	**Bethany**	*Greek* and *Latin* house of figs
0.09	**Betsy**	*Hebrew* God's oath (Elizabeth)
0.02	**Bettina**	*Hebrew* God's oath (Elizabeth)
0.12	**Betty**	*Hebrew* God's oath (Elizabeth)
0.16	**Beverly**	*English* from the beaver meadow
0.18	**Bianca**	*Italian* white
0.08	**Billie**	*English* strong willed
0.16	**Blair**	*Scottish* dweller on the plain
0.02	**Blaire**	*Scottish* dweller on the plain
0.02	**Blanca**	*Italian* white
0.02	**Blythe**	*English* joyous
0.14	**Bobbi**	*English* shining with fame; *Latin* stranger
0.02	**Bobbi-Jo**	*English* shining with fame; *Latin* stranger
0.16	**Bobbie**	*English* shining with fame; *Latin* stranger
0.02	**Bobby**	*English* shining with fame; *Latin* stranger
0.02	**Bonita**	*Spanish* pretty
0.39	**Bonnie**	*Latin*, *French*, *Scottish* good; pretty
0.03	**Brandee**	*Dutch* brandy
1.42	**Brandi**	*Dutch* brandy
0.19	**Brandie**	*Dutch* brandy
1.44	**Brandy**	*Dutch* brandy
0.02	**Breana**	*Irish* strong
0.05	**Breann**	*Irish* strong

0.19	**Breanna**	*Irish* strong
0.20	**Breanne**	*Irish* strong
0.03	**Bree**	*Latin* from the boundary line (Sabrina); *Latin* from England
0.39	**Brenda**	*English* firebrand
0.14	**Brenna**	*Irish* raven
0.05	**Brett**	*English* a Briton
0.24	**Briana**	*Irish* strong
0.47	**Brianna**	*Irish* strong
0.32	**Brianne**	*Irish* strong
0.03	**Briannne**	*Irish* strong
0.02	**Briar**	*Greek* strong
0.53	**Bridget**	*Irish* strong
0.08	**Bridgett**	*Irish* strong
0.16	**Bridgette**	*Irish* strong
0.02	**Brie**	*Latin* from the boundary line (Sabrina); *Latin* from England
0.02	**Brieanne**	*Irish* strong
0.02	**Brielle**	origin unknown, possibly an invented name
0.02	**Brienne**	*Irish* strong
0.02	**Brigette**	*Irish* strong
0.03	**Brigid**	*Irish* strong
0.06	**Brigitte**	*Irish* strong
0.09	**Britany**	*Latin* from England
0.56	**Britney**	*Latin* from England
0.08	**Britni**	*Latin* from England
0.02	**Britt**	*Latin* from England
0.04	**Britta**	*Latin* from England
0.06	**Brittaney**	*Latin* from England
0.21	**Brittani**	*Latin* from England
0.06	**Brittanie**	*Latin* from England
0.91	**Brittany**	*Latin* from England
0.02	**Britteny**	*Latin* from England
0.02	**Brittnay**	*Latin* from England
0.02	**Brittnee**	*Latin* from England
1.90	**Brittney**	*Latin* from England
0.06	**Brittni**	*Latin* from England
0.03	**Brittnie**	*Latin* from England

0.04	**Brittny**	*Latin* from England
0.03	**Bronwyn**	*Welsh* white breast
0.02	**Brook**	*English* brook
0.99	**Brooke**	*English* brook
0.02	**Bryanna**	*Irish* strong
0.02	**Bryanne**	*Irish* strong
0.02	**Bryn**	*Latin* from the boundary line (Sabrina)
0.04	**Brynn**	*Latin* from the boundary line (Sabrina)

C

0.02	**Cailin**	*Greek* lark
1.39	**Caitlin**	*Greek* pure (Katherine)
0.17	**Caitlyn**	*Greek* pure (Katherine)
0.02	**Caleigh**	*Greek* beautiful
0.03	**Caley**	*Greek* beautiful
0.02	**Cali**	*Greek* beautiful
0.02	**Calli**	*Greek* beautiful
0.20	**Callie**	*Greek* beautiful
0.04	**Cameron**	*Scottish* crooked nose
0.04	**Cami**	*Latin* young attendant
0.04	**Camilla**	*Latin* young attendant
0.28	**Camille**	*Latin* young attendant
0.02	**Cammie**	*Latin* young attendant
1.17	**Candace**	*Greek* glittering white, incandescent
0.04	**Candi**	*Greek* glittering white, incandescent
1.17	**Candice**	*Greek* glittering white, incandescent
0.06	**Candis**	*Greek* glittering white, incandescent
0.02	**Candra**	*Latin* luminescent
0.03	**Candy**	*Greek* glittering white, incandescent
0.02	**Candyce**	*Greek* glittering white, incandescent
0.02	**Caprice**	*Italian* whimsical
0.42	**Cara**	*Irish* friend
0.04	**Carey**	*Turkish* flows like water
0.08	**Cari**	*Turkish* flows like water
0.02	**Caridad**	origin unknown
0.02	**Carie**	*Irish* friend; *Turkish* flows like water
0.05	**Carina**	*Latin* keel
0.21	**Carissa**	*Latin* charity

0.54	**Carla**	*French* little and womanly
0.03	**Carlee**	*French* little and womanly
0.03	**Carlene**	*French* little and womanly
0.11	**Carley**	*French* little and womanly
0.06	**Carli**	*French* little and womanly
0.08	**Carlie**	*French* little and womanly
0.54	**Carly**	*French* little and womanly
0.02	**Carlyn**	*French* little and womanly
0.03	**Carmela**	*Hebrew* vineyard, garden
0.02	**Carmella**	*Hebrew* vineyard, garden
0.36	**Carmen**	*Latin* a song
0.26	**Carol**	*Latin* strong and womanly; *French* song of joy
0.04	**Carole**	*Latin* strong and womanly; *French* song of joy; melody
0.09	**Carolina**	*French* little and womanly
0.64	**Caroline**	*French* little and womanly
0.65	**Carolyn**	*French* little and womanly
0.02	**Carolynn**	*French* little and womanly
0.07	**Carra**	*French* little and womanly
0.91	**Carrie**	*French* little and womanly; *Latin* strong and womanly; *French* song of joy
0.05	**Caryn**	*Danish* form of Katherine: *Greek* pure, unsullied
0.10	**Casandra**	*Greek* not believed
1.16	**Casey**	*Irish* brave
0.05	**Casie**	*Irish* brave
1.75	**Cassandra**	*Greek* not believed
0.02	**Cassey**	*Greek* not believed
0.03	**Cassi**	*Greek* not believed
0.11	**Cassidy**	*Irish* clever, quick one
0.56	**Cassie**	*Greek* not believed
0.04	**Cassondra**	*Greek* not believed
0.03	**Cassy**	*Greek* not believed
0.02	**Catalina**	*Spanish* form of *Greek* pure (Katherine)
0.02	**Catharine**	*Greek* pure
0.07	**Catherin**	*Greek* pure
1.56	**Catherine**	*Greek* pure
0.05	**Cathleen**	*Greek* pure (Katherine)

0.02	**Cathrine**	*Greek* pure
0.05	**Cathryn**	*Greek* pure
0.06	**Cathy**	*Greek* pure (Katherine)
0.07	**Catrina**	*Greek* pure (Katherine)
0.03	**Cayla**	form of Katherine; *Greek* pure, unsullied
0.02	**Caylee**	form of Katherine; *Greek* pure, unsullied
0.02	**Cecelia**	*Latin* blind
0.11	**Cecilia**	*Latin* blind
0.02	**Celena**	*Latin* heavenly (Celeste)
0.12	**Celeste**	*Latin* heavenly
0.06	**Celia**	*Latin* blind
0.06	**Celina**	*Latin* heavenly (Celeste)
0.04	**Celine**	*Latin* heavenly (Celeste)
0.04	**Chanda**	*Sanskrit* the great goddess; *Punjabi* moon
0.14	**Chandra**	*Sanskrit* moonlike
0.10	**Chanel**	*English* channel
0.02	**Chanell**	*English* channel
0.04	**Chanelle**	*English* channel
0.02	**Channel**	*English* channel
0.02	**Channing**	*English* knowing and wise; *French* canal
0.32	**Chantal**	*French* a song
0.03	**Chantale**	*French* a song
0.02	**Chantalle**	*French* a song
0.02	**Chante**	*French* a song
0.29	**Chantel**	*French* a song
0.06	**Chantell**	*French* a song
0.28	**Chantelle**	*French* a song
0.02	**Chardae**	*Arabic* runaway; *Punjabi* belief in donating for charity
0.02	**Charde**	*Arabic* runaway; *Punjabi* belief in donating for charity
0.02	**Charis**	*Latin* and *Greek* charity, loving
0.04	**Charissa**	*Latin* charity, loving; *Greek* grace
0.03	**Charisse**	*Latin* charity, loving; *Greek* grace
0.35	**Charity**	*Latin* and *Greek* charity, loving
0.02	**Charla**	*French* little and womanly (Carolyn)
0.35	**Charlene**	*French* little and womanly (Carolyn)
0.02	**Charlie**	*French* little and womanly (Carolyn)
0.32	**Charlotte**	*French* little and womanly (Carolyn)

0.08	**Charmaine**	*French* little and womanly (Carolyn)
0.26	**Chasity**	*Latin* pure
0.02	**Chassidy**	*Latin* pure
0.05	**Chastity**	*Latin* pure
1.37	**Chelsea**	*English* a port
0.38	**Chelsey**	*English* a port
0.03	**Chelsi**	*English* a port
0.14	**Chelsie**	*English* a port
0.02	**Chelsy**	*English* a port
0.05	**Cherelle**	*French* beloved
0.08	**Cheri**	*French* beloved; *Latin* charity, loving
0.10	**Cherie**	*French* beloved; *Latin* charity, loving
0.04	**Cherise**	*French* beloved; *Latin* charity, loving
0.05	**Cherish**	*French* beloved; *Latin* charity, loving
0.04	**Cherrelle**	*French* beloved
0.48	**Cheryl**	*French* beloved
0.06	**Cheyenne**	*American Indian* tribal name
0.11	**Chiquita**	*Spanish* little one
0.12	**Chloe**	*Greek* blooming green bird
0.02	**Chrissy**	*Greek* a Christian, anointed one (Christina)
0.51	**Christa**	*Greek* a Christian, anointed one (Christina)
0.04	**Christal**	*Greek* brilliant glass
0.14	**Christen**	*Greek* a Christian, anointed one (Christina)
0.08	**Christi**	*Greek* a Christian, anointed one (Christina)
0.12	**Christian**	*Greek* a Christian, anointed one (Christina)
0.03	**Christiana**	*Greek* a Christian, anointed one (Christina)
0.36	**Christie**	*Greek* a Christian, anointed one (Christina)
0.11	**Christin**	*Greek* a Christian, anointed one (Christina)
7.36	**Christina**	*Greek* a Christian, anointed one
2.46	**Christine**	*Greek* a Christian, anointed one

0.65	**Christy**	*Greek* a Christian, anointed one (Christina)
0.12	**Chrystal**	*Greek* brilliant glass
0.26	**Ciara**	*Irish* black
0.02	**Ciarra**	*Irish* black
0.13	**Ciera**	*Irish* black
0.21	**Cierra**	*Irish* black
0.38	**Cindy**	*Greek* moon
0.02	**Clair**	*Latin* clear, bright
0.44	**Claire**	*Latin* clear, bright
0.07	**Clara**	*Latin* clear, bright
0.05	**Clare**	*Latin* clear, bright
0.17	**Clarissa**	*Greek* most brilliant
0.10	**Claudia**	*Latin* lame
0.02	**Codi**	*Anglo Saxon* a cushion
0.04	**Cody**	*Anglo Saxon* a cushion
0.02	**Colby**	*English* and *Danish* a coal town
0.02	**Coleen**	*Irish* girl
0.07	**Colette**	*Latin* and *French* successful in battle
0.58	**Colleen**	*Irish* girl
0.02	**Collette**	*Latin* and *French* successful in battle
0.14	**Connie**	*Latin* constant, firm
0.16	**Constance**	*Latin* constant, firm
0.06	**Cora**	*Greek* maiden
0.04	**Coral**	*Latin* coral from the sea
0.08	**Corey**	*Irish* from the hollow
0.09	**Cori**	*Irish* from the hollow
0.04	**Corie**	*Irish* from the hollow
0.03	**Corina**	*Greek* maiden
0.03	**Corinna**	*Greek* maiden
0.13	**Corinne**	*Greek* maiden
0.02	**Corissa**	*Greek* maiden
0.06	**Corrie**	*Irish* from the hollow
0.02	**Corrina**	*Greek* maiden
0.06	**Corrine**	*Greek* maiden
0.24	**Cortney**	*French* from the king's court
0.06	**Cory**	*Irish* from the hollow
0.04	**Courtenay**	*French* from the king's court
3.82	**Courtney**	*French* from the king's court

0.02	**Courtnie**	*French* from the king's court
0.03	**Crista**	*Greek* a Christian, anointed one (Christina)
0.04	**Cristal**	*Greek* brilliant glass
0.02	**Cristen**	*Greek* a Christian, anointed one (Christina)
0.03	**Cristin**	*Greek* a Christian, anointed one (Christina)
0.36	**Cristina**	*Greek* a Christian, anointed one (Christina)
0.04	**Cristy**	*Greek* a Christian, anointed one (Christina)
6.77	**Crystal**	*Greek* brilliant glass
0.02	**Crystle**	*Greek* brilliant glass
0.76	**Cynthia**	*Greek* moon

D

0.02	**Daina**	*Latin* bright, pure as day; from Denmark
0.08	**Daisy**	*Old English* eye of the day
0.02	**Dakota**	*American Indian* tribal name
0.02	**Dale**	*Old English* from the valley
0.03	**Dallas**	*English* valley
0.03	**Damaris**	*Greek* heifer; of a gentle, trusting nature
1.07	**Dana**	*Latin* bright, pure as day; from Denmark
0.03	**Danae**	*Latin* bright, pure as day; from Denmark
0.06	**Danelle**	*Hebrew* God is my judge (Danielle)
0.02	**Danette**	*Hebrew* God is my judge (Danielle)
0.02	**Dani**	*Hebrew* God is my judge (Danielle)
0.02	**Dania**	*Hebrew* God is my judge (Danielle)
0.07	**Danica**	*Slavic* morning star
0.13	**Daniel**	*Hebrew* God is my judge
0.13	**Daniela**	*Hebrew* God is my judge
0.02	**Daniele**	*Hebrew* God is my judge
0.02	**Daniell**	*Hebrew* God is my judge
0.18	**Daniella**	*Hebrew* God is my judge
8.00	**Danielle**	*Hebrew* God is my judge
0.05	**Danika**	*Slavic* morning star

0.03	**Danna**	*Hebrew* God is my judge (Danielle); from Denmark
0.03	**Dannielle**	*Hebrew* God is my judge
0.02	**Danya**	*Hebrew* God is my judge (Danielle)
0.02	**Danyel**	*Hebrew* God is my judge (Danielle)
0.04	**Danyelle**	*Hebrew* God is my judge (Danielle)
0.08	**Daphne**	*Greek* laurel tree
0.07	**Dara**	*Hebrew* compassionate
0.02	**Darby**	*English* place name "Derby," a village with a deer park
0.03	**Darci**	*Irish* dark man; *Norman* place name Arcy
0.04	**Darcie**	*Irish* dark man; *Norman* place name Arcy
0.08	**Darcy**	*Irish* dark man; *Norman* place name Arcy
0.02	**Daria**	*Greek* regal, born to be queen
0.05	**Darla**	*English* dear or loved one
0.13	**Darlene**	*French* little darling; *Old English* dear beloved
0.02	**Daryl**	*French* little darling; *Old English* dear beloved
0.03	**Davina**	*Hebrew* beloved
0.54	**Dawn**	*English* dawn
0.02	**Dawna**	*English* dawn
0.13	**Dayna**	*Latin* bright, pure as day; from Denmark
0.06	**Deana**	*Latin* divine
0.02	**Deandra**	prefix de + André
0.59	**Deanna**	*Latin* divine
0.07	**Deanne**	*Latin* divine
0.06	**Debbie**	*Hebrew* a bee
0.38	**Deborah**	*Hebrew* a bee
0.22	**Debra**	*Hebrew* a bee
0.02	**Dedra**	*Irish* sorrow; wanderer (Deidre)
0.04	**Deena**	*Hebrew* judgment
0.08	**Deidra**	*Irish* sorrow; wanderer
0.13	**Deidre**	*Irish* sorrow; wanderer
0.06	**Deirdre**	*Irish* sorrow; wanderer
0.03	**Delia**	*Greek* visible
0.02	**Delilah**	*Hebrew* brooding
0.02	**Della**	nickname for Adelaide or Adele
0.02	**Delores**	*Spanish* sorrows

0.06	**Demetria**	*Greek* goddess of grain (fertility symbol)
0.07	**Dena**	*Hebrew* vindicated
0.02	**Denae**	*Hebrew* vindicated
0.56	**Denise**	*Greek* from Dionysius, god of wine and drama
0.03	**Denisha**	origin unknown, possibly an invented name
0.07	**Desirae**	*French* to crave
0.02	**Desire**	*French* to crave
0.47	**Desiree**	*French* to crave
0.02	**Desirée**	*French* to crave
0.14	**Destiny**	*French* destiny
0.02	**Devan**	*Irish* poet; *English* from Devon
0.14	**Devin**	*Irish* poet; *English* from Devon
0.18	**Devon**	*Irish* poet; *English* from Devon
0.02	**Diamond**	*Latin* precious stone
0.88	**Diana**	*Latin* divine
0.34	**Diane**	*Latin* divine
0.12	**Dianna**	*Latin* divine
0.05	**Dianne**	*Latin* divine
0.07	**Dina**	*Hebrew* judgment
0.03	**Dionne**	*Greek* mythological daughter of heaven and earth
0.02	**Dixie**	*French* ten or tenth; a girl born in the southern USA
0.03	**Dolores**	*Spanish* sorrows
0.84	**Dominique**	*French* belonging to the Lord
0.07	**Domonique**	*French* belonging to the Lord
0.39	**Donna**	*Latin* lady, madam
0.03	**Dora**	*Greek* a gift
0.02	**Doreen**	*Irish* the sullen one
0.04	**Doris**	*Greek* from the sea
0.21	**Dorothy**	*Greek* gift of God
0.03	**Drew**	*Greek* manly, valiant, courageous, strong (Andrew)
0.02	**Dusty**	*English* brown, stone, the brown rock quarry (Dustin)

E

0.05	**Eboni**	*Greek* a hard, dark wood
0.02	**Ebonie**	*Greek* a hard, dark wood
0.46	**Ebony**	*Greek* a hard, dark wood
0.03	**Echo**	*Greek* repeated sound
0.06	**Eden**	*Hebrew* delight
0.05	**Edith**	*Old English* rich gift
0.03	**Edna**	*Hebrew* rejuvenation
0.11	**Eileen**	*Greek* a torch, light
0.03	**Elaina**	*Greek* a torch, light
0.18	**Elaine**	*Greek* a torch, light
0.04	**Elana**	*Greek* a torch, light
0.07	**Eleanor**	*Greek* a torch, light
0.15	**Elena**	*Greek* a torch, light
0.02	**Eleni**	*Greek* a torch, light
0.02	**Eliana**	*Hebrew* God has answered me
0.04	**Elicia**	*Hebrew* God's oath (Elizabeth)
0.14	**Elisa**	*Hebrew* God's oath (Elizabeth)
0.21	**Elisabeth**	*Hebrew* God's oath (Elizabeth)
0.34	**Elise**	*Hebrew* God's oath (Elizabeth)
0.21	**Elisha**	*Hebrew* God's oath (Elizabeth)
0.09	**Elissa**	*Hebrew* God's oath (Elizabeth)
0.06	**Eliza**	*Hebrew* God's oath (Elizabeth)
9.17	**Elizabeth**	*Hebrew* God's oath
0.03	**Ella**	*Old English* beautiful fairy maiden
0.35	**Ellen**	*Greek* a torch, light
0.03	**Elsa**	*German* noble one
0.04	**Elsie**	*Danish* form of Elsa: noble one
0.25	**Elyse**	*Hebrew* God's oath (Elizabeth)
0.05	**Elysia**	*Hebrew* God's oath (Elizabeth)
0.03	**Elyssa**	*Hebrew* God's oath (Elizabeth)
0.02	**Emerald**	*Old French* the green gem
0.08	**Emilee**	*German* industrious
0.04	**Emilia**	*German* industrious
0.11	**Emilie**	*German* industrious
5.11	**Emily**	*German* industrious
0.59	**Emma**	*Greek* grandmother

3.36	**Erica**	*German* honorable ruler
0.16	**Ericka**	*German* honorable ruler
0.94	**Erika**	*German* honorable ruler
4.43	**Erin**	*Irish* peace
0.03	**Erinn**	*Irish* peace
0.04	**Eryn**	*Irish* peace
0.19	**Esther**	*Persian* a star
0.03	**Eugenia**	*Greek* well-born
0.02	**Eunice**	*Greek* happy in victory
0.17	**Eva**	*Latin* life
0.02	**Evan**	*Welsh* form of John, young warrior
0.02	**Evangeline**	*Greek* bearer of good tidings
0.05	**Eve**	*Latin* life
0.22	**Evelyn**	*Celtic* pleasant
0.02	**Evette**	*Latin* life
0.02	**Evie**	*Latin* life

F

0.20	**Faith**	*English* fidelity
0.12	**Fallon**	*Irish* grandchild of the ruler
0.02	**Falon**	*Irish* grandchild of the ruler
0.03	**Fannie**	*French* free (Francis)
0.03	**Farah**	*English* beautiful, pleasant
0.02	**Faren**	origin unknown
0.04	**Farrah**	*English* beautiful, pleasant
0.02	**Farren**	origin unknown
0.06	**Fatima**	*Arabic* a daughter of Muhammed
0.03	**Fawn**	*Old French* young deer
0.03	**Faye**	*Old French* a fairy, a child blessed with good fortune
0.06	**Felecia**	*Latin* happy
0.02	**Felica**	*Latin* happy
1.09	**Felicia**	*Latin* happy
0.07	**Felisha**	*Latin* happy
0.05	**Fiona**	*Celtic* white
0.02	**Flora**	*Latin* flowering
0.04	**Florence**	*Latin* blooming
0.24	**Frances**	*French* free

0.10	**Francesca**	*French* free
0.02	**Franchesca**	*French* free
0.06	**Francine**	*French* free
0.02	**Francis**	*French* free
0.02	**Frankie**	*French* free (Francis)

G

0.05	**Gabriela**	*Hebrew* God is my strength
0.02	**Gabriell**	*Hebrew* God is my strength
0.05	**Gabriella**	*Hebrew* God is my strength
0.29	**Gabrielle**	*Hebrew* God is my strength
0.04	**Gail**	*Old English* gaiety
0.02	**Gayle**	*Old English* gaiety
0.02	**Gemma**	*Latin* jewel
0.03	**Gena**	*Latin* queen
0.03	**Geneva**	*French* juniper tree
0.19	**Genevieve**	*Celtic* white wave
0.04	**Genna**	*Arabic* small bird (Jenna)
0.02	**Georgette**	*Latin* farmer
0.07	**Georgia**	*Latin* farmer
0.03	**Georgina**	*Latin* farmer
0.03	**Geraldine**	*Old German* and *French* mighty with the spear
0.02	**Geri**	*Old German* and *French* mighty with the spear (Geraldine)
0.03	**Gianna**	*Italian* form of Jane; *Hebrew* gracious, merciful
0.24	**Gillian**	*Latin* young; *Greek* soft-haired, youthful
0.02	**Gia**	*Latin* queen (Regina)
0.63	**Gina**	*Latin* queen (Regina)
0.08	**Ginger**	*Latin* ginger
0.02	**Ginny**	*Latin* pure, virgin (Virginia)
0.02	**Giovanna**	*Italian* form of Jean; *Hebrew* gracious, merciful
0.05	**Giselle**	*German* pledge; hostage
0.03	**Gladys**	*Latin* lame; small sword
0.05	**Glenda**	*Irish* from the valley or glen
0.02	**Glenna**	*Irish* from the valley or glen

0.18	**Gloria**	*Latin* glory
0.32	**Grace**	*Latin* grace
0.02	**Greta**	*Norwegian* form of *Latin* grace
0.08	**Gretchen**	*German* form of Margaret; *Greek* a pearl
0.02	**Guadalupe**	*Spanish* from St. Mary of Guadalupe
0.02	**Gurpreet**	*Punjabi* attached to guru, religious
0.02	**Gwen**	*Welsh* white
0.07	**Gwendolyn**	*Welsh* white

H

0.02	**Hailee**	*Scottish* hero
0.22	**Hailey**	*Scottish* hero
0.45	**Haley**	*Scottish* hero
0.02	**Hali**	*Scottish* hero
0.09	**Halley**	*Scottish* hero
0.06	**Hallie**	*Scottish* hero
0.02	**Hana**	*Hebrew* gracious
0.06	**Hanna**	*Hebrew* gracious
1.20	**Hannah**	*Hebrew* gracious
0.03	**Harmony**	*Latin* complete peace
0.03	**Harpreet**	*Punjabi* loves God, devoted to God
0.02	**Harriet**	*Old French* mistress of the home
0.02	**Haylee**	*Scottish* hero
0.38	**Hayley**	*Scottish* hero
0.03	**Hazel**	*Old English* hazel tree or nut
10.31	**Heather**	*English* a heath, a plant
0.02	**Heaven**	the word used as a name
0.62	**Heidi**	*German* noble, kind
0.26	**Helen**	*Greek* a torch, light
0.07	**Helena**	*Greek* a torch, light
0.02	**Helene**	*Greek* a torch, light
0.37	**Hilary**	*Latin* cheerful
0.37	**Hillary**	*Latin* cheerful
0.02	**Holley**	*English* holly
0.05	**Holli**	*English* holly
0.18	**Hollie**	*English* holly
2.24	**Holly**	*English* holly
0.30	**Hope**	*English* trust, faith, hope

I

0.04	**Ida**	*Old German* hardworking; *Old English* prosperous
0.02	**Iesha**	*Arabic* woman
0.02	**Ikia**	*Hawaiian* form of Isaiah; *Hebrew* God is my salvation
0.02	**Ilana**	*Hebrew* tree
0.19	**India**	the name of the country as a first name
0.06	**Ingrid**	*Old Norse* a hero's daughter
0.13	**Irene**	*Greek* peace
0.08	**Iris**	*Greek* rainbow
0.06	**Isabel**	*Spanish* consecrated to God
0.09	**Isabelle**	*Spanish* consecrated to God
0.02	**Ivette**	*French* archer (Yvonne)
0.02	**Ivory**	the word as a first name
0.10	**Ivy**	*English* ivy

J

0.18	**Jacalyn**	*Hebrew* to supplant
0.02	**Jacey**	invented name, possibly from initials J and C
0.03	**Jacinda**	*Spanish* hyacinth flower
0.02	**Jacinta**	*Spanish* hyacinth flower
0.16	**Jackie**	*Hebrew* to supplant
0.10	**Jacklyn**	*Hebrew* to supplant
0.03	**Jackqueline**	*Hebrew* to supplant
0.51	**Jaclyn**	*Hebrew* to supplant
0.02	**Jaclynn**	*Hebrew* to supplant
0.02	**Jacquelin**	*Hebrew* to supplant
1.60	**Jacqueline**	*Hebrew* to supplant
0.02	**Jacquely**	*Hebrew* to supplant
0.37	**Jacquelyn**	*Hebrew* to supplant
0.03	**Jacquelynn**	*Hebrew* to supplant
0.02	**Jacquline**	*Hebrew* to supplant
0.02	**Jada**	*Spanish* jade, a precious stone
0.36	**Jade**	*Spanish* jade, a precious stone

0.43	**Jaime**	*Hebrew* supplanter
0.04	**Jaimee**	*Hebrew* supplanter
0.15	**Jaimie**	*Hebrew* supplanter
0.14	**Jami**	*Hebrew* supplanter
3.87	**Jamie**	*Hebrew* supplanter
0.03	**Jamie-Lee**	Jamie + Lee
0.02	**Jamie-Lynn**	Jamie + Lynn
0.04	**Jamila**	*Arabic* beautiful
0.03	**Jammie**	*Hebrew* supplanter
0.02	**Jan**	*Hebrew* gracious, merciful
0.28	**Jana**	*Hebrew* gracious, merciful
0.06	**Janae**	*Hebrew* gracious, merciful
0.02	**Janay**	*Hebrew* gracious, merciful
0.21	**Jane**	*Hebrew* gracious, merciful
0.07	**Janel**	*Hebrew* gracious, merciful
0.07	**Janell**	*Hebrew* gracious, merciful
0.46	**Janelle**	*Hebrew* gracious, merciful
0.02	**Janene**	*Hebrew* gracious, merciful
0.09	**Janessa**	*Hebrew* gracious, merciful
0.26	**Janet**	*Hebrew* gracious, merciful
0.05	**Janette**	*Hebrew* gracious, merciful
0.29	**Janice**	*Hebrew* gracious, merciful
0.06	**Janie**	*Hebrew* gracious, merciful
0.23	**Janine**	*Hebrew* gracious, merciful
0.02	**Janis**	*Hebrew* gracious, merciful
0.11	**Janna**	*Hebrew* gracious, merciful
0.02	**Jaqueline**	*Hebrew* to supplant
0.11	**Jasmin**	*Persian* jasmine
0.97	**Jasmine**	*Persian* jasmine
0.02	**Jaspreet**	*Punjabi* virtuous, loves virtue
0.02	**Jaylene**	origin unknown, possibly an invented name
0.11	**Jayme**	*Hebrew* supplanter
0.02	**Jaymie**	*Hebrew* supplanter
0.02	**Jayna**	*Hebrew* gracious, merciful
0.03	**Jayne**	*Hebrew* gracious, merciful
0.04	**Jazmin**	*Persian* jasmine
0.04	**Jazmine**	*Persian* jasmine
0.10	**Jean**	*Hebrew* gracious, merciful

0.03	**Jeana**	*Hebrew* gracious, merciful
0.17	**Jeanette**	*Hebrew* gracious, merciful
0.02	**Jeanie**	*Hebrew* gracious, merciful
0.06	**Jeanine**	*Hebrew* gracious, merciful
0.03	**Jeanna**	*Hebrew* gracious, merciful
0.06	**Jeanne**	*Hebrew* gracious, merciful
0.10	**Jeannette**	*Hebrew* gracious, merciful
0.05	**Jeannie**	*Hebrew* gracious, merciful
0.04	**Jeannine**	*Hebrew* gracious, merciful
0.44	**Jena**	*Arabic* small bird
0.02	**Jenae**	*Arabic* small bird
0.08	**Jenelle**	Jenny + Nell
0.13	**Jenifer**	*Welsh* white, fair
0.02	**Jeniffer**	*Welsh* white, fair
0.03	**Jenilee**	Jennifer + Lee
0.02	**Jenine**	*Hebrew* gracious, merciful
2.61	**Jenna**	*Arabic* small bird
0.02	**Jennafer**	*Welsh* white, fair
0.02	**Jennette**	*Hebrew* gracious, merciful
0.03	**Jenni**	*Welsh* white, fair
0.02	**Jennica**	*Hebrew* gracious, merciful
0.17	**Jennie**	*Welsh* white, fair
19.75	**Jennifer**	*Welsh* white, fair
0.56	**Jenny**	*Welsh* white, fair
0.03	**Jeri**	*Old German* and *French* mighty with the spear (Geraldine)
0.03	**Jerica**	origin unknown, possibly an invented name
0.02	**Jerilyn**	Jeri + Lynn
0.02	**Jerri**	*Old German* and *French* mighty with the spear
0.05	**Jerrica**	origin unknown, possibly an invented name
0.03	**Jesica**	*Hebrew* God's grace
0.03	**Jessalyn**	Jessi + Lynn
0.14	**Jesse**	*Hebrew* God's grace
0.02	**Jesseca**	*Hebrew* God's grace
0.02	**Jessenia**	*Arabic* flower (Yesenia)
0.07	**Jessi**	*Hebrew* God's grace

27.70	**Jessica**	*Hebrew* God's grace
0.55	**Jessie**	*Hebrew* God's grace
0.04	**Jessika**	*Hebrew* God's grace
0.57	**Jill**	*Latin* young; *Greek* soft-haired, youthful
0.95	**Jillian**	*Latin* young; *Greek* soft-haired, youthful
0.05	**Jo**	*Hebrew* gracious, merciful
0.06	**Joan**	*Hebrew* gracious, merciful
0.02	**Joanie**	*Hebrew* gracious, merciful
0.06	**Joann**	*Hebrew* gracious, merciful
0.58	**Joanna**	*Hebrew* gracious, merciful
0.22	**Joanne**	*Hebrew* gracious, merciful
0.36	**Jocelyn**	*German* supplanted, substituted
0.02	**Jocelyne**	*German* supplanted, substituted
0.38	**Jodi**	*Hebrew* praise
0.15	**Jodie**	*Hebrew* praise
0.20	**Jody**	*Hebrew* praise
0.04	**Joel**	*Hebrew* the Lord is winning
0.09	**Joelle**	*Hebrew* the Lord is winning
0.02	**Johana**	*Hebrew* gracious, merciful
0.16	**Johanna**	*Hebrew* gracious, merciful
0.05	**Johnna**	*Hebrew* gracious, merciful
0.03	**Joleen**	*English* he will increase
0.19	**Jolene**	*English* he will increase
0.02	**Joline**	*English* he will increase
0.02	**Jonelle**	Jon + Ella
0.08	**Joni**	*Hebrew* gracious, merciful
0.02	**Jonna**	*Hebrew* gracious, merciful
0.68	**Jordan**	*Hebrew* descending
0.04	**Jordana**	*Hebrew* descending
0.02	**Jordanna**	*Hebrew* descending
0.05	**Josee**	*Hebrew* he shall increase
0.02	**Josée**	*Hebrew* he shall increase
0.02	**Joselyn**	*German* supplanted, substituted
0.10	**Josephine**	*Hebrew* he shall increase
0.06	**Josie**	*Hebrew* he shall increase
0.02	**Joslyn**	*German* supplanted, substituted
0.32	**Joy**	*Latin* joy
0.14	**Joyce**	*Latin* joyous

0.13	**Juanita**	*Spanish* form of Joan; *Hebrew* gracious, merciful
0.10	**Judith**	*Hebrew* of Judah
0.10	**Judy**	*Hebrew* of Judah
1.15	**Julia**	*Greek* soft-haired, youthful
0.08	**Juliana**	*Greek* soft-haired, youthful
0.02	**Juliane**	*Greek* soft-haired, youthful
0.03	**Juliann**	*Greek* soft-haired, youthful
0.08	**Julianna**	*Greek* soft-haired, youthful
0.17	**Julianne**	*Greek* soft-haired, youthful
2.09	**Julie**	*Greek* soft-haired, youthful
0.03	**Juliet**	*Greek* soft-haired, youthful
0.03	**Juliette**	*Greek* soft-haired, youthful
0.04	**June**	*Latin* youthful
0.10	**Justina**	*Latin* just, honest
0.47	**Justine**	*Latin* just, honest

K

0.06	**Kacey**	*Irish* brave
0.09	**Kaci**	*Irish* brave
0.11	**Kacie**	*Irish* brave
0.03	**Kacy**	*Irish* brave
0.03	**Kady**	*Greek* pure, unsullied (Katherine)
0.04	**Kaela**	*Arabic* beloved
0.02	**Kaelyn**	*Arabic* beloved
0.07	**Kaila**	*Arabic* beloved
0.05	**Kailee**	*Arabic* beloved
0.08	**Kailey**	*Arabic* beloved
0.58	**Kaitlin**	*Greek* pure, unsullied (Katherine)
0.46	**Kaitlyn**	*Greek* pure, unsullied (Katherine)
0.03	**Kaitlynn**	*Greek* pure, unsullied (Katherine)
0.10	**Kala**	*Hindi* black; time
0.02	**Kalee**	*Sanskrit* energy
0.03	**Kaleena**	origin unknown
0.09	**Kaleigh**	*Sanskrit* energy
0.11	**Kaley**	*Sanskrit* energy
0.11	**Kali**	*Sanskrit* energy
0.04	**Kalie**	*Sanskrit* energy

0.02	**Kalli**	*Sanskrit* energy
0.03	**Kallie**	*Sanskrit* energy
0.04	**Kalyn**	*Arabic* beloved
0.04	**Kami**	*Shintoism* divine power or aura
0.04	**Kandace**	*Greek* glittering white, incandescent
0.05	**Kandice**	*Greek* glittering white, incandescent
0.02	**Kandis**	*Greek* glittering white, incandescent
0.89	**Kara**	*Danish* form of Katherine; *Greek* pure, unsullied
0.02	**Karah**	*Italian* dear one; *Irish* friend
1.02	**Karen**	*Danish* form of Katherine; *Greek* pure, unsullied
0.46	**Kari**	*Danish* form of Katherine; *Greek* pure, unsullied
0.02	**Karie**	*Danish* form of Katherine; *Greek* pure, unsullied
0.07	**Karin**	*Danish* form of Katherine; *Greek* pure, unsullied
0.11	**Karina**	*Latin* a keel
0.06	**Karine**	*Danish* form of Katherine; *Greek* pure, unsullied
0.11	**Karissa**	origin unknown, possibly an invented name
0.22	**Karla**	*French* little and womanly
0.04	**Karlee**	*French* little and womanly
0.02	**Karlene**	*French* little and womanly
0.03	**Karley**	*French* little and womanly
0.06	**Karli**	*French* little and womanly
0.03	**Karlie**	*French* little and womanly
0.06	**Karly**	*French* little and womanly
0.02	**Karmen**	*Latin* a song
0.02	**Karolyn**	*French* little and womanly
0.03	**Karri**	*Irish* dark-haired
0.04	**Karrie**	*Irish* dark-haired
0.06	**Karyn**	*Danish* form of Katherine; *Greek* pure, unsullied
0.03	**Kasandra**	*Greek* not believed
0.36	**Kasey**	*Irish* brave
0.02	**Kasi**	*Irish* brave

0.04	**Kasie**	*Irish* brave
0.12	**Kassandra**	*Greek* not believed
0.02	**Kassi**	*Greek* not believed
0.02	**Kassidy**	*Greek* not believed
0.05	**Kassie**	*Greek* not believed
0.47	**Kate**	*Greek* pure, unsullied
0.06	**Katelin**	*Greek* pure, unsullied
0.67	**Katelyn**	*Greek* pure, unsullied
0.05	**Katelynn**	*Greek* pure, unsullied
0.02	**Katerina**	*Greek* pure, unsullied
0.02	**Katey**	*Greek* pure, unsullied
0.05	**Katharaine**	*Greek* pure, unsullied
0.02	**Katharin**	*Greek* pure, unsullied
0.25	**Katharine**	*Greek* pure, unsullied
0.22	**Katherin**	*Greek* pure, unsullied
3.83	**Katherine**	*Greek* pure, unsullied
0.04	**Katheryn**	*Greek* pure, unsullied
1.58	**Kathleen**	*Greek* pure, unsullied
0.03	**Kathlyn**	*Greek* pure, unsullied
0.06	**Kathrine**	*Greek* pure, unsullied
2.46	**Kathryn**	*Greek* pure, unsullied
0.12	**Kathy**	*Greek* pure, unsullied
0.06	**Kati**	*Greek* pure, unsullied
0.02	**Katia**	*Greek* pure, unsullied
3.24	**Katie**	*Greek* pure, unsullied
0.03	**Katina**	*Greek* pure, unsullied
0.02	**Katlin**	*Greek* pure, unsullied
0.07	**Katlyn**	*Greek* pure, unsullied
1.06	**Katrina**	*Greek* pure, unsullied
0.17	**Katy**	*Greek* pure, unsullied
0.03	**Kay**	*Greek* pure, unsullied
0.03	**Kaycee**	*Irish* brave
2.18	**Kayla**	*Hebrew* a crown, a laurel
0.02	**Kayle**	*Hebrew* a crown, a laurel
0.14	**Kaylee**	*Hebrew* a crown, a laurel
0.03	**Kayleen**	*Hebrew* a crown, a laurel
0.21	**Kayleigh**	*Hebrew* a crown, a laurel
0.02	**Kaylene**	*Hebrew* a crown, a laurel
0.02	**Kayley**	*Hebrew* a crown, a laurel

0.03	**Kaylie**	*Hebrew* a crown, a laurel
0.03	**Kaylin**	*Hebrew* a crown, a laurel
0.03	**Kaylyn**	*Hebrew* a crown, a laurel
0.02	**Keara**	*Irish* dark, black
0.02	**Keeley**	*Gaelic* beautiful one
0.04	**Keely**	*Gaelic* beautiful one
0.02	**Keena**	origin unknown
0.02	**Keira**	*Irish* dark, black
0.24	**Keisha**	*African* favorite; variation of Lakeisha
0.04	**Keli**	*Irish* warrior
0.29	**Kelley**	*Irish* warrior
0.62	**Kelli**	*Irish* warrior
0.34	**Kellie**	*Irish* warrior
4.18	**Kelly**	*Irish* warrior
0.02	**Kellye**	*Irish* warrior
0.02	**Kellyn**	probably an invented name consisting of Kelly + Lynn
0.02	**Kelsea**	*Scottish* from the ship island
0.87	**Kelsey**	*Scottish* from the ship island
0.04	**Kelsi**	*Scottish* from the ship island
0.06	**Kelsie**	*Scottish* from the ship island
0.02	**Kelsy**	*Scottish* from the ship island
0.02	**Kendal**	*Celtic* ruler of the valley
0.14	**Kendall**	*Celtic* ruler of the valley
1.12	**Kendra**	*English* knowledgeable
0.02	**Kenna**	*Old English* knowledge
0.04	**Kenya**	*Hebrew* horn (of an animal)
0.02	**Kenzie**	*Scottish* the fair one
0.03	**Kera**	*Irish* dark, black
0.02	**Keren**	*Danish* form of Katherine; *Greek* pure, unsullied (Karen)
0.30	**Keri**	*Irish* dark-haired
0.29	**Kerri**	*Irish* dark-haired
0.04	**Kerrie**	*Irish* dark-haired
0.21	**Kerry**	*Irish* dark-haired
0.02	**Kesha**	*African* favorite; variation of Lakeisha
0.19	**Keshia**	*African* favorite; variation of Lakeisha
0.02	**Khadijah**	*Arabic* trustworthy
0.06	**Kia**	*African* season's beginning

0.03	**Kiana**	variant of Anna: one of grace, gracious
0.03	**Kiara**	origin unknown; possibly a variant of Kiera
0.05	**Kiera**	*Irish* dark, black
0.03	**Kierra**	*Irish* dark, black
0.03	**Kiersten**	*Greek* a Christian, anointed one (Christina)
0.06	**Kiley**	*Irish* handsome; *Western Australian Aboriginal* curled, stick or boomerang
0.09	**Kim**	*English* chief, ruler
0.02	**Kimber**	*English* chief, ruler
0.07	**Kimberlee**	*English* chief, ruler
0.37	**Kimberley**	*English* chief, ruler
0.02	**Kimberlie**	*English* chief, ruler
5.88	**Kimberly**	*English* chief, ruler
0.02	**Kindra**	*English* knowledgeable
0.02	**Kinsey**	*Old English* offspring, relative
0.19	**Kira**	*Persian* sun
0.02	**Kiran**	*Irish* black, dark
0.04	**Kirby**	*English* place name
0.11	**Kirsta**	*Greek* a Christian, anointed one
0.29	**Kirsten**	*Greek* a Christian, anointed one
0.06	**Kirstin**	*Greek* a Christian, anointed one
0.02	**Kisha**	*African* favorite; variation of Lakeisha
0.04	**Kori**	*Irish* from the hollow
0.05	**Kortney**	*French* from the king's court
0.07	**Kourtney**	*French* from the king's court
1.24	**Krista**	*Greek* a Christian, anointed one
0.09	**Kristal**	*Greek* brilliant glass
0.06	**Kristan**	*Danish* form of *Greek* a Christian, anointed one (Christina)
0.02	**Kristel**	*Greek* brilliant glass
2.96	**Kristen**	*Greek* a Christian, anointed one (Christina)
0.57	**Kristi**	*Greek* a Christian, anointed one (Christina)
0.06	**Kristian**	*Greek* a Christian, anointed one (Christina)

0.29	**Kristie**	*Greek* a Christian, anointed one (Christina)
2.22	**Kristin**	*Greek* a Christian, anointed one (Christina)
1.45	**Kristina**	*Greek* a Christian, anointed one (Christina)
0.41	**Kristine**	*Greek* a Christian, anointed one (Christina)
0.80	**Kristy**	*Greek* a Christian, anointed one (Christina)
0.08	**Kristyn**	*Greek* a Christian, anointed one (Christina)
0.14	**Krysta**	*Greek* a Christian, anointed one (Christina)
1.62	**Krystal**	*Greek* brilliant glass
0.02	**Krystel**	*Greek* brilliant glass
0.05	**Krysten**	*Greek* a Christian, anointed one (Christina)
0.02	**Krysti**	*Greek* a Christian, anointed one (Christina)
0.04	**Krystin**	*Greek* a Christian, anointed one (Christina)
0.07	**Krystina**	*Greek* a Christian, anointed one (Christina)
0.56	**Krystle**	*Greek* a Christian, anointed one (Christina)
0.02	**Krystyna**	*Greek* a Christian, anointed one (Christina)
0.25	**Kyla**	*Irish* handsome
0.14	**Kyle**	*Irish* handsome
0.10	**Kylee**	*Irish* handsome
0.02	**Kyleigh**	*Irish* handsome
0.02	**Kylene**	*Irish* handsome
0.17	**Kylie**	*Irish* handsome; *Western Australian Aboriginal* curled, stick or boomerang
0.02	**Kymberly**	*English* chief, ruler
0.07	**Kyra**	*Greek* lord or god
0.07	**Kyrie**	*Greek* lord or god

L

0.02	**La**	a popular prefix
0.02	**Lacee**	*Latin* cheerful
0.91	**Lacey**	*Latin* cheerful
0.08	**Laci**	*Latin* cheerful
0.13	**Lacie**	*Latin* cheerful
0.26	**Lacy**	*Latin* cheerful
0.03	**Ladonna**	*French* the lady
0.02	**Laila**	*Arabic* dark as night
0.02	**Laine**	*English* someone who lives near a lane
0.14	**Lakeisha**	fashionable prefix La + Aisha or Aiesha
0.02	**Laken**	origin unknown
0.02	**Lakendra**	La + Kendra
0.05	**Lakesha**	fashionable prefix La + Aisha
0.07	**Lakeshia**	fashionable prefix La + Aisha
0.02	**Lakia**	*Arabic* found treasure
0.08	**Lakisha**	fashionable prefix La + Aisha
0.12	**Lana**	*Latin* woolly
0.02	**Lani**	*Hawaiian* sky
0.02	**Laquisha**	fashionable prefix La + Aisha
0.06	**Laquita**	*Indian* quiet one
0.20	**Lara**	*Latin* shining; famous
0.02	**Larisa**	*Latin* cheerful
0.20	**Larissa**	*Latin* cheerful
0.02	**Lashanda**	La + Shanda
0.02	**Lashawna**	La + Shawna
0.06	**Lashonda**	*Greek* a bee, honey
0.02	**Latanya**	La + Tanya
0.02	**Latara**	La + Tara
0.35	**Latasha**	La + tasha (possibly from Natasha)
0.02	**Latashia**	La + tashia (possibly from Natasha)
0.03	**Latavia**	*Arabic* pleasant
0.02	**Latesha**	La + tesha (possibly from Natasha)
0.02	**Latia**	origin unknown
0.18	**Latisha**	La + tisha (possibly from Natasha);
0.11	**Latonya**	La + Tonya
0.02	**Latoria**	La + toria

0.05	**Latosha**	La + tosha
0.88	**Latoya**	*Greek* a powerful mythological deity
0.04	**Latrice**	La + element from Patrice; *Latin* of noble descent
0.02	**Latricia**	La + element from Patricia; *Latin* of noble descent
6.20	**Laura**	*Latin* laurel
0.17	**Laurel**	*Latin* laurel
8.11	**Lauren**	*Latin* laurel
0.23	**Laurie**	*Latin* laurel
0.02	**Lauryn**	*Latin* laurel
0.02	**Lawanda**	La + Wanda; variant of Lajuan, *Spanish* form of Joanna
0.03	**Layla**	*Arabic* dark as night
0.09	**Lea**	*Hebrew* to be weary
1.25	**Leah**	*Hebrew* to be weary
0.03	**Leandra**	*Latin* like a lioness
0.09	**Leann**	*English* from the meadow
0.08	**Leanna**	*English* from the meadow
0.36	**Leanne**	*English* from the meadow
0.11	**Lee**	*English* from the meadow
0.05	**Leeann**	*English* from the meadow
0.03	**Leeanne**	*English* from the meadow
0.02	**Leia**	*Hebrew* to be weary
0.28	**Leigh**	*English* from the meadow
0.03	**Leigha**	*Hebrew* to be weary
0.02	**Leighann**	*English* from the meadow
0.07	**Leila**	*Arabic* dark as night
0.02	**Leilani**	*Hawaiian* heavenly child
0.11	**Lena**	*Latin* temptress
0.05	**Leona**	*French* lionlike
0.02	**Leslee**	*English* meadowlands
0.25	**Lesley**	*English* meadowlands
1.18	**Leslie**	*English* meadowlands
0.06	**Leticia**	*Latin* gladness
0.02	**Letisha**	*Latin* gladness
0.02	**Letitia**	*Latin* gladness
0.04	**Lia**	*Hebrew* to be weary
0.04	**Liana**	*English* from the meadow

0.05	**Liane**	*English* from the meadow
0.02	**Lianna**	*English* from the meadow
0.05	**Lianne**	*English* from the meadow
0.03	**Liberty**	*Latin* free
0.02	**Lidia**	*Greek* from Lydia
0.03	**Lila**	*Hindi* free, playful will of God
0.02	**Liliana**	*Latin* lily
0.12	**Lillian**	*Latin* lily
0.07	**Lily**	*Latin* lily
0.03	**Lina**	*Latin* temptress
0.50	**Linda**	*Spanish* pretty
3.42	**Lindsay**	*English* the camp near the stream
3.42	**Lindsey**	*English* the camp near the stream
0.02	**Lindsi**	*English* the camp near the stream
0.03	**Lindsay**	*English* the camp near the stream
0.04	**Lindy**	*Spanish* pretty
0.03	**Linnea**	*Old Norse* lime tree
0.05	**Linsey**	*English* the camp near the stream
3.43	**Lisa**	*Hebrew* God's oath (Elizabeth)
0.02	**Lisa-Marie**	Lisa + Marie
0.03	**Lise**	*Hebrew* God's oath (Elizabeth)
0.02	**Lisette**	*Hebrew* God's oath (Elizabeth)
0.02	**Lissa**	*Hebrew* God's oath (Elizabeth)
0.03	**Lissette**	*Hebrew* God's oath (Elizabeth)
0.05	**Liza**	*Hebrew* God's oath (Elizabeth)
0.03	**Logan**	*Middle English* a felled tree
0.04	**Lois**	*German* famous warrior
0.02	**Lola**	*Spanish* short form of Maria de los Dolores, Mary of the Sorrows
0.03	**Loni**	*Middle English* alone
0.12	**Lora**	*Latin* laurel
0.09	**Loren**	*Latin* laurel
0.06	**Lorena**	*Latin* laurel
0.08	**Loretta**	*Latin* laurel
0.53	**Lori**	*Latin* laurel
0.02	**Lorie**	*Latin* laurel
0.02	**Lorin**	*Latin* laurel
0.04	**Lorna**	*Latin* laurel
0.11	**Lorraine**	*Latin* sorrowful

0.02	**Lorrie**	*Latin* laurel
0.03	**Louisa**	*German* famous warrior
0.09	**Louise**	*German* famous warrior
0.02	**Lourdes**	*French* place name
0.05	**Lucia**	*Latin* light
0.02	**Lucie**	*Latin* light
0.02	**Lucille**	*Latin* light
0.05	**Lucinda**	*Latin* light
0.13	**Lucy**	*Latin* light
0.02	**Luisa**	*German* famous warrior
0.03	**Luz**	*Latin* light
0.33	**Lydia**	*Greek* from Lydia
0.05	**Lynda**	*Spanish* pretty
0.02	**Lyndi**	*Spanish* pretty
0.16	**Lyndsay**	*English* the camp near the stream
0.20	**Lyndsey**	*English* the camp near the stream
0.02	**Lyndsie**	*English* the camp near the stream
0.08	**Lynette**	*Celtic* graceful
0.18	**Lynn**	*English* waterfall
0.04	**Lynne**	*English* waterfall
0.04	**Lynnette**	*Celtic* graceful
0.08	**Lynsey**	*English* the camp near the stream

M

0.02	**Mabel**	*Latin* lovable
0.11	**Mackenzie**	*Irish* son of the wise leader
0.02	**Madalyn**	*Greek* a high tower
0.02	**Madelaine**	*Greek* a high tower
0.07	**Madeleine**	*Greek* a high tower
0.22	**Madeline**	*Greek* a high tower
0.04	**Madelyn**	*Greek* a high tower
0.22	**Madison**	son of Maude; *English* good
0.16	**Maegan**	*Greek* a pearl (Margaret)
0.02	**Maeghan**	*Greek* a pearl (Margaret)
0.05	**Magan**	*Greek* a pearl (Margaret)
0.02	**Magdalena**	*Greek* tower
0.07	**Magen**	*Greek* a pearl (Margaret)
0.29	**Maggie**	*Greek* a pearl (Margaret)

0.02	**Maia**	*Old English* kinswoman; *Middle English* maiden
0.02	**Makayla**	possibly a variant of Makala; *Hawaiian* myrtle
0.02	**Malerie**	*French* armour mailed
0.02	**Malia**	*Hawaiian* form of Mary; *Hebrew* sea of sorrow
0.02	**Malika**	*Hebrew* queen
0.09	**Malinda**	*Latin* brave, martial
0.04	**Malissa**	*Greek* a bee, honey
0.02	**Mallori**	*French* armour mailed
0.06	**Mallorie**	*French* armour mailed
1.26	**Mallory**	*French* armour mailed
0.03	**Malorie**	*French* armour mailed
0.02	**Malory**	*French* armour mailed
0.03	**Mandeep**	*Punjabi* mind full of light, enlightened being
0.14	**Mandi**	form of Amanda; *Latin* worthy of love
0.02	**Mandie**	form of Amanda; *Latin* worthy of love
0.47	**Mandy**	form of Amanda; *Latin* worthy of love
0.03	**Manpreet**	*Punjabi* mind full of love
0.05	**Mara**	*Hebrew* bitter
0.07	**Maranda**	*Latin* strange, wonderful
0.06	**Marcella**	*Latin* brave, warlike
0.05	**Marci**	*Latin* brave, warlike
0.09	**Marcia**	*Latin* brave, warlike
0.06	**Marcie**	*Latin* brave, warlike
0.06	**Marcy**	*Latin* brave, warlike
0.02	**Maren**	origin unknown
1.10	**Margaret**	*Greek* a pearl
0.04	**Margarita**	*Greek* a pearl
0.02	**Margie**	*Greek* a pearl
0.04	**Margo**	*Greek* a pearl
0.03	**Margot**	*Greek* a pearl
0.03	**Marguerite**	*Greek* a pearl
0.02	**Mari**	*Hebrew* sea of sorrow
3.12	**Maria**	*Latin*, *French*, *Italian*, *Spanish*, *Swedish* of Mary; *Hebrew* sea of sorrow
0.08	**Mariah**	*Hebrew* sea of sorrow

0.03	**Mariam**	form of Mary + Ann
0.05	**Marian**	form of Mary + Ann
0.02	**Mariana**	form of Mary + Ann
0.03	**Marianna**	form of Mary + Ann
0.10	**Marianne**	form of Mary + Ann
0.02	**Maribel**	*Hebrew* beautiful but bitter
1.19	**Marie**	*Latin, French, Italian, Spanish, Swedish* forms of Mary; *Hebrew* sea of sorrow
0.02	**Marie-Claude**	Mary + Claude
0.03	**Marie-Eve**	Mary + Eve
0.02	**Marie-Pier**	Mary + Pierre
0.02	**Mariel**	*German* form of Mary; *Hebrew* sea of sorrow
0.02	**Marika**	*Slavic* form of Mary; *Hebrew* sea of sorrow
0.13	**Marilyn**	*Hebrew* descendants of Mary
0.09	**Marina**	*Latin* the sea
0.04	**Marion**	*French* form of Mary; *Hebrew* sea of sorrow
0.22	**Marisa**	*Latin* the sea
0.02	**Marisela**	*Spanish* Maris "sea" and Marcella "brave martial" or a "hammer"
0.02	**Marisha**	*Russian* short form of Mary; *Hebrew* sea of sorrow
0.04	**Marisol**	origin unknown
0.67	**Marissa**	*Latin* the sea
0.04	**Maritza**	*Arabic* blessed
0.07	**Marjorie**	*Scottish* form of Mary; *Hebrew* sea of sorrow
0.04	**Markita**	*Czech* form of Margaret; *Greek* a pearl
0.08	**Marla**	*Greek* a high tower
0.02	**Marlaina**	*Greek* a high tower
0.02	**Marlana**	*Greek* a high tower
0.03	**Marlee**	*Greek* a high tower
0.06	**Marlena**	*Greek* a high tower
0.09	**Marlene**	*Greek* a high tower
0.05	**Marley**	*Greek* a high tower
0.02	**Marly**	*Greek* a high tower
0.02	**Marnie**	*Hebrew* to rejoice

0.13	**Marquita**	*Spanish* form of Marcia: *Latin* brave, warlike
0.06	**Marsha**	*Latin* warlike
0.04	**Marta**	*Aramaic* a lady; sorrowful
0.02	**Martaha**	*Aramaic* a lady; sorrowful
0.28	**Martha**	*Aramaic* a lady; sorrowful
0.08	**Martina**	*Aramaic* a lady; sorrowful
0.04	**Martine**	*Aramaic* a lady; sorrowful
3.54	**Mary**	*Hebrew* sea of sorrow
0.06	**Maryann**	Mary + Ann
0.03	**Maryanne**	Mary + Ann
0.02	**Marybeth**	Mary + Beth
0.02	**Maryse**	*French* form of Mary; *Hebrew* sea of sorrow
0.03	**Mattie**	*Aramaic* a lady; sorrowful (Martha)
0.09	**Maura**	*Latin* dark
0.20	**Maureen**	*French* dark-skinned
0.04	**Maxine**	*Latin* greatest
0.02	**May**	*Old English* kinswoman; *Middle English* maiden
0.06	**Maya**	*Latin* great
0.04	**Mayra**	origin unknown
0.02	**Mckenna**	surname used as first name
0.05	**Mckenzie**	surname used as first name
0.93	**Meagan**	*Greek* a pearl (Margaret)
0.02	**Meagen**	*Greek* a pearl (Margaret)
0.36	**Meaghan**	*Greek* a pearl (Margaret)
9.59	**Megan**	*Greek* a pearl (Margaret)
0.04	**Meggan**	*Greek* a pearl (Margaret)
1.57	**Meghan**	*Greek* a pearl (Margaret)
0.06	**Meghann**	*Greek* a pearl (Margaret)
1.48	**Melanie**	*Greek* black, dark appearance
0.06	**Mélanie**	*Greek* black, dark appearance
0.03	**Melany**	*Greek* black, dark appearance
0.03	**Melina**	*Greek* a song
0.63	**Melinda**	*Latin* brave, martial
0.07	**Melisa**	*Greek* a bee, honey
10.23	**Melissa**	*Greek* a bee, honey
0.02	**Mélissa**	*Greek* a bee, honey
0.04	**Mellisa**	*Greek* a bee, honey

0.04	**Mellissa**	*Greek* a bee, honey
0.03	**Melodie**	*Greek* a melody
0.27	**Melody**	*Greek* a melody
0.02	**Melonie**	*Greek* black, dark appearance
0.02	**Melony**	*Greek* black, dark appearance
0.02	**Melynda**	*Latin* brave, martial
0.02	**Meranda**	*Latin* strange, wonderful
0.08	**Mercedes**	*Latin* reward, payment
0.61	**Meredith**	*Welsh* protector of the sea
0.03	**Merissa**	*Latin* the sea (Marisa)
0.02	**Meryl**	*Irish* bright sea
0.13	**Mia**	*Italian* mine, my
0.03	**Micaela**	*Hebrew* who is like God
0.03	**Micah**	*Hebrew* who is like God
0.03	**Michael**	*Hebrew* who is like God
0.15	**Michaela**	*Hebrew* who is like God
0.37	**Michele**	*Hebrew* who is like God
0.02	**Michell**	*Hebrew* who is like God
7.70	**Michelle**	*Hebrew* who is like God
0.03	**Mika**	*Hebrew* who is like God
0.04	**Mikaela**	*Hebrew* who is like God
0.02	**Mikayla**	*Hebrew* who is like God
0.03	**Mildred**	*Old English* gentle counsellor
0.32	**Milissa**	*Greek* a bee, honey
0.02	**Mina**	*Old German* love
0.03	**Mindi**	*Latin* brave, martial; *Old German* love
0.33	**Mindy**	*Latin* brave, martial; *Old German* love
0.81	**Miranda**	*Latin* strange, wonderful
0.02	**Mireille**	*Latin* wonderful
0.14	**Miriam**	*Hebrew* sea of sorrow
0.02	**Missy**	*Greek* a bee, honey
0.03	**Misti**	*English* obscure, covered with mist
0.62	**Misty**	*English* obscure, covered with mist
0.02	**Moira**	*Irish* see Mary
0.09	**Mollie**	*Irish* see Mary
0.62	**Molly**	*Irish* see Mary
0.04	**Mona**	*Gaelic* noble; *Greek* solitary
1.39	**Monica**	*Greek* solitary *Latin* advisor
0.09	**Monika**	*Greek* solitary *Latin* advisor

0.55	**Monique**	*Greek* solitary *Latin* advisor
0.81	**Morgan**	*Welsh* edge of the sea
0.02	**Moriah**	*French* dark-skinned (Maureen)
0.02	**Mylène**	*Greek* black, dark
0.04	**Myra**	*Hebrew* sea of sorrow (Miriam)
0.02	**Myriam**	*Hebrew* sea of sorrow (Miriam)

N

0.02	**Nada**	*French, Slavic* hope
0.20	**Nadia**	*French, Slavic* hope
0.21	**Nadine**	*French, Slavic* hope
0.04	**Nakia**	*Arabic* pure
0.06	**Nakita**	*Greek* victory of the people (Nicole)
0.50	**Nancy**	*Hebrew* gracious
0.33	**Naomi**	*Hebrew* beautiful, pleasant
0.03	**Natacha**	*Latin* to be born
0.03	**Natalee**	*Latin* to be born
0.10	**Natalia**	*Latin* to be born
2.18	**Natalie**	*Latin* to be born
1.97	**Natasha**	*Latin* to be born
0.05	**Natashia**	*Latin* to be born
0.14	**Nathalie**	*Latin* to be born
0.03	**Natisha**	*Latin* to be born
0.04	**Natosha**	*Latin* to be born
0.03	**Nellie**	nickname for Helen: *Greek* a torch, light
0.03	**Nia**	*Welsh* figure in *Irish* legend
0.02	**Nichelle**	blend of Michelle and Nicole
0.02	**Nichol**	*Greek* victory of the people
0.78	**Nichole**	*Greek* victory of the people
0.04	**Nicki**	*Greek* victory of the people
0.02	**Nickie**	*Greek* victory of the people
0.02	**Nickole**	*Greek* victory of the people
0.02	**Nicky**	*Greek* victory of the people
0.06	**Nicola**	*Greek* victory of the people
11.82	**Nicole**	*Greek* victory of the people
0.05	**Nicolette**	*Greek* victory of the people
0.04	**Nicolle**	*Greek* victory of the people
0.02	**Niesha**	origin unknown

0.05	**Niki**	*Greek* victory of the people
0.02	**Nikia**	*Greek* victory of the people
0.40	**Nikita**	*Greek* victory of the people
0.36	**Nikki**	*Greek* victory of the people
0.02	**Nikkita**	*Greek* victory of the people
0.05	**Nikole**	*Greek* victory of the people
0.32	**Nina**	*Spanish* girl
0.03	**Nisha**	origin unknown
0.05	**Noel**	*Latin* Christmas
0.12	**Noelle**	*Latin* Christmas
0.02	**Noemi**	origin unknown
0.09	**Nora**	short form of Eleanor; *Greek* a torch, light
0.02	**Noreen**	short form of Eleanor; *Greek* a torch, light
0.05	**Norma**	*Latin* rule, pattern
0.02	**Nyssa**	*Greek* beginning

O

0.08	**Octavia**	*Latin* eighth
0.02	**Olga**	*Old Norse* holy
0.36	**Olivia**	*Latin* olive

P

0.30	**Paige**	*English* child, young
0.87	**Pamela**	*Greek* all-honey
0.02	**Paola**	*Latin* small
0.06	**Paris**	*French* place name
0.02	**Patience**	*French* endurance
0.14	**Patrice**	*Latin* of noble descent
1.30	**Patricia**	*Latin* of noble descent
0.30	**Paula**	*Latin* small
0.02	**Paulette**	*Latin* small
0.08	**Pauline**	*Latin* small
0.02	**Pearl**	*Latin* pearl
0.05	**Peggy**	form of Margaret; *Greek* a pearl
0.05	**Penny**	*Greek* weaver
0.02	**Petra**	*Latin* rock
0.05	**Phoebe**	*Greek* the shining

0.04	**Phylicia**	*Greek* a green bough
0.03	**Phyllis**	*Greek* a green bough
0.02	**Porsche**	*Latin* an offering
0.03	**Porsha**	*Latin* an offering
0.04	**Portia**	*Latin* an offering
0.10	**Precious**	word used as a name
0.06	**Princess**	word used as a name
0.27	**Priscilla**	*Latin* from ancient times
0.04	**Priya**	*Hindi* beloved, very sweet natured

Q

0.02	**Quiana**	modernized form of Anna; *Hebrew* gracious
0.02	**Quinn**	*Old English* queen

R

0.88	**Rachael**	*Hebrew* a female sheep
0.12	**Racheal**	*Hebrew* a female sheep
5.71	**Rachel**	*Hebrew* a female sheep
0.03	**Rachele**	*Hebrew* a female sheep
0.02	**Rachell**	*Hebrew* a female sheep
0.39	**Rachelle**	*Hebrew* a female sheep
0.03	**Racquel**	*Hebrew* a female sheep
0.04	**Rae**	*Hebrew* a female sheep
0.02	**Raeann**	Rachel + Ann
0.02	**Raechel**	*Hebrew* a female sheep
0.04	**Raina**	*Old German* mighty
0.02	**Ramandeep**	origin unknown
0.03	**Ramona**	*Spanish* mighty, wise protectress
0.02	**Randa**	*Anglo Saxon* superior protection
0.02	**Randall**	*Anglo Saxon* superior protection
0.37	**Randi**	*English* shield-wolf
0.16	**Raquel**	*Hebrew* a female sheep
0.03	**Rashida**	*Turkish* the rightly guided
0.12	**Raven**	*English* like a raven
0.04	**Rayna**	*Yiddish* pure, clean
0.02	**Reanna**	Rachel + Ann
0.02	**Reba**	*Hebrew* to tie, to bind

0.03	**Rebeca**	*Hebrew* to tie, to bind
5.02	**Rebecca**	*Hebrew* to tie, to bind
0.02	**Rebeka**	*Hebrew* to tie, to bind
0.59	**Rebekah**	*Hebrew* to tie, to bind
0.02	**Reena**	*Greek* peace
0.03	**Regan**	*Latin* queen (Regina)
0.38	**Regina**	*Latin* queen
0.02	**Reina**	*Latin* queen (Regina)
0.05	**Rena**	*Greek* peace
0.04	**Renae**	*French* to be born again
0.03	**Renata**	*French* to be born again
0.04	**Rene**	*French* to be born again
0.76	**Renee**	*French* to be born again
0.04	**Renée**	*French* to be born again
0.03	**Renita**	*French* to be born again
0.03	**Reva**	*Latin* reviving
0.02	**Reyna**	*Greek* peace
0.03	**Rhea**	*Greek* a stream
0.02	**Rhianna**	*Welsh* maiden
0.09	**Rhiannon**	*Welsh* a mythological witch, nymph, goddess
0.03	**Rhoda**	variation of Rose
0.26	**Rhonda**	*Welsh* grand
0.08	**Richelle**	*German* powerful ruler
0.02	**Ricki**	*Latin* true image (Veronica)
0.07	**Rikki**	*Latin* true image (Veronica)
0.04	**Riley**	*Irish* valiant
0.13	**Rita**	*Sanskrit* brave, honest
0.09	**Roberta**	*English* shining with fame
0.81	**Robin**	*English* shining with fame
0.68	**Robyn**	*English* shining with fame
0.17	**Rochelle**	*French* from the large stone
0.02	**Rocio**	origin unknown
0.03	**Ronda**	*Welsh* grand
0.10	**Rosa**	*Latin* rose
0.04	**Rosalie**	Rose + Lee
0.02	**Rosalind**	*Spanish* fair rose
0.04	**Rosalyn**	*Spanish* fair rose
0.08	**Rosanna**	Rose + Anna

0.04	**Rosanne**	Rose + Anne
0.24	**Rose**	*Latin* rose
0.03	**Roseann**	Rose + Anne
0.02	**Roseanna**	Rose + Anna
0.02	**Roseanne**	Rose + Anne
0.04	**Rosemarie**	Rose + Marie
0.09	**Rosemary**	Rose + Mary
0.02	**Rosetta**	*French* form of Rose; rose
0.02	**Roxana**	*Persian* dawn, light
0.02	**Roxann**	*Persian* dawn, light
0.02	**Roxanna**	*Persian* dawn, light
0.23	**Roxanne**	*Persian* dawn, light
0.10	**Ruby**	*French* ruby
0.28	**Ruth**	*Hebrew* friendship
0.13	**Ryan**	*Irish* little king
0.03	**Ryann**	*Irish* little king

S

0.02	**Sabina**	*Latin* from the Sabine, a tribe in ancient Italy
0.04	**Sable**	*Middle English* rich fur
0.02	**Sabra**	*Hebrew* thorny cactus
0.84	**Sabrina**	*Latin* from the boundary line
0.02	**Sacha**	*Russian* form of Alexandra: *Greek* defender of mankind
0.29	**Sade**	*Hebrew* princess, noble
0.09	**Sadie**	*Hebrew* princess, noble
0.02	**Safiya**	*Arabic* pure, serene; best friend
0.03	**Salena**	*Latin* saline, salty
0.02	**Salina**	*Latin* saline, salty
0.16	**Sally**	*Hebrew* princess, noble (Sarah)
5.64	**Samantha**	*Aramaic* the listener
0.03	**Samara**	*Hebrew* ruled by God
0.02	**Sana**	*Arabic* top of (mountain); resplendence, brilliance
0.02	**Sandeep**	*Punjabi* enlightened being
0.02	**Sandi**	*Greek* defender of mankind (Alexandra)
0.62	**Sandra**	*Greek* defender of mankind (Alexandra)

0.13	**Sandy**	*Greek* defender of mankind (Alexandra)
0.15	**Santana**	*Spanish* saint
4.18	**Sara**	*Hebrew* princess, noble
15.68	**Sarah**	*Hebrew* princess, noble
0.02	**Sari**	*Hebrew* princess, noble
0.03	**Sarina**	form of Sarah; *Hebrew* princess, noble
0.02	**Sarita**	*Spanish* form of Sarah; *Hebrew* princess, noble
0.39	**Sasha**	*Russian* form of Alexandra; *Greek* defender of mankind
0.02	**Saundra**	*Greek* defender of mankind (Alexandra)
0.02	**Savana**	*Spanish* barren
0.03	**Savanah**	*Spanish* barren
0.07	**Savanna**	*Spanish* barren
0.54	**Savannah**	*Spanish* barren
0.02	**Scarlett**	*English* bright red color
0.07	**Selena**	*Greek* moon
0.06	**Selina**	*Greek* moon
0.16	**Serena**	*Latin* peaceful
0.02	**Serina**	*Latin* peaceful
0.02	**Shae**	*Hebrew* asked for
0.14	**Shaina**	*Hebrew* beautiful
0.02	**Shakera**	popular prefix Sha + kera
0.03	**Shakia**	popular prefix Sha + kia
0.04	**Shakira**	popular prefix Sha + kira
0.02	**Shakita**	popular prefix Sha + kita
0.02	**Shalane**	popular prefix Sha + lene
0.03	**Shalonda**	popular prefix Sha + londa
0.04	**Shameka**	popular prefix Sha + meka
0.03	**Shamika**	popular prefix Sha + mika
0.04	**Shamira**	popular prefix Sha + mira
0.35	**Shana**	*Hebrew* God is gracious
0.04	**Shanae**	*Hebrew* God is gracious
0.06	**Shanda**	*English* rambunctious
0.04	**Shandi**	*English* rambunctious
0.02	**Shandra**	origin unknown
0.03	**Shaneka**	popular prefix Sha + neka
0.02	**Shanel**	*English* channel
0.04	**Shanell**	*English* channel

0.04	**Shanelle**	*English* channel
0.02	**Shani**	*African* marvelous
0.04	**Shanika**	popular prefix Sha + nika
0.03	**Shanita**	popular prefix Sha + nita
0.33	**Shanna**	*Hebrew* God is gracious
0.03	**Shannan**	*Irish* small; wise
3.32	**Shannon**	*Irish* small; wise
0.03	**Shanon**	*Irish* small; wise
0.03	**Shanta**	*French* a song
0.02	**Shantae**	*French* a song
0.05	**Shante**	*French* a song
0.13	**Shantel**	*French* a song (Chantel)
0.09	**Shantell**	*French* a song (Chantel)
0.04	**Shantelle**	*French* a song (Chantel)
0.02	**Shaquita**	popular prefix Sha + quita
0.04	**Shara**	*Hebrew* a plain (Sharon)
0.02	**Sharayah**	popular prefix Sha + rayah
0.03	**Sharda**	*Arabic* runaway; *Punjabi* belief in donating for charity
0.04	**Shardae**	*Arabic* runaway; *Punjabi* belief in donating for charity
0.04	**Sharday**	*Arabic* runaway; *Punjabi* belief in donating for charity
0.03	**Sharde**	*Arabic* runaway; *Punjabi* belief in donating for charity
0.03	**Sharee**	*French* beloved
0.09	**Shari**	*French* beloved
0.02	**Sharita**	popular prefix Sha + rita
0.02	**Sharla**	origin unknown, possibly an invented name
0.04	**Sharlene**	*French* little and womanly (Charlene)
0.50	**Sharon**	*Hebrew* a plain
0.04	**Sharonda**	*Hebrew* a plain (Sharon)
0.02	**Sharron**	*Hebrew* a plain
0.03	**Shasta**	*American Indian* name, meaning unknown
0.03	**Shatara**	*Arabic* good, industrious; *Hindi* umbrella for protection
0.34	**Shauna**	*Hebrew* God is gracious
0.02	**Shaunda**	origin unknown

0.03	**Shaunna**	*Hebrew* God is gracious
0.02	**Shavon**	*Irish* form of Joan; *Hebrew* gracious, merciful
0.02	**Shavonne**	*Irish* form of Joan; *Hebrew* gracious, merciful
0.04	**Shawn**	*Hebrew* God is gracious
0.47	**Shawna**	*Hebrew* God is gracious
0.02	**Shawnda**	origin unknown, possibly an invented name
0.02	**Shawnna**	*Hebrew* God is gracious
0.02	**Shay**	*Hebrew* asked for
0.19	**Shayla**	*Irish* from the fairy fort
0.02	**Shaylee**	origin unknown, possibly an invented name
0.14	**Shayna**	*Hebrew* beautiful
0.05	**Shea**	*Hebrew* asked for
0.74	**Sheena**	*Irish* form of Jane; *Hebrew* gracious, merciful
0.27	**Sheila**	*Irish* form of Cecilia; *Latin* blind
0.26	**Shelby**	*English* from the ledge estate
0.21	**Shelley**	*English* from the meadow on the ledge
0.03	**Shellie**	*English* from the meadow on the ledge
0.25	**Shelly**	*English* from the meadow on the ledge
0.02	**Shena**	*Irish* form of Jane; *Hebrew* gracious, merciful
0.02	**Shenika**	origin unknown
0.03	**Shera**	*Aramaic* light
0.05	**Sheree**	*French* beloved
0.02	**Sherell**	*French* beloved (Cheryl)
0.14	**Sheri**	*French* beloved
0.02	**Sherika**	*Arabic* easterner; *Punjabi* relative
0.02	**Sherita**	origin unknown, possibly an invented name
0.17	**Sherri**	*French* beloved
0.04	**Sherrie**	*French* beloved
0.28	**Sherry**	*French* beloved
0.06	**Sheryl**	*French* beloved (Cheryl)
0.02	**Shilo**	*Hebrew* Biblical site near Jerusalem
0.03	**Shira**	*Hebrew* spring

0.12	**Shirley**	*English* from the bright meadow
0.02	**Shona**	*Irish* form of John and Jane; *Hebrew* gracious, merciful
0.02	**Shonda**	origin unknown
0.02	**Shoshana**	*Hebrew* rose
0.02	**Shyla**	*Irish* form of Cecilia; *Latin* blind (Sheila)
0.02	**Siera**	place name; *Irish* black
0.45	**Sierra**	place name; *Irish* black
0.04	**Silvia**	*Latin* forest
0.07	**Simone**	*Hebrew* one who hears
0.07	**Siobhan**	*Irish* form of Joan; *Hebrew* gracious, merciful
0.04	**Skye**	*Arabic* water giver; Scottish surname
0.05	**Sofia**	*Greek* wisdom
0.03	**Sommer**	*English* summer; summoner; *Arabic* black
0.05	**Sondra**	*Greek* defender of mankind (Alexandra)
0.20	**Sonia**	*Slavic* and *Russian* form of Sophia; *Greek* wisdom
0.11	**Sonja**	*Slavic* and *Russian* form of Sophia; *Greek* wisdom
0.29	**Sonya**	*Slavic* and *Russian* form of Sophia; *Greek* wisdom
0.24	**Sophia**	*Greek* wisdom
0.13	**Sophie**	*Greek* wisdom
1.17	**Stacey**	*Irish* form of Anastasia; *Greek* resurrection
0.15	**Staci**	*Irish* form of Anastasia; *Greek* resurrection
0.05	**Stacia**	*Irish* form of Anastasia; *Greek* resurrection
0.25	**Stacie**	*Irish* form of Anastasia; *Greek* resurrection
0.98	**Stacy**	*Irish* form of Anastasia; *Greek* resurrection
0.03	**Starla**	origin unknown
0.03	**Starr**	star
0.04	**Stefani**	*Greek* crown
0.02	**Stefania**	*Greek* crown
0.47	**Stefanie**	*Greek* crown
0.02	**Stefany**	*Greek* crown
0.03	**Stella**	*Latin* star
0.40	**Stephani**	*Greek* crown
12.39	**Stephanie**	*Greek* crown
0.03	**Stéphanie**	*Greek* crown

0.07	**Stephany**	*Greek* crown
0.03	**Stephenie**	*Greek* crown
0.02	**Stevi**	*Greek* crown
0.09	**Stevie**	*Greek* crown
0.02	**Stormy**	*Old English* impetuous by nature
0.03	**Sue**	*Hebrew* a rose, a lily
0.36	**Summer**	*English* summer
0.02	**Sunny**	*English* cheerful
0.02	**Sunshine**	word used as a first name
0.81	**Susan**	*Hebrew* a rose, a lily
0.03	**Susana**	*Hebrew* a rose, a lily
0.07	**Susanna**	*Hebrew* a rose, a lily
0.03	**Susannah**	*Hebrew* a rose, a lily
0.04	**Susanne**	*Hebrew* a rose, a lily
0.04	**Susie**	*Hebrew* a rose, a lily
0.04	**Suzanna**	*Hebrew* a rose, a lily
0.36	**Suzanne**	*Hebrew* a rose, a lily
0.03	**Suzette**	*Hebrew* a rose, a lily
0.02	**Sybil**	*Greek* prophetic
0.14	**Sydney**	*French* from the city of St. Denis
0.02	**Sylvana**	*Latin* forest
0.21	**Sylvia**	*Latin* forest
0.06	**Sylvie**	*Latin* forest
0.02	**Syreeta**	*Arabic* companion; *Hindi* good customs or tradition

T

0.25	**Tabatha**	*Greek*, *Aramaic* a gazelle
0.03	**Tabetha**	*Greek*, *Aramaic* a gazelle
0.80	**Tabitha**	*Greek*, *Aramaic* a gazelle
0.02	**Tahnee**	*English* little one
0.02	**Takia**	*Arabic* worshipper
0.09	**Talia**	*Hebrew* dew; *Greek* blooming
0.03	**Tamar**	*Hebrew* palm tree
0.87	**Tamara**	*Hebrew* palm tree
0.10	**Tameka**	origin unknown
0.04	**Tamera**	*Hebrew* palm tree
0.06	**Tami**	*Hebrew* perfection

0.14	**Tamika**	origin unknown
0.02	**Tammi**	*Hebrew* perfection
0.03	**Tammie**	*Hebrew* perfection
0.45	**Tammy**	*Hebrew* perfection
0.07	**Tamra**	*Hebrew* palm tree
0.04	**Tana**	short form of Tanya; *Slavic* fairy queen
0.02	**Taneisha**	*Hausa* Monday
0.04	**Tanesha**	*Hausa* Monday
0.18	**Tania**	*Slavic* fairy queen
0.04	**Tanis**	form of Tanya; *Slavic* fairy queen
0.18	**Tanisha**	*Hausa* Monday
0.02	**Tannis**	form of Tanya; *Slavic* fairy queen
0.85	**Tanya**	*Slavic* fairy queen
2.21	**Tara**	*Arabic* a measurement; *Aramaic* to throw, carry
0.06	**Tarah**	*Arabic* a measurement; *Aramaic* to throw, carry
0.02	**Tareva**	origin unknown
0.03	**Tarra**	*Arabic* a measurement; *Aramaic* to throw, carry
0.29	**Taryn**	*Arabic* a measurement; *Aramaic* to throw, carry
0.46	**Tasha**	form of Natasha; *Latin* to be born
0.02	**Tashia**	form of Natasha; *Latin* to be born
0.03	**Tashina**	form of Natasha; *Latin* to be born
0.03	**Tasia**	form of Natasha; *Latin* to be born
0.11	**Tatiana**	*Slavic* fairy queen
0.03	**Tatum**	*Anglo Saxon* cheerful
0.03	**Tawny**	*English* little one
0.02	**Tawnya**	*Slavic* fairy queen
0.35	**Taylor**	*English* tailor
0.07	**Tegan**	*Welsh* beautiful and fair
0.02	**Tenesha**	*Hausa* Monday
0.02	**Tenille**	French surname
0.03	**Tenisha**	*Hausa* Monday
0.02	**Tennille**	French surname
0.05	**Tera**	*Arabic* a measurement; *Aramaic* to throw, carry
0.46	**Teresa**	*Greek* to reap

0.02	**Terese**	*Greek* to reap
0.14	**Teri**	*Greek* to reap
0.15	**Terra**	*Arabic* a measurement; *Aramaic* to throw, carry
0.29	**Terri**	*Greek* to reap
0.02	**Terri-Lynn**	Terri + Lynn
0.04	**Terry**	*Greek* to reap
0.06	**Tess**	*Greek* to reap
0.23	**Tessa**	*Greek* to reap
0.02	**Thanh**	*Vietnamese* blue; *Arabic* congratulate; *Punjabi* a place, good place
0.03	**Thao**	*Vietnamese* grass; caring, concerned for parents
0.03	**Thea**	*Greek* heavenly
0.59	**Theresa**	*Greek* to reap
0.02	**Therese**	*Greek* to reap
0.02	**Thi**	*Vietnamese* poem
0.25	**Tia**	*Greek* princess
0.06	**Tiana**	*Greek* princess
0.02	**Tianna**	*Greek* princess
0.14	**Tiara**	*Latin* crown
0.03	**Tiera**	*Latin* crown
0.02	**Tierney**	*Irish* surname
0.12	**Tierra**	*Latin* crown
0.12	**Tiffani**	*Latin* trinity
0.10	**Tiffanie**	*Latin* trinity
5.69	**Tiffany**	*Latin* trinity
0.02	**Tiffiny**	*Latin* trinity
0.69	**Tina**	short form of names ending in "tina"
0.03	**Tisha**	short form of Letitia; *Latin* gladness
0.35	**Toni**	form of Antoinette; *Latin* priceless
0.05	**Tonia**	*Slavic* fairy queen
0.52	**Tonya**	*Slavic* fairy queen
0.11	**Tori**	*Japanese* bird
0.02	**Torrie**	*Japanese* bird
0.02	**Tory**	*Japanese* bird
0.09	**Tosha**	*Punjabi* armaments; *Polish* nickname for Antonina; priceless
0.30	**Tracey**	*Latin* brave

0.24	**Traci**	*Latin* brave
0.06	**Tracie**	*Latin* brave
0.86	**Tracy**	*Latin* brave
0.04	**Tressa**	*Greek* to reap
0.17	**Tricia**	form of Patricia: *Latin* of noble descent
0.12	**Trina**	nickname for Katherine: *Greek* pure, unsullied
0.39	**Trisha**	form of Patricia: *Latin* of noble descent
0.23	**Trista**	*Latin* melancholy
0.04	**Tristan**	*Latin* melancholy
0.03	**Tristen**	*Latin* melancholy
0.02	**Trudy**	short form of Gertrude
0.02	**Twyla**	born at twilight
0.03	**Tyesha**	origin unknown
0.02	**Tyisha**	origin unknown
0.03	**Tyler**	occupational surname
0.05	**Tyra**	origin unknown

U

0.03	**Ursula**	*Greek* she-bear

V

0.05	**Valarie**	*Latin* to be strong
0.06	**Valencia**	*Latin* strong and healthy
0.02	**Valene**	origin unknown, possibly an invented name
0.02	**Valentina**	*Latin* strong and healthy
0.02	**Valeria**	*Latin* to be strong
0.96	**Valerie**	*Latin* to be strong
0.02	**Vanesa**	*Greek* butterfly
4.66	**Vanessa**	*Greek* butterfly
0.03	**Vanna**	*Greek* butterfly
0.02	**Vannessa**	*Greek* butterfly
0.07	**Venessa**	*Greek* butterfly
0.02	**Vera**	*Latin* true
0.02	**Verna**	*Latin* spring-like
0.65	**Veronica**	*Latin* true image

0.05	**Veronique**	*Latin* true image
0.02	**Véronique**	*Latin* true image
0.08	**Vicki**	*Latin* victorious
0.02	**Vickie**	*Latin* victorious
0.06	**Vicky**	*Latin* victorious
2.27	**Victoria**	*Latin* victorious
0.03	**Violet**	*Old French* little purple flower
0.41	**Virginia**	*Latin* pure, virgin
0.10	**Vivian**	*Latin* alive
0.02	**Viviana**	*Latin* alive

W

0.07	**Wanda**	*German* wanderer
0.02	**Wendi**	form of Gwendolyn: *Welsh* white
0.43	**Wendy**	form of Gwendolyn: *Welsh* white
3.83	**Whitney**	*English* from the white island
0.02	**Whitnie**	*English* from the white island
0.02	**Whittney**	*English* from the white island
0.02	**Winter**	word used as a first name

X

0.02	**Xiomara**	origin unknown

Y

0.03	**Yasmin**	*Persian* jasmine
0.02	**Yasmine**	*Persian* jasmine
0.05	**Yesenia**	*Arabic* flower
0.19	**Yolanda**	*Greek* violet flower
0.07	**Yvette**	*French* archer (Yvonne)
0.17	**Yvonne**	*French* archer

Z

0.02	**Zara**	*Hebrew* dawn
0.09	**Zoe**	*Greek* life

Popular Boys Names

RATING	NAME	ORIGIN AND MEANING
	A	
4.43	**Aaron**	*Hebrew* to sing, to shine, to teach or a mountain, enlightened; *Arabic* a messenger
0.02	**Abdul**	*Arabic* son of
0.02	**Abdullah**	*Arabic* servant of Allah
0.03	**Abel**	*Hebrew* breath, evanescence
0.12	**Abraham**	*Hebrew* father of the multitude
0.03	**Abram**	*Hebrew* exalted father
8.28	**Adam**	*Hebrew* earth, man of the red earth; *Phoenician* man, mankind
0.07	**Addison**	*Old English* son of Adam
0.81	**Adrian**	*Greek* rich; *Latin* black, dark
0.03	**Adriano**	*Greek* rich; *Latin* black, dark
0.02	**Adriel**	*Hebrew* of God's congregation
0.03	**Adrien**	*French* Adrian
0.06	**Ahmad**	*Arabic* the most praised
0.04	**Ahmed**	*Arabic* most highly praised
0.04	**Aidan**	*Irish* warmth of the home
0.02	**Ajay**	*Punjabi* victorious, cannot be defeated; invented name from initials A and J
0.07	**Akeem**	*Hebrew* God will establish
0.10	**Alain**	*Celtic* harmony, peace
0.78	**Alan**	*Celtic* harmony, peace
0.47	**Albert**	*French* noble, bright
0.09	**Alberto**	*French* noble, bright
0.02	**Alden**	*Old English* old wise protector
0.02	**Aldo**	*Italian* rich
0.09	**Alec**	*Greek* helper of mankind, protector of man
0.16	**Alejandro**	*Greek* helper of mankind, protector of man
0.04	**Alessandro**	*Greek* helper of mankind, protector of man
1.29	**Alex**	*Greek* helper of mankind, protector of man
4.01	**Alexander**	*Greek* helper of mankind, protector of man

0.07	**Alexandre**	*Greek* helper of mankind, protector of man
0.09	**Alexis**	*Greek* helper of mankind, protector of man
0.05	**Alfonso**	*Italian* and *Spanish* form of *Old German* noble and eager
0.19	**Alfred**	*Old English* elfin counsellor
0.05	**Alfredo**	*Old English* elfin counsellor
0.05	**Ali**	*Arabic* greatest
0.28	**Allan**	*Celtic* harmony, peace
0.66	**Allen**	*Celtic* harmony, peace
0.08	**Alonzo**	*Spanish* form of *Old German* noble and eager
0.04	**Alphonso**	*Old German* noble and eager
0.03	**Alton**	*English* from the old town
0.02	**Alvaro**	*Latin* fair
0.25	**Alvin**	*German* beloved by all
0.02	**Amandeep**	*Punjabi* light or lamp of peace
0.02	**Amar**	*Arabic* builder; *Punjabi* immortal
0.05	**Amir**	*Arabic* prince; *Punjabi* wealthy; king's minister
0.03	**Amit**	*Arabic* the most praised; *Punjabi* unfriendly
0.03	**Ammon**	*Egyptian* the hidden
0.09	**Amos**	*Hebrew* burden
0.03	**Anders**	*Scandinavian* form of *Greek* from the east
0.61	**Andre**	*Greek* manly, valiant, courageous, strong
0.10	**André**	*Greek* manly, valiant, courageous, strong
0.03	**Andrea**	*Greek* manly, valiant, courageous, strong
0.04	**Andreas**	*Greek* manly, valiant, courageous, strong
0.13	**Andres**	*Greek* manly, valiant, courageous, strong
17.87	**Andrew**	*Greek* manly, valiant, courageous, strong
0.20	**Andy**	*Greek* manly, valiant, courageous, strong
0.22	**Angel**	*Italian* messenger
0.15	**Angelo**	*Greek* angel, a messenger or a saintly person
0.03	**Angus**	*Gaelic* very strong
0.02	**Anibal**	*Phoenician* grace of God
0.02	**Anson**	*Old English* son of a noble
1.43	**Anthony**	*Greek* flourishing; *Latin* worthy of praise
0.18	**Antoine**	*Greek* flourishing; *Latin* worthy of praise
0.05	**Anton**	*Greek* flourishing; *Latin* worthy of praise

1.27	**Antonio**	*Greek* flourishing; *Latin* worthy of praise
0.03	**Antony**	*Greek* flourishing; *Latin* worthy of praise
0.02	**Antwain**	*Arabic* form of Anthony: flourishing; worthy of praise
0.09	**Antwan**	*Arabic* form of Anthony: flourishing; worthy of praise
0.02	**Antwaun**	*Arabic* form of Anthony: flourishing; worthy of praise
0.03	**Antwon**	*Arabic* form of Anthony: flourishing; worthy of praise
0.02	**Archie**	*French* and *German* sacred and bold
0.03	**Ari**	*Hebrew* lion of God
0.03	**Aric**	*Old English* ruler
0.06	**Ariel**	*Hebrew* lion of God
0.02	**Arlen**	*Gaelic* pledge
0.02	**Armand**	*Old German* army man
0.08	**Armando**	*Old German* army man
0.05	**Arnold**	*German* strong as an eagle, eagle ruler
0.05	**Aron**	*Hebrew* to sing, to shine, to teach or a mountain, enlightened; *Arabic* a messenger
0.04	**Arron**	*Hebrew* to sing, to shine, to teach or a mountain, enlightened; *Arabic* a messenger
0.48	**Arthur**	*Gaelic* a rock, noble, lofty, hill
0.04	**Arturo**	*Spanish* and *Italian* form of *Gaelic* a rock, noble, lofty, hill
0.02	**Asher**	*Hebrew* happy blessed
0.07	**Ashley**	*Old English* one who lives at the ash-tree meadow
0.12	**Ashton**	*Old English* one who lives at the ash-tree farm
0.06	**Aubrey**	*Old French* ruler of the elves
0.03	**August**	*Latin* exalted and sacred
0.02	**Augustus**	*Latin* exalted and sacred
0.02	**Austen**	*Latin* exalted and sacred
0.93	**Austin**	*Latin* majestic, dignity; form of August
0.05	**Avery**	*Old English* leader of the elves
0.02	**Axel**	*Hebrew* father of peace

B

0.02	**Baron**	*Old English* nobleman
0.06	**Barrett**	*Old German* bear-like
0.36	**Barry**	*Welsh* form of Harry, son of Harry; *Irish* spear-like, pointed
0.02	**Bart**	*Hebrew* son of the farmer
0.02	**Barton**	*Old English* from the barley farm
0.02	**Basil**	*Latin* magnificent and kingly
0.24	**Beau**	*English* handsome
0.12	**Ben**	*Hebrew* son of my right hand
0.02	**Benito**	*Latin* blessed
0.02	**Benjamen**	*Hebrew* son of my right hand
5.22	**Benjamin**	*Hebrew* son of my right hand
0.04	**Bennett**	*Latin* little blessed one
0.04	**Bennie**	*Hebrew* son of my right hand
0.04	**Benny**	*Hebrew* son of my right hand
0.04	**Benoit**	*English* yellow-flowered plant of the rose family
0.02	**Benson**	*Hebrew* son of Benjamin
0.03	**Benton**	*Old English* moor dweller
0.18	**Bernard**	*Greek* brave bear
0.02	**Bert**	*Old English* bright
0.02	**Bilal**	*Arabic* chosen
0.04	**Bill**	*English* resolute protector
0.52	**Billy**	*English* resolute protector
0.02	**Bjorn**	*Scandinavian* bear
0.14	**Blaine**	*Irish* thin, lean
0.20	**Blair**	*Celtic* a place
0.02	**Blaise**	*Latin* stammerer
0.97	**Blake**	*English* white
0.02	**Blayne**	*Irish* thin, lean
0.03	**Bo**	*Gaelic* soft, marshy ground
0.02	**Bob**	*German* bright fame
0.82	**Bobby**	*German* bright fame
0.02	**Boyd**	*Gaelic* blond
0.39	**Brad**	*English* from the broad river crossing
0.15	**Braden**	*English* a broad lea, a meadow

0.08 **Bradford** *Old English* dweller on the broad meadow
0.02 **Bradlee** *English* a broad lea, a meadow; *English* from the broad river crossing
3.70 **Bradley** *English* a broad lea, a meadow; *English* from the broad river crossing
0.07 **Bradly** *English* a broad lea, a meadow; *English* from the broad river crossing
0.02 **Bradon** *English* a broad lea, a meadow
0.34 **Brady** *English* broad island
0.02 **Braeden** *English* a broad lea, a meadow
0.04 **Brandan** *Irish* a raven; *English* a sword
0.24 **Branden** *Irish* a raven; *English* a sword
0.02 **Brandin** *Irish* a raven; *English* a sword
12.07 **Brandon** *Irish* a raven; *English* a sword
0.03 **Brandt** *Old English* firebrand
0.03 **Brandyn** *Irish* a raven; *English* a sword
0.06 **Brant** *Old English* firebrand
0.02 **Braxton** *Anglo Saxon* Brock's town
0.04 **Brayden** *English* a broad lea, a meadow
0.02 **Braydon** *English* a broad lea, a meadow
0.63 **Brendan** *Irish* a raven; *English* a sword
0.08 **Brenden** *Irish* a raven; *English* a sword
0.13 **Brendon** *Irish* a raven; *English* a sword
0.19 **Brennan** *Irish* a raven; *English* a sword
0.03 **Brennen** *Irish* a raven; *English* a sword
1.20 **Brent** *Irish* a raven; *English* a sword
0.18 **Brenton** *Irish* a raven; *English* a sword
0.14 **Bret** *Celtic* a Breton, a native of Brittany
1.93 **Brett** *Celtic* a Breton, a native of Brittany
7.25 **Brian** *Celtic* strong; *Irish* strength, virtue
0.06 **Brice** *Welsh* form of Price, son of the ardent one; *English* son of Rice
0.02 **Britt** *English* early forms for Britain
0.03 **Britton** *English* early forms for Britain
0.02 **Broc** *Gaelic* a badger
0.33 **Brock** *Gaelic* a badger
0.02 **Broderick** *Old English* from the broad ridge
0.07 **Brodie** *Irish* ditch
0.08 **Brody** *Irish* ditch

0.04	**Bronson**	*Old English* son of the dark-skinned one
0.02	**Brook**	*Old English* from the brook
0.05	**Brooks**	*Old English* from the brook
0.50	**Bruce**	*English* from the brushwood thicket
0.04	**Bruno**	*Old English* with a dark complexion
2.90	**Bryan**	*Celtic* strong; *Irish* strength, virtue
0.23	**Bryant**	*Celtic* strong; *Irish* strength, virtue
0.43	**Bryce**	*English* son of Rice; *Welsh* form of Price, son of the ardent one
0.06	**Bryon**	*German* the cottage; *English* a bear; *English* from the cottage
0.07	**Bryson**	*Welsh* son of Bryce
0.03	**Buddy**	*Old English* herald
0.36	**Byron**	*Old French* from the cottage

C

0.02	**Cade**	origin unknown
0.06	**Cale**	*Hebrew* a dog, faithful, bold one
0.68	**Caleb**	*Hebrew* a dog, faithful, bold one
0.56	**Calvin**	*Latin* bald
0.02	**Camden**	*Old English* dweller in the winding valley
0.88	**Cameron**	*Celtic* bent nose
0.02	**Camron**	*Celtic* bent nose
0.03	**Carey**	*Old Welsh* dweller near the castle
0.78	**Carl**	*English* manly, strong; *German* farmer
0.02	**Carlin**	*Gaelic* little champion
0.06	**Carlo**	*English* manly, strong; *German* farmer
0.65	**Carlos**	*English* manly, strong; *German* farmer
0.08	**Carlton**	*Old English* from the town of the farmer
0.02	**Carmelo**	*Hebrew* vineyard or garden
0.03	**Carmen**	*Hebrew* vineyard or garden
0.02	**Carmine**	*Hebrew* vineyard or garden
0.08	**Carson**	*English* son of the family on the marsh
0.05	**Carter**	*Old English* cart driver
0.04	**Cary**	*Old Welsh* dweller near the castle
1.26	**Casey**	*Celtic* valorous; *Irish* brave
0.03	**Cassidy**	*Gaelic* clever
0.07	**Cecil**	*Latin* blind

0.23	**Cedric**	*Old English* chieftain
0.02	**Cedrick**	*Old English* chieftain
0.15	**Cerek**	origin unknown
0.05	**Cesar**	*Latin* long-haired
2.49	**Chad**	*Celtic* battle or warrior; *English* warlike
0.03	**Chadd**	*Celtic* battle or warrior; *English* warlike
0.10	**Chadwick**	*Celtic* battle or warrior; *English* warlike
0.17	**Chance**	*Old English* secretary to the throne
0.04	**Chandler**	*Old English* candlemaker
0.03	**Channing**	*English* knowing; *English* canon
4.52	**Charles**	*English* manly, strong; *German* farmer
0.16	**Charlie**	*English* manly, strong; *German* farmer
0.63	**Chase**	*English* the hunt, hunter
0.02	**Chauncey**	*Middle English* chancellor, church official
0.05	**Chaz**	*English* manly, strong; *German* farmer
0.06	**Chester**	*English* from the fortified camp
0.03	**Chet**	*English* from the fortified camp
0.13	**Chris**	*Greek* Christ-bearer
0.89	**Christian**	*Greek* Christ-bearer
0.87	**Christophe**	*Greek* Christ-bearer
28.89	**Christopher**	*Greek* Christ-bearer
0.23	**Clarence**	*Latin* famous
0.09	**Clark**	*French* scholar
0.02	**Clarke**	*French* scholar
0.05	**Claude**	*Latin* lame
0.02	**Claudio**	*Latin* lame
0.11	**Clay**	*English* a town built upon clay land
0.68	**Clayton**	*English* a town built upon clay land
0.02	**Clement**	*Latin* merciful
0.02	**Cliff**	*English* a crossing near the cliff
0.29	**Clifford**	*English* a crossing near the cliff
0.17	**Clifton**	*English* from the town near the cliffs
0.20	**Clint**	*English* a town on a hill, from the headland form
0.53	**Clinton**	*English* a town on a hill, from the headland form
0.05	**Clyde**	*Scottish* rocky eminence, heard from afar; *Welsh* warm
0.04	**Codey**	*English* a cushion

2.86	**Cody**	*English* a cushion
0.39	**Colby**	*Old English* from the black farm
0.40	**Cole**	*English* cola miner; *Latin* a man who farms cabbage
0.04	**Coleman**	*English* cola miner; *Latin* a man who farms cabbage
0.96	**Colin**	*Irish* child; *Celtic* a cub, whelp; short form of Nicholas: victory
0.17	**Collin**	*Irish* child; *Celtic* a cub, whelp; short form of Nicholas: victory
0.06	**Colt**	*Old English* from the dark town
0.03	**Colter**	*Old English* from the dark town
0.09	**Colton**	*Old English* from the dark town
0.13	**Connor**	*Irish* wise aid
0.09	**Conor**	*Irish* wise aid
0.09	**Conrad**	*German* bold, wise, counsellor
0.02	**Cooper**	*Old English* barrel maker
0.02	**Corbin**	*Latin* the raven
0.06	**Cordell**	*Old French* ropemaker
0.02	**Cordero**	*Spanish* little lamb
2.62	**Corey**	*Latin* a helmet, from the hollow
0.15	**Cornelius**	*Latin* horn
0.03	**Cornell**	*Old French* horn-colored
0.02	**Corry**	*Latin* a helmet, from the hollow
0.07	**Cortez**	*Spanish* place name or surname used as a first name
0.04	**Cortney**	*Old English* dweller in the court
2.07	**Cory**	*Latin* a helmet, from the hollow
0.07	**Coty**	*English* a cushion
0.02	**Courtland**	*Old English* dweller in the court
0.32	**Courtney**	*Old English* dweller in the court
0.02	**Coy**	*English* wood, a wooded area
1.50	**Craig**	*Celtic* from the crag or rugged rocky mass
0.02	**Cristian**	*Greek* Christ-bearer
0.03	**Cristopher**	*Greek* Christ-bearer
0.03	**Cullen**	*Gaelic* handsome
0.04	**Curt**	*Latin* short
1.31	**Curtis**	*Latin* an enclosure, court; *English* courteous
0.02	**Cyril**	*Greek* lordly

0.03	**Cyrus**	*Persian* sun

D

0.08	**Dakota**	American Indian tribal name
0.40	**Dale**	*English* a hollow, a small valley
0.22	**Dallas**	*Old English* from the waterfall
0.04	**Dallin**	*Anglo Saxon* from the dale
0.05	**Dalton**	*Old English* dweller in the town in the valley
0.15	**Damian**	*Greek* divine power or fate
0.23	**Damien**	*Greek* divine power or fate
0.04	**Damion**	*Greek* divine power or fate
0.16	**Damon**	*Greek* tamer
0.05	**Dan**	*Hebrew* God is my judge
0.27	**Dana**	*Scottish* from Denmark
0.39	**Dane**	*Norse* inhabitant of Denmark
0.04	**Danial**	*Hebrew* God is my judge
19.40	**Daniel**	*Hebrew* God is my judge
0.03	**Daniele**	*Hebrew* God is my judge
0.57	**Danny**	*Hebrew* God is my judge
0.08	**Dante**	*Latin* enduring
0.17	**Darcy**	*Irish* dark; *English* of the Arsy (Oise River)
0.02	**Darell**	*English* beloved; *English* a grove of oak trees
0.07	**Daren**	*English* a small, rocky hill
0.10	**Darin**	*English* a small, rocky hill
0.18	**Darius**	*Greek* wealthy
0.18	**Darnell**	*Old English* from the hidden niche
0.03	**Daron**	*English* a small, rocky hill
0.04	**Darrel**	*English* beloved; *English* a grove of oak trees
0.45	**Darrell**	*English* beloved; *English* a grove of oak trees
0.78	**Darren**	*English* a small, rocky hill
0.02	**Darrick**	*English* from *German* Hrodrich, famous ruler
0.08	**Darrin**	*English* a small, rocky hill
0.02	**Darrius**	*Greek* wealthy

0.50	**Darryl**	*English* beloved; *English* a grove of oak trees
0.03	**Darwin**	*Anglo Saxon* lover of the sea
0.31	**Daryl**	*English* beloved; *English* a grove of oak trees
0.05	**Dave**	*Hebrew* beloved
19.73	**David**	*Hebrew* beloved
0.05	**Davin**	*Scandinavian* brilliance of the Finns
0.04	**Davis**	*Old Scottish* son of the beloved
0.02	**Davon**	*Scandinavian* brilliance of the Finns
0.02	**Dawson**	son of David
0.02	**Dayne**	*Norse* inhabitant of Denmark
0.03	**Dayton**	*Middle English* day town; bright cheerful town
0.33	**Dean**	*English* head, leader; *English* from the valley
0.07	**Deandre**	prefix De + Andre
0.05	**Deangelo**	prefix De + Angelo
0.02	**Dejuan**	prefix De + Juan
0.02	**Delbert**	*English* bright as day
0.02	**Delvin**	*Old English* friend from the valley, proud friend
0.03	**Demarco**	prefix De + Marco
0.10	**Demarcus**	prefix De + Marcus
0.06	**Demario**	prefix De + Mario
0.02	**Demetris**	*Greek* belonging to Demeter, the *Greek* god of fertility
0.23	**Demetrius**	*Greek* belonging to Demeter, the *Greek* god of fertility
0.11	**Denis**	*English* from *Latin* and *Greek*, wild, frenzied
0.83	**Dennis**	*English* from *Latin* and *Greek*, wild, frenzied
0.03	**Denny**	*English* from *Latin* and *Greek*, wild, frenzied
0.03	**Denver**	*Old English* from the edge of the valley
0.03	**Deon**	*Greek* god of wine
0.03	**Dereck**	*English* from *German* Hrodrich, famous ruler

2.86	**Derek**	*English* from *German* Hrodrich, famous ruler
0.02	**Deric**	*English* from *German* Hrodrich, famous ruler
0.16	**Derick**	*English* from *German* Hrodrich, famous ruler
0.03	**Derik**	*English* from *German* Hrodrich, famous ruler
0.02	**Deron**	*English* a small, rocky hill
0.02	**Derrek**	*English* from *German* Hrodrich, famous ruler
0.02	**Derrell**	*English* beloved; *English* a grove of oak trees
1.22	**Derrick**	*English* from *German* Hrodrich, famous ruler
0.02	**Deshawn**	prefix De + Shawn
0.22	**Desmond**	*Old English* kindly protector
0.07	**Devan**	*Irish* poet; *English* place name
0.02	**Deven**	*Irish* poet; *English* place name
0.90	**Devin**	*Irish* poet; *English* place name
0.44	**Devon**	*Irish* poet; *English* place name
0.09	**Dewayne**	prefix De + Wayne
0.02	**Dewey**	*Old Welsh* cherished
0.21	**Dexter**	*Latin* dexterous
0.04	**Diego**	*Spanish* form of James: held by the heel, supplanter
0.19	**Dillon**	*Irish* faithful
0.02	**Dimitri**	*Greek* belonging to Demeter, the *Greek* god of fertility
0.02	**Dimitrios**	*Greek* belonging to Demeter, the *Greek* god of fertility
0.02	**Dino**	*German* little sword
0.05	**Dion**	*Greek* god of wine
0.03	**Dirk**	*Old German* famous ruler
0.04	**Domenic**	*Latin* belonging to or pertaining to God
0.04	**Domenico**	*Latin* belonging to or pertaining to God
0.39	**Dominic**	*Latin* belonging to or pertaining to God
0.10	**Dominick**	*Latin* belonging to or pertaining to God
0.11	**Dominique**	*Latin* belonging to or pertaining to God

0.14	**Don**	*Irish* brown stranger, world ruler
1.74	**Donald**	*Irish* brown stranger, world ruler
0.02	**Donavan**	*Irish* dark warrior
0.04	**Donnell**	*Celtic* brave black man
0.08	**Donnie**	*Irish* brown stranger, world ruler
0.02	**Donny**	*Irish* brown stranger, world ruler
0.17	**Donovan**	*Irish* dark warrior
0.03	**Dontae**	*Latin* enduring
0.07	**Donte**	*Latin* enduring
0.06	**Dorian**	*Celtic* stranger
1.31	**Douglas**	*Celtic* gray; *Scottish* from the dark water
0.02	**Doyle**	*Gaelic* dark stranger
0.02	**Drake**	*Latin* dragon
0.62	**Drew**	*English* sturdy; *Welsh* wise, short form of Andrew
0.08	**Drewe**	*English* sturdy; *Welsh* wise, short form of Andrew
0.12	**Duane**	*Irish* little and dark
0.08	**Duncan**	*Scottish* dark-skinned warrior
0.02	**Durell**	*Scottish-English* doorkeeper to king
0.02	**Durrell**	*Scottish-English* doorkeeper to king
4.52	**Dustin**	*English* brown, stone, the brown rock quarry
0.13	**Dusty**	*English* brown, stone, the brown rock quarry
0.02	**Dustyn**	*English* brown, stone, the brown rock quarry
0.30	**Dwayne**	*Irish* little and dark
0.17	**Dwight**	*English* modern form of De Witt, which is Flemish "blond"
0.82	**Dylan**	*Welsh* the sea

E

0.18	**Earl**	*English* nobleman
0.05	**Earnest**	*Old English* serious in intent
0.27	**Eddie**	*English* happy guardian
0.03	**Eddy**	*English* happy guardian
0.08	**Edgar**	*Old English* prosperous spearman

0.03	**Edmond**	*Old English* prosperous protector
0.05	**Edmund**	*Old English* prosperous protector
0.09	**Eduardo**	*English* happy guardian
1.84	**Edward**	*English* happy guardian
0.30	**Edwin**	*English* rich friend
0.02	**Efrain**	*Hebrew* fruitful
0.02	**Elam**	Biblical place name "the high lands"
0.02	**Eldon**	*Old English* valley of the elves
0.14	**Eli**	*Hebrew* on, up, high
0.05	**Elias**	*German* and *Dutch* form of Elijah: *Hebrew* Jehovah is God
0.16	**Elijah**	*Hebrew* Jehovah is God
0.02	**Elisha**	*Hebrew* God is salvation
0.09	**Elliot**	*English* modern form of Elijah
0.10	**Elliott**	*English* modern form of Elijah
0.03	**Ellis**	*Hebrew* God is my salvation
0.03	**Elmer**	*Old English* of famed dignity
0.02	**Elton**	*Old English* from the old estate
0.02	**Elvin**	*Old English* friend of the elves
0.02	**Elvis**	*Old Norse* all wise
0.11	**Emanuel**	*Hebrew* God is with us
0.02	**Emerson**	*Old English* son of the industrious leader
0.02	**Emery**	*Old German* industrious leader
0.02	**Emil**	*Latin* flattering
0.04	**Emilio**	*Latin* flattering
0.16	**Emmanuel**	*Hebrew* God is with us
0.02	**Emmett**	*Old German* hardworking and strong
0.02	**Emory**	*Old German* industrious leader
0.07	**Enrique**	*Spanish* form of Henry: *German* ruler of an estate
9.74	**Eric**	*Norse* honorable ruler
0.05	**Erich**	*Norse* honorable ruler
0.13	**Erick**	*Norse* honorable ruler
0.76	**Erik**	*Norse* honorable ruler
0.04	**Erin**	*Gaelic* western island
0.30	**Ernest**	*English* earnest
0.04	**Ernesto**	*English* earnest
0.02	**Errol**	*English* nobleman
0.02	**Ervin**	*Old English* lover of the sea

0.02	**Esteban**	*Spanish* form of Steven: *Greek* a crown
0.13	**Ethan**	*Hebrew* strong, firm
0.30	**Eugene**	*Greek* well-born
1.33	**Evan**	*Welsh* form of John, young warrior
0.07	**Everett**	*English* strong as a boar
0.02	**Ezekiel**	*Hebrew* strength of the Lord
0.04	**Ezra**	*Hebrew* strength

F

0.06	**Fabian**	*Latin* bean grower
0.02	**Fabio**	*Latin* bean grower
0.04	**Felipe**	*Greek* a lover of horses
0.08	**Felix**	*Latin* fortunate
0.09	**Fernando**	*Spanish* form of *Old German* world venturing
0.02	**Fletcher**	*Middle English* a feather of arrows
0.09	**Floyd**	*Welsh* gray-haired
0.02	**Forest**	*English* forest, woodsman
0.09	**Forrest**	*English* forest, woodsman
0.06	**Francesco**	*Latin* free man, *French* man
0.39	**Francis**	*Latin* free man, *French* man
0.12	**Francisco**	*Latin* free man, *French* man
0.03	**Francois**	*Latin* free man, *French* man
0.90	**Frank**	*Latin* free man, *French* man
0.05	**Frankie**	*Latin* free man, *French* man
0.24	**Franklin**	*English* free landowner
0.02	**Franklyn**	*English* free landowner
0.07	**Fraser**	*English* one who makes charcoal
0.11	**Fred**	*German* peace, king, ruler
0.14	**Freddie**	*German* peace, king, ruler
0.03	**Freddy**	*German* peace, king, ruler
0.05	**Frederic**	*German* peace, king, ruler
0.49	**Frederick**	*German* peace, king, ruler
0.14	**Fredrick**	*German* peace, king, ruler
0.02	**Fritz**	*German* form of Frederick: peace, king, ruler

G

0.58	**Gabriel**	*Hebrew* God is my strength, devoted to God
0.04	**Galen**	*Gaelic* bright
0.03	**Gareth**	*Welsh* gentle
0.11	**Garett**	*English* to watch; with a mighty spear
0.09	**Garret**	*English* to watch; with a mighty spear
0.69	**Garrett**	*English* to watch; with a mighty spear
0.02	**Garrison**	*Old French* a garrison, troops stationed at a fort
0.08	**Garry**	*English* a spear-bearer, a warrior
0.03	**Garth**	*Old Norse* from the protected enclosure
1.41	**Gary**	*English* a spear-bearer, a warrior
0.22	**Gavin**	*Welsh* little hawk
0.08	**Gene**	*Greek* well-born
0.02	**Geoffery**	*English* gift of peace
0.56	**Geoffrey**	*English* gift of peace
1.48	**George**	*Greek* a farmer, a tiller of the soil
0.52	**Gerald**	*English* a warrior; *Latin* spear-ruler
0.11	**Gerard**	*Old English* brave with a spear
0.03	**Gerardo**	*Old English* brave with a spear
0.02	**Gerrit**	*English* to watch; with a mighty spear
0.02	**Gerry**	*Old English* brave with a spear
0.04	**Giancarlo**	*Italian* form of John + Charles
0.02	**Gideon**	*Hebrew* one who fells lumber
0.11	**Gilbert**	*Old English* a man famed for his promise
0.03	**Gilberto**	*Spanish* form of Gilbert: a man famed for his promise
0.02	**Gilles**	*Greek* goatskin, a shield that protects
0.03	**Gino**	*Italian* form of John: Jehovah has been gracious
0.06	**Giovanni**	*Italian* form of John: Jehovah has been gracious
0.06	**Giuseppe**	*Italian* form of Joseph
0.19	**Glen**	*Celtic* a glen, a dale, a secluded woody valley

0.32	**Glenn**	*Celtic* a glen, a dale, a secluded woody valley
0.30	**Gordon**	*English* hill of the plains
0.03	**Grady**	*Gaelic* famous
0.11	**Graeme**	*Latin* a grain; *English* the gray home
0.40	**Graham**	*Latin* a grain; *English* the gray home
0.51	**Grant**	*English* to give, to assure; *English* great
0.03	**Grayson**	*Old English* son of the local bailiff
0.09	**Greg**	*Greek* vigilant; *Latin* watchman, watchful
0.04	**Gregg**	*Greek* vigilant; *Latin* watchman, watchful
0.03	**Greggory**	*Greek* vigilant; *Latin* watchman, watchful
3.66	**Gregory**	*Greek* vigilant; *Latin* watchman, watchful
0.02	**Griffin**	mythological animal with body of a lion and head and wings of an eagle
0.03	**Guillaume**	*French* form of William: *English* resolute protector
0.04	**Guillermo**	*Spanish* form of William: *English* resolute protector
0.04	**Gurpreet**	*Punjabi* devoted to guru or prophet
0.03	**Gustavo**	*Old Norse* staff of the Goths
0.10	**Guy**	*English* a guide; *Hebrew* valley

H

0.02	**Hakim**	*Ethiopian* doctor
0.03	**Hank**	nickname for Henry: *German* ruler of an estate
0.06	**Hans**	*Scandinavian* form of John: *Hebrew* Jehovah has been gracious
0.02	**Hardeep**	*Punjabi* loves God, devoted to God
0.02	**Harlan**	*Old English* from the land of the hare; from the territory of the army
0.07	**Harley**	*Old English* from the meadow of the hare
0.23	**Harold**	*Scottish* army-ruler; *English* soldier, short form of Harold
0.02	**Harpreet**	*Punjabi* loves God, devoted to God
0.02	**Harris**	*Old English* army man
0.14	**Harrison**	*English* Harry's son; *Old English* son of the army man

0.23	**Harry**	*Scottish* army-ruler; *English* soldier, short form of Harold
0.04	**Harvey**	*Old French* worthy of battle
0.02	**Hassan**	*Arabic* handsome
0.02	**Hayden**	*Old English* from the hedged hill
0.16	**Heath**	*English* from the heath
0.12	**Hector**	*Greek* steadfast
0.58	**Henry**	*German* ruler of an estate
0.12	**Herbert**	*Old German* glorious soldier
0.02	**Heriberto**	*Spanish* form of Herbert: glorious soldier
0.06	**Herman**	*Old German* warrior
0.02	**Hiram**	*Hebrew* noble born
0.02	**Homer**	*Greek* a pledge or security
0.02	**Horace**	*Latin* keeper of the house
0.02	**Houston**	*Anglo Saxon* the house in the town
0.19	**Howard**	*English* watchman
0.02	**Hubert**	*German* bright mind
0.06	**Hugh**	*English* intelligence
0.02	**Hugo**	*German* and *Dutch* form of Hugh: intelligence
0.02	**Humberto**	*Old German* very brilliant
0.22	**Hunter**	*Old English* a huntsman
0.02	**Huy**	*Vietnamese* glorious

I

0.04	**Iain**	*Scottish* form of John
1.63	**Ian**	*Scottish* form of John
0.02	**Ibrahim**	*Arabic* form of Abraham; *Hebrew* father of the multitude
0.02	**Imran**	*Arabic* Biblical name: host
0.05	**Ira**	*Hebrew* descendant
0.02	**Irvin**	*Old Welsh* from the white river; also Old *English* friend of the sea
0.02	**Irving**	*Old Welsh* from the white river; also Old *English* friend of the sea
0.40	**Isaac**	*Hebrew* he will laugh
0.11	**Isaiah**	*Hebrew* God is my salvation
0.04	**Ismael**	*Hebrew* God will laugh

0.06	**Israel**	*Hebrew* soldier of the Lord
0.18	**Ivan**	*Russian* form of John, grace

J

0.03	**J**	initial used as a first name
0.02	**J.**	initial used as a first name
0.04	**Jace**	invented name, possibly from initials J and C
0.41	**Jack**	short form of Jacob; nickname for John
0.09	**Jackie**	short form of Jacob; nickname for John
0.08	**Jackson**	*Old English* son of Jack
4.44	**Jacob**	*Hebrew* one who holds back another, supplanter
0.04	**Jacoby**	*Hebrew* one who holds back another, supplanter
0.03	**Jacques**	*French* form of Jacob: one who holds back another, supplanter
0.02	**Jade**	*Spanish* jade, a precious stone
0.09	**Jaime**	*Spanish* form of James
0.42	**Jake**	*Hebrew* one who holds back another, supplanter
0.02	**Jakob**	*Hebrew* one who holds back another, supplanter
0.06	**Jamaal**	*Arabic* a camel, beauty
0.24	**Jamal**	*Arabic* a camel, beauty
0.12	**Jamar**	probably a combination of prefix Ja- and suffix -mar
0.04	**Jamel**	*Arabic* a camel, beauty
0.02	**Jamelle**	*Arabic* a camel, beauty
17.18	**James**	*English* form of Jacob, held by the heel, supplanter
0.10	**Jameson**	son of James
0.72	**Jamie**	*English* form of Jacob, held by the heel, supplanter
0.02	**Jamieson**	son of James
0.05	**Jamil**	*Arabic* a camel, beauty
0.04	**Jamison**	son of James
0.05	**Jan**	*Dutch* form of John

0.02	**Jarad**	*Hebrew* to descend, descendant, one who rules
2.15	**Jared**	*Hebrew* to descend, descendant, one who rules
0.02	**Jarell**	form of Gerald: *English* a warrior; *Latin* spear-ruler
0.02	**Jaren**	*Hebrew* to sing, cry out
0.02	**Jarett**	*Hebrew* to descend, descendant, one who rules
0.02	**Jarid**	*Hebrew* to descend, descendant, one who rules
0.06	**Jarod**	*Hebrew* to descend, descendant, one who rules
0.07	**Jaron**	*Hebrew* to sing, cry out
0.02	**Jarrad**	*Hebrew* to descend, descendant, one who rules
0.18	**Jarred**	*Hebrew* to descend, descendant, one who rules
0.03	**Jarrell**	form of Gerald: *English* a warrior; *Latin* spear-ruler
0.04	**Jarret**	*Hebrew* to descend, descendant, one who rules
0.20	**Jarrett**	*Hebrew* to descend, descendant, one who rules
0.31	**Jarrod**	*Hebrew* to descend, descendant, one who rules
0.03	**Jarryd**	*Hebrew* to descend, descendant, one who rules
0.23	**Jarvis**	*Old German* keen as a spear
0.02	**Jasen**	*Greek* healer
11.93	**Jason**	*Greek* healer
0.02	**Jaspal**	*Punjabi* lives a virtuous lifestyle
0.04	**Jasper**	*Old French* stone
0.02	**Javan**	Biblical Javan is son of Japheth
0.02	**Javaris**	origin unknown
0.17	**Javier**	*Spanish* owner of the new house
0.03	**Javon**	Biblical Javan is son of Japheth
0.50	**Jay**	*English* gaius, a bird in the crow family; *English* blue jay

0.05	**Jayce**	invented name, possibly from initials J and C
0.03	**Jayme**	*English* form of Jacob, held by the heel, supplanter
0.03	**Jaymes**	*English* form of Jacob, held by the heel, supplanter
0.12	**Jayson**	*Greek* healer
0.12	**Jean**	*French* form of John: *Hebrew* Jehovah has been gracious
0.03	**Jean-Francois**	Jean + Francois
0.02	**Jean-Michel**	Jean + Michel
0.02	**Jean-Philippe**	Jean + Philippe
0.02	**Jed**	*Arabic* the hand
0.02	**Jedediah**	*Hebrew* beloved of the Lord
0.03	**Jedidiah**	*Hebrew* beloved of the Lord
0.07	**Jeff**	*English* gift of peace
0.02	**Jefferson**	*Old English* son of Jeffery
1.26	**Jeffery**	*English* gift of peace
5.53	**Jeffrey**	*English* gift of peace
0.03	**Jeffry**	*English* gift of peace
0.03	**Jerad**	*Hebrew* to descend, descendant, one who rules
0.02	**Jerald**	form of Gerald: *English* a warrior; *Latin* spear-ruler
0.03	**Jeramie**	*Hebrew* appointed by Jehovah, God will uplift
0.02	**Jeramy**	*Hebrew* appointed by Jehovah, God will uplift
0.03	**Jered**	*Hebrew* to descend, descendant, one who rules
0.02	**Jerel**	form of Gerald: *English* a warrior; *Latin* spear-ruler
0.02	**Jerell**	form of Gerald: *English* a warrior; *Latin* spear-ruler
0.02	**Jereme**	*Hebrew* appointed by Jehovah, God will uplift
0.03	**Jeremey**	*Hebrew* appointed by Jehovah, God will uplift

0.69	**Jeremiah**	*Hebrew* appointed by Jehovah, God will uplift
0.05	**Jeremie**	*Hebrew* appointed by Jehovah, God will uplift
0.02	**Jérémie**	*Hebrew* appointed by Jehovah, God will uplift
6.41	**Jeremy**	*Hebrew* appointed by Jehovah, God will uplift
0.02	**Jerimiah**	*Hebrew* appointed by Jehovah, God will uplift
0.33	**Jermaine**	*Middle English* sprout, a bud
0.02	**Jermey**	*Hebrew* appointed by Jehovah, God will uplift
0.03	**Jerod**	*Hebrew* to descend, descendant, one who rules
0.37	**Jerome**	*English* of holy name
0.03	**Jeromy**	*Hebrew* appointed by Jehovah, God will uplift
0.02	**Jeron**	form of Jerome: *English* of holy name
0.02	**Jerrad**	*Hebrew* to descend, descendant, one who rules
0.03	**Jerrell**	form of Gerald: *English* a warrior; *Latin* spear-ruler
0.08	**Jerrod**	*Hebrew* to descend, descendant, one who rules
0.75	**Jerry**	nickname for Jerome or Gerald
0.06	**Jess**	*Greek* wealthy, a gift, God exists
3.43	**Jesse**	*Greek* wealthy, a gift, God exists
0.38	**Jessie**	*Greek* wealthy, a gift, God exists
0.03	**Jessy**	*Greek* wealthy, a gift, God exists
0.17	**Jesus**	*Hebrew* God will help
0.05	**Jim**	*English* form of Jacob, held by the heel, supplanter
0.08	**Jimmie**	*English* form of Jacob, held by the heel, supplanter
0.59	**Jimmy**	*English* form of Jacob, held by the heel, supplanter
0.02	**Joaquin**	*Hebrew* God will establish
0.10	**Jody**	*Hebrew* Jehovah adds

0.24	**Joe**	*Hebrew* Jehovah adds
1.44	**Joel**	*Hebrew* God is willing, Jehovah is the Lord
0.25	**Joey**	*Hebrew* Jehovah adds
14.44	**John**	*Hebrew* Jehovah has been gracious
0.87	**Johnathan**	*Hebrew* Jehovah has been gracious
0.28	**Johnathon**	*Hebrew* Jehovah has been gracious
0.08	**Johnnie**	*Hebrew* Jehovah has been gracious
0.67	**Johnny**	*Hebrew* Jehovah has been gracious
0.02	**Johnson**	*Old English* son of John
0.41	**Jon**	*Hebrew* Jehovah has been gracious
0.05	**Jonah**	*Hebrew* dove
0.06	**Jonas**	*Hebrew* the doer
11.27	**Jonathan**	*Hebrew* Jehovah has been gracious
1.89	**Jonathon**	*Hebrew* Jehovah has been gracious
3.63	**Jordan**	*Hebrew* to descend
0.03	**Jorden**	*Hebrew* to descend
0.15	**Jordon**	*Hebrew* to descend
0.04	**Jordy**	*Hebrew* to descend
0.27	**Jorge**	*Spanish* form of George: *Greek* a farmer, a tiller of the soil
0.03	**Jory**	short form for Jordan
4.01	**Jose**	*Hebrew* Jehovah adds; *Spanish* for Joseph
0.03	**Josef**	*Hebrew* Jehovah adds
14.15	**Joseph**	*Hebrew* Jehovah adds
0.06	**Josh**	*Hebrew* Jehovah saves
18.90	**Joshua**	*Hebrew* Jehovah saves
0.02	**Joshuah**	*Hebrew* Jehovah saves
0.10	**Josiah**	*Hebrew* Jehovah supports
0.05	**Josue**	form of Joshua
0.04	**Jovan**	*Slavonic* form of John: the gift of God
0.03	**Jr**	*Latin* young
0.44	**Juan**	*Spanish* form of John; *Hebrew* Jehovah saves
0.02	**Judd**	*Hebrew* praised
0.05	**Jude**	*Hebrew* praised
0.02	**Judson**	*Old English* son of Judd
0.46	**Julian**	*Greek* soft-haired, light-bearded
0.08	**Julien**	*Greek* soft-haired, light-bearded

0.11	**Julio**	*Spanish* form of Julius; *Greek* youthful and downy-bearded
0.15	**Julius**	*Greek* youthful and downy-bearded
0.04	**Junior**	*Latin* young
0.02	**Justen**	*Latin* just, upright
11.31	**Justin**	*Latin* just, upright
0.02	**Justine**	*Latin* just, upright
0.02	**Juston**	*Latin* just, upright
0.02	**Justyn**	*Latin* just, upright

K

0.02	**Kacey**	*Celtic* valorous; *Irish* brave
0.02	**Kade**	origin unknown
0.03	**Kai**	*Hawaiian* ocean
0.03	**Kale**	*Arabic* short for Khalil: friend
0.06	**Kaleb**	*Hebrew* a dog, faithful, bold one
0.04	**Kalen**	origin unknown
0.02	**Kalin**	origin unknown
0.02	**Kalvin**	*Latin* bald
0.02	**Kameron**	*Celtic* bent nose
0.03	**Kane**	*Gaelic* fair; also warlike and tribute
0.08	**Kareem**	*Arabic* noble, exalted
0.02	**Karim**	*Arabic* noble, exalted
0.29	**Karl**	*German* form of Charles; *English* manly, strong; *German* farmer
0.06	**Kasey**	*Celtic* valorous; *Irish* brave
0.02	**Kayle**	*Hebrew* a dog, faithful, bold one
0.03	**Keaton**	*English* one who comes from Ketton
0.08	**Keegan**	*Irish* little and firey
0.06	**Keenan**	*Gaelic* little ancient one
1.74	**Keith**	*Gaelic* the wind; *Welsh* from the forest
0.09	**Kellen**	*German* surname
0.29	**Kelly**	*English* the ship on or near the river; *Irish* warrior
0.05	**Kelsey**	*Old Norse* dweller by the water
0.22	**Kelvin**	*English* a friend or lover of ships
0.02	**Ken**	nickname for names beginning with ken
0.02	**Kendal**	*Old English* from the bright valley

0.19	**Kendall**	*Old English* from the bright valley
0.02	**Kendell**	*Old English* from the bright valley
0.21	**Kendrick**	*Irish* son of Henry; *English* royal ruler
3.03	**Kenneth**	*Scottish* comely, handsome; *English* royal oath
0.17	**Kenny**	*Scottish* comely, handsome; *English* royal oath
0.17	**Kent**	*Welsh* white, bright
0.07	**Kenton**	*Old English* from the estate of the king
0.02	**Kentrell**	origin unknown
0.02	**Keon**	short form of McKeon: *Irish* well born
0.18	**Kerry**	*Gaelic* son of the dark one
0.03	**Kevan**	*Gaelic* handsome, beautiful
0.03	**Keven**	*Gaelic* handsome, beautiful
7.73	**Kevin**	*Gaelic* handsome, beautiful
0.02	**Khalid**	*Arabic* horse rider; eternal
0.02	**Khalil**	*Arabic* friend
0.08	**Kiel**	*Gaelic* a hill where the cattle graze
0.04	**Kieran**	*Irish* little and dark-skinned
0.02	**Kim**	*Greek* a hollow vessel
0.04	**Kirby**	*Old Norse* from the village of the church
0.27	**Kirk**	*Scottish* a church
0.11	**Kody**	*English* a cushion
0.03	**Kolby**	*Old English* from the black farm
0.02	**Konrad**	*German* bold, wise, counsellor
0.09	**Korey**	*Latin* a helmet, from the hollow
0.14	**Kory**	*Latin* a helmet, from the hollow
0.02	**Kraig**	*Celtic* from the crag or rugged rocky mass
0.03	**Kris**	*Greek* Christ-bearer
0.06	**Kristian**	*Greek* Christ-bearer
0.07	**Kristofer**	*Greek* Christ-bearer
0.04	**Kristoffer**	*Greek* Christ-bearer
0.04	**Kristoph**	*Greek* Christ-bearer
0.69	**Kristopher**	*Greek* Christ-bearer
0.34	**Kurt**	*German* bold, wise, counsellor
0.24	**Kurtis**	*German* bold, wise, counsellor
0.33	**Kyele**	*Gaelic* a hill where the cattle graze
8.27	**Kyle**	*Gaelic* a hill where the cattle graze
0.04	**Kyler**	*American* surname

L

0.13	**Lamar**	*Latin* from the sea
0.07	**Lamont**	*Scottish* lawyer
0.73	**Lance**	*Latin* a light spear; *German* land
0.02	**Landen**	*Old English* from the long hill
0.30	**Landon**	*Old English* from the long hill
0.06	**Lane**	*Old English* from the narrow road
0.02	**Lanny**	short form of names beginning with Lan
0.02	**Laron**	*French* a thief
0.92	**Larry**	*Latin* a laurel, a crown
0.02	**Lars**	*Scandinavian* form of Lawrence; *Latin* a laurel, a crown
0.03	**Laurence**	*Latin* a laurel, a crown
0.54	**Lawrence**	*Latin* a laurel, a crown
0.03	**Layne**	*Old English* from the narrow road
0.06	**Lazaro**	*Hebrew* God will help
0.72	**Lee**	*English* field, meadow; short form of Leo, Leon, Leroy, Leslie, Leigh
0.03	**Leif**	*Old Norse* beloved
0.02	**Leigh**	*English* field, meadow; short form of Leo, Leon, Leroy, Leslie, Leigh
0.05	**Leland**	*Old English* from the meadowland
0.12	**Leo**	*Latin* lion
0.21	**Leon**	*Greek* form of Leo, lion; *French* lion-like
0.28	**Leonard**	*English* form of *German*, strong as a lion
0.03	**Leonardo**	*English* form of *German*, strong as a lion
0.02	**Leonel**	*English* lion cub
0.15	**Leroy**	*Old French* king
0.13	**Leslie**	*English* small meadow, a dell; *Scottish* from the gray fortress
0.09	**Lester**	*Latin* from the camp of the legion
0.36	**Levi**	*Hebrew* joined to, attendant upon; *Hebrew* joined in harmony
0.17	**Lewis**	*Welsh* lionlike, lightning
0.14	**Liam**	*Irish* form of William: *English* resolute protector; *English* to bind, tie

0.03	**Lincoln**	*Old English* from the settlement by the pool
0.03	**Lindsay**	*Old English* the linden trees near the water
0.02	**Lindsey**	*Old English* the linden trees near the water
0.10	**Lionel**	*English* lion cub
0.15	**Lloyd**	*Welsh* gray-haired
0.47	**Logan**	*English* a felled tree; *Irish* from the hollow
0.10	**Lonnie**	nickname for Lawrence: *Latin* a laurel, a crown
0.07	**Loren**	form of Lawrence: *Latin* a laurel, a crown
0.11	**Lorenzo**	*Spanish* and *Italian* form of Lawrence: a laurel, a crown
0.05	**Lorne**	familiar form of Lawrence
0.51	**Louis**	*English* famous in battle
0.02	**Lowell**	*Old English* little beloved one
0.09	**Luc**	*English* form of *Latin* Lucius: light
0.02	**Luca**	*English* form of *Latin* Lucius: light
0.71	**Lucas**	*English* form of *Latin* Lucius: light
0.02	**Luigi**	*English* famous in battle
0.45	**Luis**	*English* famous in battle
0.05	**Lukas**	*English* form of *Latin* Lucius: light
0.97	**Luke**	*English* form of *Latin* Lucius: light
0.04	**Luther**	*Old German* famous warrior
0.10	**Lyle**	*English* from the island
0.03	**Lyndon**	*Old English* dweller at the hill of the linden tree
0.03	**Lynn**	*Old Welsh* from the waterfall

M

0.02	**Mack**	*Irish* and *Gaelic* son of
0.06	**Mackenzie**	*Irish* son of the wise leader
0.02	**Madison**	*Old English* son of the mighty warrior
0.02	**Malachi**	*Hebrew* angel
0.18	**Malcolm**	*Arabic* a dove
0.04	**Malik**	*Arabic* king; angel, divine messenger; *Punjabi* lord or master
0.02	**Mandeep**	*Punjabi* mind full of light
0.20	**Manuel**	form of Emanuel: *Hebrew* God is with us

0.88	**Marc**	*Latin* warlike; *Italian* form of Mark
0.03	**Marc-Andre**	Marc + Andre
0.03	**Marc-André**	Marc + André
0.10	**Marcel**	*English* short form of Marc and Marcus; *Latin* little and warlike; *Italian* form of Marcel
0.02	**Marcello**	*English* short form of Marc and Marcus; *Latin* little and warlike; Italian form of Marcel
0.20	**Marco**	*Latin* Mars, warlike
0.07	**Marcos**	*Latin* Mars, warlike
1.73	**Marcus**	*Latin* Mars, warlike
0.47	**Mario**	*Latin* warlike; *Italian* form of Mark
0.03	**Marion**	form of Mark: *Latin* Mars, warlike
5.39	**Mark**	*Latin* warlike; *Italian* form of Mark
0.02	**Marko**	*Latin* warlike; *Italian* form of Mark
0.04	**Markus**	*Latin* warlike; *Italian* form of Mark
0.03	**Marlin**	*English* little falcon
0.11	**Marlon**	*English* little falcon
0.03	**Marques**	*French* a sign, a mark
0.12	**Marquis**	*Old French* a nobleman
0.02	**Marquise**	*Old French* a nobleman
0.23	**Marshall**	*English* steward, horse-keeper
0.02	**Martell**	*English* one who uses a hammer
0.62	**Martin**	*English* warlike; *Latin* akin to Marcus
0.05	**Marty**	*English* warlike; *Latin* akin to Marcus
0.27	**Marvin**	*Old English* famous friend
0.23	**Mason**	*English* a mason, a worker in stone
0.02	**Massimo**	*Italian* the greatest
0.92	**Mathew**	*Hebrew* gift of God
0.17	**Mathieu**	*Hebrew* gift of God
0.03	**Matt**	*Hebrew* gift of God
24.13	**Matthew**	*Hebrew* gift of God
0.03	**Matthieu**	*Hebrew* gift of God
0.45	**Maurice**	*Latin* dark-skinned
0.03	**Mauricio**	*Spanish* form of Maurice; *Latin* dark-skinned
0.24	**Max**	*Latin* great, most excellent
0.02	**Maxime**	*Latin* great, most excellent

0.03	**Maximilian**	*Latin* great, most excellent
0.14	**Maxwell**	*Latin* great, most excellent
0.02	**Mckay**	*Scottish* son of fire
0.27	**Melvin**	*Gaelic* polished chief
0.02	**Merle**	*Old French* famous
0.03	**Mervin**	*Old English* lover of the sea
0.29	**Micah**	*Hebrew* who is like God
32.37	**Michael**	*Hebrew* who is like God
0.77	**Micheal**	*Hebrew* who is like God
0.16	**Michel**	*Hebrew* who is like God
0.02	**Michele**	*Hebrew* who is like God
0.03	**Mickey**	*Hebrew* who is like God
0.25	**Miguel**	*Hebrew* who is like God
0.02	**Mikael**	*Hebrew* who is like God
0.02	**Mikal**	*Hebrew* who is like God
0.05	**Mike**	*Hebrew* who is like God
0.02	**Mikeal**	*Hebrew* who is like God
0.03	**Mikel**	*Hebrew* who is like God
0.02	**Mikhail**	*Hebrew* who is like God
0.22	**Miles**	*Latin* a warrior, a soldier
0.07	**Milton**	*Old English* dweller at the farmstead of the mill
0.02	**Mitch**	*Hebrew* who is like God (Michael)
0.07	**Mitchel**	*Hebrew* who is like God (Michael)
1.01	**Mitchell**	*Hebrew* who is like God (Michael)
0.03	**Mohamed**	*Arabic* praised
0.06	**Mohammad**	*Arabic* praised
0.06	**Mohammed**	*Arabic* praised
0.03	**Moises**	*Spanish* form of Moses; *Greek* drawn from the water
0.02	**Monte**	*Latin* a hill, a mountain
0.02	**Montez**	*Spanish* surname: dweller in the mountains
0.02	**Monty**	*Latin* a hill, a mountain
0.25	**Morgan**	*Celtic* one who lives near the sea
0.07	**Morris**	form of Maurice: *Latin* dark-skinned
0.04	**Moses**	*Greek* drawn from the water
0.02	**Moshe**	form of Moses: *Greek* drawn from the water
0.03	**Muhammad**	*Arabic* praised

0.05	**Murray**	*Scottish* sailor
0.02	**Mustafa**	*Arabic* superior, royal
0.18	**Myles**	*Latin* a warrior, a soldier
0.04	**Myron**	*Greek* fragrant essence

N

4.06	**Nathan**	*Hebrew* gift of God
0.07	**Nathanael**	*Hebrew* gift of God
0.06	**Nathanial**	*Hebrew* gift of God
0.09	**Nathanie**	*Hebrew* gift of God
1.24	**Nathaniel**	*Hebrew* gift of God
0.03	**Nathen**	*Hebrew* gift of God
0.17	**Neal**	*English* a champion
0.48	**Neil**	*English* a champion
0.20	**Nelson**	*Gaelic* son of Neal
0.03	**Nevin**	*Gaelic* nephew
10.98	**Nicholas**	*Greek* victory of the people
0.02	**Nicholaus**	*Greek* victory of the people
0.05	**Nick**	*Greek* victory of the people
0.03	**Nicklaus**	*Greek* victory of the people
0.17	**Nickolas**	*Greek* victory of the people
0.02	**Nicola**	*Greek* victory of the people
0.28	**Nicolas**	*Greek* victory of the people
0.11	**Nigel**	*English* night, dark
0.07	**Nikolas**	*Greek* victory of the people
0.02	**Nikolaus**	*Greek* victory of the people
0.23	**Noah**	*Hebrew* rest, peace
0.08	**Noel**	*English* to be born, the Nativity, born at Christmas
0.13	**Nolan**	*Irish* famous, noble
0.16	**Norman**	*English* a man from the North

O

0.09	**Oliver**	*Latin* an olive tree
0.02	**Olivier**	*French* form of Oliver: an olive tree
0.19	**Omar**	*Arabic* long life, first son, highest, follower of the Prophet
0.02	**Oren**	*Gaelic* pale
0.16	**Orlando**	*English* from the pointed land
0.02	**Orry**	*Latin* the Orient
0.10	**Oscar**	*Old Norse* divine spearman
0.02	**Osvaldo**	*Spanish* form of Oswald; *Old English* with power from God
0.05	**Otis**	*Old German* prosperous; *Greek* with acute hearing
0.02	**Otto**	*Old German* prosperous, wealthy
0.18	**Owen**	*Welsh* variation of Eugene, well born

P

0.04	**Pablo**	*Spanish* form of Paul; *Latin* small
0.02	**Paolo**	*Latin* small
0.02	**Paris**	*Greek* in legend a king of Troy
0.10	**Parker**	*Old English* guardian of the park
0.02	**Pascal**	*Italian* born at Easter or Passover
0.02	**Pasquale**	*Italian* born at Easter
4.45	**Patrick**	*Latin* a patrician, a person of noble descent
3.68	**Paul**	*Latin* small
0.02	**Paulo**	*Latin* small
0.02	**Payton**	*Old English* from the estate of the warrior
0.11	**Pedro**	*Spanish* form of Peter
0.02	**Percy**	*Old French* valley prisoner
0.17	**Perry**	*Middle English* from the pear tree
0.02	**Pete**	*Greek* a rock
2.08	**Peter**	*Greek* a rock
1.27	**Philip**	*Greek* a lover of horses
0.10	**Philippe**	*Greek* a lover of horses
1.61	**Phillip**	*Greek* a lover of horses

0.03	**Pierce**	*Anglo French* form of Peter
0.14	**Pierre**	*Greek* a rock
0.02	**Pierre-Luc**	Pierre + Luc
0.02	**Pietro**	*Greek* a rock
0.36	**Preston**	*English* from the priest's estate
0.02	**Prince**	*Latin* first, chief

Q

0.19	**Quentin**	*Latin* fifth; *Old English* from the estate of the queen
0.11	**Quincy**	*Old French* from the estate of the fifth son
0.07	**Quinn**	*Irish* wise
0.05	**Quintin**	*Latin* fifth
0.17	**Quinton**	*Latin* fifth

R

0.11	**Rafael**	*Spanish* form of Raphael; *Hebrew* God has healed
0.02	**Raheem**	*Punjabi* God
0.02	**Rahim**	*Arabic* merciful; *Punjabi* forgiveness
0.02	**Rahul**	*Arabic* traveler
0.18	**Ralph**	*Old Norse* counsel wolf
0.12	**Ramon**	*Spanish* form of Raymond; *English* wise protection
0.02	**Ramsey**	*Old English* from the island of the ram
0.07	**Randal**	*English* superior protection; *English* shield-wolf
0.64	**Randall**	*English* superior protection; *English* shield-wolf
0.03	**Randell**	*English* superior protection; *English* shield-wolf
0.06	**Randolph**	*Old English* shield-wolf
0.91	**Randy**	*English* superior protection; *English* shield-wolf
0.05	**Raphael**	*Hebrew* God has healed
0.02	**Rashaad**	*Arabic* guider, wisdom
0.13	**Rashad**	*Arabic* guider, wisdom

0.02	**Rashawn**	origin unknown
0.03	**Rasheen**	origin unknown
0.08	**Raul**	*French* form of Randolph: *Old English* shield-wolf
0.02	**Ravi**	*Hindi* benevolent
0.17	**Ray**	*English* wise protection
1.17	**Raymond**	*English* wise protection
0.02	**Raynard**	*Old German* wise and hard, bold, courageous
0.05	**Reece**	*Old Welsh* rash, ardent
0.05	**Reed**	*English* red-haired
0.02	**Reese**	*Old Welsh* rash, ardent
0.02	**Regan**	*Gaelic* little king
0.03	**Reggie**	*Old English* powerful and mighty
0.04	**Reginal**	*Old English* powerful and mighty
0.34	**Reginald**	*Old English* powerful and mighty
0.02	**Regis**	*Latin* kingly, regal
0.09	**Reid**	*English* red-haired
0.02	**Reinaldo**	*Spanish* form of Reginald: powerful and mighty
0.02	**Rémi**	possibly a form of Roman: *Latin* a person from Rome
0.02	**Remi**	possibly a form of Roman: *Latin* a person from Rome
0.11	**Rene**	*English* to be reborn, to revive
0.08	**Reuben**	*Hebrew* behold, a son
0.05	**Rex**	*Latin* king
0.03	**Rhett**	*Old English* a small stream
0.03	**Rhys**	*Old Welsh* rash, ardent
0.02	**Rian**	*Irish* little king
0.26	**Ricardo**	*English* powerful, rich ruler
0.02	**Riccardo**	*English* powerful, rich ruler
5.32	**Richard**	*English* powerful, rich ruler
0.10	**Rick**	*English* powerful, rich ruler
0.14	**Rickey**	*English* powerful, rich ruler
0.02	**Rickie**	*English* powerful, rich ruler
0.60	**Ricky**	*English* powerful, rich ruler
0.03	**Rico**	*English* powerful, rich ruler
0.22	**Riley**	*German*, *Dutch* a small stream; *Irish* valiant

0.05	**Robbie**	*German* bright fame
0.03	**Robby**	*German* bright fame
16.11	**Robert**	*German* bright fame
0.21	**Roberto**	*German* bright fame
0.19	**Robin**	*German* bright fame
0.04	**Rocco**	short form of Richard
0.09	**Rocky**	*Old English* rock; the well near the rock
0.23	**Roderick**	*German* famous ruler
0.02	**Rodger**	*English* famous, noble warrior
0.54	**Rodney**	*English* from the island clearing
0.02	**Rodolfo**	*Spanish* form of Rudolph: famous wolf
0.05	**Rodrick**	*German* famous ruler
0.02	**Rodrigo**	*Spanish* and *Italian* form of Roderick: famous ruler
0.53	**Roger**	*English* famous, noble warrior
0.12	**Roland**	*German* from the famous land
0.04	**Rolando**	*German* from the famous land
0.05	**Roman**	*Latin* a person from Rome
0.04	**Ron**	*Scottish* wise, judicious
1.52	**Ronald**	*Scottish* wise, judicious
0.24	**Ronnie**	*Scottish* wise, judicious
0.02	**Ronny**	*Scottish* wise, judicious
0.05	**Roosevelt**	*Dutch* field of roses
0.19	**Rory**	*Irish* red king
0.02	**Roscoe**	*Scottish* from the deer forest
0.55	**Ross**	*English* woods, meadow; *English* red; *Scottish* headland
0.35	**Roy**	*English* king
0.04	**Royce**	*Old English* song of the king
0.09	**Ruben**	*Hebrew* behold, a son
0.02	**Rudolph**	*Old German* famous wolf
0.05	**Rudy**	*Old German* famous wolf
0.02	**Rufus**	*Latin* red-haired
0.03	**Russel**	*English* red
0.80	**Russell**	*English* red
0.12	**Rusty**	*Old French* red-haired
14.98	**Ryan**	*Irish* little king
0.03	**Rylan**	*English* dweller on hill where rye is grown
0.02	**Ryne**	form of Ryan: *Irish* little king

S

0.03	**Salvador**	*Latin* to be saved
0.07	**Salvatore**	*Latin* to be saved
0.07	**Sam**	*Hebrew* God has heard
0.02	**Samir**	*Arabic* entertainer
0.03	**Sammy**	*Hebrew* God has heard
0.02	**Samson**	*Hebrew* child of the sun
2.58	**Samuel**	*Hebrew* God has heard
0.03	**Sandeep**	*Punjabi* enlightened being
0.02	**Sandy**	nickname for Alexander: *Greek* helper of mankind, protector of man
0.02	**Santiago**	form of Saint Diego (James): held by the heel, supplanter
0.02	**Sasha**	nickname for Alexander: *Greek* helper of mankind, protector of man
0.03	**Saul**	*Hebrew* asked for
0.02	**Schuyler**	*Dutch* a shelter
0.02	**Scot**	*English* Scotsman
4.34	**Scott**	*English* Scotsman
0.08	**Scotty**	*English* Scotsman
0.02	**Seamus**	*Irish* form of James: held by the heel, supplanter
4.29	**Sean**	*Irish* form of John
0.10	**Sebastian**	*Greek* venerable
0.04	**Sebastien**	*Greek* venerable
0.03	**Sébastien**	*Greek* venerable
0.03	**Serge**	*Latin* attendant
0.13	**Sergio**	*Italian* form of Serge; *Latin* attendant
0.92	**Seth**	*Hebrew* garment; appointed; *Syriac* appearance
0.02	**Shad**	*Punjabi* happy-go-lucky
2.22	**Shane**	*Irish* form of John
0.15	**Shannon**	*Irish* small and wise
0.02	**Sharif**	*Arabic* honest, noble
0.81	**Shaun**	*Irish* form of John
0.02	**Shavar**	origin unknown
3.08	**Shawn**	*Irish* form of John

0.10	**Shayne**	*Irish* form of John
0.08	**Shea**	*Gaelic* ingenious, courteous and regal
0.05	**Shelby**	*English* from the ledge estate
0.22	**Sheldon**	*English* protected kill
0.07	**Sherman**	*English* shearer
0.10	**Sidney**	short for Saint Denys, derived from Dionysius, the *Greek* god of wine
0.03	**Silas**	*Latin* forest dweller
0.02	**Simeon**	*French* form of Simon; *Latin* he heard
0.35	**Simon**	*Latin* he heard
0.05	**Skylar**	*Dutch* a shelter
0.11	**Skyler**	*Dutch* a shelter
0.04	**Solomon**	*Hebrew* man of peace
0.05	**Sonny**	son or boy
0.61	**Spencer**	*English* steward, administrator, butler
0.03	**Spenser**	*English* steward, administrator, butler
0.02	**Stacey**	*Latin* firmly established
0.02	**Stacy**	*Latin* firmly established
0.32	**Stanley**	*English* a stony meadow
0.22	**Stefan**	*Greek* a crown
0.02	**Stefano**	*Greek* a crown
0.02	**Steffen**	*Greek* a crown
0.13	**Stephan**	*Greek* a crown
0.04	**Stephane**	*Greek* a crown
4.98	**Stephen**	*Greek* a crown
0.04	**Stephon**	*Greek* a crown
0.07	**Sterling**	*Old English* of value
0.20	**Steve**	*Greek* a crown
9.64	**Steven**	*Greek* a crown
0.02	**Stevie**	*Greek* a crown
0.10	**Stewart**	*English* a steward
0.32	**Stuart**	*English* a steward
0.02	**Sundeep**	*Punjabi* light or enlightened being
0.02	**Syed**	*Arabic* master, chief
0.04	**Sylvain**	*Latin* forest dweller
0.05	**Sylvester**	*Latin* from the forest

T

0.04	**Tad**	nickname for Thaddeus: *Greek* courageous; *Latin* praiser
0.02	**Tai**	*Vietnamese* money, prosperity
0.02	**Talon**	origin unknown
0.20	**Tanner**	*English* leather worker
0.02	**Tariq**	origin unknown
0.02	**Tate**	*American Indian* windy
0.02	**Taurean**	astrological name: Taurus
0.02	**Tavares**	origin unknown
0.03	**Tavaris**	origin unknown
0.74	**Taylor**	*English* tailor
0.07	**Ted**	familiar form of names beginning with "ed"
0.06	**Teddy**	familiar form of names beginning with "ed"
0.02	**Terance**	*Latin* smooth
0.02	**Terell**	*German* belonging to Thor; martial
0.17	**Terence**	*Latin* smooth
0.39	**Terrance**	*Latin* smooth
0.02	**Terrel**	*German* belonging to Thor; martial
0.26	**Terrell**	*German* belonging to Thor; martial
0.30	**Terrence**	*Latin* smooth
0.98	**Terry**	*Latin* smooth
0.08	**Thaddeus**	*Greek* courageous; *Latin* praiser
0.03	**Theo**	*Greek* divine gift
0.35	**Theodore**	*Greek* divine gift
0.02	**Theron**	*Greek* hunter
6.49	**Thomas**	*Hebrew* a twin
0.02	**Tim**	*Greek* to honor God
0.02	**Timmothy**	*Greek* to honor God
0.03	**Timmy**	*Greek* to honor God
6.39	**Timothy**	*Greek* to honor God
0.02	**Titus**	*Greek* of the giants
0.03	**Tobias**	*Hebrew* goodness of God
0.09	**Toby**	nickname for Tobias
0.89	**Todd**	*English* fox

0.05	**Tom**	*Hebrew* a twin
0.05	**Tomas**	*Hebrew* a twin
0.02	**Tommie**	*Hebrew* a twin
0.28	**Tommy**	*Hebrew* a twin
0.63	**Tony**	short form for Anthony: *Greek* flourishing; *Latin* worthy of praise
0.02	**Torrence**	*Irish* form of Terrence; *Latin* smooth
0.02	**Torrey**	*Old English* from the tower
0.05	**Tory**	*Old English* from the tower
0.02	**Trace**	*Greek* harvester
0.06	**Tracy**	*Greek* harvester
3.43	**Travis**	*Latin* crossroads
0.02	**Tremaine**	*Old Cornish* from the house of stone
0.02	**Tremayne**	*Old Cornish* from the house of stone
0.25	**Trent**	*Latin* torrent
0.22	**Trenton**	*Latin* torrent
0.03	**Trever**	*Celtic* prudent
1.55	**Trevor**	*Celtic* prudent
0.11	**Trey**	*Middle English* third born
0.39	**Tristan**	*Celtic* tumult, noise; *Welsh* sorrowful
0.83	**Troy**	*Irish* foot soldier
0.02	**Tuan**	*Vietnamese* handsome appearance
0.02	**Tucker**	*Old English* one who fulled, teased and burled cloth
0.08	**Ty**	*British* a house
0.02	**Tye**	*British* a house
5.57	**Tyler**	*English* maker of tiles
0.06	**Tylor**	*English* maker of tiles
0.07	**Tyree**	origin unknown
0.07	**Tyrel**	*German* belonging to Thor; martial
0.13	**Tyrell**	*German* belonging to Thor; martial
0.03	**Tyron**	*Greek* sovereign; *Irish* land of Owen
0.40	**Tyrone**	*Greek* sovereign; *Irish* land of Owen
0.50	**Tyson**	*English* firebrand

U

0.03	**Ulysses**	*Greek* wrathful
0.02	**Uriah**	*Hebrew* God is my light

V

0.04	**Van**	*Dutch* "of" or "from"
0.04	**Vance**	*Middle English* from the grain fan
0.03	**Vaughn**	*Old Welsh* small one
0.13	**Vernon**	*Latin* spring-like, youthful
0.02	**Vicente**	*Spanish* form of Vincent; *Latin* victor, conqueror
0.62	**Victor**	*Latin* victor, conqueror
0.02	**Vijay**	origin unknown
0.03	**Vince**	*Latin* victor, conqueror
0.88	**Vincent**	*Latin* victor, conqueror
0.03	**Vincenzo**	*Latin* victor, conqueror
0.05	**Virgil**	*Latin* rod or staff bearer
0.02	**Vito**	*Latin* alive
0.02	**Vladimir**	*Old Slavic* powerful warrior

W

0.28	**Wade**	*English* to wade; from the river crossing
0.04	**Wallace**	*Old English* Welshman
0.52	**Walter**	*German* powerful warrior
0.34	**Warren**	*English* preserver, defender
0.04	**Waylon**	*English* from the land by the road
0.52	**Wayne**	*English* a way; wagoner
0.08	**Wendell**	*German* wanderer
1.23	**Wesley**	*English* the west meadow
0.03	**Westley**	*English* the west meadow
0.11	**Weston**	*English* from the western estate
0.09	**Whitney**	*Old English* a small piece of land near water
0.04	**Wilbert**	*Old English* wall fortification; bright willows
0.04	**Wilfred**	*Old German* resolute for peace
0.03	**Wilfredo**	*Italian* form of Wilfred: resolute for peace
0.06	**Will**	*English* resolute protector
0.03	**Willard**	*Old English* resolutely brave
9.78	**William**	*English* resolute protector

0.60	**Willie**	*English* resolute protector
0.03	**Willis**	*English* resolute protector
0.08	**Wilson**	*Old German* son of William
0.04	**Winston**	*Old English* from the friend's town
0.06	**Wyatt**	*Old French* form of Guy; *English* a guide; *Hebrew* valley

X

0.17	**Xavier**	*Arabic* bright

Y

0.02	**Yusuf**	*Arabic* form of Joseph: Jehovah adds
0.04	**Yves**	*Scottish* archer

Z

0.03	**Zacharia**	*Hebrew* the remembrance of the Lord
0.10	**Zachariah**	*Hebrew* the remembrance of the Lord
0.02	**Zacharie**	*Hebrew* the remembrance of the Lord
4.16	**Zachary**	*Hebrew* the remembrance of the Lord
0.17	**Zachery**	*Hebrew* the remembrance of the Lord
0.09	**Zackary**	*Hebrew* the remembrance of the Lord
0.11	**Zackery**	*Hebrew* the remembrance of the Lord
0.10	**Zane**	form of John: *Hebrew* Jehovah has been gracious
0.02	**Zechariah**	*Hebrew* the remembrance of the Lord

Section III

Unusual Names

• • • • GIRLS • • • •

A

Aadriyanda
Aaih
Aaisha
Aaisna
Aalia
Aaliyah
Aaltina
Aalya
Aamie
Aandrea
Aarai
Aaren
Aariak
Aarianne
Aarica
Aarika
Aarin
Aarius
Aaron-Nicole
Aartee
Aarti
Aaryn
Aase-Marie
Aasha
Aashley
Aasiya
Aatifa
Aayshah
Abagael
Abagail
Abageal
Abalonia
Abanessa
Abani
Abasha
Abbe
Abbegail
Abbegale
Abbelyn
Abbi
Abbi-Lynn
Abbigail
Abbigale
Abbigayle
Abby Joy
Abbye
Abbylene
Abdullah
Abebech
Abeer
Abegail
Abeliris
Abena
Abeni
Aberian
Abethal
Abgail
Abia
Abidah
Abidiya
Abidjan
Abiella
Abigail-Rebecca
Abigale
Abigaliy
Abigayil
Abigayl
Abigayle
Abilene
Abilynn
Abimbola
Abir
Abira
Abirami
Abiramy
Abisai
Abish
Abla
Aboni
Abosede
Abra
Abraham
Abralyn
Abrar
Abria
Abriana
Abriel
Abrigayle
Abril
Abyssinia
Acacia
Acadia
Aceria
Achia
Acie
Aconderia
Acrua
Adéle
Adabell
Adacia
Adaela
Adah
Adaiah
Adaina
Adair
Adairis
Adalena
Adalia
Adalin
Adalyn
Adamari
Adana
Adanna
Adaora
Adaria
Adarsh
Adash
Adawna
Adayshia
Addaleigh
Adde
Addi
Addison
Addrienne
Addy
Adeana
Adebe
Adebimpe
Adebola
Adebrean
Adedoyin
Adeela
Adeen
Adeena

Adefolakemi
Adehlia
Adel
Adela
Adelade
Adelaida
Adelaide
Adelei
Adelheid
Adeliade
Adelicia
Adelin
Adelina
Adelindda
Adelita
Adelivette
Adell
Adella
Adelle
Adelyn
Adelynn
Aden
Adena
Adene
Adenia
Adenike
Adeola
Adessa
Adetola
Adetoun
Adeyinka
Adhwa
Adi
Adia
Adianez
Adie
Adiena
Adieren
Adila
Adilene
Adinna
Adira
Adisa
Adivel
Adiyo
Adlay
Adleaida
Adlene
Adlenia
Adlin
Adlyne
Adonica
Adonna
Adonysha
Adora
Adoree
Adra
Adranah
Adrea
Adream
Adreana
Adreanna
Adreika
Adren
Adrena
Adrenne
Adri
Adriann
Adriannette
Adrie
Adrieanna
Adriel
Adriela
Adriele
Adrien
Adriena
Adriene
Adrienna
Adrieon
Adrin
Adrina
Adriona
Adron
Adry
Adryan
Adryanne
Adweena
Adwoa
Aeelyn
Aeisha
Aelicia
Aelise
Aelissa
Aeliya
Aelwynn
Aerial
Aeriale
Aerica
Aerikka
Aerin
Aerinne
Aeriona
Aerione
Aeris
Aeron
Aerreadnea
Aersta
Aeryal
Aesha
Afaf
Afaq
Afara
Afe
Afeefa
Affiea
Affin
Affton
Afhton
Afifa
Afiya
Africa
Afrin
Afsa
Afsheen
Aftan
Aftine
Aftyn
Afua
Aganetha
Agata
Agelkidimitria
Agie-Lois
Aginah
Aglaia
Aglena
Agnés
Agnelia
Agnes Mae
Agnie
Agnieszka
Agrora
Ah-Ran
Ahakoa
Ahalaine
Ahalia
Aheesha
Ahjah
Ahlam
Ahleesha
Ahmad
Ahmana
Ahmeena
Ahmphayv
Ahna
Ahnansa
Ahneysha

Ahrissa
Ahsamon
Ahtaesha-Daniell
Ahteasha
Ahuoiza
Ai
Aibhne
Aicha
Aida
Aidan
Aiden
Aidin
Aiehsa
Aieisha
Aiesha
Aieshia
Aigher
Aigner
Aijalon
Aikatereina
Aikaterini
Aikia
Aiko
Aileene
Ailema
Ailene
Ailet
Aili
Ailil
Ailish
Aillson
Ailsa
Aily
Ailys
Aimée
Aimee Beth
Aimeé
Aimee-Jo
Aimee-Lynn
Aimee-Marie
Aimey
Aimi
Aimie
Aimory
Aimy
Aina
Ainadi
Aine
Ainge
Aingeal
Ainslee
Ainslie
Ainsly
Aipaupau
Airan
Aire
Aireal
Aireka
Airen
Airesa
Airiel
Airien
Airika
Airily
Airiona
Airiss
Airistea
Airl
Airmia
Airraka
Airyn
Aisat
Aishah
Aishat
Aishia
Aislann
Aisleen
Aislin
Aisling
Aislinn
Aislyn
Aislynn
Aissata
Aissatou
Aissette
Aisylin
Aitana Yuk
Aitza
Aivi
Aixa
Aiyanna
Aiysha
Ajà
Ajabeyang
Ajah
Ajahnique
Ajanikiya
Ajaran
Ajda
Ajene
Ajeshia
Ajha
Ajia
Ajolee
Akacia
Akaisha
Akala
Akamia
Akasha
Akaya
Akeah
Akeala
Akeema
Akeina
Akeisha
Akeita
Akela
Akelia
Akeliah
Akemi
Akemy
Akenele
Akerria
Akeshia
Akessiah
Aketa
Akethya
Aketia
Akeya
Akeyla
Akeysha
Akia
Akiata
Akiba
Akiela
Akiko
Akila
Akilah
Akilha
Akina
Akira
Akiria
Akirra
Akisha
Akista
Akora
Akosua
Akquana
Akshara
Akta
Akua
Akua Difie
Akyia
Akyra
Al-Hnouf

Alaa
Alacia
Alacie
Alacsia
Aladene
Alaena
Alahbayith
Alahna
Alain
Alaina-Kaye
Alainah
Alaine
Alainna
Alair
Alaire
Alais
Alaisha
Alan
Alana-Jean
Alana-Lynn
Alana-Marie
Alanah
Alanda
Alandis
Alandra
Alandria
Alane
Alanea
Alani
Alania
Alanis
Alannah
Alanoud
Alanta
Alanya
Alaquarya
Alarice
Alaricsa
Alasha
Alawna
Alaylea
Alayne
Alaysha
Alaysia
Alaythea
Alazandria
Alba
Albamary
Albany
Albarru
Alberta
Albina
Albreena
Albrey
Aldéa
Alda
Aldea
Aldena
Aldene
Aldia
Aldina
Aldonia
Aldora
Aldrena
Aléa
Aleace
Aleafia
Aleaha
Aleana
Aleara
Alease
Aleasha
Aleashea
Aleasia
Aleata
Aleatha
Aleaya
Alechea
Alechia
Alecisha
Alecsa
Aleczandria
Aleda
Alee
Aleea
Aleece
Aleema
Aleen
Aleena
Aleene
Aleesa
Aleesand
Aleese
Aleeshia
Aleeshya
Aleeta
Aleeyah
Alegria
Alehra
Aleia
Aleice
Aleicia
Aleida
Aleigh
Aleigha
Aleighsha
Aleis
Aleisa
Aleix
Alejandr
Alejandrina
Alejandro
Aleksandra
Aleksandra-Andrea
Aleksandria
Alelea
Alelia
Alenay
Alenda
Alene
Aleni
Alenna
Aleria
Aleris
Ales
Alesa
Alesandra
Alesandrea
Alescia
Alese
Aleshea
Alesheal
Aleska
Alessa
Alessand
Alessandra-Fernandes
Alessia
Aleta
Aletha
Alethea
Alethia
Aletia
Aletrice
Alex-Ann
Alexande
Alexander
Alexanderia
Alexandrina
Alexandrine
Alexcis
Alexdrandia
Alexes
Alexey
Alexi

Alexian
Alexie
Alexiea
Alexina
Alexis Bernadett
Alexisia
Alexius
Alexsandra
Alexsia
Alexus
Alexx
Alexxandra
Alexxis
Alexys
Alexyss
Alexzand
Alexzandra
Alexzandrea
Alexzandria
Aleya
Aleydi
Aleysha
Aleyssa
Alezis
Alfred
Alfreda
Alften
Ali Nichole
Ali Rae
Aliah
Aliana
Alianna
Alica
Alicakylene
Alican
Alice-Jamilla
Alicea
Alicen
Aliceson
Alicha
Alicha-Lynn
Alichia
Alicia Elana
Alicia Marie
Alicia Nicole
Alicia-Ann
Alicia-Jane
Alicia-Rae
Alician
Alicie
Aliciea
Alicja
Alicya
Alicyn
Alie
Aliea
Aliece
Aliecia
Aliena
Alies
Aliese
Aliesha
Aliesha-Jean
Alieshia
Aliette
Aliisa
Alile
Alillian
Alima
Alimah
Alinda
Alis
Alisabet
Alisabeth
Alisan
Alisane
Aliscia
Alisé
Àlise
Alisen
Alisha-Lynn
Alisha-Marie
Alishah
Alishaye
Alishea
Alishia-Iona
Alishya
Alison Megan
Alisondra
Alisse
Alissia
Alisson
Alisun
Alisyn
Alisza
Alithra
Alitsha
Alivette
Alivia
Alixandra
Alixandria
Alixendr
Alixiand
Alixis
Aliyaali
Aliyah
Aliye
Aliyyah
Alizabet
Alizabeth
Alize
Alka
Alkeensha
Alkeeta
Alkeshia
Allaina
Allaire
Allana
Allanah
Allandrya
Allanna
Allayna
Allea
Alleana
Allecia
Alleetta
Allegra
Allen
Allena
Allene
Allenecia
Alleneeka
Alleniece
Allesha
Allesse
Alli
Allic
Allicen
Allicia
Allidah
Allieta
Allina
Allis
Allisa
Alliscia
Allise
Allisen
Allisha
Allisia
Allissa
Allissarae
Allisson
Allisyn
Allitha
Allix
Allona

Allura
Allurie
Ally
Allyce
Allycia
Allylam
Allyn
Allysa
Allysceaioun
Allyscia
Allyse
Allysha
Allysia
Allysobn
Allyson-Kate
Allyss
Allyssa
Allyssen
Allysun
Almarie
Almea
Almeda
Almeera
Almesha
Almeta
Almira
Almire
Alnellys
Alodia
Aloma
Alona
Alonda
Alondra
Alonna
Àlonna
Alonnah
Alonzia
Alouque
Aloysia
Alpa
Alpha
Alphia
Alquavia
Alquleeaha
Alrick
Alsha
Alsharifa
Alsheree
Alsheri
Alshley
Alta
Alta-Aza
Altagracia
Altamead
Altamese
Altermease
Altha
Althaea
Althea
Althenia
Althia
Altina
Altomesh
Altosha
Altricia
Alunya
Alva
Alvanna
Alvel
Alveta
Alvieda
Alvina
Alvincia
Alvinesha
Alvira
Alvita
Alvona
Alwin
Alwyn
Alxis
Aly
Alyassa
Alybia
Alycen
Alycetta
Alycisa
Alyea
Alyese
Alyeshia
Alyia
Alyicia
Alyisa
Alyisha
Alyn
Alyna
Alyne
Alynne
Alyosha
Alyrea
Alys
Alysabeth
Alyscia
Alysea
Alysen
Alyshah
Alyss
Alyssa-Dawn
Alyssaann
Alyssha
Alyssia
Alysson
Alysyn
Alyvia
Alyx
Alyxandr
Alyzee
Alzbeta
Amélie
Ama
Ama Lynda
Amá
Amabel
Amada
Amadi
Amaia
Amaisha
Amaka
Amal
Amale-Nassima
Amalia
Amalie
Amalis
Amaly
Amamda
Aman
Amana
Amanada
Amanah
Amanda Ann
Amanda Christine
Amanda Dee
Amanda Isa
Amanda Jo
Amanda Rose
Amanda Sundrae
Amanda-Constance
Amanda-Crystal
Amanda-Jane
Amanda-Jean
Amanda-Jeanne
Amanda-Jillian
Amanda-Lea
Amanda-Lee

Amanda-Lisa
Amanda-Lyn
Amanda-Lynn
Amanda-Marie
Amanda-Mary
Amanda-Rae
Amanda-Rai
Amandah
Amandajo
Amandalee
Amandalyn
Amandi
Amandine
Amandip
Amands
Amandy
Amane
Àmanekina
Amanie
Amanjot
Amanjoyt
Amann
Amanna
Amara
Amarae
Amarah
Amaranta
Amardeep
Amarelys
Amari
Amarilis
Amarilys
Amarisa
Amarissa
Amarita
Amarjit
Amarjot
Amarprit
Amarris
Amarta
Amary
Amarylis
Amaryllis
Amaya
Amayah
Ambar
Amber Elizabeth
Amber Jo
Amber Lynn
Amber-Ann
Amber-Ashley
Amber-Dawn
Amber-Lea
Amber-Lee
Amber-Leigh
Amber-Lynn
Amber-Rae
Amber-Rose
Amber-Sue
Ambereen
Amberely
Amberia
Amberise
Amberle
Amberlea
Amberlee
Amberley
Amberlie
Amberlie-Gail
Amberlyn
Amberlynn
Amberzina
Ambilena
Ambor
Ambra
Ambre
Ambré
Ambrea
Ambree
Ambreia
Ambrey
Ambria
Ambrie
Ambriell
Ambrosha
Ambrosia
Ambry
Ambur
Ambyr
Ambyre
Amdra
Amdrea
Ame
Ameachel
Amealia
Ameasha
Amecia
Amee
Ameedah
Ameena
Ameera
Amegan
Ameia
Ameila
Ameisha
Amelda
Amelia-Rosa
Ameliz
Amellia
Amely
Amena
Amenaghawon
Amenda
Amenh
Amera
Amerah
Amerberle
America
Americus
Amerie
Amerlea
Amerlie
Ameron
Amery
Amesa
Amesha
Ameshia
Amethyst
Ametra
Amey
Amia
Amie Joe
Amié
Amie-Lee
Amiee
Amiee-Leigh
Amielia
Amiet
Amigayle
Amii
Amijo
Amiko
Amil
Amilet
Amilia
Amilie
Àmilie
Amillia
Amilyn
Aminah
Aminda
Amindia
Aminta
Aminte
Amio
Amir

Amira
Amirah
Amisha
Amishia
Amita
Amitha
Amitoz
Amity
Ammanda
Ammanda-Beth
Ammanuella
Ammaris
Ammeline
Ammerisa
Ammi-El
Ammie
Ammy
Amna
Amnada
Amne
Amneshia
Amnesty
Amninder
Amnit
Amoi
Amondine
Amonise
Amoreena
Amorette
Amorie
Amorrette
Amorrey
Amory
Amoryn
Amoury
Amreen
Amrinder
Amrit
Amrita
Amrith
Amritpal
Amritpreet
Amrutha
Amsbry
Amuen
Amy-Ann
Amy-Caroline
Amy-Jo
Amy-Lea
Amy-Leen
Amy-Lise
Amy-Lynn
Amy-Marie
Amye
Amyelita
Amyko
Amylia
Amylyn
Amythyst
An
Anà
Ana-Alic
Ana-Alicia
Ana-Lei
Ana-Loui
Ana-Maria
Ana-Marie
Anaar
Anabel
Anabela
Anabelle
Anabelsy
Anadel
Anadeli
Anadelia
Anadine
Anadrian
Anaeli
Anaeliz
Anaely
Anagé
Anagensy
Anah
Anahi
Anaiah
Anaily
Ànaise
Anaiya
Anaka
Analee
Analeis
Analena
Analesa
Anali
Analia
Analicia
Analidis
Analiese
Analilia
Analis
Analisa
Analise
Analisha
Analisia
Analissa
Anals
Analy
Anam
Anamari
Anamaria
Anamarie
Anamaris
Anamary
Ananay
Ananda
Anandalilia
Anandy
Anansa
Anar
Anara
Anarie
Anaseini
Anastasha
Anastasi
Anastasia
Domino
Anastasia Jasmin
Anastasia-Marie
Anastasj
Anastassia
Anastasy
Anastayc
Anastazia
Anasthia
Anasuya
Anaszia
Anatashia
Anatava
Anau
Anayancy
Anays
Ancellnita
Anchal
Anchan
Ancille
Ande
Andea
Andee
Andeidre
Andelin
Andeline
Andelyn
Andera
Anderà
Andersen
Anderson

Andi
Andi-Christina
Andianna
Andie
Andilyn
Andin
Andina
Andjellia
Andleeb
Andonia
Andra-Lynn
Andrah
Andraia
Andranae
Andranetta
Andranette
Andranique
Andranita
Andraya
Andraya-Lynn
Andréa
Andréne
Andrea De Fatima
Andreà
Andrea-Fiorella
Andrea-Lynn
Andrea-Nicole
Andreah
Andreaka
Andreal
Andrealiş
Andreana
Andreane
Andreanna
Andreanne
Andrée
Andrée-Anne
Andrée-Claude
Andrée-Eve
Andree-Anne
Andree-Michelle
Andreea
Andrei
Andreia
Andreina
Andreitt
Andreja
Andreka
Andrell
Andrelle
Andrena
Andreo
Andres
Andressa
Andretta
Andrew
Andrewa
Andri
Andriana
Andrianna
Andriea
Andrieka
Andrietta
Andrija
Andrika
Andrina
Andris
Andromahie
Andromeda
Aneacia
Aneasha
Aneccia
Anecia
Anedra
Aneeka
Aneela
Anees
Aneesa
Aneesah
Aneesha
Aneeta
Aneicia
Aneidah
Aneisha
Aneka
Anel
Anela
Aneli
Anelia
Anelisa
Anelle
Aneris
Aneschia
Aneseh
Anesha
Aneshia
Anesia
Anessa
Anessia
Aneste
Anestie
Anesty
Aneta
Anetra
Anett
Anette
Anfia
Angala
Angalena
Angalina
Anganita
Angdeep
Ange
Angee
Angel-Jane
Angela-Marie
Angelaine
Angelais
Angelanell
Angelanette
Angelaquis
Angèle
Angèlique
Angelea
Angeleah
Angelealee
Angeleana
Angelee
Angeleen
Angeleigh
Angelena
Angelene
Angeles
Angeli
Angelian
Angeliana
Angelici
Angelie
Angelika
Angeliqu
Angelita
Angelitt
Angeliz
Angell
Angella
Angellica
Angelmarie
Angelnett
Angelpreet
Angelyn
Angelyna
Angelynn
Angen
Angenett
Angenette

Angenise
Angey
Angi
Angial
Angielee
Angielina
Angila
Angilique
Angionette
Angjhan
Angle
Anglea
Angleana
Anglia
Angy
Anh
Anh-Tuyet
Anhelica
Anhquynh
Anhthy
Ani
Aniabelys
Aniasha
Anica
Anicarin
Anicia
Anick
Anie
Aniela
Anielica
Aniellia
Anielyn
Aniger
Anik
Anikka
Aniladys
Anilec
Anina
Anique
Anisa
Anisah
Anise
Anisia
Aniska
Anisled
Anissa
Anita-Ida
Anitha
Anitia
Anitra
Aniva
Anivah
Anja
Anja-Ani
Anjala
Anjali
Anjalicia
Anjalyn
Anjana
Anjane
Anjanetta
Anjanette
Anjani
Anjean
Anjeet
Anjela
Anjelic
Anjelina
Anjeliqu
Anjelita
Anjella
Anjellaca
Anjenette
Anjila
Anjilen
Anjillica
Anjli
Anjni
Anjoli
Anju
Anjulee
Anjuli
Anjulie
Anka
Ankita
Anlecta
Ann Britt
Ann Marie
Ann-Alexandra
Ann-Mari
Ann-Marie
Ann-Renee
Anna Clair
Anna Claudia
Anna Ellen
Anna Gail
Anna Leah
Anna Lena
Anna Maria
Anna Marie
Anna May
Anna-Bel
Anna-Bell
Anna-Dawn
Anna-Katherine
Anna-Leigh
Anna-Lise
Anna-Mar
Anna-Margrethe
Anna-Maria
Anna-Marie
Anna-Maude
Anna-Miriam
Anna-Theresa
Annabel
Annabell
Annabella
Annabelle
Annah
Annajean
Annaka
Annakaleena
Annakaye
Annakriseljeen
Annalaura
Annalea
Annalece
Annalecia
Annalee
Annaleigh
Annalice
Annalicia
Annalie
Annaliese
Annalis
Annalisa
Annalise
Annalissa
Annalisse
Annalyn
Annamae
Annamari
Annamaria
Annamieke
Annaquista
Annarita
Annasha
Annastacia
Annastashia
Annastasia
Annavel
Anne Clair
Anne Nicol
Anne-Andree
Anne-Christine
Anne-Denise

Anne-Elizabeth
Anne-Lydie
Anne-Mar
Anne-Margret
Anne-Michelle
Anne-Rachel
Anne-Sophie
Anne-Yara
Annegillette
Anneka
Anneke
Annelies
Anneliese
Annelisa
Annelise
Annelize
Annella
Annelys
Annemari
Annerys
Annescia
Annesha
Annesly
Annessa
Annetine
Annett
Annetta
Anngela
Anni
Annica
Annicca
Annicia-Louise
Annick
Annicka
Annie-Claude
Annie-Laurie
Anniecia
Annielanet
Annielissa
Anniena-Elvira
Annieshia
Annika-B
Annikki
Annina
Annis
Annisa
Annise
Annisha
Annissa
Annissia
Annjanette
Annjelina
Annjulie
Annjuline
Annley
Annlizeth
Annora
Annslea
Anntanell
Anntanette
Anntenia
Anntwaunett
Annunziata
Anny
Anoise
Anona
Anosha
Anouk
Anouska
Anquanece
Anquanette
Anquinette
Anraya
Anrielle
Ansa
Anshanta
Ansley
Anslie
Ansonia
Ansonya
Antaneice
Antanett
Antania
Antanis
Antanisha
Antasia
Antaya
Antea
Anteaus
Antelee
Antelma
Anteniqua
Anteshia
Antha
Anthea
Anthelesia
Antheria
Anthia
Anthlesia
Anthonette
Anthonia
Anthonisha
Anthony
Anthoula
Antia
Antigone
Antigoni
Antineska
Antinett
Antionet
Antionetta
Antioniquie
Antiwonette
Antoine
Antoineet
Antona
Antonell
Antonella-Anna
Antonenett
Antonesha
Antoneshia
Antonett
Antonette
Antonice
Antonietta
Antonina
Antoniqu
Antonise
Antonisha
Antonnea
Antonnia
Antonya
Antoya
Antranet
Antrell
Antrianna
Antrisa
Antronette
Antwanett
Antwanette
Antwannette
Antwawnett
Antwoinette
Antwonette
Antwoniek
Anu
Anudeep
Anue
Anuj
Anunciata
Anunziata
Anupa
Anuradha
Anureet
Anutka
Anvita

Anwyn
Any
Anyana
Anycea
Anyea
Anyenid
Anyiri
Anynya
Anysah
Anyse
Aoi
Aondrea
Aophonie
Aparna
Aphrodite
Aphtin
Aphton
Apolline
Apollonia
Apolonia
Applonia
Appoline
Appollonia
Appoloina
Apree
Aprele
Aprelle
Apriell
Aprielle
April-Dawn
April-Grace
April-Lynn
April-Sue
Aprila
Aprile
Aprili
Aprill
Apryle
Aqua
Aquaisha
Aquana
Aquanda
Aquanetta
Aquanitta
Aquarius
Aquasia
Aquavia
Aquaysha
Aqueehal
Aquiala
Aquila
Aquilla
Aquina
Aquisha
Aquita
Aquitha
Àqwela
Ara
Araba
Arabany
Arabella
Arabia
Araceli
Aracelis
Araceliz
Aracelly
Aracely
Aradhna
Arae
Arah
Araina
Araly
Araminta
Aramis
Aramys
Aranais
Aranpreet
Aranza
Araseli
Arbor
Arby
Arcadia
Arcelia
Archana
Archevia
Archithia
Ardelia
Ardell
Ardelle
Arden
Ardice
Ardis
Ardith
Ardrekra
Ardrey
Areal
Areatha
Areeba
Areej
Arefa
Arelia
Arelis
Areliz
Arelys
Aremanda
Arendtina
Areolynn
Aresha
Aretha
Areti
Arezou
Arfeen
Argiro
Ari
Aria
Ariadne
Arial
Ariale
Arian
Arianae
Ariann
Arias
Ariba
Arica
Aricelda
Aricelis
Aricka
Aridia
Arie
Arieal
Arieana
Arieann
Arieauna
Ariela
Ariell
Ariella
Ariellia
Arien
Arienne
Arieon
Aries
Aries-Anne
Arika
Arina
Arinn
Arion
Aris
Arisa
Arisha
Arissa
Arista
Aristea
Arit
Arizbel
Arjorie
Arjumand

Arkeia
Arkela
Arkeria
Arkesha
Arkeshia
Arla
Arlaine
Arlana
Arlee
Arleen
Arlen
Arlena
Arlenis
Arleshia
Arletha
Arlethea
Arlethia
Arlett
Arlette
Arley
Arlicia
Arlillie
Arlin
Arlina
Arlinda
Arline
Arlis
Arlisa
Arliss
Arllah
Arlouise
Arly
Arlyn
Arlyne
Arlyse
Arlysse
Armanda
Armani
Armel
Armena
Armenda
Armeta
Armie
Arminda
Armine-Theresa
Arneatha
Arnel
Arnell
Arnella
Arnelle
Arneris
Arnesha
Arnethen
Arnetta
Arnica
Arniika
Arnisha
Arnishia
Arnita
Arolis
Aronika
Arontrica
Arooj
Arpeeneh
Arran
Arren
Arria
Arrica
Arriel
Arrielle
Arriely
Arrienne
Arriet
Arrion
Arrita
Arrolynn
Arryn
Arryone
Arsadia
Arsala
Arsimmer
Artamishie
Artansas
Artavia
Artell
Artemis
Artesha
Artesia
Artessa
Arteviah
Arthea
Arthuoro
Arthurine
Arti
Articia
Artie
Artiesha
Artillia
Artimissia
Artisha
Artisia
Artrina
Artti
Artyra
Arunjot
Arvella
Arvelle
Arverna
Arveta
Arvinder
Arvinderjit
Arwa
Arwah
Arwen
Aryandalavanna
Aryann
Aryanna
Aryantee
Arycca
Aryel
Aryka
Aryn
Arzela
Arzina
Asa
Asako
Asal
Asami
Asayshia
Asbell
Asberg
Aschlee
Asees
Asenath
Ashadore Jenning
Ashala
Ashalee
Ashalei
Ashana
Ashanta
Ashantae
Ashante
Ashanti
Ashanty
Ashara
Ashauna
Ashaunta
Ashayla
Ashby
Ashden
Asheda
Ashelee
Ashelei
Asheleigh
Asheley

Ashely Do Rego
Asher
Ashera
Asheria
Ashia
Ashica
Ashika
Ashira
Ashiya
Ashkea
Ashkia
Ashlan
Ashlay
Ashle
Ashlée
Ashleah
Ashleann
Ashleay
Ashlee Jamille
Ashlee-Ann
Ashlee-B
Ashlee-Irene
Ashleen
Ashleene
Ashlen
Ashley Ann
Ashley Ashawndr
Ashley Danielle
Ashley Hope
Ashley Jan
Ashley Lyne
Ashley Patrice
Ashley Quonsha
Ashley Rae
Ashley Shardaa
Ashley Sherriee
Ashley-Ann
Ashley-Anne
Ashley-Carlen
Ashley-Charlene
Ashley-Dawn
Ashley-Jean
Ashley-Lee
Ashley-Lyn
Ashley-Lynn
Ashley-Lynne
Ashley-Marie
Ashley-Nicole
Ashley-Rae
Ashley-Rayne
Ashley-Rosanne
Ashley-Susan
Ashlianne
Ashliegh
Ashlii
Ashlin
Ashline
Ashling
Ashliy
Ashlley
Ashlye
Ashlynne
Ashnoor
Ashonti
Ashriah
Ashsheé
Ashta
Ashtain
Ashtan
Ashtar
Ashten
Ashthon
Ashtian
Ashtyn
Ashwini
Asiah
Asian
Asil
Asima
Asimina
Asinate
Asiray
Asiyih
Asjenquetta
Aslyne
Asma
Asmaa
Asmarth
Asna
Asonte
Aspacia
Asrai
Assia
Assunta
Assuntina
Assyria
Asta
Astaisha
Aster
Asthon
Astin
Aston
Astonti
Astra
Astrea
Astrid
Astrid-Maria
Astrida
Astrik
Asuka
Asya
Asyett
Aszurdee
Aszure
Atalaya
Atanacia
Atavia
Ateasa
Ateasha
Ateisa
Ateja
Ateya
Athanasia
Athanya
Athea
Athene
Athenea
Athida
Athina
Atia
Atia-Akhtar
Atiba
Atina
Atisha
Atiya
Atlantis
Atlee
Atneciv
Atoke
Atoria
Atosha
Atoshia
Atrena
Atrice
Atsuko
Attia
Attiah
Attracta
Atur
Aua
Auana
Auberi
Aubernay
Aubery
Aubin

Aubray
Aubre
Aubrea
Aubreah
Aubreé
Aubreee
Aubrei
Aubrey Anna
Aubrey-L
Aubri
Aubria
Aubrianne
Aubriegh
Aubry
Auburn
Aubyn
Auctorina
Aucuria
Audaisha
Audean
Audeina
Audra-Anne
Audray
Audrea
Audrée
Audree
Audrey-Christina
Audrey-Lea
Audri
Audria
Audriana
Audrianna
Audrianne
Audrick
Audrie
Audrin
Audrina
Audris
Audry
Audrya
Auerila
Augino
Augumn
August
Augusta
Augustin
Augustina
Augustine
Aujolie
Auketia
Aulia
Aumbrea
Auna
Aunastasia
Aundrea
Aundrean
Aundria
Aunique
Aunna
Auntwanique
Aunyea
Aunyeah
Aura
Auralee
Auralei
Aurea
Aureal
Aurèle
Aurelia
Aurelie
Aurellia
Auria
Aurica
Auriel
Aurielle
Aurina
Auroosa
Ausalena
Ausha
Ausley
Ausma
Austen
Austi
Austina
Australia
Austri
Austyn
Ausuade
Auta
Autaumn
Authena
Autom
Autraya
Auttumn
Autum
Autum Dawn
Autume
Auxilia
Auyante
Ava-Marie
Avada
Avae
Avais
Avalon
Avaly
Avani
Avanna
Avanthi
Avanti
Avarelle
Avarie
Avary
Avé
Aveeta
Avelea
Avera
Averi
Averiel
Averil
Averill
Averlia
Averyl
Avi
Avia
Aviana
Avianca
Aviance
Aviandai
Avica
Àvierre
Avigail
Avila
Avion
Avionladoris
Avis
Avital
Aviva
Avneet
Avni
Avon
Avonell
Avra
Avri
Avril
Avrilia
Avrillia
Avy
Awareness
Awna
Axie
Aya
Ayah
Ayako
Ayan
Ayana
Ayauna

Aydi
Aydon
Ayecia
Ayeesha
Ayelet
Ayianna
Ayiesha
Ayisha
Ayishah
Aylana
Ayleen
Aylene
Aylessa
Aylissa
Aymee
Aymie
Aynsley
Aynsley-Danielle
Ayofini
Ayonna
Ayra
Ayrea
Ayrika
Aysa
Ayse
Aysha
Ayshah
Ayshe
Aysia
Aysian
Aytza
Ayyusue
Azada
Azalee
Azalia
Azeema
Azelee
Azeneth
Azia
Aziah
Azin
Azinna
Aziya
Aziz
Aziza
Azizah
Azkaa
Aznie
Azra
Azur-Dee
Azura
Azure
Azure Dee
Azuré
Azuree
Azzie
Azziza

B

Ba Kendra
Baaron
Babandeep
Babe
Babhita
Babonga
Baby
Bacardi
Bach-Tuyet-Thi
Bacogie
Badriah
Bahar
Baiesha
Bailee
Bailley
Baillie
Bailly
Baily
Baint
Baleigh
Bali
Balita
Baljinder
Ballqiss
Balpreet
Balreet
Balwinder
Bambi
Banah
Banan
Bandna
Bandy
Banesa
Banesha
Banessa
Banisha
Banita
Banressa
Banyan
Baotram
Baraa
Barbara Ann
Barbara Jane
Barbara Jean
Barbara-Ann
Barbara-Ellen
Barbara-Jean
Barbarit
Barbarita
Barbeeleen
Barbette
Barbi
Barbie
Barbra
Barbraann
Bari
Barina
Barinder
Barneet
Barnetta
Baroness
Baronessa
Barrett
Barri
Barrie
Barroso
Barrun
Bartelyne
Baseemah
Basirat
Bassira
Bassma
Basya
Bathy
Batia
Batrina
Batya
Baubie
Baxter
Baye
Bayla
Baylee
Baylie
Bayly
Baytee
Bea
Beata
Beatrica
Beatris
Beaudry
Becca
Bechele
Bechocho
Beck
Becka

Becke
Beckett
Beckey
Beckhila
Becki
Beckie
Becky-Lee
Beda
Bee
Beena
Beige
Beisan
Bekki
Bekki-Anne
Bektu
Bela
Belarrialaronni
Belec
Belen
Belenda
Belinda Rose
Belinda-Michelle
Belindra
Belinette
Belit
Belkis
Belkys
Bella
Bella-Aurora
Belladonna
Bellamy
Belle
Belle-Rae
Belynda
Ben
Bendalynn
Benea
Benediza
Beneisha
Beneshea
Beneta
Benge
Beniesha
Benish
Benishia
Benissa
Benitta
Benjamin
Benjulie
Bennicia
Bennilyn
Bennita
Benvenidavalent
Beonca
Bera
Beradette
Beraiah
Beratrice
Berenice
Berenid
Berenis
Beril
Berit
Beritshia
Berkeley
Berkley
Berla
Berlinda
Berline
Berling
Berlyn
Berlyne
Berna
Bernadet
Bernadett
Bernadetta
Bernadin
Bernadine
Bernardette
Bernatta
Bernavela
Bernedette
Bernessa
Bernice
Bernie
Bernilya
Bernise
Bernita
Beronica
Berrastina
Berta
Bertarose
Bertholette
Bertita
Bertrona
Berty
Beryl
Besa
Bess
Bessie
Bessie-Lyn
Besty
Betelguese
Beth Ann
Beth-Ann
Beth-Anne
Beth-Lynn
Betha
Bethan
Bethane
Bethanee
Bethaney
Bethani
Bethania
Bethann
Bethanne
Bethanney
Bethannie
Bethe
Bethea
Bethenie
Betheny
Bethia
Bethney
Bethzaida
Betia
Betina
Betmarie
Betsabe
Betsey
Bette
Bettie
Betty-Jo
Betty-Joe
Bettye
Bettyjo
Bettylou
Bety
Betzaida
Betzaira
Beulah
Bevalee
Bevan
Bevany
Beverlee
Beverley
Beverley-Carol
Beverlianne
Beverly-Ann
Bevin
Bevin-Alexis
Beyamita
Beyonca
Bhakti
Bhamimi
Bhardeep

Bharkha
Bharti
Bhavika
Bhavna
Bhavnett
Bhavpreet
Bhumi
Bhupali
Biana
Biancia
Bianey
Bianka
Bibi
Bich
Bieisha
Bighton
Bijah
Bilaine
Bilan
Bilaugn
Bilee
Billi
Billie Elizabeth
Billie Jo
Billie-Jean
Billie-Jo
Billiejo
Billy
Billy-Jo
Bimbola
Bina
Bindiya
Binny
Binta
Bionca
Biranda
Birgy
Birrilla
Bismah
Bita
Bitonnica
Bittney
Bituin
Bivian
Biyaya
Bjanka
Blaine
Blair-Ann
Blaise
Blake
Blakeley
Blakely
Blakesley
Blanaid
Blanche
Blandine
Blane
Blasha
Blayke
Blayne
Blayre
Blaze
Blenda
Bliss
Blisse
Bliythe
Blondell
Blqees
Bluma
Blyss
Blyth
Bo
Bobbi-Ann
Bobbi-Lee
Bobbi-Lynn
Bobbi-Marie
Bobbi-Sue
Bobbie-Ann
Bobbie-Jean
Bobbie-Jo
Bobbie-Jon
Bobbie-Laine
Bobbie-Rae
Bobbiejo
Bobbijo
Bobbilee
Bobbisue
Bobby-Joe
Bobbye
Bobbylee
Bobette
Bobi
Bobie
Bobie Jean
Bobijo
Bobilee
Boderek
Bodiel
Boen
Bohdanna
Boipuso
Boishea
Bolanle
Bomond
Bond
Bonetta
Bonifacia
Boniqua
Bonnell
Bonney
Bonni
Bonnie-Jean
Bonnie-Joan
Bonnie-Lee
Bonnielo
Bonnin
Bonny
Bonny-Jo
Bontranique
Bophanawy
Boua
Bowdrie
Bowie
Bozica
Bracha
Brachell
Bracy
Bradee
Bradi
Bradie
Bradlee
Bradley
Bradly
Brady
Braegan
Braelyn
Braie
Brambhanee
Brand
Branda
Brandace
Brandala
Brandalyn
Brandalynn
Brande
Brande-Leigh
Brandei
Brandeli
Brandell
Brandelle
Brandelynn
Branden
Brandi Alexandri
Brandi-Lee
Brandi-Lynn
Brandice

Brandice-Lynn
Brandie-Leigh
Brandii
Brandily
Brandilyn
Brandilynne
Brandin
Brandis
Brandise
Brandlin
Brandlyn
Brandolyn
Brandon
Brandy Jea
Brandy-Lee
Brandy-Lyn
Brandy-Lynn
Brandye
Brandylyn
Brandyn
Branell
Brani
Branigan
Brann
Branndie
Brannigan
Brantley
Branyell
Brattany
Brauwin
Brayden
Braylee
Brazillia
Brchell
Bre-Ann
Bre-Anna
Bre-Anne
Brea
Brea-Ann
Breah
Breanda
Breauna
Breaunne
Breawna
Breay
Breayantey
Brecca
Brecka
Brecken
Breckin
Bree-Anne
Breea
Breean
Breeana
Breeann
Breeanna
Breeanne
Breeauna
Breelyn
Breena
Breesha
Breeze
Breezie
Brehan
Brei
Breiana
Breiann
Breigh
Breighann
Breila
Breina
Breionna
Brekke
Brena
Brenda Jean
Brenda-Lee
Brenda-May
Brendalee
Brendali
Brendaly
Brendalys
Brendan
Brendell
Brenden
Brendette
Brendie
Brendyl
Brenesha
Breneshia
Brenie
Brenisha
Brenlee
Brenley
Brenna Eli
Brenna-Lynn
Brennagh
Brennah
Brennan
Brennicka
Brennin
Brent
Brentan
Breon
Breona
Breonna
Brescia
Bresha
Breshay
Breshia
Bret
Bretele
Bretny
Bretta
Brette
Bretteny
Brettin
Brettiney
Brettlyn
Brettney
Brettnie
Bretton
Brevity
Breya
Breyan
Breyana
Breyann
Breyden
Breyn
Bri-Anna
Bria
Briahna
Brian
Briand
Brianda
Briane
Briann
Briannalee
Brianne-Katherine
Brianni
Briannon
Briauna
Bricole
Briddgett
Bridger
Bridgete
Bridgid
Bridgit
Bridgitte
Bridgot
Bridi
Bridnee
Bridney
Briéaunna
Brie-Anne
Brieann

Brieanna
Briena
Brienna
Brieon
Brier
Briet
Brieta
Brietta
Brieyonna
Briget
Brigett
Briggette
Briggitte
Brigham
Bright
Brighton
Brigit
Brigitta
Brihoney
Briian
Brijida
Brilyn
Brin
Brina
Brinda
Brindi
Brindy
Brinia
Brinlee
Brinly
Brinn
Brinna
Brinnan
Brinttne
Briona
Brione
Brionna
Brionnaambreniq
Brionne
Briony
Brisa
Brishetta
Brissa
Bristanerica
Bristelle
Bristian
Bristol
Bristy
Brit
Brita
Britana
Britanee
Britaney
Britani
Britanica
Britanie
Britanii
Britanni
Britanny
Britanny Kathry
Britatani
Britenee
Briteny
Britia
Britianey
Britiany
Britiney
Britini
British
Britkney
Britley
Britlyn
Britnay
Britne
Britnee
Britnei
Britney-Ann
Britnie
Britny
Britnye
Briton
Britt-Lise
Brittainny
Brittainy
Brittamy
Brittan
Brittana
Brittana Deone
Brittane
Brittanee
Brittania
Brittaniee
Brittanikay
Brittann
Brittanni
Brittannie
Brittanny
Brittany Ann
Brittany Anne
Brittany-Ann
Brittanyne
Britte
Brittell
Britten
Brittenee
Britteney
Brittenie
Brittenty
Brittiani
Brittianni
Brittiany
Brittin
Brittina
Brittıne
Brittiné
Brittinee
Brittiney
Brittini
Brittiny
Brittlin
Brittlynn
Brittnaye
Brittne
Brittnea
Brittneigh
Brittney-Janell
Brittney-Marie
Britton
Brittoni
Brittony
Brittyne
Brityn
Brityne
Brizelda
Brneda
Brocade
Brocha
Brock
Brodi
Brodie
Bronia
Brontay
Bronwen
Bronwin
Bronwynn
Brookanne
Brooke Ash
Brooke Elizabeth
Brooke-Lynn
Brookelle
Brookelyn
Brookelynn
Brookie
Brooklin
Brooklyn
Brooklynn

Brooks
Bruce
Brudael
Bruleigh
Bruna
Brunet
Brunetta
Bruni
Brunina
Brushea
Bruttany
Brya
Bryan
Bryana
Bryann
Bryar
Bryauna
Bryce
Bryceann
Brycie
Bryden
Brydie
Bryley
Bryna
Bryndi
Bryndis
Bryneé
Brynesha
Brynishia
Brynna
Brynnan
Brynne
Bryony
Brysen
Brysie
Brytnea
Brytni
Bryton
Bryttani
Bryttany
Bryttine
Bryttney
Bsmah
Buffy
Bukunola
Bunroeun
Burcu
Burgandy
Burgundy
Burnadett
Burnell
Burnette
Bushra
Butlyne
Byesha
Bylon

C

C J
C. J.
Ca
Ca Lescuia
Càellen
Cabrea
Cabrieal
Cabrina
Cabrinie
Cacelia
Cacey
Cacharelle
Cache
Cachea
Cachet
Cachet Georgette
Caci
Cacy
Cadence
Cadera
Cadi
Cadie
Cadine
Cadori
Cady
Caela
Caelee
Caeleigh
Caeley
Caeli
Caelie
Caelin
Caelyn
Caeri
Caesha
Caeville
Caffee
Cagney
Cahela
Cahlie
Caia-Alexandra
Caihla
Caila
Caileigh
Cailen
Cailene
Cailey
Caili
Cailie
Cailon
Caily
Cailyn
Cailynn
Caira
Caisse
Caisseylynne
Caitlan
Caitland
Caitlandt
Caitlen
Caitlinn
Caitlynn
Caitria
Caitrin
Caity
Cakimme
Cala
Calais
Calan
Calandra
Calasanz
Caldonia
Caledonia
Calee
Caleen
Caleena
Caleida
Caleine
Caleisha
Calen
Calene
Caletta
Calha
Caliann
Calico
Calie
Calin
Calina
Calinda
Calise
Calisha
Calissa
Calista
Calitia
Calizzcia

Calla
Callae
Callahan
Callan
Callee
Calleen
Callen
Calletta
Calley
Callia
Callie-Jean
Calliope
Callista
Callrissa
Callula
Cally
Callyn
Calogera
Calretha
Calrissian
Calsi
Calvary
Calvert
Calvina
Calvine
Calvinetta
Calyn
Calynn
Calypso
Calysta
Cam
Camala
Camara
Camber
Camberleigh
Camberry
Cambie
Cambrea
Cambree
Cambri
Cambria
Cambridge
Cambrya
Camealia
Camecia
Camela
Camelia
Camelita
Camella
Camellia
Camellia Charlot
Camemisha
Cameo
Cameran
Cameren
Cameri
Cameria
Camesha
Cameshia
Camey
Camia
Camie
Camila
Camile
Camilia
Camill
Camillia
Camillie
Camilyn
Camin
Camio
Camisha
Cammay
Cammi
Cammille
Cammy
Camria
Camrin
Camrion
Camron
Camry
Camryn
Camy
Camyll
Camylle
Cana
Canaa
Canace
Canda
Candace-Cherry
Candal
Candalyn
Candance
Candas
Candee
Candelle
Candes
Candiace
Candianc
Candias
Candice Ann
Candice-Jade
Candice-Lynda
Candida
Candide
Candie
Candiese
Candince
Candise
Candiss
Candist
Candita
Candle
Candon
Candrce
Candus
Candys
Candyse
Candyss
Canea
Canei
Caneika
Caneisha
Canesha
Caneyl
Canice
Canietha
Canilla
Canise
Canisha
Cannearly
Cannelle
Cansus
Cantarra
Cantrell
Cantrella
Cao
Caoimhe
Cappi
Caprece
Capri
Capricia
Caprie
Caprina
Caprise
Capritta
Capucine
Cara Lyn
Cara Mia
Cara-Ann
Cara-Celeste
Cara-Dawn
Cara-Joy
Cara-Lee
Cara-Lynn

Cara-Lynne
Caragh
Carah
Caralea
Caralee
Caralia
Caralin
Caraline
Caralyn
Caranda
Caravaughn
Carcia
Cardi
Cardin
Carea
Carece
Careema
Careen
Careena
Carel
Carely
Caren
Carenna
Caress
Caress Franciea
Caress Kayleigh
Caressa
Caresse
Caretha
Caretrice
Carey-Ann
Carey-Jo
Carey-Lynn
Careyelle
Careylynn
Cari-Ann
Cari-Lee
Carianne
Caricathelin
Carice
Carida
Cariel
Carileen
Carilena
Carilis
Carilynne
Carima
Carime
Carimee
Carimisha
Carin
Carine
Carine
Catherine
Carinne
Carisa
Carisia
Carissa Ma
Carisse
Carita
Carl
Carla De F
Carla-Dawne
Carlaena
Carlan
Carlana
Carlandra
Carle
Carleah
Carleen
Carleena
Carleesia
Carleeza
Carleigh
Carlen
Carlena
Carlenna
Carleta
Carletha
Carlethe
Carletta
Carley-Rae
Carlia
Carlianne
Carlicia
Carlin
Carlina
Carlinda
Carline
Carling
Carliqua
Carlis
Carlise
Carlisha
Carlisia
Carlissa
Carlissia
Carlista
Carlita
Carliyle
Carllen
Carlonda
Carlota
Carlotta
Carlreca
Carltissa
Carly-Ann
Carly-Mae
Carly-Marie
Carly-Rae
Carlye
Carlyjo
Carlyle
Carlyne
Carlynn
Carlyse
Carlysle
Carma
Carmaine
Carmaletta
Carmalit
Carmalita
Carmalla
Carman
Carmarit
Carmel
Carmelia
Carmelina
Carmelit
Carmelita
Carmelitha
Carmelitia
Carmelle
Carmellia
Carmellita
Carmen Gloria
Carmene
Carmenysol
Carmesa
Carmesha
Carmeva
Carmi
Carmill
Carmilla
Carmin
Carmine
Carmisha
Carmon
Carmynn
Carnella
Carnesha
Carnesia
Carnette
Carnika
Carnisha
Carnnel

Carnola
Carnthia
Carol Ann
Carol Anne
Carol Charlene
Carol-Ann
Carol-Anne
Carol-Lin
Carol-Lynn
Carol-Marie
Carola
Carolan
Carolane
Carolann
Carolanne
Carole-Anne
Carolee
Carolin
Carolyn-Ann
Carolyn-Annette
Carolyne
Carolynne
Caron
Carone
Carpathia
Carradine
Carrah
Carrara
Carre
Carres
Carress
Carressa
Carrey
Carri
Carrianne
Carrie-Ann
Carrie-Anne
Carrie-Jeanne
Carrie-Lee
Carrie-Lynn
Carrieann
Carrin
Carrine
Carrington
Carris
Carrisa
Carrisann
Carrissa
Carrita
Carrol
Carroll
Carroll-Dawn
Carrolyn
Carron
Carrona
Carronda
Carry
Carsen
Carsha
Carshara
Carshell
Carshena
Carsina
Carson
Cartaya
Carter
Cartier
Cartila
Cartina
Carvina
Carweina
Cary
Caryann
Carybel
Caryl
Caryne
Carynn
Carysa
Caryssa
Carzette
Casadee
Casandri
Casasi
Casaundr
Casaundra
Cascilla
Cascy
Casey-Ann
Casey-Lynn
Cashara
Casharell
Casharri
Cashea
Cashena
Cashundra
Casi
Casianne
Casidee
Casidy
Casilyn
Casimir
Casimira
Casinda
Casondra
Casoundra
Cass
Cassa
Cassadi
Cassadie
Cassadina
Cassady
Cassan
Cassandra Jane
Cassandra-Nicole
Cassandre
Cassanndra
Cassanora
Cassanudra
Cassaoundra
Cassaphia
Cassaund
Cassaundra
Cassaundra-Leigh
Cassaundra-Marie
Casseday
Cassee
Cassia
Cassiddy
Cassidee
Cassidi
Cassidie
Cassie-Rae
Cassiope
Cassiopeia
Cassioph
Cassiopi
Cassiopia
Cassity
Casslyn
Cassondr
Cassondra Mia
Cassondria
Cassundra
Cassy Bernice
Cassye
Casteel
Castling
Casy
Cataline
Catarina
Cate
Cateel
Cateka
Catelyn
Cateria

Caterina
Caterine
Catey
Catharin
Catharina
Catheirn
Cathenne
Catheren
Catherina
Catherine Elizabeth
Catherine-Ann
Catherine-Anna
Catherine-Jo
Catheryn
Cathi
Cathie
Cathleana
Cathlin
Cathryne
Cathy Rose
Cathy-Lee
Catia
Catiana
Catie
Catillie
Catina
Catisha
Catissa
Catlain
Catlaina
Catlin
Catlyn
Catlynn
Catreece
Catreena
Catrelle
Catrenia
Catrice
Catricia
Catrin
Catrina-Rae
Catrine
Catrinia
Catriona
Catroina
Catryn
Catteeka
Cattiah
Caty
Cauline
Caurie
Cautauqua
Cautlin
Cavasi
Cawanda
Cayce
Cayci
Caylei
Cayleigh
Caylen
Cayley
Caylie
Caylin
Caylyn
Cayse
Caysie
Caytee
Cazzi
Cérise
Ceaimontese
Ceaira
Ceairra
Cealyne
Ceanda
Ceanne
Ceara
Cearaa
Cearia
Cearra
Cearrow
Cebre
Cebryna
Ceceilia
Ceceli
Cecelyn
Cecette
Cecil
Cecila
Cécile
Cecile
Cecilea
Cecilia Shaquind
Cecille
Cecillia
Cecily
Ceclia
Cedar
Ceddrea
Ceddrina
Cedes
Cedra
Cedreka
Cedrica
Cedricka
Cedrina
Cee
Ceejay
Ceiaira
Ceiara
Ceiffawn
Ceil
Ceila
Ceilagh
Ceileh
Ceileigh
Ceilena
Ceilia
Ceilidh
Ceilidh-Anne
Ceilidhe
Ceina
Ceira
Ceire
Ceirra
Ceje
Celani
Celaunce
Celebrity
Celene
Celenia
Celes
Celesia
Celesley
Celest
Celesta
Celestia
Celestial
Celestin
Celestina
Celestine
Celestinea
Celeta
Celiana
Celica
Celicia
Celidah (Kailie)
Celie
Celiegh
Celiet
Céline
Celine-Loppi
Celines
Celisa
Celisha
Celisia

Celissa
Celisse
Celissia
Celize
Cella
Celless
Celriece
Celsea
Celsey
Celustia
Celynn
Celysse
Cena
Cenda
Cendi
Cendra
Cendy
Cenise
Cenora
Centeria
Centerria
Centia
Centrelle
Cenzina
Ceola
Cepi
Cera
Ceradwyn
Cerance
Cerea
Cerena
Cerese
Ceri
Ceria
Cerice
Cericia
Ceridwen
Cerissa
Cerria
Cerrina
Cerrita
Cervana
Cervia
Cervice
Ceryce
Cescelie
Cescily
Cesery
Cesilie
Cesira
Cessna
Cestau
Cetoria
Ceyda
Ceyma
Cezanne
Cha Raé
Chabeli
Chabley
Chabli
Chablis
Chabre
Chabreka
Chabrielle
Chacyne
Chadae
Chadaye
Chade
Chadene
Chae
Chaela
Chaeli
Chaella
Chaena
Chaffonda
Chafone
Chahrazad
Chai
Chainey
Chaire
Chairel
Chairity
Chairty
Chaitra
Chaive
Chaka
Chakai
Chakara
Chakaria
Chakeia
Chakeitha
Chakena
Chakia
Chakila
Chakina
Chakira
Chakriya
Chakyra
Chala
Chalace
Chalamar
Chalanda
Chalandi
Chalanta
Chalcie
Chalece
Chalee
Chaleeta
Chalena
Chalene
Chalese
Chalet
Chalette
Chali
Chalia
Chalice
Chalie
Chaliese
Chalise
Chalisfaith
Chalissa
Chalisse
Challa
Challaine
Challis
Challysse
Chalnique
Chalonda
Chalry
Chalsey
Chalyce
Chalyn
Chalysse
Chamaikha
Chamali
Chamara
Chamaria
Chamberlain
Chambray
Chambre
Chameira
Chameka
Chamel
Chamelia
Chamelle
Chameron
Chamia
Chamika
Chamila
Chamille
Champagne
Champange
Chan
Chana
Chana Marie
Chanae

Chanaye
Chanbopha
Chance
Chanci
Chancoria
Chancy
Chandal
Chandaley
Chandalynn
Chandee
Chandel
Chandell
Chandelle
Chandelyn
Chandesia
Chandi
Chandi-Taren
Chandice
Chandie
Chandler
Chandni
Chandon
Chandre
Chandrea
Chandrelle
Chandrenie
Chanea
Chaneà
Chanecqu
Chaneé
Chanekka
Chanele
Chanesse
Chanetta
Chaney
Chaneyll
Chani
Chania
Chanice
Chaniece
Chanika
Chanille
Chanin
Chaning
Chaniqué
Chanisa
Chanise
Chanisty
Chanita
Chanity
Chankyna
Chann-Veasna
Channa
Channell
Channelle
Channen
Channity
Channon
Chanovia
Chanquita
Chanrath
Chanresmey
Chansey
Chanta
Chantaal
Chantae
Chantael
Chantai
Chantal-Anita
Chantal-Christine
Chantal-Lynn
Chantal-Marie
Chantal-Mélanie
Chantall
Chantara
Chantaraî
Chantasia
Chantay
Chantaye
Chanté
Chantea
Chanteau
Chantee
Chanteese
Chantel-Jacqueline
Chantel-Lee
Chantel-Marie
Chantela
Chantele
Chantella
Chantelle-May
Chantelsha
Chanter
Chantey
Chantez
Chantha
Chanthasone
Chanthear
Chantiel
Chantielle
Chantil
Chantila
Chantill
Chantille
Chantilly
Chantini
Chantle
Chantlet
Chantoya
Chantra
Chantrel
Chantrell
Chantrelle
Chantress
Chantri
Chantrice
Chantriel
Chantrill
Chanvir
Chanyell
Chapman
Chaquana
Chaquanta
Chaquéta
Chaquerr
Chaquita
Chaquoya
Char
Char'nea
Chara
Charai
Charamy
Charanne
Charasika
Charayah
Charbel
Chard"a
Charda
Chardai
Chardaie
Charday
Chardé
Chardee
Chardese
Chardesia
Chardiera
Chardon
Chardonay
Chardonnay
Charee
Chareese
Chareka
Charelis
Charell

Charelle
Charena
Charesa
Charese
Chari
Charice
Charie
Charie Ann
Chariety
Charika
Charily
Charina
Charine
Chariot
Charisa
Charise
Charish
Charisha
Charisma
Charissee
Charista
Charita
Chariti
Charity Ann
Charkelia
Charkeshia
Charlaine
Charlamagne
Charlanda
Charlanna
Charlaunda
Charlcey
Charlci
Charle
Charlea
Charlee
Charlee-Ann
Charleen
Charleesa
Charleig
Charleigh
Charlena
Charles
Charlese
Charlest
Charlestine
Charlet
Charlett
Charletta
Charlette
Charley
Charli
Charli-Anne
Charlice
Charlien
Charlina
Charline
Charlis
Charlise
Charlita
Charlott
Charlotte Amelie
Charlsey
Charlsie
Charly
Charlyn
Charlyne
Charlynn
Charma
Charmain
Charmalique
Charman
Charmar
Charmara
Charmayne
Charmeen
Charmeka
Charmene
Charmese
Charmian
Charmin
Charmine
Charmion
Charmisa
Charmon
Charmyn
Charna
Charnan
Charndeep
Charnell
Charnella
Charnelle
Charneshea
Charneshia
Charnesia
Charney
Charnez
Charniece
Charniecia
Charniqua
Charnise
Charnita
Charnprit
Charnyar
Charolett
Charolette
Charolotte
Charon
Charonda
Charonia
Charray
Charriet
Charron
Charry
Charsetta
Charsha
Chartavia
Charteir
Charteshia
Chartrice
Chartyle
Charu
Charvanda
Charvel
Charvenisia
Charviel
Charvielle
Charvon
Charyl
Charyssa
Charysse
Charzetta
Chasa Dee
Chasadie
Chasady
Chase
Chashea
Chasidy
Chasiti
Chaslee
Chaslie
Chaslyn
Chasmine
Chassandra
Chassedi
Chassey
Chassie
Chassitty
Chassity
Chassy
Chasta
Chastady
Chastidy
Chastin
Chastinty

Chastitie
Chastney
Chasty
Chasya
Chatara
Chatare
Chatavia
Chatele
Chatelle
Chatia
Chatisa
Chatoni
Chattni
Chaucey
Chauncey
Chauncie
Chauncy
Chaundra
Chaundre
Chaunell
Chaunetta
Chauneva
Chaunna
Chaunta
Chauntay
Chaunte
Chauntel
Chauntell
Chauntell-Leese
Chauntelle
Chauté
Chavà
Chavah
Chavarra
Chavarria
Chave
Chavé
Chavel
Chaveli
Chavette
Chavgney
Chaviva
Chavon
Chavondria
Chavonne
Chavvis
Chawna
Chawntelle
Chaya
Chayla
Chaylea
Chaylene
Chaymar
Chayndon
Chaynique
Chayra
Chazalyn
Chazaray
Chazlit
Che
Chéla
Chélynn
Chéron
Chealyn
Cheanay
Cheapell
Chearease
Chebony
Chebrise
Chee
Cheelou
Cheerell
Cheerish
Cheeroke
Cheetara
Cheiree
Cheivs
Chekeria
Chekesha
Chekesheia
Chekina
Chekita
Chela
Chelah
Chelaina
Chelan
Cheland
Chelann
Chelbi
Chelby
Chelcie
Chelcy
Chele
Chelese
Chelesia
Chelica
Chelie
Chelisa
Chelise
Chellante
Chelle
Chelli
Chellie
Chellise
Chellsie
Chelsa
Chelsae
Chelse
Chelsea Nicole
Chelsea-Anne
Chelsea-Lee
Chelsea-Lyn
Chelsee
Chelsei
Chelsia
Chelsice
Chelta
Chelynne
Cheme
Chemeka
Chemeo
Chenara
Chenda
Chendra
Chenee
Cheneil
Cheneka
Chenell
Chenelle
Chenesha
Chenesia
Chenessa
Chenetta
Chenice
Chenika
Chenille
Chenita
Chenna
Chennel
Chennistique
Chenoa
Chentell
Chenterra
Chequita
Cher
Chera
Cheralee
Cheranda
Cheranne
Cherdee
Chere
Cherea
Cherece
Cheredean
Cheree
Chereena

Chereese
Cherei
Chereise
Chereka
Cherekia
Cherell
Cherena
Cheresa
Cherese
Cheresse
Cheri-Lee
Cheri-Lyn
Cheriah
Cherial
Cherice
Cherida
Cheriese
Cherieth
Cherika
Cherilee
Cherilyn
Cherina
Cherine
Cherion
Cherishe
Cherissa
Cherisse
Cherita
Cherith
Cherity
Cherkedria
Cherkita
Cherl
Cherlande
Cherlene
Cherlie
Cherlina
Cherline
Cherlinne
Cherlisa
Cherly
Cherlyn
Cherlyne
Chermaine
Chermarie
Cherna
Chernell
Cherniara
Cherokee
Cheron
Cherra
Cherrell
Cherrellee
Cherretta
Cherri
Cherrice
Cherrideth
Cherrie
Cherrise
Cherrish
Cherritta
Cherry
Cherry-Lynn
Chersti
Chertonne
Chertrese
Chery
Cheryce
Cheryl-Ann
Cheryl-Anne
Cheryl-Lee
Cheryl-Lyn
Cheryl-Lynn
Cheryl-Lynne
Cherylann
Cheryle
Cherylee
Cheryline
Cherylinn
Cheryll
Cherylyn
Cherylynn
Cheryn
Cheryse
Cherysh
Chesea
Cheslee
Chesney
Chessa
Chessica
Chessie
Chestimo
Chestina
Chestine
Chetara
Chetarah
Chetaria
Chetney
Chettranee
Chevarlyn
Chevaun
Chevaunne
Chevella
Chevelle
Chevellia
Chevon
Chevonna
Chevonne
Chey
Cheyan
Cheyana
Cheyann
Cheyanne
Cheyene
Cheyenna
Cheyla
Cheylyn
Cheylynne
Cheyna
Cheyne
Cheyrie
Chez
Chezare
Chhorvy
Chi
Chi-Anna
Chiah
Chian
Chianne
Chianti
Chiara
Chiavani
Chiavonne
Chicaro
Chidi
Chidonna
Chie
Chiffon
Chiffonne
Chika
Chikara
Chikita
Chikona
Chila
Chilena
Chilise
Chilquella
Chimaria
Chimene
Chimere
Chimon
China
Chinaedu
Chinaetta
Chinasa
Chinda

Chinea
Chinequa
Chinequia
Chinesia
Chineva
Ching
Chiniceia
Chiniqua
Chiniree
Chinita
Chinna
Chinwa
Chinwendu
Chinyere
Chioma
Chiqueta
Chiquila
Chiquite
Chiquith
Chiquitha
Chiquitia
Chiquitta
Chira
Chiree
Chiri
Chirstina
Chisa
Chisana
Chistina
Chitara
Chitarra
Chitoria
Chiveon
Chivon
Chivonne
Chloé
Chloee
Choana
Choi-Hung
Chole
Cholla
Chomonique
Chonda
Chonkita
Chontavia
Chontel
Choung
Chrelle
Chriquita
Chris
Chrisana
Chrisandra
Chrisanna
Chrisceda
Chrisha
Chrishaunda
Chrisheena
Chrishelle
Chrishia
Chrishmia
Chrisie
Chrislena
Chrisline
Chrislyn
Chrisnata
Chrisoula
Chrissa
Chrisseanda
Chrissee
Chrissie
Chrisstina
Chrisstine
Chrissy-Lee
Christa Antonina
Christa-Lee
Christable
Christain
Christalene
Christalin
Christall
Christalyn
Christan
Christanna
Christar
Christeen
Christeena
Christeia
Christel
Christele
Christell
Christella
Christelle
Christena
Christene
Christener
Christey
Christi-Anne
Christia
Christiaan
Christian-Ann
Christiane
Christiané
Christiann
Christianna
Christianne
Christianni
Christie K.
Christie-Anne
Christie-Lee
Christienne
Christillia
Christina Marie
Christina Thao
Christina-Antonette
Christina-Lee
Christina-Lyn
Christina-Lynn
Christina-Maria
Christina-Marie
Christina-Myra
Christine Marie
Christine-Domenica
Christine-Marian
Christine-Soohie
Christinea
Christineq
Christinia
Christinie
Christinna
Christle
Christleen
Christline
Christmas
Christna
Christol
Christoleena
Christon
Christonia
Christophe
Christopher
Christy-Ann
Christy-Lee
Christy-Leigh
Christyann
Christyl
Christyn
Christyna
Christyne
Chrisy
Chrniesa
Chrsten
Chryl
Chrysa

Chryseis
Chryslee
Chrysovalant
Chrysta
Chrystal A
Chrystele
Chrysten
Chrystie
Chrystina
Chrystine
Chrystle
Chrystyna
Chuntavia
Chvonne
Chyann
Chyanna
Chyanne
Chyemen
Chyle
Chyleina Kay
Chyloe
Chylynn
Chyna
Chyncia
Chyra
Chyrese
Chystal
Ciaara
Ciana
Ciarrah
Cibely
Cicara
Ciccika
Cicelie
Cicely
Cicilie
Cicily
Cidney
Ciéra
Cieara
Ciearra
Cieba
Cielle
Ciendel
Cienna
Ciequnita
Cieria
Cierrah
Cigdem
Cigi
Ciji
Cilea
Cileece
Cilena
Cilia
Cilicia
Cimber
Cimberly
Cindal
Cindee
Cindel
Cindell
Cindi
Cindl
Cindy Lee
Cindy-Lea
Cindy-Lee
Cindyl
Cinee
Cinnamon
Cinnesha
Cinnomon
Cinthia
Cinthya
Cinthyia
Cintia
Cintrece
Cinzia
Ciprianna
Cira
Cira-Lauren
Cirena
Ciressa
Cireya
Citikita
Cj
Cjardae
Ckeisha
Ckenzie
Ckeyairra
Cladretta
Claimise
Claire-Helene
Claire-Jehanne
Claire-Marie
Claire-Simone
Clairesa
Clairessa
Clairissa
Clanétt
Clancy
Clara Rose
Clarabeth
Clarecia
Claresa
Claressa
Claribel
Clarica
Clarice
Claridean
Clarina
Claris
Clarisa
Clarissa-Anne
Clarissia
Claritza
Clarizza
Clarlice
Clarrisa
Clarrissa
Classie
Claudean
Claudee
Claudette
Claudex
Claudia-Marisa
Claudiane
Claudie-Anne
Claudine
Claunese
Clautid
Clea
Clea Rose
Cleana
Clearinda
Cleaverose
Cleavet
Clecia
Clelia
Cleo
Cleoandra
Cleopatra
Cleotia
Cleriese
Cleshaeasheniqu
Cletecia
Cleteria
Cletta
Cliesha
Cliffina
Cliftina
Climistina
Clinnisia
Clinshonda
Clintrail
Clio

Clique
Clista
Cloded
Cloe
Clondia
Clorinda
Clorissa
Clothia
Clover
Clyde
Clydie
Coacoa
Coady
Coatni
Cobby
Cobi
Cobie
Coburn
Cocha
Coco
Codeine
Codey
Codie
Cody-Ann
Coe
Coel
Coelina
Coetta
Colando
Colbey
Colbi
Colbie
Coleece
Colemesha
Colena
Colene
Coley
Colice
Colil
Colinda
Colleen-Denise
Colleene
Collen
Collenn
Collett
Collina
Collins
Colombina
Coloya
Colton
Colynn
Comfort
Commisyon
Conceptia
Concetta
Concettina
Concha
Conchita
Conciana
Condriah
Conelia
Conesha
Conisha
Conitha
Conneilla
Connelly
Conni
Connie-Lee
Connie-Stephanie
Connor
Conor
Consheena
Conshett
Constanc
Constantina
Constinteen
Consuela
Consuela Kijafka
Consuella
Consuelo
Consula
Contessa
Contessica
Conzuelo
Cookie
Coquina
Cora-Lee
Coral-Dawn
Coralea
Coralee
Coralene
Coralia
Coralie
Coralito
Corall
Coralle
Corallee
Coralyn
Coranna
Corastonza
Corazon
Corbi
Corby
Cordae
Cordaye
Cordelia
Cordett
Cordia
Cordilia
Coree
Coreen
Coreena
Coren
Corena
Corene
Coressa
Coreta
Coretta
Corette
Corey-Jo
Cori Ann
Cori-Ann
Corian
Coriann
Corianne
Coribbia
Corilee
Corin
Corinda
Corine
Corinee
Corinn
Corinna-Christine
Corinthia
Corinthian
Corisa
Corki
Corlee
Corley
Corlisa
Corlise
Corliss
Corneatia
Corneilla
Cornelia
Cornelie
Cornelius
Corney
Cornie
Cornisha
Coronda
Corra
Corral
Corran

Correen
Corren
Correta
Corretta
Correy
Corri
Corrie-Ann
Corrieann
Corrigan
Corrin
Corrinn
Corrinna
Corrinne
Corritha
Corronica
Corry
Corryn
Corsha
Cortia
Cortinee
Cortisha
Cortiya
Cortlin
Cortnea
Cortnee
Cortneia
Cortni
Cortnie
Cortnie Jeankuul
Cortny
Corttney
Corvatus
Corvette
Coryawn
Coryelle
Coryn
Corynn
Corynna
Cosby Gabrielle
Cosette
Cossette
Costadina
Costandeana
Coti
Cottia
Coty
Coty-Lynne
Courntey
Coursheka
Courtena
Courtenay Leigh
Courtene
Courteney
Courteny
Courtlann
Courtlyn
Courtnaé
Courtnay
Courtnee
Courtnei
Courtney J
Courtney Mccall
Courtney Nicole
Courtney-Anne
Courtney-May
Courtni
Courtny
Courtonie
Coveannda
Coy
Coyona
Cozetta
Craesha
Craig
Craionna
Cranisha
Crassa
Crassandra
Crescentia
Creshia
Cressend
Cressida
Cressie
Crestina
Creta
Crete
Cricket
Crickett
Crimson
Cris
Crisandr
Crishann
Crislin
Crislyn
Crisondra
Crissa
Crissean
Crissie
Crissteena
Crissy
Crista Eve
Crista-Lee
Cristabe
Cristalie
Cristalina
Cristalle
Cristan
Cristee
Cristeen
Cristel
Cristela
Cristelia
Cristella
Cristelle
Cristhie
Cristi
Cristi-Rae
Cristia
Cristian
Cristiane
Cristie
Cristilyn
Cristin Ann
Cristina Gabriel
Cristina-Valentina
Cristince
Cristine
Cristle
Cristle Ly
Cristy-Lee
Cristyn
Cristyna
Crisvett
Crisy
Critin
Cruz
Cruzanna
Crylal
Crysta
Crysta-Lynn
Crystal Ly
Crystal'
Crystal-Ann
Crystal-Anne
Crystal-Dawn
Crystal-Jean
Crystal-Leah
Crystal-Lee
Crystal-Lynn
Crystal-Lynne
Crystal-Marie
Crystal-Rose
Crystala
Crystaldawn
Crystale

Crystale-Tea
Crystalee
Crystalin
Crystalina
Crystaline
Crystall
Crystaly
Crystalyn
Crystalynn
Crystan
Crystel
Crystelia
Crysthelle
Crysti
Crystin
Crystina
Crystine
Crystl
Crystole
Crystoria
Crystrl
Crysty
Crystyl
Csilla
Ctatiania
Cubbette
Culcemaria
Culcinea
Cumilla
Curemia
Curie
Curteca
Curtessa
Curtina
Curtis
Curtisa
Curtisha
Curtissa
Curtkeya
Curtrica
Curtrisa
Curtteria
Cusheena
Cushena
Cy
Cyara
Cybel
Cybil
Cybill
Cycelie
Cydavia
Cydnea
Cydney
Cydnie
Cyhene
Cyle
Cylena
Cylenthia
Cylie
Cylshen
Cymberly
Cymone
Cyna
Cynda
Cyndal
Cyndale
Cyndall
Cyndel
Cyndi
Cyndia
Cyndle
Cyndy
Cynecia
Cynedra
Cyneta
Cynethia
Cynethress
Cynetria
Cyniece
Cynithia
Cynquitta
Cyntauria
Cyntel
Cynteria
Cyntheria
Cynthiana
Cynthiann
Cynthya
Cyntoria
Cyntrale
Cyntreia
Cyntrell
Cyrell
Cyrena
Cyrene
Cyrina
Cyrstal
Cythia
Czardae

D

D Lexis
D'andra
D'angela
D'ara
D'arci
D'jolani
D'laney
D'neil
D'neile
D'quenly
D'shae
D'shawn
D'vorah
Da Janeé
Da Lishua
Da Rae
Da Silva
Da Tisha
Dàjanai
Dàjuana
Dànae
Dàquetta
Daana
Daanard
Dabbitha
Dabeq
Dabney
Dabraesha
Dabriel
Dacarla
Dacee
Dacia
Dacie
Dackeri
Dacylla
Dadeve
Dadreinne
Dae
Daeleen
Daelena
Daelin
Daelyn
Daelynn
Daeryl
Daesha
Daeshavon
Daeshawntia
Dafany
Dafna
Dafne
Dafney
Dafny
Dafydd

Dagdianamai
Dagmar
Dagnanna
Dagne
Dagney
Dagny
Daguse
Dahlia
Dahne
Dahnielle
Dai
Daiana
Daichon
Daicy
Daidre
Daidrelle
Daih Syafi
Daija
Daijon
Daikehsa
Daile
Daileen
Daimi
Daimy
Dainelle
Dainna
Daiquire
Daiquiri
Daira
Dairac
Dairar
Daire
Daisey
Daisha
Daishaw
Daishia
Daisia
Daisy Lynn
Daisy-Marie
Daisyred
Daitrice
Daizzee
Daj'sha
Daja
Dajan
Dajmila
Dajon
Dajona
Dak
Dakeavia
Dakia
Dakiesha
Dakima
Dakisha
Dakotah
Daksha
Dakshana
Dalacey
Dalanda
Dalaney
Dalania
Dalanna
Dalavanh
Dalayna
Dalcie
Daleashanti
Dalecia
Dalee
Daleena
Daleisha
Daleleana
Dalena
Dalene
Daleney
Daletha
Dalia
Daliah
Dalialah
Dalibel
Dalida
Dalila
Dalilia
Dalin
Dalina
Dalinda
Daline
Dalishya
Dalisia
Dalissia
Dalla
Dallan
Dallyce
Dalon
Daloris
Dalpreet
Dalrajkaur
Dalresha
Dalton
Dalvessa
Dalvina
Dalvine
Dalyce
Dalyn
Dalynn
Dalynna
Dalys
Damali
Damalyn
Damanjeet
Damar
Damara
Damarius
Damary
Damarys
Damee
Dameeka
Damesha
Dameshia
Damesia
Dametia
Dametra
Dametrahl
Damie
Damien
Damilet
Damilie
Damita
Damitria
Damla
Dammei
Damnira
Damona
Damonella
Damonica
Damryz
Dana-Lee
Dana-Lynn
Dana-Rae
Danael
Danah
Danahé
Danai
Danaia
Danalee
Danaliz
Danalle
Danan
Danarra
Danay
Danayla
Danays
Danchi
Dandrea
Dane
Danea
Daneal

Danealle
Danean
Danee
Daneel
Daneen
Daneesha
Daneil
Daneila
Daneille
Daneka
Danel
Danela
Danele
Danelia
Danell
Danella
Danene
Danesca
Danesha
Danesis
Danessa
Danetra
Danett
Danetta
Dang
Dani-Rio
Daniah
Danial
Danialle
Danica-Marie
Danice
Danicia
Danida
Danie
Daniel-Marie
Daniela-Rachela
Danièle
Danielé
Danielle Bell
Danielle Marie
Daniellé
Danielle-Elizabeth
Danielle-Marie
Danielle-Marie-Nicole
Daniene
Danier
Daniesha
Danietra
Danijela
Danika-Jeannelle
Danila
Danille
Danilyn
Danina
Danine
Danion
Danis
Danisha
Daniss
Danit
Danita
Danitra
Danitza
Daniyel
Daniyka
Daniz
Danja
Danlie
Dann
Dannae
Dannah
Dannaica
Danne
Danneley
Dannell
Dannella
Dannelle
Danneta
Dannetta
Dannette
Danni
Dannibelle
Dannie
Danniece
Danniele
Danniell
Danniella
Dannikka
Dannikwa
Dannille
Dannis
Dannisha
Dannita
Dannon
Danny
Dannyis
Danrisha
Dansell
Danshantal
Dante
Dantelle
Danti
Dantia
Dantzel
Dany
Danyae
Danyail
Danyaile
Danyal
Danyale
Danyea
Danyele
Danyell
Danyella
Danyetta
Danyiell
Danyle
Danyse
Daphane
Daphaney
Daphanie
Daphany
Dapheney
Daphna
Daphnee
Daphney
Daphnie
Daphnique
Daphny
Daquisha
Daracar
Darah
Daraka
Daralea
Daralee
Daralyn
Daralynn
Darbi
Darbra
Darcee
Darcel
Darcell
Darcelle
Darcey
Darchann
Darchel
Darchell
Darcie-Louise
Darcie-Lynn
Dardani
Darden
Dardhielle
Dareth
Darian

Darianne
Darice
Dariel
Darielle
Darien
Darika
Daril
Daril-Lynn
Darilyn
Darilynn
Darin
Darisha
Dariss
Daritza
Darka
Darkeitha
Darkeyenna
Darlean
Darleen
Darlena
Darlene-Lee
Darlenia
Darletha
Darlin
Darline
Darling
Darlnisha
Darly
Darlynn
Darmecia
Darmeta
Darneatr
Darneisha
Darneishia
Darnel
Darnell
Darnella
Darnelle
Darnesha
Darneshia
Darnesia
Darnice
Darniece
Darnisha
Darnita
Darnshell
Darnycesia
Darnyell
Darolann
Daron
Daronica
Daronice
Darquetta
Darquise
Darquita
Darra
Darragh
Darrah
Darrel
Darrell
Darrelle
Darreshia
Darria
Darrica
Darricka
Darriel
Darrielle
Darrika
Darris
Darryl
Darrylan
Darryll
Darryllann
Darrynne
Darsella
Darsey
Darshani
Darshay
Darshinee
Darshpal
Darthula
Darvette
Darya
Daryia
Daryl-Ann
Daryl-Anne
Daryle-A
Daryn
Dasema
Dasha
Dashavia
Dashawn
Dashawna
Dashawnda
Dashay
Dashe
Dashell
Dashika
Dashka
Dashweil
Dasie
Dasya
Datemiea
Datha
Datina
Datoria
Datrice
Datrina
Daughtry
Dauna
Dauren
Dautti
Dava
Davalyn
Davalynn
Davannah
Davean
Davee
Daveena
Daveisha
Davelyn
Daveon
Davesia
Davette
Davey
Davi
Daviana
David
Davida
Davida-Michal
Davidaa
Davie
Davika
Davin
Davinder
Davineen
Davinna
Davisha
Davita
Davon
Davona
Davonda
Davonna
Davria
Dawana
Dawandrea
Dawanna
Dawin
Dawn-Marie
Dawna-Lee
Dawna-Marie
Dawne
Dawnee
Dawnele
Dawnell
Dawnelle

Dawnesha
Dawni
Dawniell
Dawnielle
Dawnisha
Dawniss
Dawnlynn
Dawnn
Dawnna
Dawnrae
Dawnya
Dawnyale
Dawnyell
Day
Daya
Dayana
Dayanelli
Dayanna
Dayce
Daydrey
Daygun
Dayja
Dayla
Daylan
Dayle
Daylean
Daylee
Daylene
Daylina
Daylix
Daylon
Daymi
Daymon
Daynalee
Dayneisha
Daynna
Daysa
Daysha
Dayshana
Dayshaun
Daysi
Dayton
Dayurmveance
Dayva
Dazha
Dazholi
Dborra
De
De Andrea
De Anna
De Anne
De Edra
De Kosha
De Lena
De Neica
De Nesha
Déanne
Déesha
Déja
Désha
Désirée
Détana
Dea
Dea Annie
Deaana
Deabra
Deadra
Deahanna
Deamber
Deamra
Dean
Deana-Gail
Deana-Marie
Deandre
Deandrea
Deandria
Deane
Deangela
Deangelina
Deaniell
Deanisha
Deann
Deanna-Elizabet
Deanna-Lee
Deanndra
Deannia
Deanquanette
Deanqunette
Deardra
Dearest
Dearndra
Deasha
Deatra
Deaudra
Deaundra
Deavon
Deaz
Debbi
Debbra
Debby
Debecca
Debi
Debilene
Debonaire
Debora
Deborah Inza
Deborah-Georgiana
Deborrah
Debra-Ann
Debrah
Debrasue
Debrea
Debrena
Debria
Debrielle
Debrina
Debroah
Debyn
Decarra
Decassia
December
Dechanta
Decherra
Decinia
Dedo
Dedreecka
Dedria
Dedrick
Dedricka
Dee
Dee Anna
Deéanna
Dee-Ajra
Dee-Dee
Dee-Jay
Deea
Deeandra
Deeann
Deeanna
Deeanne
Deeba
Deeddra
Deedee
Deedra
Deedrie
Deela
Deeleon
Deeniece
Deeon
Deeona
Deepa
Deepika
Deerika
Deetra
Deetta

Deezya
Defana
Dehagony
Dehlila
Deidrea
Deija
Deiona
Deirdra
Deirdree
Deisha
Deisi
Deitra
Deive
Deja
Dejanelle
Dejanira
Dejarley
Dejon
Dejuana
Dekariss
Dekeana
Dekedra
Dekendra
Dekenya
Dekfisha
Dekoda
Dekota
Del
Del Vina
Del-Rae
Delacey
Delache
Delaina
Delaine
Delainey
Delaka
Delana
Delane
Delaney
Delania
Delanya
Delayna
Delayne
Delaynie
Delcatha
Delea
Deleani
Deleasia
Delecia
Deleena
Deleila
Delena
Delenya
Deleon
Delesha
Delexious
Delfina
Delicia
Delight Lynn
Delika
Delila
Delilia
Delina
Delinda
Déline
Delisa
Delisha
Delissa
Deljorak
Delkeisha
Dell
Dellaina
Dellia
Dellores
Delma
Delmar
Delmarie
Delmys
Delonda
Delonna
Deloraid
Deloria
Delories
Deloris
Delorise
Delphia
Delphine
Delpreet
Delsa
Delsey
Delsina
Delta
Delte
Deltoria
Deltra Tat
Deluxious
Delvina
Delvonda
Delysha
Delyte
Delzee
Demarae
Demarice
Demeatrice
Demeeka
Demeka
Demesha
Demeta
Demeteria
Demetra
Demetra-Eleana
Demetric
Demetrice
Demetris
Demetrish
Demetrius
Demi
Demiah
Demilya
Demilyn
Deminee
Demisha
Demitra
Demonica
Demonique
Denaé
Denali
Denalie
Denara
Denashah
Denay
Denea
Denean
Denecia
Denee
Deneé
Deneen
Deneenesmerelda
Deneesha
Deneichia
Deneil
Deneisha
Deneishia
Deneka
Denelle
Denequia
Denesha
Deneshia
Denetra
Denetress
Denetri
Denetria
Deneuve
Deney
Denfana
Deni

Denica
Denice
Denicia
Denie
Deniece
Deniele
Denielle
Deniesha
Denika
Denile
Denille
Denine
Deninnea
Denis
Denisecia
Denish
Denishia
Denisse
Denita
Denitra
Denitrika
Denity
Deniz
Denna
Dennarah
Dennee
Denni
Dennielle
Dennis
Dennise
Denone
Denora
Denver
Denyelle
Denyka
Denys
Denyse
Deolinda
Deon
Deona
Deondra
Deonjala
Deonna
Deonne
Deonyia
Depree
Deqa
Dequandrea
Dequilla
Dequisha
Dequita
Dequoai
Deramise
Derandre
Derbie
Dercas
Derek
Derekia
Derenda
Derhonda
Deriantae
Derica
Dericka
Derika
Derisha
Derita
Dernesha
Deronna
Derrericka
Derrica
Derricka
Derrie
Derrika
Derrina
Dervina
Desaire
Desantis
Desara
Desarae
Desarai
Desaraie
Desaray
Desaré
Desarea
Desaree
Desarie
Desedria
Desendra
Desenia
Deserae
Deseraé
Deserai
Deseray
Desere
Deseree
Deseret
Deseri
Deserie
Deserrae
Deserray
Desert
Desha
Deshae
Deshailia
Deshan
Deshanda
Deshandra
Deshane
Deshannon
Desharia
Deshaun
Deshaundra
Deshawn
Deshawna
Deshawndra
Deshay
Deshaydia
Desheania
Desheka
Deshell
Deshima
Deshona
Deshonda
Deshonna
Desiana
Desiarae
Desirée
Desira
Desirah
Desiray
Desiraye
Desirée
Desirea
Desireé Iris
Desirey
Desjaray
Deslann
Deslin
Desma
Desmond
Desmonee
Desmontay
Desni
Desonia
Despina
Desra
Desray
Desree
Dessa
Desserie
Dessert
Dessie
Dessirae
Dessire
Dessylin
Desta

Destanee
Destanie
Destannie
Destany
Destara
Desteni
Destin
Destine
Destinee
Destiney
Destini
Destinie
Destnie
Destry
Desttine
Desty
Destyn
Destyni
Detasha
Detria
Detrick
Dev Hari
Deva
Deva Marie
Devane
Devanese
Devangi
Devanie
Devany
Devaughn
Develyn
Deven
Devena
Deveney
Devenje
Devera
Deverae
Deverell
Deverie
Deverne Alexis
Deveyn
Devi
Deviessia
Devika
Devilakhen
Devina
Devinanne
Devine
Devita
Devlin
Devola
Devolya
Devona
Devonda
Devonna
Devora
Devorah
Devra
Devree
Devrie
Devyn
Dewanyelle
Dewi
Dewilla
Dewuana
Deyanira
Deysi
Deza
Dezarae
Dezaray
Dezare
Dezembra
Dezerae
Dezeray
Dezere
Dezerea
Dezerie
Dezi
Dezia
Dezila
Dezirae
Deziree
Dezireé
Dezorae
Dezra
Dezrae
Dezyrae
Dezzie
Dhadra
Dhaima
Dhanika
Dhanisha
Dhanishta
Dhanya
Dhara
Dharshini
Dhiffon
Dhiya
Dhoha
Dhriti
Di'anna
Dia
Diahann
Diahanna
Diamanto
Diamisha
Diamo'n
Diamonia
Diamonique
Dian
Diana-Antonella
Diana-Frances
Diana-Kieu-Anh
Diana-Marie
Diana-Tim
Dianah
Dianalyn
Dianarose
Dianatris
Dianca
Diandra
Diandra-Leigh
Dianelis
Dianely
Dianelys
Dianett
Diania
Dianie
Dianielle
Dianita
Diann
Diannah-Marie
Diantha
Dianys
Diara
Diarra
Diaset
Diba
Dicie
Didiane
Didja
Dieanna
Diedra
Diedre
Dielle
Diem
Dienecia
Dienna
Diera
Dierdra
Dierdre
Diesha
Dietlind
Dietrich
Dieudonne
Dieumise

Digna
Dihana
Dihanna
Dilanne
Dilayna
Dilcia
Dilease
Dilek
Diletta
Dilpreet
Dima
Dimein
Dimeshia
Diminique
Dimisha
Dimitra
Dimitria
Dimonica
Dimple
Dina-Marie
Dinah
Dineen
Dineet
Dineka
Dinesti
Dinieca
Dinora
Dinorah
Diocelina
Dion
Diona
Diondra
Diondrea
Dione
Dionee
Dionisia
Dionitia
Dionna
Dionte
Dionysus
Dipa
Diquee
Diquetta
Diracé
Dirk
Disa
Disha
Dishae
Dishay
Disheia
Disheka
Dishon
Ditza
Diva
Diveeta
Divine
Divionne
Divya
Diya
Djuana
Dlolly
Dnetra
Doa
Doan
Doanne
Dochelle
Doha
Dollina
Dollmeshia
Dollsh'n
Dolly
Dolmesha
Domanesha
Domanick
Domaniqu
Domanique
Domanique Johani
Domeneque
Domenica
Domeniqu
Domenique
Domimique
Domineque
Domini
Dominic
Dominica
Dominick
Dominigue
Dominik
Dominika
Dominikk
Dominiqua
Dominiquic
Dominixe
Domino
Dominoque
Dominqueka
Dominuque
Dominyika
Domique
Domminique
Domna-Athanasia
Domnicka
Domonica
Domonice
Domoniqu
Dona
Donail
Donalea
Donalisa
Donatha
Doncha
Dondi
Dondra
Dondrea
Dondrecka
Dondreea
Doneese
Doneila
Doneille
Doneisha
Donell
Donella
Donelle
Donera
Donesha
Doneshia
Donessa
Doneta
Donetta
Donette
Dongbin
Doni
Donia
Donica
Donice
Donielee
Doniella
Donielle
Donika
Donise
Donisha
Donishia
Donita
Donitrae
Donlee
Donmonique
Donn-Telina
Donna Lynn
Donna-Mae
Donna-Marie
Donnaica
Donnalee
Donnalen

Donnan
Donnanique
Donneisha
Donnell
Donnelle
Donnelly
Donneta
Donnette
Donni
Donnica
Donnie-Marie
Donniecka
Donnielle
Donnika
Donnise
Donnisha
Donnita
Donnyale
Donrell
Donshae
Donsherlyn
Donshiwa
Dontai
Donterria
Dontia
Dontorya
Dontoya
Donya
Donyale
Donyce
Donyell
Donyuell
Dooinise
Dorali
Doralie
Doralisa
Doraluz
Doraly
Doralynn
Doran
Dorathy
Dorbie
Dorca
Dorcas
Dore
Dorece
Doree
Doreece
Doreshia
Doressa
Doretha
Doretta
Dorettie
Dorey
Dori
Dori-Anne
Dorian
Doriann
Dorianne
Dorie
Doriene
Dorika
Doriley
Dorilis
Dorina
Dorinda
Dorion
Dorita
Doritha
Dorla
Dorlene
Dorlores
Dornez
Dorota
Dorotha
Dorothea
Dorothee
Dorrah
Dorrie
Dorrie-Anne
Dorsal
Dorsel
Dortha
Dorthea
Dorthey
Dorthia
Dorthy
Dory
Doryann
Doshie
Dosithée
Dossie
Dottie
Douaa
Dove
Doveann
Dovevann
Dovie
Dovina
Doyinsola
Dracie
Draeshell
Drandel
Drayton
Dreama
Dreamarie
Dreann
Dreanna
Drema
Drenae
Dreunna
Drewzella-Er
Drianne
Drissia
Dru
Drue
Druscilla
Drusilla
Dsesirea
Dshayna
Dsyvette
Duana
Dudlyne
Dulce
Dulcia
Dulcie
Dunai
Dunielle
Duong
Durenda
Durriya
Dustee
Dusti
Dustie
Dustin
Dustina
Dustine
Dustyn
Duwana
Dvonndrea
Dwan
Dwanda
Dwania
Dwayna
Dwdoshema
Dwight
Dwina
Dwjuana
Dy Anne
Dy-Esha
Dyamante
Dyan
Dyana
Dyane
Dyani
Dyann

Dyanna
Dydell
Dyeasha
Dyeshay
Dylan
Dylana
Dymita
Dynasdy
Dynasti
Dynelle
Dynesha
Dynika
Dynirie
Dyona
Dyshadrick
Dyshanetta
Dyshanta
Dyshawn
Dyshia
Dyvonne
Dywonda
Dywris
Dzaja
Dze
Dzidra

E

Élinn
Élise
Élyse
E.
Eadaoin
Eadyn
Ean
Earial
Earlecia
Earlena
Earlene
Earline
Earlisha
Earllene
Earnasha
Earnestine
Earnisha
Earon
Eartha
Easha
Easkie
Eastan
Easter
Eastlyn
Easton
Eban
Ebanee
Ebanie
Ebany
Ebbony
Ebelyn
Ebone
Ebonee
Eboney
Eboni'
Ebonique
Ebonisha
Ebonnee
Ebonni
Ebonnie
Ebonque
Ebonye
Eborah Anne
Ebularia
Ed Resha
Eda
Edabel
Edan
Edana
Eddrena
Edelina
Edelmira
Edelyne
Edene
Edibet
Edid
Edie
Edite
Editha
Edlin
Edline
Edlisha
Edlyn
Edlyne
Edneisha
Ednita
Edora
Edrian
Edricka
Edrie
Edrine
Edwena
Edwin
Edwina
Edwine
Edwyna
Edy
Edyn
Effie
Efia
Efthimia
Eftihia
Egdallys
Eghosa
Ehren
Eichelle
Eida
Eiesha
Eilat
Eilene
Eilleen
Eillen
Eilyn
Eiman
Eimy
Eir
Eirann
Eirca
Eisha
Ejoli
Eka
Ekaterina
Ekatrinna
Ekeira
Ekeya
Ekmal
Ekta
El'arcenia
Elaa
Elah
Elain
Elainia
Elainna
Elais
Elan
Eland
Elane
Elania
Elanie
Elanit
Elanna
Elanor
Elanore
Elashia
Elauna
Elayesha
Elayna

Elayne
Elba
Elbonie
Elbony
Elda
Eldora
Eldris
Eldynn
Ele
Eleacia
Eleah
Eleana
Eleanor-Francis
Eleanore
Elease
Eleasha
Eleata
Elecia
Electa
Electra
Eleesha
Elefteria
Eleftheria
Elegence
Eleia
Eleisha
Elektra
Elemjah
Elen
Elenee
Elenoa
Elenor
Elenora
Eleny
Eleonor
Eleonora
Eleonore
Elesebet
Elesha
Eleshia
Elesia
Elesthe
Eleticia
Eleuthera
Elexious
Elexis
Elexius
Eleysse
Elfi
Elfirma
Elham
Eli
Elia
Elia Melisa
Eliabeth
Eliane
Elianna
Elianne
Elibel
Elicea
Elida
Elif
Eligance
Eligia
Elihu
Eliisa
Elijah
Elika
Elimichell
Elin
Elina
Elinda
Eling
Elinor
Elinora
Eliot
Eliotta
Elisa Rae
Elisabet
Elisabethe
Elisabetta
Elisabette
Elisandra
Eliscia
Elise-Anne
Elisebet
Elisheba
Elisheva
Elishia
Elishua
Elisia
Elismari
Elisse
Elita
Elitia
Elivia
Eliya
Eliz
Eliz Vanessa
Elizabee
Elizabeth Ann
Elizabeth Evelyn
Elizabeth Marie
Elizabeth-Amanda
Elizabeth-Ann
Elizabeth-Anne
Elizabeth-Ashley
Elizabeth-Hien
Elizabeth-Joy
Elizaida
Elizalina
Elize
Elizea
Elizebeth
Elkannah
Elke
Ellaina
Ellaine
Ellamarie
Ellana
Ellarie
Elldie
Elle
Ellecia Dawn
Elleda
Ellen-Mae
Ellena
Ellene-Hera
Ellery
Ellesha
Ellet
Ellexia
Elli
Ellianne
Ellice
Ellicia
Ellie
Elliott
Ellis
Ellisa
Ellise
Ellisha
Ellishya
Ellison
Ellissa
Ellisya
Ellna
Ellsbeth
Ellsie
Ellsy
Elly
Ellyce
Ellyn
Ellyse
Ellysia

Ellyssa
Elmasei
Elna
Elneatria
Elnesa
Elnora
Elodie
Elois
Eloisa
Eloise
Elonda
Elora
Elosia
Elrinda
Elsabeth
Elsbeth
Elsey
Elsha
Elsheara
Elsja
Elspeth
Elsy
Elthea
Eltoria
Eluvia
Elva
Elvelin
Elvera
Elvia
Elvina
Elvira
Elyana
Elyanna
Elyannah
Elyce
Elyci
Elycia
Elynore
Elysa
Elysabeth
Elysha
Elyshia
Elysin
Elysse
Elyssia
Elyzebet
Elzbieta
Ema
Emaan
Emalea
Emalee
Emalie
Eman
Emanda
Emanise
Emanuela
Emanuelle
Emanulynne
Ember
Emberly
Embre
Emby
Emeleigh
Emeli
Emelia
Emelie
Emeline
Emely
Emelyn
Emerante
Emerie
Emerisa
Emerlee
Emerson
Emery
Emi
Emica
Emiglia
Emiko
Emilea
Emilene
Emiley
Emili
Emiliana
Emilianne
Emilie-Ann
Emilie-Jeanne
Emilieane
Emiline
Emilis
Emillie
Emilly
Emily Jane
Emily-Ann
Emily-Jane
Emily-Jean
Emily-Marie
Emilyann
Emilyn
Emine
Emiy
Emiyann
Emliana
Emma Catherine
Emma Elizabeth
Emma Lee
Emma-Jane
Emma-Kate
Emma-Lea
Emma-Lee
Emma-Lily
Emmajean
Emmalee
Emmaleigh
Emmalene
Emmali
Emmalie
Emmaliese
Emmaline
Emmaly
Emmalyn
Emmalyse
Emmanuela
Emmanuella
Emmanuelle
Emmeline
Emmelline
Emmelyne
Emmery
Emmi
Emmilly
Emmilou
Emmy
Emmylou
Emoani
Emorfiu
Emory
Empriss
Emrie
Emry
Emueje
Emunah
Emy
Emylee
Emylinda
Emylou
Emzhei
Ena
Enas
Enass
Enayat
Endea
Endera
Endia
Endura
Endya

Endyia
Eneida
Enelida
Engelica
Engie
English
Enibokun
Enid
Enide
Eniley
Eniola
Enise
Enishia
Enith
Enjaneek
Enjolee
Enjoli
Enjoli'
Enjoli-A
Enjolia
Enjuli
Enna
Enne
Ennovy
Enobi
Enoha
Enslatta
Enza
Eomenii
Eonie
Ephie
Equailla
Equesei
Equida
Equila
Equilla
Erasmia
Ercia
Eredith
Ereka
Erena
Erendira
Erenie-M
Erenis
Eri
Eria
Erian
Eriane
Eric
Erica De Fatima
Erica Lynn
Erica Pauline
Erica-Isabel
Erica-Lynn
Erical
Ericca
Erich
Ericia
Ericika
Erick
Erie
Erieal
Erieanna
Eriel
Erienne
Erikah
Erikka
Erikus
Erin-Lynne
Erina
Erine
Erinetta
Erinne
Eriqa
Eris
Erla
Erlana
Erlene
Erlenne
Erlina
Erlinda
Erma
Ermelinda
Ermina
Erminda
Erminia
Ermite
Ermithe
Ernecia
Ernelia
Ernestin
Ernestina
Ernestine
Ernisha
Erolida
Eron
Erondalyn
Eroulla
Eroya
Errica
Erricca
Errin
Errollyn
Erum
Eryal
Erykia
Erykka
Eryn-Jean
Erynn
Erynne
Erzulie
Esabia
Eseoghene
Eseta
Esha
Eshe
Esi
Eslynne
Esme
Esmerald
Esmeralda
Esmerazda
Esmerelda
Esohe
Espe
Espedaniza
Esperans
Esperanta
Esperanz
Esperanza
Esra
Essa
Essence
Essie
Esson
Estee
Estefania
Estela
Estella
Estelle
Estephanie
Ester
Esther Grace
Esthur
Estibaliz
Estrela
Estrella
Eternity
Etha
Ethel
Etienne
Etorya
Etoy
Etta
Eugenie
Eugenina

Eugina
Eulaisha
Eulalia
Eulalya
Eun Ah
Eun-Joo
Euna
Eunique
Euphemia
Eureka
Eurekia
Eurica
Eurice
Eurika
Eustacia
Eva Lena
Eva Marie
Eva-Alaine
Eva-Marie
Evagelia
Evah
Evah-Sheng
Evalea
Evalee
Evalys
Evamarie
Evana
Evanalison
Evanesa
Evangelia
Evangelica
Evangelina
Evangelynn
Evanie
Evann
Evanna
Evanne
Evanthia
Evany
Evar
Evdokia
Evealyson
Eveania
Eveca
Eveleena
Evelia
Evelim
Evelina
Eveline
Evelisa
Evelisse
Evella
Evelyca
Evelyn Mariel
Evelyna
Evelynn
Evelynne
Evenie
Everaridis
Evergreen
Everica
Everline
Evett
Evexzia
Evey
Evia
Evies
Evika
Evin
Evinn
Evionne
Evita
Evlynn
Evon
Evonda
Evoni
Evonia
Evonne
Evonsk
Evony
Evthokia
Evunea
Evvanne
Evy
Evyan
Evymaris
Evyn
Evynne
Ewa
Ewelina
Exsodier
Eyaggelia
Eydie
Eylenna
Eylin
Eyman
Eyna
Eyvonne

F

Faaria
Faatima
Fabia
Fabian
Fabiana
Fabielle
Fabiene
Fabienne
Fabiola
Fabreanne
Fadia
Fadora
Fadwa
Faerlyn
Fahema
Fahim
Fahreen
Fahren
Fahria
Faigy
Faiola
Fairen
Fairicy
Fairuz
Faiza
Fajer
Falakika
Falan
Faleisha
Falen
Falena
Falene
Falesha
Faleshia
Falicia
Falin
Falina
Falisa
Falisha
Fallan
Fallen
Fallenlee
Falleshia
Fallyn
Falonne
Falyn
Falynn
Falynne
Fameedah
Famie
Fana
Fanchon
Fanci
Fancy

Fanelissa
Fanesia
Fani-Fay
Fania
Fanny
Fanta
Fantasha
Fantashia
Fantashialealan
Fantasia
Fanteema
Fara
Fareen
Farhana
Farhanah
Farheen
Farica
Farida
Fariha
Farihah
Farima
Farin
Farinah
Farinaz
Faring
Faron
Faronn
Farra
Farrahn
Farran
Farrel
Farren-Lee
Farren-Nora
Farress
Farrin
Farris
Farrisa
Farron
Farron-Leigh
Farryn
Farshawn
Faryn
Farzaana
Farzama
Farzana
Farzaneh
Farzeen
Farzina
Fasha
Fashidatnafisat
Fashionette
Fasiha
Fata Fehi Huiam
Fatafehi
Fatai
Fateisha
Fatema
Fathema
Fathimah
Fathma
Fatimah
Fatimah-Fawzi
Fatime
Fatin
Fatina
Fatma
Fattin
Fatu-Ma
Faun
Fauna
Faunché
Fausta
Fauve
Fauzia
Faviana
Faviola
Fawna
Fawnna
Fay
Faydra
Fayette
Faykita
Faylena
Faylynn
Faynita
Fayrell
Fayshon
Faytandria
Fayte
Faythe
Fazia
Fazlin
Feather
February
Fedah
Federica
Fedna
Feena
Fehoko
Fekadu
Feleasha
Feleina
Feleisha
Felesha
Felia
Felice
Felichia
Felicia-Joy
Felicialee
Feliciamae
Felicita
Feliciti
Felicity
Felicya
Felina
Felipe
Felisa
Felisca
Felishia
Felisiana
Felissa
Felita
Felixia
Feliza
Felizia
Fellcia
Fellishia
Fellyn
Felon
Felteena
Felysia
Female
Fendy
Feneisha
Fenta
Fereshteh
Ferheen
Ferila
Ferin
Ferlia
Ferlisa
Fern
Fernalia
Fernanda
Fernanda De Araujo
Fernande
Ferni
Feroza-Mohamed
Ferran
Ferrante
Ferrell
Ferren
Ferresha
Ferrin
Ferris

Ferron
Ferryl
Feryall
Feryn
Feven
Feyla
Fiamma
Ficki
Fidelia
Fielding
Fiera
Fiero
Fiesta
Fifi
Filicia
Filiz
Fillal
Filomena
Finessa
Finisa
Finita
Fionna
Fiorella
Fiorenza
Fiorina
Fiorisela
Firstina
Fitore
Fittonia
Flanders
Flanice
Flavia
Flawna
Fleasia
Fleater
Flechia
Fleicia
Fleishia
Fleming
Flena
Fleur
Fllaza
Fllonxa
Floichar
Flor
Flora De L
Floralee
Floreisha
Floren
Florence-Helene
Florencia
Florency
Florendra
Floria
Floriana
Florie
Florina
Florinda
Florisa
Florisis
Flossie
Flozelly
Fnan
Fonchona
Fondericka
Fondrica
Fonta
Fontane
Fontavia
Fontayne
Fontella
Fontianna
Forrest
Fotina
Fotini
Fowlen
Fowz
Fradel
Frady
Frain
Fran
Françoise
Franca
France
Francee
Franceine
Franceline
Francenia
Frances-Arnnie
Francesca Lucian
Franceska
Francess
Francessca
Francesta
Franceta
Francetta
Francheca
Franchelle
Franches
Francheska
Franchesker
Franchessca
Franchestka
Franchisca
Franchiska
Franchon
Franci
Francia
Francies
Francin
Francina
Francisc
Francisca
Francise
Franciska
Francne
Francois
Francoise
Frande
Frandrika
Franetha
Franjellica
Frank
Franka
Frankeisha
Franki
Frankia
Franklin
Frankorrnie
Franlicia
Franline
Frannie
Franny Lee
Franshawn
Franshesca
Fransis
Franterria
Frantessa
Franzannie
Franzene
Frashan
Frazia
Freadreya
Frecnhelle
Fred
Freda
Fredda
Freddi
Freddie
Fredelyne
Frederica
Fredericka
Frederique
Fredia
Fredikia
Fredlyn

Fredreca
Fredreka
Fredrica
Fredricka
Fredrika
Freedom
Freeha
Freema
Freesia
Freida
Freisha
Frences
Frencesc
Frencesca
Frencesea
Frenchesca
Frenchy
Frencien
Frenecia
Freshanda
Freshta
Freya
Frida
Frieda
Friendella
Friezi
Fristina
Fritzi
Fritzline
Fritzy
Fuatino
Fuchsia
Fulisha
Fung
Funmilola
Furtuna
Fushia
Fylesha

G

G.
Gaberal
Gaberiel
Gabielle
Gabirela
Gabreill
Gabrela
Gabrial
Gabriala
Gabriel
Gabriele
Gabrille
Gabrina
Gabryanna
Gaby
Gacia
Gael
Gaelen
Gaelle
Gaetan
Gaetana
Gaètane
Gaetanne
Gaganbir
Gagandeep
Gaganjot
Gaibrell
Gaildresha
Gaileen
Gaisha
Gaiti
Gaitlin
Gaitri
Gaitrie
Gakeshia
Galaxy
Galayna
Gale
Galen
Galena
Galina
Galit
Galyn
Gami
Gamocha
Gandria
Ganelle
Gao
Garan
Garbrielle
Garcelle
Garen
Garene
Garilyn
Garmeika
Garmeisha
Garnet
Garnetta
Garra
Garrian
Garrica
Garryn
Gary
Garyn
Gassia
Gauri
Gawenageho
Gayatri
Gaybriel
Gayla
Gaylaine
Gaylen
Gaylyn
Gaynell
Gea
Geamaury
Geanette
Geania
Geanine
Geanna
Geannine
Geda
Geena
Geeta
Geetanjali
Geetha
Geethen
Geetika
Geisha
Gelareh
Geline
Gelya
Gemilea
Gemini
Gemmina
Gemy
Genaah
Genan
Genara
Genave
Genavive
Gene
Genea
Geneall
Genece
Genee
Geneen
Geneice
Geneieve
Geneline
Genell
Genelle
Genera
Generra
Genesa

Genesee
Genesia
Genesis
Genessia
Genet
Geneve
Genever
Geneveve
Geneviève
Genevie
Genevieve-Marie
Genevievre
Geney
Geni
Genia
Genice
Genie
Geniel
Genieve
Genifer
Geniirae
Genine
Genis
Genise
Genisus
Genita
Genna-Lynn
Gennell
Genni
Gennie
Gennifer
Gennifur
Genny
Genoa
Genobia
Genola
Genora
Genoveva
Gense

Gentle Alice
Gentrie
Gentry
Genvieve
Geoffrey
Geordann
Georgaline
Georgann
Georganna
Georganne
George
Georgean
Georgeann
Georgeanne
Georgena
Georgeta
Georgett
Georgiaellie
Georgiana
Georgianna
Georgianne
Georgie
Georjetta
Geovon
Geovonna
Gera
Gera-Lee
Gerah
Gerald
Geraldin
Geralyn
Gerarda
Gerardviane
Gerda
Gerdeline
Gereda
Geria
Gerica
Gericaha

Gerika
Gerilyn
Gerilynn
Geris
Gerisa
Gerlande
Gerlene
Gerlia
Gerline
Germa
Germaine
Germanie
Germaya
Germine
Gernea
Gernia
Gerri
Gerrianna
Gerrica
Gerrielin
Gerrilyn
Gerrish
Gerritje
Gerry
Gerry-Ann
Gerrylee-Ann
Gertrude
Geryah
Gesenia
Gesine
Gessel
Getaura
Getenesh
Getoria
Geurda
Geurlyne
Geveniève
Gevonna
Gewana

[illegible]
Ghislain
Ghislaine
Ghnami
Gialicia
Giana
Gianina
Gianinna
Gianni
Giannina
Gianny
Gianoula
Giavanna
Giavonna
Gideann
Gienah
Gierla
Giesela
Gila
Gilana
Gilda
Gilenia
Gili
Gilian
Gilit
Gillette
Gilliane
Gillianne
Gillie
Gillyan
Gimica
Gin
Gin-Ning
Gina Maria
Gina Marie

marie
inah
Ginale
Ginamarie
Ginea
Gineen
Ginel
Ginell
Ginelle
Ginessa
Ginette
Ginger-Anne
Ginger-Rose
Gini
Ginia
Ginie
Ginika
Ginja
Ginjer
Ginneisha
Ginneva
Ginney
Ginni Feralicia
Ginnie
Giny
Gioany
Giovana
Giovanni
Giovene
Gipsy
Gira
Girlaine
Girlande
Girlie
Girline
Gisel
Gisela
Gisèle
Gisele
Gisell
Gisella
Giselmis
Gisenia
Gissa
Gisselle
Gita
Gitel
Giulia
Giuliana
Giulianna
Giuseppa
Giuseppina
Gixsy
Gizelle
Gizzryl
Gladia
Gladis
Gladiz
Gladnishia
Glanda
Glandalis
Glavita
Gleeta
Glena
Glenara
Glendalis
Glendaly
Glennda
Glennesha
Glennetta
Glennie
Glennis
Glennisha
Glennishia
Glenora
Glentoria
Gleny
Glenyale
Glenys
Glikerya
Glimer
Glinert
Glitter
Gloria-Daniela
Gloriah
Gloriana
Gloribel
Gloriela
Glorisha
Glory
Gloryvette
Glydes
Glynis
Glynitra
Glynnis
Glynshonda
Golda
Golden
Goldie
Goldilu
Goldshua
Gopi
Gorane
Gordana
Gordon
Gorete
Gorvette
Gorys
Grace Akosua
Grace-Wing-Yun
Gracea
Graceann
Gracemika
Gracia
Gracie
Graciela
Gracy
Granetta
Granisha
Grashondra
Grasilia
Grayce
Graylin
Grayson
Grazia
Graziella
Grazyna
Grechi
Greer
Gregan
Gregshawn
Greide
Greneshia
Grenisha
Gretchin
Grete
Gretel
Grethe
Gretna
Gretta
Gretter
Grevonica
Grianne
Grisel
Griselda
Griselys
Grissel
Grissele
Grissely
Gristina
Grossi
Guadalup
Guadulupe
Guankita
Guataesha
Gudelia

Gudrun
Gueline
Guely
Guerda
Guerla
Guerline
Guerlyne
Guermila
Guertha
Guetheleen
Guiliana
Guiliann
Guillaine
Guinevere
Guinevieve
Guiomar
Guiselle
Gulaine
Gurdaman
Gurjit
Gurkirat
Gurlaine
Gurminder
Gurpinder
Gurraj
Gursharan
Gurveen
Gurvinder
Guyla
Guylaine
Guylene
Guylynn
Gwen Delynn
Gwenda
Gwendaline
Gwendaly
Gwendalyn
Gwendela
Gwendolen
Gwendoline
Gwendoly
Gwendylan
Gwenetta
Gwenette
Gwenevere
Gwenisha
Gwenita
Gwenivere
Gwenn
Gwenness
Gwennetta
Gwenyth
Gwinda
Gwinn
Gwyn
Gwyneth
Gwynn
Gwynne
Gwynnevere
Gylaina
Gyllian
Gyna
Gynell
Gypsy
Gysel

H

Hélena
Hélène
Héléné
Ha Lea
Habiba
Habon
Hadar
Hadas
Hadassah
Hadden
Haddie
Hadeal
Hadeel
Hadeer
Haden
Hadlee
Hadley
Haedy
Haeley
Haeli
Haendel
Haera
Hafeeza
Hafsah
Hagen
Hager
Hai Lee
Haifa
Hailea
Haili
Hailie
Hailley
Haily
Haitel
Hajer
Hakima
Hala
Halanna
Halcea
Halcyn
Halcyon
Halecia
Halee
Haleen
Haleh
Halei
Haleigh
Halena
Halie
Haliegh
Haliema
Halima
Halime
Halina
Halle
Hallee
Halleh
Hallei
Hallette
Halley-Rose
Halli
Halliday
Hally
Hallye
Halsi
Halston
Hamishia
Hanah
Hanako
Hanamay
Hanan
Haneen
Hang
Hanh
Hani
Hania
Hanife
Hanin
Hannah-Rachelle
Hannalee
Hanne
Hannelore
Hanni
Hannon
Hans

Haona
Harbour
Haria
Hariklia
Harit
Harjit
Harjot
Harkiran
Harlee
Harleen
Harley
Harleyanne
Harly
Harman
Harmani
Harmanjot
Harmanpreet
Harmonie
Harolaina
Harolyn
Harper
Harri
Harriett
Harrietta
Harrison
Harsimran
Hartley
Harvir
Haseena
Hasheptsu
Hashia
Hasina
Hassina
Hassonah
Hatham
Hatice
Hattie
Hau
Hava
Havalee
Havelah
Haven
Havilah
Havonna
Havvah
Hawa
Hawley
Hawra
Hawwa
Hawwii
Haydee
Haydelisa
Hayden
Haye-Man
Hayhlee
Hayley-Brooke
Hayli
Haylie
Hayriye
Haytung
Haze
Hazel-Ann
Hazen
Heath
Heather Ann
Heather Lee
Heather Nicole
Heather-Anne
Heather-Marie
Heather-Rose
Heatherlee
Heatherly
Heathshia
Heaven'le
Heavenly
Heavyn
Heba
Hebah
Hedaya
Hedi
Hedy
Heejab
Hei Min
Heida
Heide
Heidi Lynn
Heidiann
Heidie
Heidilin
Heidy
Heigh
Heike
Heili
Heiporo
Hekmat
Hela
Helah
Helaina
Helaine
Helal
Helana
Helayna
Helayne
Heldy
Heleana
Heleena
Helen Alexis
Helen Ishbel
Helena-Nicole
Helenh
Helenna
Helga
Heli
Helicia
Helina
Hellanna
Hellen
Hellen Morto
Heloise
Helon
Helsa
Helsy
Hema
Hend
Hendy
Henita
Henna
Hennreitta
Hennrietta
Henri
Henrietta
Henriette
Henry
Henya
Hera
Herbreka
Herce
Herissa
Herjot
Herkena
Herlinda
Hermalina
Hermina
Herminia
Hero
Hersha
Hershelle
Hester
Heta
Hetal
Heureuse
Heven
Heyam
Hiapatia
Hiba
Hibah

Hibbat-Ul-Mannan
Hidee
Hidi
Hiedi
Hien
Hien Dieu
Hifa
Hikima
Hila
Hilairy
Hilaree
Hilarie
Hilary-Ann
Hilda
Hildy
Hiliary
Hilit
Hillarie
Hilleary
Hilleri
Hillery
Hillianne
Hilliary
Hillory
Himali
Himani
Hina
Hind
Hinda
Hindy
Hinid
Hira
Hirax
Hiromi
Hissa
Hlee
Ho-Yan
Ho-Yu
Hoa
Hoa-Mo-Faleono
Hoai
Hoai-Huong
Hoaimi
Hoang
Hoangmai
Hodan
Hodda
Hoeuth
Hoi
Hokinely
Hokunani
Holda
Holie
Holl-Lee
Holladay
Hollan
Holland
Hollee
Holleh
Hollenda
Holli-Anna
Holli-Lyn
Holliann
Hollianne
Hollie-Lynn
Hollinda
Hollis
Hollisto
Hollond
Holly Ann
Holly Katherine
Holly Lee
Holly-Ann
Holly-Anne
Holly-Anne-Lynn
Holly-Marie
Hollyanne
Hollyce
Holyce
Honalee
Honesty
Honey
Hong
Hong Thanh
Hong-An
Hong-Hanh
Honna
Honor
Honora
Honore
Honorine
Honour
Hopey
Hopi
Hordlen
Hosanna
Hoshelle
Hoshoma
Houda
Houry
Houssniah
Houston
Howneshia
Hrauna
Hrisovalantou
Hua-Wah
Huberta
Huda
Hughberta
Huguett
Huguette
Hui
Hulda
Hullena
Hullirose
Hulya
Huma
Humaira
Humera
Hunter
Huong
Hussai
Huu
Huynh
Huyul
Hyacinth
Hyam
Hyang
Hycinth
Hyekyeng
Hylann
Hylee
Hyturia
Hyun
Hyun-Jeong
Hyunjung

I

I Eshia
I'eisha
I'keishi
Iakita
Ianda
Iasha
Ibelisse
Ibinka
Ibis
Ibrittnay
Ibtesam
Ibtihaj
Ibtihal
Icésha

Icela
Ichrissheena
Icilma
Icy
Idahaili
Idai
Idairy
Idalia
Idalmi
Idalmys
Idamae
Idanelly
Idania
Idarine
Idaya
Idella
Idolioia
Idonesit
Idongesit
Idys
Ieachia
Ieaisha
Ieesha
Ieisha
Ielise
Iericha
Ieschia
Ieshia
Ifeoma
Ifeyinka
Iffat
Ifioma
Iglesia
Igmarie
Iiasha
Iieshia
Iisha
Ijaune
Ijeoma
Ikaisha
Ikeisha
Ikesha
Ikeshia
Ikram
Ila
Ilalee
Ilane
Ilani
Ilasa
Ildaco
Ilea
Ileah
Ileaha
Ileana
Ileanea
Ileena
Ileene
Ileia
Ilena
Ilene
Ilese
Ileshia
Ilez
Ili
Iliana
Ilianexsi
Iliani
Ilicia
Ilisha
Ilissa
Ilizzibet
Illiana
Illona
Illsheia
Illyse
Ilona
Ilsa
Ilse
Ilvia
Ilycia
Ilyne
Ilyona
Ilysa
Ilyse
Ilysha
Ilyssa
Imadelle
Iman
Imane-Hassiba
Imani
Imara
Imari
Imaris
Imee
Imelda
Imene
Immaculate
Immaculee
Immarie
Imninder
Imogen
Imogene
Impreet
Ina
Inanna
Inderial
Inderjeet
Inderjit
Inderpreet
Indiana
Indigo
Indira
Indra
Indya
Ineida
Ineka
Inekia
Inelis
Ines
Inez
Infinie
Ing-Tyng
Inga
Ingela
Inico
Inisha
Inna
Innana
Innis
Innogen
Inocia
Inyabelise
Ioanna
Iola
Iolanda
Iona
Iosha
Ipek
Ira
Iracema
Iraida
Iram
Iranda
Iranelly
Irantzu
Irayiza
Ireashia
Ireda
Irena
Irena-Marie
Iresha
Iretha
Irfana
Iriana
Iriel
Irien

Irika
Irina
Irisa
Irisha
Irissa
Irlanda
Irlene
Irma
Irnise
Irona
Irriccarichardia
Irum
Iruma
Irvie
Irvishia
Isa
Isabeau
Isabel-Marie-Aline
Isabeli
Isabella
Isable
Isadora
Isaiah
Isairis Maria
Isamarie
Isana
Isara
Isaura
Isavel
Isbel
Ischia
Isela
Isha
Ishana
Ishanda
Ishaney
Ishani
Ishaun
Ishdip
Isheka
Ishenda
Ishvir
Isiah
Isis
Isla
Islamiyat
Islay
Ismaris
Ismat
Isobel
Isra
Isreal
Issaline
Issetta
Istiahnah
Italia
Italy
Itamara
Itavia
Iteche
Ithaca
Itilia
Itta
Itzamarie
Iva
Ivana
Ivania
Ivania Maria
Ivanka
Ivanna
Iveline
Ivelis
Ivelisse
Ivellss
Iverline
Ivete
Iveth
Ivetlisse
Ivevalry
Ivey
Ivon
Ivonne
Ivori
Ivorlene
Ivree
Ivy-Rose
Ivyie
Iwalani
Iwona
Ixis
Ixland
Iyana
Iyanna
Iyisha
Iyoko
Iza
Izabella
Izabelle
Izaida
Izaria
Izbia
Izelle
Izena
Iznatia

J

J Nora
J-Lynn
J.
J.j.
Ja
Ja Ché
Ja Kenda
Ja Kesha
Ja Meka
Ja Neva
Ja Teka
Jàmica
Jànae
Jànelle
Jàteira
Ja-Mese
Jaànell
Jaad
Jaala
Jaanai
Jabalia
Jabbianca
Jabeen
Jac-E
Jacara
Jace
Jacee
Jacelle
Jacely
Jacelyn
Jacelynn
Jacenda
Jacenta
Jacey-Lee
Jaci
Jacie
Jaciel
Jacilyn
Jacilynn
Jacinth
Jacinthe
Jack
Jackalene
Jackalyn
Jackalynn
Jackee
Jackeline

Jackelyn
Jackeria
Jacki
Jackia
Jackie-Lynn
Jackilee
Jackilyn
Jacklin
Jacklyne
Jacklynn
Jackolyn
Jackquel
Jackquelyn
Jackquelynn
Jackquetta
Jackquilyn
Jackqulyn
Jacky
Jackysha
Jacleen
Jaclin
Jacline
Jaclyne
Jacob
Jacoba
Jacolbia
Jacolby
Jacolea
Jacolyn
Jacolyne
Jacoria
Jacoueline
Jacoyia
Jacqlyn
Jacqlynne
Jacqu-Lynne
Jacqualin
Jacqualine
Jacqualyn

Jacquanecia
Jacquas
Jacquay
Jacque
Jacque Lyn
Jacqué
Jacquee
Jacqueena
Jacqueice
Jacqueine
Jacquel
Jacqueleen
Jacquelène
Jacquelene
Jacqueline Dian
Jacqueline-Isabel
Jacqueline-Yvette
Jacquelyne
Jacquelynlea
Jacquelynne
Jacquena
Jacqueria
Jacquetta
Jacqui
Jacquil
Jacquiline
Jacquilyn
Jacquise
Jacquita
Jacqulin
Jacqulyn
Jacqulynn
Jacqutta
Jacuita
Jacy
Jacylin
Jacynthe
Jadah
Jadda

Jade-Ann
Jadea
Jadeann
Jadee
Jadeemerald
Jaden
Jadera
Jadi
Jadie
Jadielyn
Jadienne
Jadira
Jadrianne
Jadrien
Jady
Jae
Jae Ce
Jaeda
Jaede
Jaedra
Jael
Jaela
Jaelee
Jaeleen
Jaelie
Jaelithe
Jaelle
Jaelynn
Jaemie
Jaena
Jaennae
Jaennett
Jaffree
Jafra
Jagaia
Jagdeep
Jagdip
Jagruti
Jahaidia

Jahaira
Jaharra
Jahayra
Jahdai
Jahida
Jahira
Jahitza
Jahkiisha
Jahla
Jahlea
Jahmelia
Jahmil
Jahmilla
Jahmonique
Jahna
Jahnasseh
Jahnaya
Jahnelizza
Jahnelle
Jahvonda
Jahyraika
Jahzeel
Jahzinga
Jai
Jaica
Jaida
Jaide
Jaiden
Jaika
Jaileen
Jailyn
Jaima
Jaime-Lee
Jaime-Lyn
Jaime-Lynn
Jaimeclaire
Jaimee-Lynn
Jaimey
Jaimi

Jaimini
Jaimmie
Jaimy
Jain
Jaine
Jainy
Jaira
Jaisa
Jaissa
Jajuana
Jakala
Jakea
Jakeela
Jakeida
Jakeisia
Jakeita
Jakela
Jakelia
Jakell
Jakena
Jaketta
Jakevia
Jakia
Jakie
Jakiya
Jakki
Jakkia
Jaklene
Jaklyn
Jakobee
Jakorra
Jalane
Jalanna
Jalaya
Jalayna
Jalea
Jaleah
Jalean
Jalee
Jaleen
Jaleh
Jaleisa
Jalene
Jaley
Jaliegh
Jalilah
Jalileh
Jalin
Jalina
Jalinda
Jaline
Jalisa
Jalisia
Jalohn
Jalpa
Jalynn
Jama
Jamacia
Jamaica
Jamaina
Jamaisa
Jamalis
Jamalyn
Jamara
Jamaria
Jamarra
Jamasa
Jamase
Jamay
Jamea
Jamecia
Jamee
Jamee-Beth
Jamee-Lee
Jameela
Jameelah
Jameeliah
Jameice
Jameila
Jameisha
Jameisy
Jameka
Jamela
Jamelia
Jameliah
Jamell
Jamella
Jamelle
Jamely
Jamelya
Jamen
Jamene
Jameria
Jamerica
James
Jamese
Jamesha
Jameshia
Jameshyia
Jamesia
Jamesica
Jamessa
Jameta
Jamethia
Jametta
Jamey
Jami Ryan
Jami-Lyn
Jami-Lynn
Jamia
Jamiann
Jamiaya
Jamica
Jamicyn
Jamie Lynn
Jamie-Jo
Jamie-Leigh
Jamie-Lyne
Jamie-Marie
Jamie-Montana
Jamie-Rae
Jamie-Raye
Jamiela
Jamielee
Jamielynn
Jamiera
Jamieshala
Jamieson
Jamii
Jamika
Jamilah
Jamilee
Jamilia
Jamiliah
Jamilla
Jamillah
Jamillariana
Jamille
Jamillia
Jamilya
Jamilyn
Jamilynn
Jamin
Jamina
Jamira
Jamirah
Jamireal
Jamis
Jamise
Jamisha
Jamison
Jammi
Jammisha
Jamnesha
Jamora
Jamoy

Jamy
Jamya
Jamye
Jamyla
Jamyra
Jan Ette
Jana-Leigh
Janaca
Janacha
Janadine
Janaé
Janaea
Janaeh
Janaesia
Janah
Janai
Janail
Janaire
Janairy
Janaki
Janale
Janalee
Janalisa
Janalyn
Jananie
Janarleen
Janases
Janaya
Janaye
Jancie
Jandee
Jandel
Jandin
Jandra
Jandy
Janea
Janeal
Janean
Janeann
Janece
Janecia
Janee
Janeé
Janeely
Janeen
Janeia
Janeice
Janeika
Janeil
Janeiro
Janeisha
Janeka
Janele
Janelis
Janella
Janelle Ma
Janellis
Janelly
Janely
Janelys
Janenicole
Janese
Janesey
Janeshia
Janeta
Janete
Janett
Janetta
Janey
Jani
Jania
Janica
Janicce
Janick
Janicka
Janieasha
Janiece
Janiel
Janielle
Janiesa
Janik
Janika
Janilee
Janille
Janina
Janique
Janise
Janisha
Janissa
Janita
Janitza
Janive
Janizzette
Janjay
Janka
Jankea
Jannah
Jannartha
Janneke
Jannel
Jannell
Jannelle
Jannellies
Jannet
Janneth
Jannette
Jannie
Janniece
Jannifer
Jannika
Jannike
Jannina
Jannis
Jannisha
Janny
Jannyne
Janon
Janora
Janour
Jansen
Jansi
Janssen
Jante
Jantinee
Jantony
Janu
January
Janue
Janus
Jany
Janyce
Janyll
Janyn
Janyne
Japera
Japhneia
Jaqkela
Jaqua
Jaquaia
Jaquala
Jaquandra
Jaquane
Jaquanna
Jaquay
Jaquel
Jaquelin
Jaquelle
Jaquelyn
Jaquetta
Jaquice
Jaquiese
Jaquilla
Jaquin
Jaquina
Jaquinda
Jaquinta

Jaquita
Jaquline
Jaqulynne
Jaquorya
Jaquoya
Jaqutia
Jara
Jarah
Jaralyn
Jarcelyn
Jardan
Jardine
Jaree
Jarelis
Jarell
Jarelle
Jaren
Jarene
Jari
Jaria
Jariar
Jarica
Jarina
Jarita
Jaritza
Jarixa
Jarlene
Jarllyn
Jarneà
Jarnicia
Jarnita
Jarrika
Jarrine
Jarushia
Jarvé
Jaryn
Jarynet
Jasaline
Jasamane
Jasamine
Jasan
Jasbina
Jasbrine
Jasdeep
Jaselyn
Jasey
Jashae
Jashala
Jashona
Jashonte
Jasie
Jasime
Jasjeet
Jasjit
Jaskia
Jaskiran
Jaskirat
Jasleen
Jasline
Jasma
Jasmain
Jasmaine
Jasman
Jasme
Jasmeen
Jasmeet
Jasmen
Jasmene
Jasmina
Jasmira
Jasmit
Jasmyn
Jasmyne
Jasna
Jasneet
Jasolin
Jason
Jasonya
Jaspar
Jasparit
Jasper
Jassary
Jassenya
Jassi
Jassica
Jassie
Jassma
Jassmine
Jassy
Jasveen
Jasvinder
Jaswinder
Jatalia
Jatanna
Jatanya
Jatara
Jataria
Jatarra
Jatea
Jatia
Jatiame
Jatoiya
Jatori
Jatoria
Jauniece
Jaunkita
Jaunna
Jauquette
Jauquiline
Jauveone
Javacia
Javairia
Javana
Javanna
Javda
Javeeka
Javel
[illegible]
Ja[illegible]
Ja[illegible]
Jav[illegible]
Javon
Javonda
Javonna
Javonne
Javonya
Jawairiya
Jawana
Jawanna
Jawn
Jaya
Jayanthi
Jayanti
Jaycee
Jaycelyn
Jaycey
Jaycie
Jayda
Jayde
Jaydee
Jaydelle
Jaydesha
Jaydi
Jaye
Jayelene
Jaykelia
Jayla
Jaylah
Jaylan
Jayleana
Jaylee
Jayleen
Jaylyn
Jaylynn
Jaymee
Jaymee-Leigh

Jaymes
Jaymi
Jaymi-Lee
Jaymie-Ann
Jaymie-Lynne
Jaymini
Jayml
Jaymne
Jayn
Jaynae
Jaynee
Jaynie
Jaynita
Jaynne
Jayran
Jayzin
Jazelle
Jazleen
Jazlyn
Jazlynn
Jazmen
Jazminjune
Jazminn
Jazmone
Jazmyn
Jazmyne
Jazmyné
Jazsmine
Jazsmyne
Jazze
Jazzel
Jazzele
Jazzimine
Jazzlin
Jazzlyn
Jazzma
Jazzman
Jazzmin
Jazzmine
Jazzmon
Jazzmyn
Jazzy
Jeagan
Jealande
Jean-Ann
Jean-Christy
Jean-Ely
Jean-Marie
Jeanalise
Jeanann
Jeancie
Jeane
Jeaneane
Jeaneen
Jeaneia
Jeanell
Jeanelle
Jeanene
Jeanete
Jeanetta
Jeaneva
Jeania
Jeanide
Jeaninne
Jeanita
Jeanitra
Jeanitta
Jeanmarie
Jeannalyn
Jeanné
Jeanne-Marie
Jeannett
Jeannetta
Jeanney
Jeannie Marie
Jeannik
Jeannina
Jeannita
Jeannot
Jeanny
Jeantelle
Jeany
Jeauline
Jecely
Jee
Jeena
Jeesica
Jeevitha
Jeffrey
Jehan
Jehann
Jehn-Ai
Jehna
Jehnese
Jeimara
Jekina
Jekira
Jelaina
Jelaine
Jelea
Jeleann
Jeleis
Jelena
Jelissa
Jem
Jemaica
Jemece
Jemelia
Jemesha
Jemi
Jemia
Jemika
Jemila
Jemima
Jemimah
Jemma
Jemyka
Jen
Jena-Lee
Jenacee
Jenaé
Jenafer
Jenah
Jenai
Jenal
Jenalee
Jenaleigh
Jenalieg
Jenalle
Jenan
Jenavy
Jenay
Jendi
Jendisa
Jene
Jenea
Jenean
Jeneanne
Jenee
Jeneen
Jenees
Jeneffer
Jeneice
Jeneka
Jenel
Jenelea
Jenell
Jenelle-Lara
Jenelly
Jenely
Jenene
Jenesia
Jenesis
Jenessa
Jenesse
Jenet

Jenetta
Jenette
Jenettie
Jeneva
Jeneviev
Jenevieve
Jeni
Jeni-Lee
Jenia
Jenica
Jenice
Jenicia
Jenicka
Jeniece
Jenifer-Nicole
Jeniffier
Jenifre
Jenika
Jenille
Jenilyn
Jenin
Jenines
Jenipher
Jeniqua
Jenique
Jenis
Jenise
Jenisha
Jenisly
Jenissa
Jenita
Jenna Christine
Jenna-Celeste
Jenna-D
Jenna-Dee
Jenna-Lea
Jenna-Lee
Jenna-Lyn
Jenna-Lynn
Jenna-Marie
Jenna-May
Jenna-Rae
Jennae
Jennafre
Jennah
Jennaka
Jennalaine
Jennalea
Jennalee
Jennalynn
Jennarae
Jennat
Jennawave
Jennawaye
Jennay
Jennaya
Jenne
Jenné
Jenneca
Jennee
Jennefer
Jenneffer
Jennel
Jennell
Jennelle
Jennely
Jennene
Jenner
Jennery
Jennesia
Jennet
Jennetta
Jenneve
Jennexis
Jenney
Jenni-Fer
Jenni-Leila
Jenni-Lynn
Jennia
Jennicke
Jennie Ann
Jenniele
Jennielee
Jennielle
Jennier
Jennifer Ann
Jennifer Joylen
Jennifer K
Jennifer Lee
Jennifer Marie
Jennifer Mary
Jennifer Patrici
Jennifer Rose
Jennifer-Amanda
Jennifer-Ann
Jennifer-Anne
Jennifer-Ashley
Jennifer-Jean
Jennifer-K
Jennifer-Lauren
Jennifer-Lee
Jennifer-Lori
Jennifer-Lynn
Jennifer-Lynne
Jennifer-Marlene
Jennifer-Rose
Jenniferanne
Jenniferleigh
Jenniferq
Jenniferr
Jennifeur
Jenniffe
Jenniffer
Jenniffier
Jennifier
Jennika
Jennilea
Jennilee
Jennilie
Jennilin
Jennilyn
Jennilynn
Jennine
Jenniphe
Jennipher
Jenniprim
Jennisa
Jennise
Jennisse
Jennita
Jennora
Jenntille
Jenny Marie
Jenny-Lee
Jenny-Lyn
Jenny-Lynn
Jennyfer
Jennylinn
Jennyne
Jensie
Jensine
Jensyn
Jentie
Jentra
Jentré
Jentri
Jentry
Jeny
Jenyce
Jenyfer
Jenyse
Jeorgi
Jepinder
Jequila
Jequita
Jera

Jerai
Jeralee
Jeralyn
Jeramia
Jeran
Jeree
Jereelyn
Jerel
Jerelyn
Jeremi
Jeremy
Jerenda
Jerhonda
Jeri Ann
Jeri-Ann
Jerian
Jerianne
Jerice
Jericha
Jericho
Jericka
Jerico
Jeriel
Jerika
Jerikay
Jerilee
Jerilenrose
Jerilynn
Jerima
Jerimî
Jerina
Jerinda
Jeris
Jerisha
Jerlaina
Jerlyn
Jermaine
Jerman
Jermasa
Jermecia
Jermia
Jermice
Jermicia
Jermika
Jermila
Jernice
Jerniette
Jeron
Jeronise
Jerra
Jerrece
Jerri-Ann
Jerri-Lynn
Jerriann
Jerricca
Jerrice
Jerrid
Jerrie
Jerrika
Jerrilee
Jerrilyn
Jerring
Jerritt
Jerry
Jerryn
Jersey
Jerusha
Jerylin
Jerzy
Jesabel
Jesaca
Jesalyn
Jesamy Jah'n
Jescenia
Jesenia
Jeserika
Jeseyria
Jesi
Jesicca
Jesie
Jesika
Jesilyn
Jesinie
Jesiree
Jesleen
Jeslin
Jesly
Jesmin
Jesni
Jess
Jessa
Jessa-Lyn
Jessa-Lynn
Jessaca
Jessah
Jessaira
Jessalynn
Jessamie
Jessamyn
Jessanne
Jessara
Jessca
Jesscia
Jessé
Jesse-Lee
Jesse-Lyn
Jessee
Jesselyn
Jesselynn
Jessencia
Jessey
Jesshaye
Jesshia
Jessi-Lee
Jessi-Lynn
Jessi-Ma
Jessia
Jessica Amieliend
Jessica Ashley
Jessica Clare
Jessica Da Costa
Jessica Diane
Jessica Ly
Jessica May
Jessica-Ann
Jessica-Anne
Jessica-Bohee
Jessica-Caroline
Jessica-Dawn
Jessica-Jean
Jessica-Lauren
Jessica-Leah
Jessica-Lee
Jessica-Leigh
Jessica-Lynn
Jessica-Lynne
Jessica-Marie
Jessica-Rae
Jessica-Rhae
Jessica-Therese
Jessicalynn
Jessicca
Jessicia
Jessicka
Jessidee
Jessie-Lee
Jessie-Lynn
Jessie-Rae
Jessieann
Jessieca
Jessilee
Jessilyn
Jessilynn
Jessimar
Jessiqa

Jessiqua
Jessire
Jessiya
Jesslyn
Jesstyne
Jessy
Jessyca
Jessye
Jessyica
Jessyka
Jessynda
Jestine
Jestle
Jestyn
Jesuis
Jesula
Jesusita
Jetaime
Jeton
Jetta
Jettie
Jeunesse
Jeunyde
Jeva
Jevette
Jevon
Jevonie
Jewel
Jewell
Jewelle
Jewellee
Jexsenia
Jez
Jezabel
Jezami
Jezeble
Jezel
Jezele
Jezell
Jezika
Jezreal
Jezzelin
Jha-Nata
Jhamelia
Jhana
Jhancie
Jhanelle
Jhaniqua
Jhannaria
Jhannell-Lori
Jharin
Jhauntel
Jhenique
Jhenna
Jheri
Jheria
Jherria
Jhilma
Jhonna
Jhonte
Jhordan
Jiana
Jianina
Jianna
Jicelia
Jiely
Jigna
Jihan
Jihane
Jikeeta
Jikeka
Jil
Jilaine
Jilda
Jilian
Jiliann
Jilianna
Jilianne
Jilienne
Jiline
Jilisa
Jillaine
Jillana
Jillane
Jillayne
Jilleash
Jilleen
Jillene
Jillenne
Jilliane
Jilliann
Jillianne
Jillie
Jillienne
Jillion
Jillissa
Jilliyn
Jilynn
Jimae
Jimaria
Jimella
Jimella-Tashio
Jimena
Jimetrice
Jimi
Jimilonda
Jimisha
Jimiyah
Jimmeka
Jimmet
Jimmicia
Jimmie
Jimmy
Jimysha
Jina
Jinae
Jinan
Jinavisa
Jinda
Jinell
Jinelle
Jinessa
Jinette
Jinewa
Jinger
Jingle
Jingwen
Jinhwa
Jinicka
Jinna
Jinnalee
Jinney
Jinnie
Jinny
Jinohn
Jisele
Jishena
Jissele
Jitana
Jitashio
Jiyun
Jkina
Jky
Jmelvonna
Jo Ann
Jo Anna
Jo Anne
Jo Dee
Jo Ell
Jo Ellen
Jo Hanna
Jo Marie
Jo Quona
Jo Tasha
Jo'shanda
Jo-Ana

Jo-Anie
Jo-Ann
Jo-Anna
Jo-Anne
Jo-Annie
Jo-Dell
Jo-Elle
Jo-Ellen
Jo-Leah
Jo-Lee
Jo-Lene
Jo-Lyen
Joahanne
Joahnin
Joahnna
Joana
Joana Da Costa
Joana Marie
Joananne
Joandra
Joane
Joaneil
Joanelle
Joangie
Joani
Joanie Marie C
Joanmarie
Joannah
Joannanette
Joannel
Joannie
Joannxe
Joany
Joaris
Joayn
Jobeth
Jobina
Jobita
Jobrina
Jocarra
Jocavett
Jocelin
Joceline
Jocelle
Jocelynn
Jocelynne
Joci
Jocia
Jocinta
Joclyn
Joconda
Jocqueline
Jodee
Jodele
Jodene
Jodeva
Jodi Ann
Jodi Anne
Jodi Mae
Jodi Winifred
Jodi-Ann
Jodi-Lee
Jodi-Lynn
Jodi-Mae
Jodi-Marie
Jodianne
Jodilynn
Jodine
Jody Ann
Joe
Joe-Anne
Joeana
Joeane
Joeanna
Joeanne
Joei Lynna
Joeina
Joelana
Joelee
Joeleen
Joelene
Joeli
Joeline
Joell
Joella
Joèlle
Joellen
Joely
Joelyn
Joelyne
Joeneena
Joenie
Joesett
Joesetta
Joesphine
Joetta
Joette
Joey
Joezette
Johanan
Johannah
Johanne
Johannie
Joharah
Johashis
Johna
Johnathan
Johnda
Johneatha
Johnecia
Johnel
Johnele
Johnell
Johnelle
Johnesha
Johnetra
Johnetta
Johnette Latrice
Johni
Johnica
Johnie
Johnique
Johnisha
Johnishi
Johnita
Johnittia
Johnnetta
Johnnette
Johnnie
Johnnise
Johnny
Johnquia
Johnquita
Johonna
Johvanne
Joi
Joia
Joice
Joicy
Joie
Joielle
Joinesse
Joismaly
Jojuana
Jokeirra
Jokho Roon
Jolaine
Jolan
Jolana
Jolanda
Jolande
Jolander
Jolane
Jolanna
Jolanta
Jolayne

Jolé
Jolea
Jolean
Joleane
Jolee
Joleigh
Jolena
Jolène
Jolenna
Joley
Joli
Joliba
Jolibeth
Jolie
Joliene
Jolin
Jolina
Jolinda
Jolissaint
Jolleane
Jolleen
Jollie
Jolnar
Jolyn
Jolyne
Jolynn
Jolynne
Jomana
Jomarie
Jomayra
Jomeka
Jometa
Jona
Jonachi
Jonae
Jonah
Jonai
Jonalyn
Jonann
Jonasia
Jonathan
Joncie
Jonda
Jondell
Jondrea
Jone
Joneeka
Joneen
Joneika
Joneisha
Jonel
Jonell
Jonella
Jonetta
Jonette
Joni-Lee
Jonica
Jonie
Jonielee
Jonika
Jonina
Joniqua
Jonique
Jonisha
Jonita
Jonlyn
Jonmalet
Jonmekya
Jonmeliah
Jonmisha
Jonnell
Jonnette
Jonnica
Jonnie
Jonnie-Lyn
Jonnika
Jonnita
Jonquelo
Jonquila
Jonsie
Jonszhell
Jonta
Jontae
Jontaé
Jontaya
Jontece
Jontel
Jontell
Jontelle
Jontia
Jontila
Jontrice
Jontue
Jonyelle
Jonyssa
Joo
Joquala
Joquela
Joquita
Jorae
Joraven
Jorcelyn
Jordaeshia
Jordain
Jordanae
Jordanashleigh
Jordane
Jordann
Jordanne
Jorden
Jordenne
Jordi
Jordin
Jordon
Jordonna
Jordyn
Jordyne
Joree
Joregne
Jorelis
Jorganna
Jori
Jori-Ann
Jorian
Jorianna
Jorie
Jorin
Jorina
Jorine
Jorita
Jorja
Joronica
Jory
Josabet
Josalon
Josalyn
Josalynn
Josanna
Josanne
Josaphine
Joscelyn
Jose
Josee-Anne
Josee-Lynn
Josefa
Josefina
Josefine
Joseha
Josei
Joseline
Joselle
Joseph
Josephen
Josephin
Josephina
Josette

Josetts
Josey
Josha
Joshalin
Joshalynn
Joshana
Joshelle
Joshetta
Joshlene
Joshlin
Joshlyn
Joshsalin
Joshua
Joshyln
Josi
Josiane
Josianne
Josie Joy
Josie-Marie
Josielina
Josilyn
Josina
Josipa
Joslin
Josline
Joslynn
Joslynne
Joslyz
Josmerie
Josna
Josphine
Joss
Jossada
Jossalyn
Josselyn
Josselynne
Jossie
Josslyn
Jostina
Josue
Josy
Josyln
Jotara
Joti
Joulie
Joumana
Jounie
Jourdan
Journey
Journie
Jouvon
Jova Lee
Jovado
Joval
Jovan
Jovana
Jovanie
Jovanna
Joveda
Jovena
Jovian
Jovida
Jovita
Jovon
Jovonda
Jovonia
Jovonna
Jovonne
Jowanna
Jowell
Joy Anna
Joy Lynne
Joy-El
Joy-Kay
Joy-Lynn
Joya
Joyann
Joyanna
Joyanne
Joycelyn
Joycelynn
Joye
Joyeeta
Joyelle
Joyhanna
Joyia
Joyl
Joyleen
Joylene
Joylin
Joylyn
Joylynn
Joynee
Joyneika
Joysel
Joytika
Joytonia
Joyvina
Jozee
Jozette
Juànna
Ju'neka
Jua
Juana
Juana Marie
Juandalyn
Juaneice
Juanequà
Juanisha
Juanquail
Juanquill
Juanquinetta
Juawana
Jubie
Juchita
Judana
Jude
Judelkys
Judine
Judishea
Judit
Judite
Judith Elizabeth
Judith-Louise
Judline
Judyann
Judyanna
Judyta
Jue Cindar
Juel
Julaine
Julayne
Jule
Juleana
Julee
Juleen
Juleia
Juleidy
Julene
Jules
Julet
Juli
Juli-Ann
Julia Beth
Julia Enid
Julia-Yveline
Juliaana
Juliaetta
Julian
Julianda
Julica
Julie Ann
Julie Anna
Julie Anne
Julie-Ann
Julie-Anne

Julie-Lyn
Julie-Mae
Julieann
Julieanna
Julieanne
Juliemil
Julien
Juliene
Julienne
Julija
Julina
Julisa
Julise
Julissa
Julixa
Julleen
Jullena
Jullet
Jullian
Jullianna
Jullie
July
Julyel
Jumana
Jumanji
Jumily
Jun
Juna
Junchun
Junechae
Junell
Junelle
Junette
Junia
Junie
Juniet
Junlee
Junuen
Juranne
Jurelle
Jurema
Juretta
Jusbeer
Juselle
Jussan
Justa
Justayne
Juste
Justeen
Justene
Justice
Justicia
Justin
Justinna
Justy
Justyna
Justyne
Juwanda
Juwita
Jyllian
Jyme
Jymeela
Jyna
Jynelle
Jynice
Jyntri
Jyoti
Jyssica
Jyvonda

K

K C
K'lyn
K-Leigh
K.c.
Ka
Ka Lynne
Ka Tara
Ka Teira
Ka Tina
Kàshay
Kaala
Kaalyn
Kaamil
Kaara
Kaari
Kaarina
Kabria
Kabrina
Kabryna
Kace
Kacee
Kacelyn
Kachia
Kachina
Kachine
Kachiri
Kachonda
Kacia
Kacindra
Kacindy
Kacye
Kadee
Kadeen
Kadeidra
Kadeisha
Kadeja
Kaden
Kadena
Kadesha
Kadeshia
Kadey
Kadi
Kadian
Kadie
Kadieann
Kadieros
Kadreana
Kae
Kaedi
Kael
Kaela-Dawn
Kaelacey
Kaelah
Kaelea
Kaelee
Kaeleen
Kaeleigh
Kaelen
Kaelena
Kaeley
Kaeli
Kaelie
Kaelin
Kaelly
Kaely
Kaelynn
Kaesha
Kaeti
Kaetlin
Kaetlyn
Kaffee
Kagiso
Kagney
Kagni
Kahadija
Kahalia
Kahandi
Kahdejah
Kahdijah
Kahea
Kahla
Kahlae
Kahle

Kahlea
Kahlei
Kahley
Kahlia
Kahlil
Kahlin
Kahmeise
Kahra-Lyn
Kahsaandra
Kai
Kaia
Kaiala
Kaidi
Kaieyesha
Kaija
Kailagh
Kailah
Kailani
Kaile
Kaile-Anne
Kaileen
Kailei
Kaileigh
Kailen
Kaili
Kailie
Kailin
Kailla
Kaillie
Kaily
Kailye
Kailyn
Kailynn
Kaira
Kairi
Kairra
Kaisa
Kaisha
Kaishawn
Kaissie
Kaite
Kaiti-Jo
Kaitia
Kaitisha
Kaitlan
Kaitland
Kaitlen
Kaitlind
Kaitlinn
Kaitlyn-Rae
Kaitlynne
Kaitrina
Kaity
Kaity-Elyse
Kaiya
Kaj
Kaja
Kajal
Kajel
Kajsa
Kajuan
Kajuana
Kalae
Kalah
Kalahn
Kalai
Kalan
Kalana
Kalani
Kalcy
Kalea
Kalean
Kaleatak
Kaleen
Kalei
Kaleigha
Kaleisha
Kalen
Kalena
Kalene
Kalere
Kalesha
Kaleshia
Kalesia
Kalesta
Kaleyne
Kalîi
Kalia
Kalia Amani
Kalicea
Kalida
Kaliegh
Kalika
Kalima
Kalimah
Kalin
Kalina
Kalinda
Kalinna
Kaliopi
Kalisa
Kalisha
Kalishandra
Kalissa
Kalisse
Kalista
Kalla
Kallamity
Kallan
Kalle
Kallee
Kallen
Kallilah Shunque
Kallipe
Kallison
Kallista
Kally
Kallyn
Kalmia
Kalolaina
Kalonda
Kalondra
Kalsey
Kalteke
Kalunga
Kalvilena
Kalvin
Kalvinisha
Kaly
Kalyen
Kalyna
Kalynda
Kalynn
Kalysa
Kama
Kamae
Kamala
Kamalah
Kamalie
Kamaljit
Kamany
Kamara
Kamari
Kamaria
Kamarie
Kamber
Kamberly
Kambria
Kambriall
Kambrie
Kambriea
Kambry
Kameela
Kameelah
Kameka

Kameko
Kamela
Kamella
Kamellia
Kameo
Kamerin
Kameron
Kamesha
Kameshia
Kamesia
Kamey
Kamia
Kamiaalma
Kamiana
Kamie
Kamika
Kamil
Kamila
Kamilah
Kamilia
Kamilie
Kamilla
Kamille
Kamillia
Kamini
Kaminia
Kamira
Kamisha
Kamishia
Kamita
Kamleesh
Kammeron
Kammie
Kammy
Kamren
Kamrica
Kamrie
Kamron
Kamryn
Kamshia
Kamy
Kamyron
Kana
Kanae
Kanakathurka
Kanako
Kanan
Kanasha
Kanathy
Kanatineshon
Kanaya
Kanbao
Kanchan
Kanda
Kandalsiha
Kandance
Kandas
Kandess
Kandhi
Kandi
Kandia
Kandie
Kandies
Kandin
Kandirae
Kandise
Kandislee
Kandle
Kandra
Kandus
Kandy
Kandyce
Kandyse
Kaneasha
Kaneesha
Kaneisha
Kanesha
Kaneshia
Kanetta
Kanhnilla
Kanice
Kaniesha
Kanika
Kanisha
Kanishia
Kanita
Kanitha
Kanitra
Kanlyn
Kanna
Kanoy
Kansas
Kansis
Kantrel
Kantrice
Kanya
Kanynta
Kanza
Kaori
Kaori Alejandra
Kapiolani
Kapree
Kaprice
Kaprincess
Kaprisha
Kar
Kar-Man
Kara-Ann
Kara-Lea
Kara-Lee
Kara-Leigh
Kara-Lis
Kara-Lyn
Kara-Lynn
Karac
Karalee
Karaline
Karalyn
Karalyne-Patricia
Karalynn
Karalynne
Karamea
Karamee
Karamiea
Karamjit
Karan
Karandeep
Karanne
Karas
Karee
Kareé
Kareece
Kareema
Kareemah
Kareena
Kareisha
Karelee
Karelia
Karelle
Karem
Karema
Karen Ann
Karena
Karendeep
Karene
Karenjit
Karenlee
Karenna
Karennea
Karese
Karess
Karessa
Karesse
Karey
Kari Ane
Kari Lyn

Kari-Ann
Kari-Anne
Kari-Lyn
Kari-Lynn
Karia
Kariann
Karianne
Karica
Karice
Karicka
Karidi
Karien
Kariesha
Karilla
Karily
Karilyana
Karilyn
Karilynn
Karima
Karimah
Karime
Karin-Alycia
Karinda
Karindeep
Karinichole
Karinna
Karinne
Karintha
Karis
Karisa
Karisha
Karishma
Karisma
Karissima
Kariza
Karja
Karl
Karle
Karlea
Karleen
Karleigh
Karlen
Karlena
Karlenn
Karletta
Karli-Jo
Karlie-Michelle
Karlijn
Karlin
Karlina
Karling
Karlisha
Karlisia
Karlita
Karlitha
Karlla
Karlon
Karlyan
Karlye
Karlyn
Karlynn
Karma
Karman
Karmel
Karmela
Karmin
Karmonique
Karmoya
Karmyla
Karmyn
Karna
Karnesha
Karnisha
Karnissa
Karnit
Karnyta
Karnza
Karol
Karolann
Karolayna
Karolin
Karolina
Karoline
Karolynn
Karon
Karonia
Karra
Karrah
Karrah-Lauren
Karren
Karrena
Karrin
Karrina
Karrine
Karris
Karrisa
Karrissa
Karronda
Karry
Karryanne
Karryn
Karsa
Karsandra
Karsheena
Karss
Karsten
Karstin
Kartier
Kartika
Karvenina
Kary
Karyanne
Karyen
Karyl
Karylin
Karynda
Karyne
Karynel
Karynn
Karys
Karysa
Karyss
Kasa
Kasaaundra
Kasacha
Kasander
Kasandria
Kasani
Kasaundra
Kasci
Kasee
Kasey-Ann
Kasha
Kashae
Kashalene
Kashannon
Kashara
Kashawn
Kashawna
Kasheena
Kasheia
Kasheka
Kashema
Kashena
Kashia
Kashica
Kashiel
Kashina
Kashinda
Kashlie
Kashmear
Kashmia
Kashmira
Kashunna
Kasia
Kasidy

Kasinda
Kasmira
Kasondra
Kasone
Kasonya
Kasoundra
Kassadi
Kassandr
Kassandra-Elyse
Kassandre
Kassandré
Kassatria
Kassaundra
Kasse
Kassey
Kassia
Kassidee
Kassidi
Kassidie
Kassie-Lee
Kassiope
Kassiopiya
Kassondr
Kassondra
Kassy
Kastin
Kastle
Kastyn
Kasy
Kataceya
Katacha
Katalin
Katana
Katanna
Katara
Kataria
Katariin
Katarina
Kataruh
Kataryna
Katarzyn
Katarzyna
Katasha
Katassy
Kataun
Katayun
Katchaya
Katdie
Kate Lynn
Kate-Lynn
Kate-Lynne
Kateana
Katee
Kateé
Katee-Maree
Katelan
Kateland
Katelen
Katelind
Katelinn
Katelun
Kately
Katelyn Jean
Katelyn-Ann
Katelynd
Katelyne
Katelynne
Katera
Kateri
Kateria
Katerine
Katernia
Katerra
Katerri
Kateryna
Katesha
Kateshia
Katessa
Kathaleah
Kathaleen
Kathalena
Katharina
Katharyn
Kathe
Katheleen
Kathelina
Katheline
Kathena
Katherina
Katherine Anne
Katherine-Jean
Katherine-Margaret
Katherine-Maria
Katherine-Nicole
Kathern
Katheryne
Kathi
Kathia
Kathiana
Kathie
Kathijah
Kathleen Maria
Kathleen-Jo-Anne
Kathleena
Kathleene
Kathlena
Kathlene
Kathlene-Lee
Kathlin
Kathlynn
Kathneicela
Kathrein
Kathrene
Kathrin
Kathrina
Kathryn-Marie
Kathryn-Rose
Kathryna
Kathryne
Kathrynn
Kathrynne
Kathylee
Kathyn
Kathyrialy
Kathyrn
Kati Lynn
Kati-Jo
Katiana
Katibel
Katidja
Katie Elizabeth
Katie Jo
Katie Lynn
Katie Marie
Katie-Anne
Katie-Beth
Katie-Jo
Katie-Lynn
Katie-Lynne
Katie-Ma
Katie-Marie
Katieann
Katiera
Katiesha
Katilin
Katilyn
Katinia
Katinka
Katinna
Katir
Katira
Katiria
Katirra
Katisha

Katiusca
Katja
Katlain
Katland
Katlynd
Katlynn
Katlynne
Katony
Katonya
Katora
Katori
Katoria
Katosha
Katoya
Katra
Katracia
Katrece
Katreena
Katrelle
Katrena
Katresia
Katresse
Katria
Katriana
Katrica
Katrice
Katricia
Katriena
Katrijn
Katrila
Katrin
Katrina-Anne
Katrina-Lyn
Katrine
Katringa
Katrinia
Katrinka
Katriona
Katrise
Katrisha
Katryn
Katryna
Kattie
Kattiya
Kattrice
Kattryna
Katty
Katura
Katurah
Katuria
Katya
Katyana
Katyann
Katye
Katyia
Katylin
Katymae
Katyria
Kau
Kaula
Kaulona
Kaur
Kaurel
Kaurice
Kaurie
Kausarjahan
Kaveecia
Kavie
Kavina
Kavindra
Kavita
Kavitha
Kavonne
Kawaii
Kawan
Kawana
Kawania
Kawanica
Kawanis
Kawanna
Kawya
Kay Cee
Kay De
Kay Lisha
Kay-Dee
Kay-Leigh
Kaya
Kayana
Kayanta
Kayawna
Kayce
Kayci
Kaycie
Kayde
Kaydee
Kaydeina
Kaydi
Kaye
Kaye Dee Lee
Kayelene
Kayelyn
Kayhla
Kayhlin
Kayia
Kayie
Kayion
Kayko
Kayla-Amanda
Kayla-Amber
Kayla-Lyn
Kayla-Lynn
Kaylah
Kaylan
Kaylanne
Kaylea
Kayleah
Kaylei
Kaylen
Kaylena
Kayler
Kaylha
Kayli
Kaylia
Kaylie-Anne
Kaylie-Marie
Kayliegh
Kaylieh
Kaylla
Kayln
Kaylon
Kayly
Kaylynn
Kaylynne
Kayona
Kayondra
Kayra
Kayress
Kayse
Kaysea
Kaysee
Kaysen
Kaysha
Kayshia
Kaysie
Kayte
Kaytee
Kayti
Kaytie
Kaytlyn
Kaytron
Kaz
Kazandra
Kazeray
Kazia
Kazuko
Kc

Kcee
Kdie
Ke Ala O Ka
Ke Andra
Ke Asha
Ke Lynda
Ke Yana
Kéell
Kéyonna
Kea
Keacha
Keagan
Keah
Keaira
Keairra
Keairrah
Keala
Kealey
Keali
Keallie
Keally
Kealy
Kealyn
Keamoni
Keana
Keandra
Keandrea
Keanna
Keannette
Kearah
Kearby
Kearia
Kearney
Kearra
Kearsa
Kearsten
Kearstie
Kearstin
Keary
Keasha
Keathann
Keaton
Keaty
Keaundra
Keaunna
Kebra
Kebrasha
Kechaundra
Kechelle
Kechia
Kecia
Kedelim
Kedly
Kedna
Keea
Keeanna
Keebra
Keegan
Keeghan
Keeisha
Keela
Keelan
Keeleigh
Keeli
Keelie
Keelin
Keely-Jo
Keenan
Keenya
Keeosha
Keera
Keerthika
Keesha
Keeshond
Keesje
Keetara
Keetly
Keeva
Keewanda
Keeyetta
Kefira
Kefon
Kegan
Kehara
Kehau
Kei
Keiana
Keiandrea
Keiannah
Keiara
Keiartra
Keicha
Keichelle
Keidri
Keiera
Keierra
Keigan
Keighen
Keighla
Keighlagh
Keikanne
Keiko
Keila
Keilah
Keilan
Keilani
Keilee
Keileigh
Keilonda
Keily
Keimari
Keimocia
Keimonty
Keina
Keion
Keionda
Keionna
Keiosha
Keir
Keiren
Keiria
Keirora
Keirra
Keirrià
Keirsten
Keirsten Lee
Keisa
Keisha-Marie
Keishae
Keishah
Keishara
Keishaun
Keishauna
Keishawn
Keishia
Keishuna
Keitcha
Keitha
Keitra
Keitriana
Keivonna
Keiynna
Kejina
Kejuana
Kekesha
Kela
Kelby
Kelcey
Kelci
Kelcie
Kelcy
Kelda
Keldi
Keldyn
Keleigh
Kelia

Kelia-Marie
Keliana
Kelie
Kelilah
Kelilyn
Kelin
Kelise
Kelisha
Kelita
Kelitha
Kella
Kellan
Kellar
Kelle
Kellee
Kelleen
Kelleigh
Kellen
Kellene
Kelli Ann
Kelli Anne
Kelli-Ann
Kellianne
Kellin
Kellina
Kelline
Kellisha
Kelloryn
Kellsey
Kellsie
Kellsy
Kellvonyia
Kelly-Ann
Kelly-Anne
Kelly-Lee
Kelly-Louise
Kelly-Lynn
Kellyann
Kellyce
Kellyjo
Kellynie
Kellys
Kelsay
Kelsee
Kelsei
Kelsey-Kathleen
Kelsey-Lee
Kelsiann
Kelsye
Kelti
Keltie
Keltie-Lynne
Kelty
Kelva
Kelvona
Kelyn
Kelynne
Kemandra
Kemary
Kemberly
Kembrie
Kemeonta
Kemesha
Kemet
Kemia
Kemish
Kemny
Kena
Kenalee
Kenan
Kenanna
Kenara
Kenda
Kendahl
Kendalla
Kendalle
Kendel
Kendele
Kendell
Kendelle
Kendera
Kendia
Kendice
Kendis
Kendl
Kendra-Lee
Kendra-Leigh
Kendrah
Kendralla
Kendrea
Kendri
Kendria
Kendrick
Kendrie
Kendrya
Kendyl
Kendyle
Kendyll
Keneasha
Kenecia
Keneisha
Keneka
Kenesha
Keneshia
Kenetra
Kenetta
Kengal
Keni
Kenia
Kenik
Kenisha
Kenita
Kenize
Kenjele
Kenley
Kennah
Kennara
Kenndra
Kenneather
Kennedie
Kennedy
Kennesha
Kenneshia
Kenneth
Kennetha
Kennethea
Kennetta
Kenni
Venniesha
Kennifer
Kennisha
Kennitra
Kenoinda
Kenokia
Kenon
Kenqueta
Kensey
Kenshanetha
Kenshia
Kensi
Kensie
Kensta
Kentae
Kentaro
Kenten
Kenteria
Kentilya
Kentoyia
Kentra
Kentreia
Kentrel
Kentrell
Kentucka
Kentura
Kentyata
Kenuana

Kenyada
Kenyana
Kenyarda
Kenyarta
Kenyata
Kenyatta
Kenyattaantinav
Kenyeal
Kenyetta
Kenyo
Kenyona
Kenyonna
Kenyota
Kenythia
Kenzi
Kenzy
Keo Rea
Keoisha
Keokesey
Keokia
Keola
Keon
Keona
Keondra
Keonea
Keonia
Keonna
Keophokham
Keosha
Keoyma
Keraly
Kerbie
Kerby
Kereishah
Kereka
Kerensa
Kerenza
Kerey
Keri Ann
Keri-Ann
Keri-Anne
Keri-Beth
Keri-Dawn
Keri-Iynn
Keri-Lee
Keri-Lyn
Keri-Lynn
Keria
Kerian
Keriann
Kerianne
Keriayn
Kerie
Kerilee
Kerilyn
Kerilynn
Kerin
Kerina
Keris
Kerisa
Kerissa
Keristen
Kerith
Kerline
Kerlyn
Kerlyne
Kernita
Kerra
Kerrel
Kerri Samant
Kerri-Ann
Kerri-Anne
Kerri-Lee
Kerri-Lyn
Kerri-Lynn
Kerri-Lynne
Kerri-Michelle
Kerria
Kerriann
Kerrianne
Kerricka
Kerrie Christin
Kerrieal
Kerrilee
Kerrilyn
Kerrin
Kerrine
Kerris
Kerrisa
Kerrissa
Kerrlka
Kerry-Ann
Kerryann
Kersha
Kershaw
Kershra
Kersten
Kerstin
Kerston
Kersty
Kerstyn
Kertina
Kertreeka
Kertrina
Kery
Kerye
Kerys
Kerzdenn
Kesa
Kesandra
Keschia
Keshaana
Keshandra
Keshawn
Keshawna
Keshayla
Keshisa
Keshlyn
Keshondra
Keshonna
Kesi
Kesia
Kesley
Keslie
Keslyn
Keslynn
Kess
Kess-Sandra
Kessa
Kessey
Kessi
Kessia
Kester
Kestrel
Kesun
Ketere
Keteria
Keterine
Ketha
Ketia
Ketisha
Ketleine
Ketlin
Ketmanee
Ketmany
Ketonya
Ketra
Ketrial
Ketsia
Kettelie
Ketteline
Kettia
Ketty
Ketura
Keturah
Kety

Keuandea
Keva
Kevan
Keveannasha
Keverynne
Kevi
Kevida
Kevilin
Kevin
Kevina
Kevinanita
Kevinique
Kevisia
Kevleen
Kevlynn
Kevone
Kevonna
Kevyn
Kewanna
Keya
Keyànna
Keyah
Keyaira
Keyairra
Keyana
Keyanna
Keyarah
Keyasha
Keyata
Keyatta
Keyaun
Keyauna
Keyera
Keyetta
Keyla
Keylallare
Keyle
Keyleigh
Keyli
Keynetta
Keynna
Keyocko
Keyoina
Keyoisha
Keyona
Keyonda
Keyondra
Keyonia
Keyonna
Keyonndra
Keyonnie
Keyontae
Keyosha
Keyoudra
Keyousha
Keyra
Keyronda
Keysala
Keysha
Keysharia
Keyshonda
Keyshondra
Keytin
Keyuana
Keyunna
Keyvette
Keywanda
Keyyana
Kezia
Keziah
Khacy
Khadeeja
Khadeirdre
Khadeja
Khadejah
Khadejha
Khadija
Khahifa
Khaki
Khala
Khaleedah
Khaleil
Khaley
Khali
Khalia
Khalika
Khalila
Khalilah
Khalillah
Khalish
Khambrel
Khambri
Khamphan
Khandace
Khandi
Khandice
Khanhnge
Khanoni
Khara
Kharingt
Kharisma
Kharla
Kharman
Kharyssa
Khatija
Khatira
Khatrina
Khawla
Khaydra
Khayla
Khaylae
Khema
Khendra
Kheondra
Khera
Kherstin
Khesha
Khiara
Khierstyn
Khierta
Khinna
Khioanna
Khira
Khloé
Khlood
Khollah
Kholood
Khom
Khoral
Khrisandra
Khrishawna
Khrishia
Khrista
Khristal
Khristanna
Khristen
Khristian
Khristie
Khristin
Khristina
Khristine
Khristy
Khrysta
Khrystale
Khrysten
Khrystianne
Khrystle
Khrystyna
Khushbu
Khyber
Khyla
Ki
Kiaalicia
Kiah
Kiaha
Kiaira

Kiajuana
Kialani
Kiameshia
Kiami
Kiandra
Kianicole
Kianie
Kianna
Kiantae
Kiante
Kiantela
Kianti
Kiara-Patrice
Kiaria
Kiaro
Kiarra
Kiasha
Kiashia
Kiauna
Kiaundra
Kiauntae
Kiawanna
Kiayis
Kideana
Kieanna
Kiearea
Kiela
Kielce
Kiele
Kieley
Kielly
Kiely
Kielyn
Kielynneé
Kieonta
Kieosha
Kieraire
Kieran
Kierann
Kierea
Kiereese
Kieri
Kierin
Kierria
Kierstan
Kierstin
Kierston
Kierstyn
Kiesha
Kieshla
Kievia
Kieya
Kifah
Kiffani
Kiffin
Kiffini
Kifi
Kigan
Kiia
Kiira
Kiiran
Kiirsten
Kijahfha
Kijanda
Kijhana
Kijonna
Kiki
Kikora
Kila
Kilby
Kilden
Kile
Kilea
Kilee
Kileen
Kilina
Killishandra
Killoran
Kilynn
Kim Anh
Kim Loan
Kim-Chi
Kim-Hoa
Kim-Susan
Kimaya
Kimball
Kimbaly
Kimbela
Kimbelyn
Kimberely
Kimberle
Kimberlea
Kimberlei
Kimberleigh
Kimberleta
Kimberli
Kimberly Ann
Kimberly Diane
Kimberly Jane
Kimberly Nicole
Kimberly-Ann
Kimberly-Anne
Kimberly-Elizabeth
Kimberly-Star
Kimberlye
Kimberlyn
Kimberlynn
Kimberlynne
Kimbery
Kimbra
Kimbre
Kimbreley
Kimbrelinda
Kimbria
Kimchi
Kimdria
Kimea
Kimeko
Kimeley
Kimera
Kimerberlyanne
Kimery
Kimesha
Kimetha
Kimi
Kimia
Kimika
Kimiko
Kimle
Kimme
Kimmie
Kimona
Kimothy
Kimpreet
Kimra
Kimver
Kimy
Kimyatta
Kimyetta
Kimyuara
Kina
Kinda
Kindal
Kindale
Kindall
Kindi
Kindle
Kindsey
Kinesha
Kinga
Kingdra
Kingkham
Kingsley
Kinisha
Kinleigh

Kinley
Kinnetra
Kinny
Kinsie
Kinsley
Kinya
Kinyada
Kinyata
Kinyona
Kinyorri
Kinyuana
Kinzie
Kiona
Kionia
Kionna
Kionne
Kiosha
Kiosta
Kira Marie
Kira-Lee
Kira-Lynn
Kiralae
Kiraleigh
Kiran-Jyot
Kiran-Preet
Kirandeep
Kiranjot
Kiranpreet
Kiranveer
Kirat
Kirbi
Kirbie
Kirbie Sabrina
Kirchele
Kiree
Kireen
Kiren
Kirendeep
Kirenia
Kirenpreet
Kiress
Kiretta
Kiri
Kiria
Kiriakoula
Kirin
Kirn
Kirnjeet
Kirrah
Kirsha
Kirsi
Kirssan
Kirssy
Kirstan
Kirsteen
Kirsti
Kirstian
Kirstie
Kirstina
Kirsty
Kirstyn
Kirti
Kirtisha
Kisa
Kisaana
Kisani
Kisca
Kishandra
Kishaverdine
Kishori
Kismet
Kissie
Kista
Kistea
Kisti
Kit
Kit-Yee
Kita
Kitina
Kitna Rone
Kitrina
Kitsel
Kittie
Kitty
Kiwàna
Kiwana
Kiwanis
Kiyana
Kiyaniah
Kiyo
Kiyoko
Kiyomi
Kiyomia
Kiyosha
Kiza
Kizzi
Kizzie
Kizzy
Kjelsie
Kjersten
Kjersti
Kjerstin
Kladeh
Klana
Klancy
Klara
Klaralee
Klarika
Klarisa
Klarise
Klarissa
Klarrisa
Klary
Klaudija
Klaundreia
Kleo
Kleresa
Klicia
Klinque
Klista
Kloe
Kluane
Klyse
Knanh Linh
Knashena
Knea
Kneessa
Knesia
Knessa
Kniya
Knshanaha
Koa
Koah
Kobi
Kodi
Kodi-Lyn
Kodie
Kody
Koedi
Koelli
Kohonah
Kohrine
Kojuana
Kokarea
Kolay
Kolbie
Kolby
Kolette
Koli
Kolina
Kolyn
Komal
Konane
Koni
Konia
Konishia

Konnie
Konny
Konstadina
Konstance
Konstantina
Kookie
Koontida
Kora
Koral
Koralie
Koran
Kordria
Koree
Koreen
Koreena
Korelle
Koren
Korena
Korenn
Korey
Kori-Lynn
Koriday
Korie
Korin
Korina
Korine
Korinna
Korinne
Kormichia
Kornelia
Korrell
Korri
Korria
Korrie
Korrin
Korrina
Korrine
Korrinne
Kortnay
Kortnee
Kortni
Kortnie
Kortny
Kory
Koryn
Korynne
Kosasi
Kosha
Koshia
Kostadina
Kostandina-Dina
Kotera
Koundienetia
Kourtnee
Kourtnee-Louise
Kourtni
Kourtny
Kourtynie
Koya
Kraesly
Kratain
Kratina
Kratrina
Kraystaly
Kreisten
Krenda
Krenshentond
Kresandra
Kresence
Kresenda
Kreshia
Kreshonda
Krestlyn
Kreszentia
Krigina
Krigles
Krina
Kris
Krisa
Krisanda
Krisandra
Krisann
Kriscelda
Krischele
Krisean
Krisha
Krishana
Krishawn
Krishelle
Krishena
Krishina
Krishna
Krisi
Krisia
Krisina
Krisitin
Krisly
Krislyn
Krisrie
Krissa
Krissandra
Krissie
Krissina
Krissy
Krista-Anne
Krista-Lee
Krista-Louise
Krista-Lynn
Kristabel
Kristain
Kristaine
Kristale
Kristalee
Kristaline
Kristall
Kristalyn
Kristalynn
Kristana
Kristanna
Kristeé
Kristeen
Kristeena
Kristell
Kristelle
Kristena
Kristene
Kristey
Kristi Lyn
Kristi Zea M
Kristi-Ann
Kristi-Chantel
Kristi-Dawn
Kristi-Lee
Kristi-Lynn
Kristian-Hope
Kristiana
Kristiann
Kristianna
Kristianne
Kristiannhe
Kristie-Anne
Kristien
Kristienne
Kristiin
Kristiina
Kristill
Kristilyn
Kristin Whitney
Kristin-Anne
Kristin-Lori
Kristina-Alexandra
Kristina-Ann
Kristina-Antoinette
Kristina-Joy

Kristina-Lynn
Kristinarae
Kristinia
Kristinna
Kristl
Kristle
Kristlyn
Kristol
Kriston
Kristonia
Kristopher
Kristra
Kristy-Ann
Kristy-Anne
Kristy-Lee
Kristy-Lynn
Kristy-Lynne
Kristyana
Kristylee
Kristyna
Kristyne
Krisy
Krisytal
Krisztina
Kritzia
Krizia
Krizti
Krstina
Krupa
Krupalatha
Krupali
Krustyn
Krychell
Krychond
Kryistien
Krysanne
Krysha
Krysia
Kryslyn
Krysta-Lee
Krysta-Leigh
Krystah
Krystal Le
Krystal Verlene
Krystal-Ann
Krystal-Elaine
Krystal-Lee
Krystal-Louise
Krystal-Lynn
Krystal-Mari
Krystal-Rose
Krystalanne
Krystale
Krystaleen
Krystalin
Krystalina
Krystall
Krystalo
Krystan
Krystee
Krystelle
Krysten-Ashley
Krysten-Lea
Krysten-Leigh
Krystene
Krystia
Krystiana
Krystianne
Krystie
Krystie-Ling
Krystil
Krystine
Krystinia Marie
Krystl
Krystlea
Krystlelea
Krystn
Krystol
Krysty
Krystyiana
Krystyl
Krystyn
Krystyne
Kryzell
Kryzysia
Ksenia
Kshawnda
Kshe
Kshena
Ksi
Ktina
Ktreese
Kuannika
Kuiana
Kulani
Kuljet
Kulwinder
Kumari
Kumarie
Kumiko
Kung
Kunjita
Kunyu
Kurbie
Kurchelle
Kurdustan
Kurren
Kursten
Kurstin
Kurtiza
Kurtress
Kurtricia
Kurtrina
Kuturah
Kuwanya
Kwanaiya
Kwaneisha
Kwanetta
Kwastina
Ky
Kya
Kyan
Kyana
Kyann
Kyanna
Kyarra
Kyaunda
Kyeisha
Kyela
Kyera
Kyerra
Kyesha
Kyeshia
Kyeshu
Kylah
Kylara
Kylarra
Kylea
Kyleagh
Kyleé
Kylee-Rayne
Kyleen
Kyleene
Kylen
Kyler
Kyley
Kyli
Kylia
Kylii
Kylle
Kyllie
Kyly
Kylynne
Kym
Kymberle
Kymberlee

Kymberli
Kymberlie
Kymburlee
Kymmberleigh
Kyna
Kynda
Kyndal
Kyndall
Kyndi
Kyndra
Kyndria
Kyneesha
Kyni
Kynisha
Kynsha
Kynthia
Kyomi
Kyona
Kyonda
Kyonna
Kyrah
Kyria
Kyriaki
Kyriakoula
Kyriann
Kyricka
Kyrie Eleison
Kyrima
Kyrina
Kyris
Kyrisma
Kyrsta
Kyrstal
Kyrsten
Kyrstin
Kysa
Kysha
Kyshona
Kyshonda
Kyshyhia
Kystonal
Kyteva
Kyu
Kyung

L

L Tannae
L'erin
L'oreal
L'tina
L. Zebulun
Léa
La Channa
La Chelle
La Deana
La Donna
La Juanta
La Keisha
La Kenya
La Keshia
La Kia
La Kiesha
La Kirah
La Kita
La Kresha
La Manuel
La Meka
La Quaia
La Quanta
La Quesha
La Quita
La Rae
La Resha
La Rhonda
La Rita
La Rohnda
La Shaina
La Shanda
La Shante
La Shauna
La Shawn
La Shawnda
La Shea
La Sheena
La Shon
La Shonda
La Staishà
La Tarsha
La Tasha
La Tazia
La Tesa
La Tina
La Tisha
La Tonya
La Tosha
La Toshia
La Toya
La Toyia
La Trasha
La Trice
La Trina
La Vanity
La Vega
La Vera
La Von
La Wanda
La'cheer
La'darah
La'jeana
La'keisha
La'kia
La'petra
La'quisha
La'sandra
La'shay
La'shona
La'teesh
La'tesha
La'toya
La'wrease
La-Dominque
La-Donna
La-Nai
La-Tasha
Laana
Laani-Merike
Laanita
Laaquarius
Labella
Laberta
Laboni
Laborah
Labridget
Labriel
Labrina
Labrisha
Labritney
Lacanda
Lacandace
Lacandice
Lacarsia
Lacassie
Lace
Lacé
Laceisha
Lacelei
Lacella
Lacelle
Lacene
Laceria
Lacey-Anne
Lacey-Jay
Lacey-Lee
Lachana

Lachanda
Lachandice
Lachandra
Lachanta
Lachante
Lachanze
Lachara
Lacharle
Lache
Lachea
Lacheal
Lachele
Lachell
Lachelle
Lachen
Lachere
Lacherika
Lacheryl
Lacheya
Lachisha
Lachlan
Lachona
Lachristie
Lacia
Lacinda
Laclassia
Lacola
Lacole
Laconya
Lacosta
Lacoya
Lacrasha
Lacreash
Lacrecia
Lacresha
Lacreshia
Lacricia
Lacrisha
Lacrissa
Lacrista
Lacristal
Lacuanda
Lacy-B
Lacy-Leigh
Lacynda
Lacynthia
Ladaisa
Ladaishia
Ladara
Ladaseha
Ladasha
Ladashia
Ladassa
Ladavia
Ladawn
Ladawna
Ladaysha
Ladeanna
Ladeena
Ladeidra
Ladell
Ladesha
Ladina
Ladira
Ladli
Ladona
Ladonne
Ladonya
Ladraya
Ladreama
Laebony
Laekin
Lael
Laela
Laena
Laerica
Laerika
Laesha
Laetitia
Lafarra
Lafaryn
Lafay
Lafayette
Laferia
Laferra
Lafonta
Lafoya
Lafrancesa
Lagan
Lagara
Lageisha
Lagina
Lagracia
Lahaina
Lahkina
Lahoma
Lahomer
Lahrissa
Lai
Lai-Yee
Laia
Laici
Laikan
Laiken
Laikyn
Lailah
Laimeya
Laina
Laine-Marie
Lainee
Lainey
Laiqita
Laira
Lairen
Lais
Laiza
Lajaneze
Lajeania
Lajeanna
Lajewell
Lajharra
Lajohna
Lajohnda
Lajonee
Lajoy
Lajuan
Lajuanna
Lajunan
Lakaarî
Lakair
Lakaisha
Lakandis
Lakasha
Lakateria
Lakayla
Lakazia
Lakecia
Lakedra
Lakeela
Lakeena
Lakeenna
Lakeenya
Lakeeserous
Lakeesha
Lakeetah
Lakeia
Lakeila
Lakein
Lakeita
Lakeitha
Lakeithia
Lakell
Lakelly
Lakena
Lakenya
Lakera

Lakeseia
Lakesha-Sky
Lakeshia Rachell
Laketa
Laketha
Laketia
Laketrice
Laketta
Lakeva
Lakevia
Lakevier
Lakeya
Lakeyba
Lakeysha
Lakeyvia
Lakezia
Lakiah
Lakiayh
Lakier
Lakiesha
Lakietha
Lakilla
Lakin
Lakindra
Lakinja
Lakinya
Lakishia
Lakita
Lakitra
Lakitri
Lakitta
Lakivia
Lakiyn
Lakonya
Lakranda
Lakreshia
Lakrisha
Lakrista
Lakshmi
Lakwanya
Lakwanza
Lakyla
Lakyra
Lakyria
Lalaine
Lalani
Lalisha
Lalita
Lalonie
Lama
Lamanda
Lamatia
Lamaya
Lameanya
Lamees
Lameise
Lameka
Lamelia
Lamesha
Lameshia
Lametria
Lamia
Lamiah
Lamika
Lamina
Lamisha
Lamona
Lamonda
Lamondria
Lamonica
Lamontavia
Lamthong
Lamuria
Lamya
Lan
Lan-Anh
Lanae
Lanance
Lanarcis
Lanation
Lanatta
Lanavia
Lanay
Lancee
Landa
Landis
Landon
Landora
Landra
Landrea
Landria
Lane
Lanecia
Lanee
Laneece
Laneetca
Laneil
Laneise
Laneisha
Laneita
Laneka
Lanell
Lanesha
Laneshe
Lanessa
Lanesse
Lanetra
Lanetta
Lanette
Laney
Laneya
Lang
Langa
Langakali
Langatoli
Langdon
Langi
Lanice
Lanidra
Lanie
Laniece
Lanieka
Laniesha
Lanika
Lanis
Lanise
Lanisha
Lanisse
Lanita
Lanna
Lannette
Lannie
Lanona Mae
Lanquinda
Lansea
Lanta
Lantya
Lany
Lanza
Laoawanda
Laporcha
Laporche
Laporscha
Laporsha
Laportia
Laprincess
Laqeita
Laquai
Laquainta
Laquaita
Laquana
Laquanda
Laquandra
Laquanna
Laquanta
Laquanya

Laquay
Laquaya
Laquaysha
Laqueen
Laqueena
Laqueeta
Laqueinta
Laqueisha
Laquelita
Laquenda
Laquenette
Laquese
Laquesha
Laqueshia
Laquesta
Laqueta
Laquetta
Laquia
Laquiata
Laquice
Laquiche
Laquida
Laquiesha
Laquilla
Laquilvia
Laquina
Laquinda
Laquinta
Laquira
Laquise
Laquitsha
Laquitta
Laqunda
Laquonda
Laquondra
Laqusha
Laqushia
Laqutia
Lar'cynthia
Laradon
Larae
Larah
Larah-Natalie
Larain
Laraine
Laramie
Laranda
Laranie
Laray
Laree
Lareesa
Lareesea
Lareina
Lareisha
Larema
Laren
Larena
Larendalys
Laresa
Laresha
Lareva
Larhonda
Lari
Larianna
Larianne
Laricka
Lariesha
Larika
Larin
Larina
Larinette
Lariss
Larissa-Chantel
Larissas
Larissia
Larita
Laritza
Larizza
Lark
Larkin
Larkyn
Larmie
Larnecia
Larnette
Larnise
Laronda
Larosa
Larose
Larosia
Larra
Larreatta
Larrecia
Larren
Larrin
Larrisa
Larrissa
Larsandra
Lartice
Larua
Laryn
Laryssa
Lasable
Lasadra
Lasandra
Lasaundra
Lasha
Lashabla
Lashadrian
Lashae
Lashai
Lashaia
Lashala
Lashameeka
Lashameka
Lashana
Lashanay
Lashand
Lashandoline
Lashandra
Lashane
Lashanna
Lashannon
Lashannova
Lashanta
Lashante
Lashaquonta
Lashara
Lasharda
Lashareesha
Lasharo
Lashaun
Lashauna
Lashaunda
Lashaundra
Lashaune
Lashaunna
Lashaunta
Lashawda
Lashawn
Lashawnd
Lashawnda
Lashawndra
Lashawne
Lashawnia
Lashay
Lashaya
Lashayla
Lashda
Lashea
Lasheasha
Lasheena
Lasheika
Lasheka

Lashelia
Lashell
Lashelle
Lashemia
Lashena
Lashera
Lasheree
Lasheri
Lasheryl
Lashiedra
Lashika
Lashikka
Lashima
Lashina
Lashirelle
Lashon
Lashonde
Lashondia
Lashondra
Lashonna
Lashonta
Lashonya
Lashunda
Lashunta
Lashunte
Lashuntrice
Lashyia
Lasierra
Lasimone
Laska-Da
Lasonda
Lasonja
Lasonya
Lassell
Lastacia
Lastameon
Lastarsha
Latacha
Latacia
Latai
Lataisha
Latalia
Latana
Latandra
Latangela
Latangelia
Latania
Latanna
Latanua
Latarra
Latarsha
Latascha
Lataura
Latausha
Latavya
Lataya
Lataysha
Latea
Lateara
Lateasha
Lateashia
Latecia
Latedra
Lateefa
Lateefah
Lateemia
Lateesha
Latehia
Lateia
Lateicia
Lateisha
Lateka
Latela
Latena
Latequa
Laterakia
Lateria
Laterica
Laterra
Laterria
Laterrica
Latesa
Lateshia
Latessa
Lathea
Lathelia
Lathena
Latiancian
Latice
Laticia
Latiere
Latiesha
Latifa
Latifah
Latiffany
Latifia
Latika
Latilya
Latima
Latina
Latipha
Latique
Latisa
Latishia
Latissa
Latissha
Latitia
Lativa
Latiya
Latoccia
Latodyon
Latoia
Latoira
Latoiya
Latoko
Latona
Latoni
Latonia
Latonna
Latonshia
Latora
Latorio
Latorray
Latorreia
Latorya
Latoshia
Latotla
Latoyia
Latoyleia
Latoyo
Latoyra
Latoyria
Latraci
Latraia
Latranece
Latravia
Latreana
Latrece
Latrecia
Latreece
Latreese
Latreka
Latrell
Latrena
Latrenda
Latrenia
Latresa
Latrese
Latresh
Latresha
Latressa
Latreva
Latrichia
Latriece
Latrikia
Latrina

Latrisha
Latrophia
Latroya
Latryce
Latsha
Lattista
Latu
Latwana
Latwanda
Latwaunda
Latya
Latyra
Lauana
Lauchlin
Laudan
Laudelina
Laudelyf
Lauire
Launa
Laundrea
Laur
Laura Alex
Laura Amanda
Laura Ann
Laura Elizabeth
Laura Lea
Laura Lee
Laura Lynn
Laura Lynne
Laura-Ann
Laura-Ashley
Laura-Beth
Laura-Lee
Laura-Lily
Laura-Lin
Laura-Marie
Laura-Michelle
Laurae
Laurah
Lauraine
Lauralea
Lauralee
Laurali
Lauraly
Lauralynn
Lauran
Laurann
Laure
Laureana
Laureen
Laureena
Laurel Ann
Laurel-Ann
Laureli
Laurelin
Laurell
Laurelle
Lauren Beth
Laurena
Laurence
Laurenda
Lauressa
Laurette
Lauri
Laurian
Laurica
Laurice
Lauricia
Laurie Ann
Laurie-Ann
Laurie-Anne
Lauriel
Laurien
Laurin
Laurinda
Laurine
Laurisa
Laurissa
Laurita
Laurra
Laurrane
Laurren
Laury
Lauvana
Lavada
Lavanda
Lavangala
Lavantez
Lavara
Laveda
Lavell
Lavender
Lavera
Lavern
Laverna
Laverne
Laverta
Lavesha
Laveshia
Lavetria
Lavetta
Lavette
Lavina
Lavinia
Lavinna
Lavisha
Lavisia
Lavithia
Lavon
Lavonda
Lavonder
Lavondria
Lavone
Lavonia
Lavonica
Lavonn
Lavonna
Lavonne
Lavonnie
Lavonya
Lavoryia
Lawana
Lawanna
Lawanne
Lawanza
Laweania
Lawntore
Lawrie
Lawynda
Laya
Layce
Laycee
Layci
Layda
Layfeete
Layken
Layli
Laymon
Layna
Layne
Layonda
Layton
Laytoya
Lazandria
Lazara
Lazaraly
Lazarita
Lazedra
Lazet
Laziah
Le Andra
Le Ann
Le Anna
Le Anne
Le Keshia
Le Shanda

Le Tasha
Le 'Ticia
Le Treasha
Léah
Léjoan
Léonsha
Létisha
Leà
Leafa
Leah Marie
Leah-Anne
Leah-Marie
Leaha
Leahan
Leairra
Leakana
Leala
Lealaena
Lealani
Lealofi
Leamber
Leambra
Leana
Leandia
Leandre
Leandrea
Leandria
Leane
Leanecia
Leanessa
Leanette
Leannah
Leannda
Leanndra
Leanndrea
Leannie
Leanore
Leaonzia
Leaora
Leaphy
Leara
Leasa
Leashalea
Leashea
Leather
Leatina
Leatrice
Leaunder
Leaundra
Leavodis
Lecara
Lechet
Lechina
Lecia
Lecretia
Leda
Ledeatha
Lededra
Ledwina
Lee Ann
Lee Anna
Lee-Ann
Lee-Anna
Lee-Anne
Lee-Tara
Leea
Leeah
Leeallie
Leean
Leeandra
Leeandre
Leeanna
Leeat
Leeba
Leekohnnia
Leela
Leelund
Leelynn
Leemor
Leena
Leenise
Leerika
Leesa
Leesandra
Leesha
Leeson
Leeta
Leetana
Leeza
Leeza-Leigh
Lehandrea
Lehanna
Lehanne
Lehti
Lei
Leiah
Leiane
Leianne
Leiçhelle
Leida
Leigan
Leigeilyn
Leigh Ann
Leigh Anna
Leigh Anne
Leigh-An
Leigh-Ann
Leigh-Anna
Leigh-Anne
Leighah
Leighan
Leighana
Leighandra
Leighanna
Leighanne
Leigherin
Leighia
Leighnia
Leighton
Leihren
Leilah
Leilena
Leilia
Leina
Leisa
Leisel
Leisha
Leisly
Leith
Leizel
Lejontae
Lejoy
Lejoya
Lejoyce
Lekasha
Lekeathia
Lekeisha
Lekeithia
Lekell
Lekenia
Lekesha
Lekeshia
Lekesia
Lekeyia
Lekeyra
Lekicia
Lekina
Lekira
Lekisha
Lekita
Lela
Lelah
Leland
Lelani
Lelania
Lelauna

Lele
Leleona
Lelia
Lelita
Lellany
Lelonni
Lelsie
Lema
Leman
Lemas-Ali
Lemelia
Lemisha
Lena-Joy
Lenae
Lencola
Lendsey
Lendsi
Lendsy
Lene
Lenea
Lenece
Lenedra
Lenee
Leneice
Lenelle
Lenesha
Lenette
Leni
Lenica
Lenifer
Lenika
Lenisa
Lenise
Lenita
Lenna
Lenneal
Lennette
Lennie
Lennon
Lennoria
Lennox
Lenora
Lenore
Lenses
Lensey
Lenya
Lenys
Lenzie
Leo
Leola
Leolen
Leonda
Leondra
Leonela
Leonette
Leonia
Leonie
Leonna
Leonor
Leonora
Leonta
Leontine
Leora
Leosha
Lepa
Lepaula
Leporsche
Leprecious
Lequandra
Lequira
Lequisa
Lequisha
Lequita
Lera
Lerae
Lerah
Leranda
Lerhonda
Lerin
Lerinna
Lerosa
Leroyce
Lerryn
Lesa
Lesa-Anne
Lesalynn
Lesasha
Leschia
Lesha
Leshae
Leshande
Leshandra
Leshara
Leshaun
Leshay
Leshell
Leshenda
Leshia
Leshundra
Leshya
Lesia
Lesle
Leslea
Lesleigh
Lesley Anne
Lesley-Ann
Lesley-Anne
Lesleyanne
Lesli
Lesli Beth
Leslie Ann
Leslie Anne
Leslie Jo
Leslie-Ann
Leslie-Anne
Leslie-Debra
Lesline
Lesly
Leslye
Lesondra
Lessie
Leta
Letamra
Letara
Letasha
Letashia
Letasiah
Letaviah
Letecia
Leteisha
Leteres
Leteshia
Letetia
Letha
Lethanne
Letice
Letichia
Leticia-Barreira
Letigre
Letina
Letishia
Letisia
Letiticia
Letitisha
Letiza
Letizia
Letonia
Letosa
Letoya
Letrease
Letrice
Letrina
Letrinka
Letrisia
Lettechia
Letticia

Lettie
Letty
Leung
Leusandra
Leva
Levashia
Levay
Levedra
Leverne
Levi-Eleshia
Levia
Levida
Levina
Levita
Levitticus
Levonie
Lewis
Lexa
Lexanna
Lexanne
Lexi
Lexie
Lexine
Lexis
Lexy
Leya
Leyah
Leyda
Leyden
Leyicet
Leyla
Leyna
Leynee
Leysa
Leyton
Leza
Lezith
Lezlee
Lezleigh
Lezley-Ann
Lezlie
Lezora
Lezzie
Lhatoria
Li
Liahna
Lian
Liana D
Liandrea
Lianette
Liang
Liann
Liante
Liany
Lianys
Libbie
Libby
Librea
Libya
Licha
Lichelle
Licia
Licina
Lickarisa
Licole
Lida
Lidice
Lidona
Lieana
Lieetta
Lien
Lien Chau
Liereen
Lierin
Liesbeth
Liesel
Lieselot
Liesl
Liette
Ligaya
Ligia
Ligorina
Lii
Liisa
Likeshia
Likita
Lil
Lilah
Lili
Lilia
Liliam
Lilian
Liliane
Lilianna
Lilibeth
Liliceta
Lilith
Lilla
Lillahi
Lillee
Lilli
Lilliah
Lilliam
Lilliana
Lillie
Lillieana
Lilly
Lilnetta
Liltera
Liltoynta
Lily-Anna
Lilyanne
Lilybeth
Limay
Limberle
Limira
Lin
Linda Maria
Linda-Marie
Lindareina
Linday
Lindee
Lindell
Linden
Lindi
Lindie
Lindita
Lindley
Lindsay-Ann
Lindsay-Anne
Lindsay-Lee
Lindsayjean
Lindsea
Lindsee
Lindseylee
Lindsie
Lindsley
Lindylee
Lindze
Lindzee
Lindzie
Line
Lineasha
Linelle
Linese
Linette
Ling
Linh
Linique
Linita
Linn
Linna
Linnaea
Linnell
Linnet
Linnette

Linnie
Linnora
Linora
Linose
Linsay
Linsday
Linsi
Linsie
Linsy
Linze
Linzee
Linzey
Linzi
Linzie
Linzy
Liona
Liondra
Lionela
Liquita
Liqunta
Lira
Lisa Ann
Lisa Jean
Lisa Marie
Lisa Melia
Lisa-Ann
Lisa-Anne
Lisa-Felicia
Lisa-Lyn
Lisabel
Lisabeth
Lisabette
Lisamari
Lisandra
Lisanne
Lisbeb
Lisbell
Lisbet
Lisbeth
Lisbett
Lise-Anne
Liseet
Lisel
Lisesel
Liset
Liseth
Lisha
Lishana
Lishanna
Lishara
Lishelle
Lishunda
Lisiane
Lisl
Lismarie
Lismaris
Lismary
Lisnet
Lisolette
Lissa Mari
Lissandra
Lissandre
Lisset
Lissete
Lissett
Lissey
Liszt
Lita
Litah
Litho
Litia
Litillya
Litisha
Livia
Liwayway
Liz
Liz Mary
Liza Flory
Liza Marie
Liza May
Lizabeth
Lizandra
Lizanne
Lizbet
Lizbeth
Lizbett
Lizeidy
Lizena
Lizet
Lizete
Lizeth
Lizett
Lizette
Lizmarie
Lizna
Lizveth
Lizzette
Lizzie
Lizzieann
Lizzu
Ljubica
Llarelis
Llarely
Llatsmin
Llee
Lliana
Lloni
Lluvia
Lnir
Loa
Loan
Lochie
Lochrey
Locita
Lockietta
Locquett
Lodema
Lodi
Loene-Mae
Loi
Loistein
Lok-Yee
Lola Jean
Lolita
Lolomai
Loma
Lona
Lona-Des
London
Loneise
Lonell
Lonetta
Lonette
Loni-Kay
Lonie
Loniesha
Lonisha
Lonna
Lonnece
Lonnetta
Lonni
Lonnie
Lonniea
Lonnisha
Loody
Lopa
Lopamudra
Lora-Lea-Louna
Lorabeth
Lorae
Lorah
Loraie
Loraina
Loraine
Lorainne
Loralee

Loraleen
Loraleigh
Loralie
Loralyn
Loran
Loranda
Lorane
Loranesha
Lorann
Loranna
Loranne
Lore
Loreah
Loreal
Loreanet
Loreanne
Loredana
Loree
Loreen
Loreena
Loreilein
Loreithia
Lorel
Lorelee
Lorelei
Loreli
Lorell
Lorelle
Lorenda
Lorene
Lorenika
Lorenis
Lorenza
Lorenzcia
Lorenzina
Loreon
Loresley
Loressa
Lorette
Lorey
Lori Ann
Lori Beth
Lori Chamar
Lori Lou
Lori-Ann
Lori-Anne
Lori-Beth
Lori-Jeanne
Lori-Lynn
Lori-Lynne
Loria
Lorial
Lorian
Loriana
Loriane
Loriann
Lorianna
Lorianne
Lorians
Loribeth
Lorieanna
Loriel
Lorien
Lorienne
Lorijene
Lorile
Lorilee
Lorimar
Lorin Eliz
Lorina
Lorinda
Lorine
Lorinna-Dee
Lorisa
Lorissa
Lorita
Loriza
Lorn
Lorna-Mae
Lorra
Lorrain
Lorraina
Lorralin
Lorrece
Lorren
Lorrena
Lorretta
Lorri
Lorrie-Kunthala
Lorrie-Lyne
Lorrin
Lorrine
Lorrisa
Lorrissa
Lorry
Lortoya
Lory
Loryn
Losaline
Losira
Lotoya
Lottie
Lotty
Loty
Lou
Lou-Ann
Lou-Anne
Louane
Louann
Louanna
Louanne
Loucretia
Loudi
Loudry
Louella
Louelsie
Louis
Louisa-Marie
Louise-Victoria
Louisena
Louissy
Louiszelene
Louizette
Loukia
Loulwah
Louna
Louneda
Louneska
Loura
Louraine
Lourdjine
Louree
Lourene
Lourica
Lourie
Lourisa
Lourlye
Lousheanne
Lousheba
Louveisha
Louvenia
Lovani
Love
Loveal
Lovecia
Loveleen
Lovell
Lovely
Lovena
Lovestacia
Loveta
Lovetta
Lovette
Lovie
Lovina
Lovis

Lovna
Loxley
Loyola
Loyretta
Loys
Lporcha
Ltrice
Lu Ann
Lu Hana
Lu Liesha
Lua
Luana
Luann
Luanne
Luba
Lubna
Lubomyra
Luccia
Lucciana
Lucelle
Lucelynne
Lucerito
Lucero
Lucette
Luchandria
Luchawndra
Luci
Luciadefatima
Luciana
Luciann
Lucienne
Lucila
Lucilia
Lucilla
Lucine
Lucious
Lucja
Luckshi
Lucky
Lucresha
Lucretia
Lucrezia
Lucyana
Ludeen
Ludmiar
Ludmilla
Ludmyla
Ludney
Ludy
Luedelle
Luella
Luellen
Luemma
Lufarrah
Luidalys
Luindia
Luisa Maria
Luisana
Lukhveer
Lul
Lula
Lulu
Lulzime
Lumary
Luna
Lunden
Lundy
Lunetta
Lunise
Luonna
Lupe
Lupita
Luqueasha
Lura
Lurcora
Lurdes
Lurene
Lurka
Lurquoise
Lurys
Luseane
Lushelle
Lushiera
Lushus
Lusinda
Lutavia
Lutricia
Luv
Luvia
Luvinda
Luwana
Luz Damari
Luzalma
Luzmary
Luzmeralys
Luzmila
Lvecruietia
Ly-Julie
Lyane
Lyanna
Lyanne
Lybia
Lyda
Lydel
Lydi
Lydiana
Lydiann
Lydianne
Lyer
Lyia
Lyl
Lyla
Lyllian
Lylun
Lyly
Lymari
Lyn
Lyna
Lynada
Lynaia
Lynann
Lynar
Lynashley
Lyndae
Lyndal
Lynde
Lyndee
Lyndell
Lynden
Lyndian
Lyndie
Lyndin
Lyndsay-Ann
Lyndsea
Lyndsee
Lyndsi
Lyndsy
Lyndz
Lyndze
Lyndzee
Lyndzi
Lyndzie
Lyne
Lynea
Lyneah
Lynee
Lyneek
Lyneisha
Lynell
Lynelle
Lynelly
Lynesha
Lynett
Lynetta
Lynettie
Lynikia

Lyningra
Lynise
Lynita
Lynkahn
Lynlee
Lynley
Lynna
Lynnae
Lynndsay
Lynne-Suzanne
Lynnea
Lynnee
Lynnel
Lynnelle
Lynnesha
Lynnesia
Lynnita
Lynnsey
Lynnsie
Lynntay
Lynnze
Lynnzi
Lynora
Lynsay
Lynsee
Lynsi
Lynsie
Lynsy
Lyntje
Lyntrell
Lynyssa
Lynz
Lynzey
Lynzi
Lynzie
Lyonda
Lyra
Lyric
Lyrica
Lyricia
Lyrissa
Lys
Lysa
Lysandra
Lysanne
Lysbeth
Lysette
Lysley
Lysondra
Lyssa
Lyssette
Lytia
Lytisha
Lyvon
Lyza
Lyzette
Lyzzet

M

M'kaila
Ma
Ma Kayla
Ma'ata
Maaike
Maalika
Maaria
Maat
Mabeliss
Mabry
Mac
Mac Kenzie
Macaela
Macala
Macalaigh
Macdala
Macelia
Macenzie
Macey
Machaela
Machaka
Machealle
Machele
Machell
Machella
Machelle
Machia
Maci
Macie
Maciel
Maciena
Mackay
Mackayla
Mackenna
Mackensi
Mackensie
Mackenzee
Mackenzi
Mackenzia
Mackenzy
Mackline
Maclaria
Macon
Macquria
Macrae
Macrina
Macy
Madais
Madaleine
Madalena
Madalene
Madalin
Madaline
Madalit
Madaloynn
Madalyne
Madalynn
Maddalena
Maddelyn
Maddi
Maddie
Maddie-Jo
Maddilyn
Maddison
Maddlin
Maddy
Madeha
Madelain
Madelein
Madelen
Madelene
Madeliene
Madelin
Madelina
Madella
Madelon
Madelyne
Madelynn
Madelynne
Madelynne Rae
Madhavi
Madi
Madie
Madigan
Madiha
Madilyn
Madina
Madisen
Madison Hillary
Madissen
Madisyn
Madjelyn
Madlene
Madline
Madlyn

Madolyn
Madonna
Madonna-Amelda
Madrena
Madysen
Madyson
Mae
Maegen
Maegon
Maelea
Maelen
Maelle
Maeona
Maethel
Maeve
Magali
Magalie
Magalita
Magaly
Magalyn
Magalys
Magann
Magarret
Magda
Magdala
Magdalaina
Magdalen
Magdalene
Magdalina
Magdaline
Magdalis
Magdalyn
Magdelena
Mageline
Magge
Maggee
Maggen
Maggi
Maggiemae
Maggin
Maggy
Maghan
Maghen
Maghie
Magi
Magin
Magnolia
Magon
Maguire
Magy
Magyn
Maha
Mahagony
Mahalia
Maham
Mahara
Mahasen
Mahasheta
Mahdia
Mahdirah
Maheen
Mahera
Mahima
Mahlah
Mahnaz
Mahogani
Mahoganie
Mahogany
Mahogny
Mahogony
Mahreen
Mahri
Mahriah
Mahryah
Mahsa
Mahvish
Mahwish
Mai
Maia Danielle
Maiada
Maida
Maidelyn
Maider
Maigan
Maigen
Maighan
Maija
Maika
Maikala
Maike
Maikenya
Maiko
Maile
Mailee
Maileigh
Mailekuuipo
Mailin
Mailinh
Maily
Mailyn
Mailynh
Mailynn
Maira
Mairead
Mairim
Mairin
Maisah
Maisey
Maishiyah
Maisie
Maite
Maitia
Maiya
Maja
Majal
Majalisa
Majalyn
Majayla
Majduleen
Majestica
Majida
Majidah
Majorie
Majory
Makaela
Makala
Makaley
Makalita
Makandrine
Makara
Makaya
Makeda
Makeesha
Makeila
Makeitha
Makel
Makell
Makelle
Makensie
Makenzie
Makenzie Leeann
Makesha
Makeshia
Maketha
Makeya
Makeyia
Makia
Makiko
Makila
Makisha
Makita
Makkedah
Mala
Malaak

Malac
Malahat
Malaika
Malaine
Malainie
Malak
Malana
Malanie
Malaree
Malari
Malarie
Malary
Malaurie
Malaya
Malayna
Malea
Maleah
Maleaha
Malee
Maleeka
Maleigha
Maleka
Malena
Malenna
Malery
Malese
Malessa
Maleta
Maleyah
Malfrie
Malgarita
Mali
Maliaka
Maliasha
Maliea
Maliesha
Maliha
Malikah
Malikia
Malin
Malina
Maline
Malini
Malinna
Malirie
Malisa
Malisha
Malisia
Malissia
Malka
Malkresha
Mallari
Mallarie
Mallary
Mallauri
Mallee
Mallerie
Mallerie-Anne
Mallery
Malley
Mallica
Mallisa
Mallony
Malloree
Malloreigh
Mallory Ev
Malora Marie
Maloree
Malorey
Malori
Malree
Malrie
Malthyde
Maltoria
Malurie
Malvi
Malwanh
Maly
Malyn
Malynda
Malynne
Malysah
Malyssa
Mama
Mamanda
Mamie
Mamiesha
Mamta
Man Wan
Manal
Manali
Manange
Manar
Manayra
Manda
Mandalyn
Mande
Mandee
Mandelin
Mandi-Jean
Mandi-Lynn
Mandica
Mandijo
Mandilyn
Mandip
Mandisa
Mandolin
Mandolyn
Mandra
Mandy-Ashley
Mandy-Lee
Mandylyn
Maneesha
Manefa
Maneka
Manelive
Manelle
Manessa
Manewa
Mangai
Mangeliz
Mangita
Manhattan
Manice
Manige
Manijeh
Manik
Manika
Manikdeep
Manila
Manileuth
Maninder
Manisa
Manisha
Manita
Manivanh
Manja
Manjinder
Manjot
Manjyot
Mankeerut
Manmeet
Manna
Manoli
Manolia
Manon
Manoucheka
Manouchka
Manouheca
Manpreett
Manpriet
Manreet
Manroop
Manroop-Kaur
Mansai
Mansi

Mantrioe
Manuchka
Manuela
Manuela-Marlene
Manuelita
Manvi
Manvinder
Manvir
Maomi
Maple
Mapuana
Maquesha
Maquisha
Maquita
Mar Leigha
Mar'kesh
Marah
Maraia
Maraim
Marainda
Maral
Maralda
Maralea
Maralee
Maralyn
Maramatha
Marandia
Marandy
Marayda
Maraysa
Marbella
Marbely
Marc
Marcail
Marcarsha
Marcdaluse
Marcedes
Marcee
Marceil
Marcel
Marcela
Marcelen
Marcelin
Marcelina
Marceline
Marcell
Marcelle
Marcello
Marcena
Marcene
Marcey
Marcha
Marchanis
Marchard
Marchelle
Marchessa
Marchette
Marci Lyn
Marcia-L
Marciale
Marciela
Marcile
Marcilena
Marcilene
Marcilla
Marcina
Marckline
Marco
Marcuelia
Mardel
Mardeliza
Mardi
Maread
Mareale
Maredith
Maree
Mareen
Marelou
Marene
Maresa
Maresha
Mareshah
Maressa
Maret
Marfa
Margalyn
Margan
Margaret Ann
Margaret Frances
Margaret Megan
Margaret-Ann
Margaret-Mary
Margaretha
Margarett
Margarette
Margarit
Margaritta
Margaux
Marge
Margeaux
Margeauy
Margeely
Margel
Margelande
Margeline
Margene
Margerete
Margery
Margetta
Margey
Margherita
Margineka
Margorie
Margrena
Margret
Margrete
Margueri
Marguerita
Margueritte
Marguita
Marguriete
Margurite
Margwine
Marià-Sol
Mari-Lyn
Maria Adelinapaz
Maria Alejandra
Maria Belen
Maria Delcarmen
Maria Eugenia
Maria Graz
Maria Isabel
Maria Jose
Maria Luisa
Maria Neni
Maria Star
Maria-Angelica
Maria-Assunta
Maria-Carmela
Maria-Cathy
Maria-Christina
Maria-Cristina
Maria-Ingrid
Maria-Louise
Maria-Ludwika
Maria-Mary-Ann
Maria-Saroja
Maria-Teresa
Maria-Vanessa
Mariachiara
Mariaines
Mariam-Ward
Mariama

Mariame
Mariane
Marianella
Mariann
Marianne Loretta
Mariarosa
Mariarosa-Assunta
Maribella
Maribeth
Marible
Maribou
Marica
Maricar
Maricarmen
Maricel
Maricela
Maricell
Maricella
Maricellis
Maricelly
Maricely
Maricka
Maricsa
Marida
Marie Clai
Marie-Andrée
Marie-Annique
Marie-Astrid
Marie-Céline
Marie-Catherine
Marie-Chantal
Marie-Christiane
Marie-Christine
Marie-Claire
Marie-Daphne
Marie-Elyse
Marie-Etta
Marie-France
Marie-France-Veronique
Marie-Francoise
Marie-Ginette
Marie-Hélène
Marie-Helene
Marie-Jean
Marie-Jeanne
Marie-Joelle
Marie-Josee
Marie-Josée
Marie-Line
Marie-Lise
Marie-Louise
Marie-Lyne
Marie-Lynn
Marie-Manon
Marie-Manon-Eve
Marie-May
Marie-Michele
Marie-Michèle
Marie-Michelle
Marie-Paule
Marie-Pierre
Marie-Soleil
Marie-Sylvie
Marie-Therese
Marie-Yvonne
Marieka
Marieke-Lise
Mariela
Marieline
Mariella
Marielle
Marielle-Brigitte
Mariellen
Marielna
Marielsie
Mariely
Marielys
Mariem
Marienne
Mariepier
Mariesa
Mariesha
Mariessa
Marieta
Marietta
Mariette
Marieve
Mariève
Mariha
Marija
Marijana-Valentina
Marijke
Marijoyce
Marikia
Mariko
Marile
Marilee
Marilena
Marilin
Marilise
Marilou
Marilu
Marily
Marilyn-Jennie
Marilyn-Renée
Marilyne
Marilynn
Marilys
Marin
Marina-Saba
Marinda
Marindi
Marine
Mariney
Marinieves
Mario
Mariolive
Maris
Marisabel
Marisel
Mariseli
Marisella
Marishelle
Marishka
Marisia
Mariska
Marison
Marita
Maritha
Maritie
Maritsa
Marivel
Marivette
Marixa
Mariya
Mariza
Marizabet
Marizela
Marizeny
Marizol
Marja
Marjaé
Marjaliese
Marjan-Monireh
Marjanna
Marjie
Marjoe
Marjohn
Marjolaine
Marjory
Mark

Marka
Markasa
Markashie
Markeeda
Markeesha
Markeeta
Markeidra
Markeila
Markeisha
Markeita
Markeka
Markela
Markell
Markelle
Marken
Markerat
Markeria
Markesha
Markeshia
Marketa
Marketha
Marketta
Markeva
Marki
Markia
Markie
Markiessha
Markieta
Markila
Markisha
Markishia
Markitha
Markketta
Marko
Marky
Marlainna
Marlanea
Marlania
Marlanna
Marlayna
Marleah
Marleasa
Marleen
Marleine
Marlen
Marlenes
Marlenna
Marlenne
Marlent
Marleny
Marlesa
Marlese
Marley-Anne
Marleyda
Marleys
Marli
Marlicia
Marlie
Marlina
Marlinda
Marline
Marlis
Marlisa
Marlise
Marlisha
Marlissa
Marlo
Marlon
Marlowe
Marlyn
Marlyne
Marlys
Marmee
Marna
Marnaté
Marnda
Marne
Marnecia
Marnee
Marnette
Marney
Marni
Marnina
Marnique
Maron
Marqeita
Marqel
Marquashia
Marque
Marqueda
Marquedia
Marquee
Marqueita
Marquell
Marquenda
Marquerite
Marqueritte
Marquet
Marqueta
Marquett
Marquetta
Marquette
Marquia
Marquida
Marquiet
Marquietta
Marquieva
Marquilla
Marquinta
Marquise
Marquisha
Marquisia
Marquitra
Marquitta
Marquittia
Marquiva
Marra
Marranda
Marriah
Marrian
Marriann
Marrianne
Marrie
Marrika
Marrina
Marrion
Marrisa
Marrissa
Marrissia
Marriza
Marry
Marsa
Marsali
Marschar
Marsdena
Marsedez
Marsee
Marseilles
Marshae
Marshaé
Marshaleise
Marshana
Marshatta
Marshay
Marshayla
Marshebya
Marshel
Marshele
Marshell
Marshelle
Marshia
Marshiela
Marshika
Martavia
Marte
Marteen

Marteka
Martene
Martesha
Martha Ann
Martha Maria
Marthan
Marthasely
Marthe
Marthesia
Marthina
Marthine
Marthy
Marti
Martice
Martie
Martika
Martilyn
Martina-Francesca
Martina-Ivka
Martinia
Martiniq
Martino
Martisha
Martiza
Martosia
Martoya
Martrica
Martrina
Marty
Martyjo
Martyne
Maruca
Marva
Marvell
Marvella
Marvelle
Marvely
Marvet
Marvetta
Marvette
Marvia
Marvina
Marwa
Marwah
Marwyn
Mary Ann
Mary Beth
Mary Caitlynn
Mary Cathe
Mary Clair
Mary Crystal
Mary Delsi
Mary Elisa
Mary Elisabeth
Mary Eliza
Mary Elizabeth
Mary Ellen
Mary Grace
Mary Helen
Mary Jane
Mary Jean
Mary Jo
Mary Kate
Mary Katheri
Mary Lee
Mary Lou
Mary Lynn
Mary-Ann
Mary-Anne
Mary-Beth
Mary-Claire
Mary-Elizabeth
Mary-Ellen
Mary-Jean
Mary-Jo
Mary-Joe
Mary-Juen
Mary-Katherine
Mary-Lee
Mary-Lou
Mary-Lynn
Mary-Rose
Mary-The
Marya
Maryalice
Maryam
Maryan
Maryana
Maryane
Marybell
Marycatherin
Marycathry
Marycruz
Maryellen
Maryetta
Marygel
Maryie
Maryjane
Maryjoy
Maryka
Marykatherine
Maryke
Maryl
Marylanna
Marylee
Marylin
Maryline
Marylise
Maryllyn
Marylou
Marylouise
Marylu
Maryluz
Marylynn
Maryn
Maryon
Maryori
Maryrena
Maryrose
Marysa
Marysara
Maryselee
Marysol
Maryssa
Marysue
Marytery
Maryum
Masako
Masha
Mashanda
Mashanna
Mashara
Mashayla
Mashedia
Mashelle
Mashia
Mashie
Mashikka
Maslande
Masline
Masoko
Massey
Massiel
Mastane
Masumi
Masyl
Matanya
Matavara
Matefia
Mateya
Mathangi
Mathdany
Mathew
Mathilda
Mathilde

Mathisse
Matia
Matijames
Matilda
Matilde
Matina
Matisha
Matiya
Matosha
Matoya
Matrese
Matrisha
Mattasyn
Matte
Mattea
Matthew
Matti
Mattison
Mattissee
Matty
Matye
Matylda
Maud
Maude
Maudeline
Maudie
Maudlen
Maura Eliz
Maurade
Mauraine
Maureena
Mauri
Mauria
Maurice
Maurie
Mauriel
Mauriell
Maurisa
Maurissa
Maurita
Maury
Mausharri
Mava
Maverannemarie
Mavis
Mawusi
Max
Maxi
Maxie
Maxime
Maxina
Maxna
Maxyne
Mayada
Mayangi
Maycruz
Maydalyn
Maydelin
Maye
Mayebelle
Mayela
Maygan
Maygen
Mayleen
Maylen
Maylene
Maylin
Maylon
Maylynn
Maylynne
Mayme
Mayo
Mayola
Mayre
Mayriya
Maysha
Mayssia
Maytal
Mayte
Maytee
Mayu
Mayuko
Mayumi
Mayuri
Mayurika
Mayve
Mc
Mc Kayla
Mc Kensi
Mc Kenzie
Mc Kinzie
Mcallister
Mccaley
Mccall
Mcclaine
Mcdonna
Mckay
Mckayla
Mckayle
Mckee
Mckel
Mckell
Mckella
Mckelle
Mckendra
Mckenize
Mckensey
Mckensie
Mckensy
Mckenzey
Mckenzie-Jay
Mckinlie
Mckinna
Mckinsey
Mckinzie
Mckinzy
Mcquada
Me Linda
Me Lisa
Me Litta
Mécaila
Me-Me-Keau
Meadow
Meagain
Meagann
Meaghan-Lynn
Meaghann
Meaghen
Meagin
Meagna
Meagon
Meahgan
Meara
Mecah
Mecall
Mecca
Mechell
Mechelle
Meckenzie
Meclas
Mecoe
Mecole
Medalie
Medea
Medetia
Medija
Medina
Medjine
Medlyne
Mee
Meegan
Meeghan
Meehan
Meeka
Meekayle
Meeme

Meena
Meenah
Meenakshi
Meera
Meesha
Meetra
Meg
Megahn
Megan Elizabeth
Megan Lyn
Megan-Elaine
Megan-Lee
Megan-Sara
Megann
Meganne
Megantaylor
Megara
Megean
Megen
Meggann
Meggi
Meggie
Meggie Elizabeth
Meggin
Meggy
Megha
Meghan-Lyn
Meghana
Meghane
Meghann-Jean
Meghanne
Meghara
Meghean
Meghen
Meghna
Megin
Megon
Megumi
Megun
Megyn
Meha
Mehana
Meher
Mehgan
Mehgen
Mehlissa
Mehnaz
Mehreen
Mehtab
Mehvish
Mehwish
Mei
Mei-Kar
Meica
Meiche
Meichelle
Meigan
Meighan
Meighen
Meika
Meiken
Meila
Meilani
Meilin
Meira
Meiratiferet
Meirav
Meiri
Meisha
Meji
Mejka
Mekaela
Mekala
Mekayla
Mekco
Mekeda
Mekell
Mekenna
Mekenzie
Mekka
Mela
Melady
Melaina
Melaine
Melainie
Melamie
Melana
Melandie
Melanee
Melaney
Melani
Melania
Melanie Roxann
Melanie-Alexandra
Melanie-Ann
Melanie-Anne
Melanie-Dawn
Melanie-Susan
Mélanisé
Melannie
Melarie
Melayne
Melba
Melbina
Melda
Mele
Melea
Meleah
Meleena
Meleia
Meleisha
Melena
Melendy
Melene
Melerie
Melesha
Meleshia
Meli
Melia
Meliah
Melicia
Melida
Melika
Mélina
Melinda-Sue
Meline
Melinna
Mélisa
Melisa René
Melisa-Costa
Melisand
Mélisandréé
Melise
Melisha
Melishea
Melishia
Melisia
Melissa Ann
Melissa Da Silva
Melissa Janashay
Melissa-Amber
Melissa-Anne
Melissa-Dawn
Melissa-Dulcé
Melissa-Jayne
Melissa-Lee
Melissa-Louise
Melissa-Lynn
Melissa-Lynne
Melissa-Natalie
Melissa-Olivia
Melissa-Robyn
Melissa-Roein
Melissa-Stella
Melissa-Sue

Melissia
Melita
Melizah
Melkevia
Mellanie
Mellary
Mellinda
Mellisa-Dawn
Mellodi
Mellody
Mellonie
Mellony
Melodee
Melodey
Melodi
Mélodié
Melody-Ann
Melond
Melonee
Meloney
Meloni
Melorie
Melory
Melsheena
Melva
Melvellaneia
Melvina
Melvonna
Melyndasue
Melynn
Melynne
Melysa
Melyssa
Memoree
Memorie
Memoucheka
Mena
Menah
Menancha
Menda
Mendon
Mendy
Menika
Menina
Menyon
Meocha
Meon-Margaret
Meonna
Mequail
Mequelle
Mequila
Mequisha
Merary
Meray
Mercede
Mercedez
Mercella
Merci
Mercia
Mercie
Mercy
Merdie
Meredeth
Meredithe
Meredy
Meredyth
Meredythe
Meregon
Merehan
Mereika
Merella
Merescil
Meriah
Meriari
Meribeth
Merica
Merideth
Meridith
Merie
Merielle
Merilu
Merin
Merina
Merinda
Meris
Merisa
Merisha
Merita
Meritt
Meriwether
Merland
Merlenda
Merline
Merlissa
Merlyne
Merna
Merran
Merri
Merriam
Merribeth
Merrick
Merridee
Merrie
Merrilee
Merrill
Merrillee
Merrilyn
Merrin
Merrisa
Merrissa
Merritt
Merron
Merry
Merryn
Mersadi
Mersadie
Mershawn
Mervat
Mery
Meryam
Meryle
Meschell
Mesha
Meshal
Meshell
Meshelle
Meshia
Meshiale
Meshiel
Meshonda
Metara
Metaxia
Metta
Mette
Metti
Meuset
Mevelyn
Meyada
Meyber
Meygan
Meylin
Meyosha
Mezella
Mhairi
Mi
Mièisha
Mi'kia
Mià
Miaela
Miagen
Miah
Miaka
Mialy
Miama
Miami
Miana

Miante
Miatta
Mic Kayla
Mica
Micaella
Micai
Micaiah
Micaiesha
Mical
Micala
Micalé
Micalyne
Micayla
Micca
Miceala
Micelle
Micha
Michael-
Michaelagh
Michaele
Michaelene
Michaelia
Michaelina
Michaell
Michaella
Michaelyn
Michaheala
Michaila
Michaira
Michal
Michala
Michalann
Michale
Michalene
Michalina
Michalisha
Michalle
Michaltal
Michanda
Michandra
Michawn
Michayla
Miche
Micheaelle
Micheal
Micheal-Eliz
Micheala
Michealanne
Michecarine
Michel
Michela
Michelda
Michelene
Micheleona
Michelia
Michelina
Micheline
Michella
Michelle Dawn
Michelle De Sousa
Michelle Opal
Michelle-Lee
Michelle-Lynn
Michelle-Marie
Michelle-Mona
Michellene
Michellerae
Michellyn
Michely
Michelyn
Micheyla
Michianna
Michica
Michieala
Michiko
Michiyo
Michole
Michon
Miciala
Micka
Mickael
Mickaela
Mickala
Mickayla
Mickeel
Mickeeya
Mickell
Mickelle
Mickeria
Mickey
Micki
Mickia
Micklee
Micky
Mickya
Micola
Micole
Micolette
Micquel
Micquivia
Micralyn
Midaliz
Midgalia
Midori
Miea
Mieasha
Mieha
Mieke
Miekela
Mieko
Miesha
Migdalia
Migdilia
Mignon
Migoalia
Miguelina
Miguelita
Mihia
Miia
Mija
Mika Brean
Mikaella
Mikah
Mikail
Mikaila
Mikala
Mikalene
Mikalovna
Mikalyn
Mikasha
Mikaya
Mikayle
Mikeà
Mikeisha
Mikeita
Mikel
Mikela
Mikele
Mikell
Mikella
Mikelle
Mikenzie
Mikenzy
Mikerline
Mikerra
Mikesha
Mikeya
Mikhaela
Mikhail
Mikhaila
Mikhala
Mikhalea
Mikhelle
Miki
Mikia

Mikiala
Mikie
Mikiela
Mikise
Mikita
Mikka
Mikkel
Mikki
Mikkicia
Mikkie
Mikkya
Mikla
Miko
Mikol
Mikyàla-Sad
Mikyla
Mikyn
Mikyria
Mikysha
Mila
Milady
Milagro
Milagros
Milala
Milan
Milana
Miland
Milande
Milane
Milani
Milanka
Milanna
Milanne
Milasro
Milawaty
Milay
Milca
Milcah
Mildrene
Mildreys
Milegra
Milena
Milène
Milenia
Milenny
Milenys
Milessa
Mili
Milica
Milika
Milinda
Milini
Milison
Milkan
Milla
Millanne
Millicent
Millie
Millini
Million
Millisa
Millissa
Milou
Miltoneisha
Milvette
Milynda
Mimi
Mimma
Min
Minakshi
Minaly
Minde
Mindee
Mindie
Mindon
Mindona
Mindus
Mindy Sue
Mindyanne
Mindylee
Mine
Minerva
Mineta
Mineth
Minett
Ming-Lai
Mingzohn
Minh
Minhdoan
Minike
Minju
Minke
Minna
Minnette
Minnie
Minnita
Minouche
Minsun
Minyaka
Miqueilia
Miquel
Miquela
Miquelle
Miquesha
Miquia
Mira
Miracle
Miracle Faith
Mirada
Mirae
Miraida
Miranada
Miranda Lee
Mirandeé
Mirandia
Mircale
Mirelida
Mirelis
Mirella
Mirelle
Mirelys
Miressa
Mirette
Mireya
Mireyda
Miri
Miria
Miriah
Miriam-Nadim
Miriame
Mirian
Mirinda
Mirisa
Mirissa
Mirjana
Mirjanna
Mirka
Mirlaine
Mirland
Mirlanda
Mirlande
Mirlando
Mirlege
Mirline
Mirna
Mirnouve
Miron
Mironda
Miroslava
Mirranda
Mirrisa
Mirtha
Mirushe
Miryam
Miryame
Miryan

Miryha
Misato
Mischa
Mischel
Mischelle
Misha
Mishae
Mishael
Mishaela
Mishalen
Mishana
Mishanda
Mishaun
Mishauna
Mishay
Mishayla
Mishell
Mishelle
Misheri
Mishka
Misia
Misled
Misleidi
Misogi
Miss
Missilin
Missty
Mistao
Mistee
Misteree
Mistey
Misti-Jo
Mistianna
Mistie
Mistin
Mistina
Mistral
Misty-Ann
Misty-Dawn
Mistylynn
Misun
Mita
Mitasha
Mitchell
Mitchelle
Mithsue
Mitra
Mitzi
Mitzie
Miuriel
Miya
Miyauna
Miyelin
Miyoko
Miyoshi
Miyquishaa
Miyuki
Mjari
Moanalee
Mobashar
Mobolanle
Mocha
Modanna
Modavia
Modeline
Moena
Mohani
Mohoghany
Mohogony
Moinique
Moisha
Molina
Molique
Molissia
Molita
Mollee
Molley
Molli
Mollissa
Molly Ann
Monaa
Monaca
Monae
Monah
Monay
Monchell
Mondi
Mondia
Mondica
Mone
Monea
Monee
Moneeke
Moneena
Moneik
Moneka
Monelle
Monesha
Moneshea
Moneshia
Monester
Monet
Monetta
Monic
Monica Ale
Monica Elizabeth
Monica-Lynn
Monica-Tracy
Monice
Monicia
Monicka
Monida
Moniece
Moniek
Monielle
Monifa
Monija
Monik
Monika-Juliette
Monikia
Monikue
Monina
Moninder
Moniqua
Monique Alexandr
Monique-Madelaine
Moniquea
Moniqueca
Moniquic
Moniquie
Moniree
Monise
Monisha
Monisola
Monita
Monnie
Monnikha
Monrobina
Montana
Montanna
Montavia
Montazia
Montekka
Montika
Montine
Montira
Montoiyalatrece
Montorria
Montoya
Montra
Montreal
Montrese
Montserrat

Monuzza
Monvon
Monya
Monyatta
Monymolyka
Monyra
Moorea
Mora
Moracine
Moraima
Moranda
Morea
Morgaine
Morgan Michelle
Morgan-Janelle
Morgana
Morgane
Morganfae
Morgann
Morganna
Morganne
Morganne Amelia
Morgen
Morghan
Morgyn
Moria
Moriell
Morissa
Morley
Mormarie
Morning
Morning-Kay
Morningstar
Morouje
Morriah
Morrisa
Morrisha
Morroco
Morrow
Mortana
Morufatadeola
Moryn
Mos'ira
Mosessa
Moshana
Moska
Mossina
Motika
Mounirah
Mount
Moushumi
Mouzaya
Moweza
Moya
Moynica
Moyra
Mozella
Mozhdeh
Mren
Mrlissa
Mryamn
Ms
Mshea
Mtheresa
Mubeen
Mubrouka
Muge
Mui
Mui-Ling
Mukami
Mumtaz
Muneeba
Muneet
Muniq
Munira
Munirah
Muqietta
Muranda
Muriah
Muriel
Murissa
Murla
Murlande
Murlene
Murphy
Murti
Musfirah
Musherrah
Muslie
Mutinta
My
Mya
Myah
Myanah
Myanda
Mycala
Mycca
Mychael
Mychal
Mychele
Mychelle
Myda
Mydra
Myeisha
Myesha
Myeshia
Myesia
Myhesha
Myiesha
Myisha
Myka
Mykael
Mykaela
Mykal
Mykaleen
Mykeda
Mykel
Mykela
Myken
Mykenzie
Mykeria
Mykia
Mykle
Myla
Mylady
Mylaine
Mylana
Mylatesha
Mylee
Myleka
Mylekia
Mylenda
Mylene
Myles
Mylesia
Myliece
Mylinda
Mylinh
Mylisia
Mylissa
Mylkia
Mylla
Myllissa
Mynde
Mynie
Mynina
Mynthia
Myong
Myraida
Myran
Myranda
Myreda
Myrela
Myrena
Myresha

Myria
Myriade
Myriah
Myriam-Esther
Myriame
Myriane
Myrissa
Myrlande
Myrline
Myrna
Myrnise
Myrta
Myrtha
Myrtice
Myrtle
Myrtle-R
Myschelle
Mysha
Myslene
Mystee
Mysti
Mystic
Mystie
Mystique
Mytia
Mytisha
Myulinda
Myvahna
Myya

N

Na Coral
Na Tasha
Nàkeisha
Nàquasha
Na-Tasha
Naadira
Naazneen
Nabeeha
Nabeela
Nabihah
Nabila
Nabilah
Nabilla
Nacala
Nacarra
Nacaya
Nacellie
Nachalah
Nachante
Nachel
Nachelle
Nachiele
Nacie
Nacola
Nacolbie
Nacole
Nacona
Naconie
Nacosta
Nacrina
Nacy
Nadà
Nadea
Nadean
Nadeana
Nadeau
Nadeen
Nadege
Nadège
Nadeges
Nadeige
Nadeisha
Nadelene
Nadely
Nadene
Nadezdha
Nadge
Nadhege
Nadhrah
Nadien
Nadika
Nadina
Nadira
Nadirah
Nadisha
Nadiya
Nadiyah
Nadja
Nadjema
Nady
Nadya
Nadyne
Nadzine
Naeelah
Naeisha
Naema
Nafey
Nafia
Nafisa
Nafisabanu
Nafisah
Naghieli
Nagla
Naheed
Naheemah
Nahir
Nahkeeta
Nahkia
Nahma
Nahomie
Nahrain
Nahreen
Nahtasha
Nahvon
Nahyun
Naiara
Naida
Naidene
Naija
Naike
Naikeya
Naila
Nailah
Naileen
Naima
Naimah
Naimi
Naina
Nairobi
Nairoby
Naisha
Naitore
Naivi
Naja
Najah
Najia
Najla
Najma
Najtassa
Najuk
Najwa
Nakala
Nakale
Nakayla
Nakea
Nakeanya
Nakedra
Nakeebra
Nakeema
Nakeesha
Nakeeta
Nakeia
Nakeidra

Nakeisha
Nakeita
Nakeithra
Nakeitra
Nakeitress
Nakeitta
Nakeittia
Nakenyia
Nakeria
Nakesha
Nakeshea
Nakeshia
Naketa
Naketrease
Naketta
Nakeysha
Nakiesha
Nakieta
Nakilia
Nakima
Nakina
Nakisha
Nakitha
Nakitia
Nakitta
Nakoa
Nakomi
Nakona
Nakrischia
Naksha
Nakyta
Nalani
Nalanie
Nalany
Nalesia
Naleta
Nalicia
Nalin
Nalisa
Nalka
Nalleli
Nalleyly
Nallinie
Nalwanga
Naly
Nalyn
Nambuusi
Namibia
Namika
Namita
Namneet
Nana
Nanami
Nance
Nancee
Nancey
Nanci
Nancie
Nancye
Nandani
Nandanie
Nandi
Nandie
Nandini
Nandria
Nanette
Nanise
Nanna
Nannie
Nansee
Nantonia
Nanyamka
Naoko
Naoma
Naomi Anne
Naomie
Naomy
Naonna
Naovanni
Naphaphone
Naphtali
Naphtoya
Naquania
Naquesha
Naquima
Naquita
Naquitta
Nara
Narah
Naranja
Narcissa
Narecia
Narelle
Naretaresha
Nareth
Narette
Narges
Nargis
Narinna
Narisa
Narissa
Narkita
Narrey
Narsha
Nartisha
Nary
Nasa
Nasareli
Nasasha
Naseem
Nasha
Nashadra
Nashae
Nashana
Nashanda
Nashata
Nashauna
Nashaunda
Nashawn
Nashay
Nasheena
Nasheeta
Nasheka
Nasheyn
Nashley
Nashounda
Nashua
Nashuana
Nashwa
Nasia
Nasiha
Nasira
Nasiya
Nasreen
Nasrin
Nassira
Nassrein
Nastasha
Nastashia
Nastasia
Nastasija
Nastasji
Nastassa
Nastassia
Nastassj
Nastassja
Nastassja-Jade
Nastazia
Nastiassia
Naswanna
Nasya
Nata
Nataasha
Natachar
Natachia
Natacia

Natadra
Nataha
Natajha
Natale
Natalea
Natalee-Rose
Nataleen
Nataleigh
Natali
Natalie-Jeanne
Natalie-Judith
Natalija
Natalina
Natalka
Natalle
Natallia
Natallie
Natallye
Nataly
Natalya
Natalyn
Natane
Natania
Natanis
Natanya
Natasa
Natascha
Natasha Kimberly
Natasha-Concetta
Natasha-Helena
Natasha-Irene
Natasha-Lynn
Natashah
Natashea
Natasheal
Natashiea
Natashja
Natashoia
Natasia
Natassa
Natassha
Natasshia
Natassia
Natassija
Natassja
Natasza
Natausha
Natavia
Nataviya
Natawsha
Nataya
Natayla
Nate
Nateé
Nateela
Natelie
Natena
Natesha
Natessia
Nathalia
Nathalie C
Nathaly
Nathan
Nathania
Nathania-Anne
Nathaniel
Nathasa
Nathasha
Nathassha
Nathen
Nathenia
Nathsa Rashida
Natia
Natianaquail
Natice
Naticha
Natika
Natira
Natishia
Nativia
Natividad
Natkisha
Natkyta
Natlie
Natoia
Natoriea
Natoshia
Natoya
Natrailya
Natrese
Natricia
Natsha
Natsumi
Nattachas
Nattalie
Nattie
Nattliee
Nature
Naudia
Naureen
Nausheen
Naushin
Nautasha
Nava
Navada
Navah
Navanna
Navannah
Navaz
Navdeep
Navedeep
Navesha
Navette
Navida
Navika
Navina
Navita
Navjeet
Navjit
Navjot
Navjote
Navjyot
Navneet
Navona
Navraj
Navreet
Nawal
Naya
Nayasheree
Nayda
Naydee
Nayel
Nayeli
Nayha
Naylet
Nayletha
Naylia
Nayllibi
Nayo
Nayomee
Nayrobi
Naytalia
Naz
Nazanin
Nazeema
Nazelene
Nazerath
Nazeria
Nazia
Nazish
Nazleen-Nisha
Nazlie
Nazmia
Nazneen

Nbelah
Ndidi
Neacy
Neala
Nealee
Nealie
Neama
Neardsheama
Neary
Neather
Neca
Nechama
Nechesa
Nechole
Necia
Necie
Necoe
Necole
Neda
Nedenia
Nedra
Neecha
Needra
Needrawraw
Neeka
Neekan
Neelam
Neeley
Neelie
Neely
Neema
Neena
Neeral
Neeru
Neesha
Neeti
Neetu
Nefer
Nefertari
Nefertia
Nefertiti
Nefretiri
Negail
Negar
Neha
Nehemie
Neicole
Neicoya
Neida
Neidra
Neikeishia
Neil-Jeremy
Neila
Neilani
Neile
Neisha
Nejla
Nejuan
Nekarah
Nekeeda
Nekeena
Nekeisha
Nekelia
Nekema
Nekesha
Nekeshia
Nekia
Nekiesha
Nekisha
Nekita
Nekitah
Nektaria
Nekweyah
Nekyanne
Nekysha
Nela
Nelcy
Nelda
Neleigh
Neli
Nelia
Nelicia
Nelida
Nelie
Nelina
Nelisha
Nelissa
Nell
Nella
Nelle
Nelli
Nellianne
Nellina
Nellshida
Nellsy
Nelly
Nellyda
Nelmary
Nelsha
Nelsi
Nelsy
Nena
Nenweh
Neomi
Neota
Nephaterria
Nephatira
Nephrateries
Nequa
Nequita
Nereida
Nereyda
Nerina
Nerissa
Nerissa-Anne
Nerland
Nerlange
Nerli
Nerline
Nermeen
Nesa
Nesha
Neshia
Neshie
Neshonda
Nesiah
Neslie
Neslihan
Nesly
Nesreen
Nesreia
Nessa
Nesseika
Nessrine
Neta
Netanis
Netanya
Netasawh
Netasha
Netassha
Netlora
Netra
Netta
Netti-An
Nettia
Nettie
Neurtha
Neuza
Neva
Nevada
Neve
Nevein
Nevia
Nevin
Nevra
Ney-Tang

Neya
Neyanna
Neyla
Neysa
Nga
Ngaire
Ngaluahoe
Ngan
Ngo
Ngoc
Ngoc-Vicky
Ngozi
Nguyen
Nguyet́
Nhi
Nhia
Nhoc
Nhu
Niabi
Niacora
Niah
Niambi
Niara
Niarisa
Nicalia
Nicci
Niccola
Niccole
Niccolo
Nichel
Nichell
Nichola
Nicholas
Nicholet
Nicholette
Nicholey
Nicholle
Nickalina
Nickcole
Nickeia
Nickelle
Nickenya
Nickesha
Nickeshia
Nicketa
Nickette
Nickey
Nickeya
Nickhole
Nickia
Nickila
Nickisha
Nickita
Nickiya
Nickol
Nickola
Nickoli
Nicoel
Nicol
Nicola-Kerry
Nicolbi
Nicole De Jesus
Nicole Elizabeth
Nicole Louis
Nicole Mae
Nicole Suzette
Nicolé
Nicole-Marie
Nicole-Renee
Nicolena
Nicolene
Nicoleshay
Nicolet
Nicolett
Nicoletta
Nicoli
Nicolina
Nicoline
Nicollet
Nicollette
Nicolyn
Nicomi
Nicoole
Nicoshia
Nicoya
Nida
Nida-Fatima
Nidal
Nidhi
Nidi
Nidia
Nieasha
Niecole
Niefrae
Nieha
Nieve
Nifateria
Nigarsultan
Nigel
Nigeria
Nigham
Nigui
Nihah
Niina
Niinortey
Nija
Nijah
Nijeria
Nijill
Nika
Nikado
Nikaela
Nikai
Nikaila
Nikara
Nikasha
Nikcola
Niké
Nikea
Nikedà
Nikedia
Nikeesha
Nikeeta
Nikeisha
Nikell
Nikesha
Niketa
Nikete
Niketrica
Niketris
Nikeya
Nikeyshal
Nikicia
Nikida
Nikiesha
Nikikita
Nikilona
Nikipa
Nikira
Nikiriya
Nikisha
Nikita Lynnette
Nikitia
Nikitress
Nikiya
Nikka
Nikkeria
Nikkeya
Nikki-Lee
Nikki-Marie
Nikkia
Nikkie
Nikkisha
Nikkitress
Nikkoel
Nikkole

Nikkolette
Nikky
Nikoal
Nikohl
Nikol
Nikola
Nikolene
Nikoletta
Nikolina
Nikolle
Niktia
Nikyta
Nila
Nilalini
Nilam
Nilamdeep
Nilani
Nilda
Nileela
Nilena
Nilesia
Nilka
Nillybeth
Nilsa
Nilufar
Nilufer
Nilza
Nima
Nimali
Nimira
Nimrat
Nimrata
Nina-Kristina
Ninadeniene
Ninafiora
Ninashka
Ninfa
Nini
Ninja
Ninosca
Ninoshka
Ninsenre
Ninya
Nioemi
Niokah
Niomi
Nipawan
Niquita
Niquitta
Niquole
Nirakone
Nirlande
Nirma Cristina
Nirosha
Niroshi
Nirusha
Nirva
Nisa
Nishali
Nisheka
Nishell
Nishkala
Nishma
Nisreen
Nissa
Nissi
Nita
Nita Maria
Nitasha
Niteisha
Nitika
Nitisha
Nitishia
Nitza
Niukayla
Niurka
Niveen
Nivia
Niya
Niyya Alexanderi
Nizbeth
Njemeh
Njeri
Nkaonyia
Nkauj
Nkechi
Nkieta
Nkolika
Nkoyo
Nneka
Nnenna
Nnolika
Noa
Noadia
Noala
Nocola
Noehmi
Noelani
Noelia
Noella
Noellelyn
Noemie
Noémie
Noemy
Noffah
Noha
Nohemi
Noida
Noire
Nolan
Nolina
Nolwazi
Nomalizwe
Nomi
Nomiki
Nomusa
Nona
Nonah
Noni
Nonie
Nonya
Noopur
Noor
Noor-Han
Nooreen
Noorin
Nora Abdulmohsen
Nora Ann
Nora-Lynn
Norady
Norah
Norah Jane
Noraimi
Noralee
Norali
Norangelice
Norciss
Nordia
Noreaka
Noreena
Noren
Norene
Nori
Noria
Norico
Norileen
Norita
Norma-Jean
Normaeli
Normandy
Normarie
Norrice
Norshawna
Norshawndra

Norwanna
Noshin-Naz
Nosipho
Noslen
Nostacia
Notel
Notoyia
Nouha
Nour
Noura
Nova
Nova-Laine
Novadawn
Novalee
Novela
Novelle
November
Novia
Novka
Novprit
Nozomi
Ntawnis
Ntozakehelen
Nubia
Nuchanad
Nue
Nuithia
Nukrica
Nulise
Nunziata
Nur Jannah
Nura
Nuraisha
Nurechia
Nureen
Nurhuda
Nuria
Nurin
Nurul
Nurul Naki
Nusaibah
Nusheen
Nuvia
Nxida
Ny
Nya
Nyah
Nyann
Nyanna
Nychelle
Nycohle
Nycole
Nycolle
Nyda
Nyderra
Nydia
Nydra
Nyeisha
Nyema
Nyesha
Nyeshia
Nyeta
Nyia
Nyiajah
Nyiesha
Nyisha
Nyjole
Nykea
Nykeadra
Nykeia
Nykele
Nykeva
Nykia
Nykita
Nykki-Lynn
Nykol
Nykole
Nyla
Nylah
Nyleen
Nyna
Nyoka
Nyome
Nyomi
Nyomie
Nyota
Nypsia
Nyra
Nyrie
Nysheena
Nyssarose
Nytasha
Nytosha

O

O'dasha
O'hara
Oak
Oakes
Oakley
Oanh
Oares
Oatoya
Obadiah
Obafemi
Oberlina
Obery
Obvianca
Ocairis
Ocatavice
Ocean
Oceanne
Oceon
Octavier
Octavisis
Octeria
Octivia
October
Odaemin
Odalis
Odalys
Odarkor
Odelia
Odessa
Odette
Odevilia
Odilia
Odipsy
Odisis
Odline
Odree
Odysa
Odyssey
Ofarrah
Ofelia
Officiana
Ofina
Ohio
Oiga
Okeshia
Okevia
Oksana
Okwuchelu
Ola
Olabisi
Oladele
Olahya
Olajuwon
Olawumi
Oleaha
Oleara
Olena
Olenka
Olesya

Olicia
Olimpiada
Olin
Oliva
Olive
Olivea
Oliveti
Olivetta
Olivia Elizabeth
Olivia-Helena
Olivia-Teresa
Ollicia
Ollie
Olmela
Olnee
Olowan
Olubusayo
Olufolakemi
Olufunmilayo
Olunda
Oluseun
Oluwatomi
Oluyemisi
Olympia
Olyndia
Olyvia
Oma
Omaira
Omara
Omarack
Omaris
Omayra
Omeaike
Omega
Omesha
Ometela
Omni
Omnique
Omnisha
Omolola
Omotayo
Ona
Onajah
Ondalee
Ondrea
Ondriea
Oneasha
Oneida
Onelie
Oneretta
Onietha
Onisha
Onna
Ontavia
Onya
Onyeka
Onyx
Onzanikka
Opal
Opale
Ophelia
Ophilia
Ophra
Ophrahstine
Oprah
Oqudra
Oqueria
Ora
Ora-Lea
Oralia
Oralis
Orangina
Oreal
Orean
Oreana
Orenda
Oreoia
Oressa
Oreteria
Oriana
Orie
Oriel
Orielle
Orisa
Orisel
Orissa
Orit
Oritisha
Orkia
Orla
Orlanda
Orlando
Orli
Orlinda
Orly
Orly-Elinor
Ornesha
Orpha
Orquidea
Orquidia
Orsolya
Ortavia
Orveline
Orveta
Orysia
Oryssa
Orytnell
Osa
Oshay
Osheka
Osia
Osie
Oslyne
Otila
Otisha
Otishia
Otoius
Otolose
Otria
Ottilie
Oudeline
Ouida
Oulaivone
Oun'janiese
Outi
Owahchige
Owna
Ozea
Ozella
Ozlem
Oznites

P

Pa
Padocia
Padra
Padrina
Paegan
Paeter
Paetra
Page
Pagen
Pagi
Pagona
Pahsa
Paisley
Paisleyann
Paivi
Paj
Pajcic
Pakoya
Palesa
Pallavi
Palma-Angela

Palmer
Palmida
Paloma
Pam
Pam-Marie
Pamala
Pamalee
Pamela-Charity
Pamela-Dawn
Pamella
Pamila
Pamilla
Pammie
Pamula
Panagiota
Panayiota
Panayota
Pandora
Pang
Panganga
Panit
Pankita
Panmany
Panolgiota
Panorea
Paradise
Paraskevi
Paraskivoula
Parasty
Parbir
Parchell
Pardeep
Paria
Paries
Parinaz
Parisa
Parise
Parisia Jordan
Pariss
Parissa
Parker
Parlie
Parminder
Parminder-Kaur
Parneet
Parpreet
Parrice
Parris
Partica
Parul
Parveen
Parvinder
Parvjit
Parylee
Parys
Paryse
Pascal
Pascale
Pascalleaimee
Pascha
Paschel
Pasean
Pasha
Pashaun
Paskel
Pasng
Pasqua
Passion
Passionette
Pat
Patamery
Patches
Paterialee
Patisha
Patona
Patraillia
Patrease
Patrece
Patreka
Patrell
Patresa
Patrese
Patrica
Patriceia
Patricia De Fatima Da Silva
Patricia-Anne
Patricia-Cecilia
Patricia-Lynn
Patricja
Patrick
Patricka
Patriece
Patrika
Patrikia
Patrina
Patrisha
Patrishia
Patrizia
Patrizzia
Patrnnia
Patronia
Patryce
Patrysia-Beatka
Patsy
Patti
Patti-Lyn
Pattie
Pattrice
Patty
Paul
Paula-Cristina
Paula-Natalia
Paule
Paulena
Pauletha
Pauletta
Paulina
Pauline-Celina
Pauline-Myriam
Pauline-Suzanne
Paulinique
Paulisa
Paunit
Pausefunei
Pavan
Pavandeep
Pavia
Paviale
Pavielle
Pavina
Pavithra
Pavitra
Pavla
Pavneet
Pawan
Pawangjit
Payal
Payden
Payengcha
Payton
Pazely
Peagan
Peareita
Pearlie
Pearlita
Pecola
Pedelia
Peelar
Peggy-Sue
Peige
Pektra
Peky
Pema
Penci

Pendle
Penelope
Penelopie
Penina
Peninnah
Pennee
Penney
Penni
Penni-Lee
Pennie
Penny-Jo
Penny-Laine
Pennylynn
Penthes
Pepper
Perdita
Peri
Periscia
Perisha
Perita
Perla
Perline
Perm
Perniecia
Pernilla
Pernisha
Perrette
Perri
Perriann
Perrie
Perrin
Perry
Persephanie
Persephone
Pertisha
Peshonna
Pessie
Petchulla
Petesha
Petiqueshandre
Petrina
Petrine
Petroa
Petrona
Petronella
Petronia
Petyah
Peyton
Phadra
Phadre
Phadren
Phae
Phaedra
Phaidra
Phala
Phalena
Phallen
Phallon
Phally
Phalon
Phan
Phanchipa
Phara
Pharin
Phénecia
Pheara
Phebe
Pheldrique
Phelesha
Phelisia
Phemi
Phenisha
Pheobe
Pheona
Pherrin
Phetmanie
Phiannon
Philadelphia
Philca
Philette
Philica
Philicia
Philida
Philip
Philippa
Philisha
Phillip
Phillipa
Phillippa
Phillis
Philomena
Philonna
Philycia
Phimphone
Phlice
Phoenix
Phoi
Pholy
Phonmalay
Photina
Phrankee
Phronsie
Phryne
Phteca
Phuchia
Phung
Phuong
Phurtura
Phyatasa
Phylecia
Phylesia
Phylis
Phylisha
Phylisia
Phyllecia
Phyllicia
Phyllisia
Phyllisjo
Physlicia
Pia
Pia Tanish
Pia-Lauren
Piara
Pieper
Pierce
Piere
Pierinna
Pierreline
Pierrette
Pieter
Pietra
Pietre
Pietrina
Pilar
Pilimilose
Pimpilar
Pinelopi
Pinkey
Pinkie
Pinra
Piper
Pipiena
Pleasants
Pleshette
Poi
Pola
Polly
Polo
Ponmaly
Ponter
Pooja
Poonam
Poonum
Poorvi
Poppy
Porcha

Porchai
Porchare
Porche
Porchia
Porchsa
Porchusa
Porcsha
Porcshe
Pornampa
Pornepnn
Porscha
Porschà
Porschea
Porschecia
Porschee
Porschia
Porshà
Porshai
Porshay
Porshe
Porshia
Portiea
Portland
Poshà
Pourche
Pousha
Prabhjot
Prachi
Pracilla
Prairie
Praise
Praveen
Prea
Precida
Precious Dominiq
Precious Turquoi
Preet
Preethi
Preeti
Preety
Preeya
Prema
Prentice
Presadani-Helessage
Prescill
Prescilla
Presious
Presley
Preya
Preytrice
Prianka
Pricila
Pricilla
Pride
Primitiva
Princcess
Princess Judah
Princetta
Princie
Princilla
Prineikai
Printellina
Prisca
Priscella
Priscila
Priscill
Priscilla-Ashley
Priscille
Priscillia-Hope
Prisella
Prisila
Prisma
Pritha
Pritika
Priya-Nitu
Priyanka
Priyanta
Procia
Promila
Promise
Providence
Provvidenza
Prubjoth
Prudence
Puja
Punamdeep
Punampreet
Puneet
Puneetjo
Punghwa
Pura
Purificacion
Purnata
Purnice
Purvi
Puttaporn
Puyuk Vera

Q

Qairul
Qauntilla
Qeysha
Qiana
Qiarra
Qihui
Qmetee
Qquani
Quachell
Qualisha
Qualonda
Quamika
Quana
Quanatrenae
Quanda
Quandra
Quandreka
Quanecia
Quanee
Quaneisha
Quanesha
Quanesia
Quanika
Quanikka
Quanikki
Quanique
Quanisha
Quanishia
Quanita
Quanricka
Quansha
Quantara
Quantay
Quantel
Quantenique
Quanteria
Quanterria
Quantiara
Quantinish
Quantisha
Quantrina
Quantyce
Quanza
Quara
Quarnisha
Quashanda
Quashawdna
Quasheca
Quateka
Quatella
Quatesha
Quatonja
Quaunteka

Quavetta
Quawanica
Quay
Quayla
Quayshaw
Quazina
Quazma
Queen
Queena
Queenda
Queenetta
Queenie
Queenika
Queeta
Quehona
Queira
Queisha
Queli
Quella
Quellencia
Quenchell
Quenell
Quenessa
Quenest
Quenetta
Quenikka
Quenisha
Quenishia
Quenna
Quentin
Quentrese
Querie
Queshia
Queshonda
Quetelinne
Queteria
Quetty
Qui'lencia
Quian
Quianna
Quichell
Quierra
Quin
Quina
Quinae
Quinanna
Quinby
Quincey
Quinci
Quincy
Quindara
Quindelyn
Quindolyn
Quineda
Quineisha
Quineita
Quinesha
Quineshia
Quinesia
Quinetta
Quinika
Quiniksha
Quinisha
Quinita
Quinleia
Quinlin
Quinna
Quinndara
Quinnesse
Quinnette
Quinntina
Quinshanna
Quinshetta
Quinta
Quintamar
Quintaneshia
Quintanna
Quintara
Quintavia
Quintella
Quinteria
Quintia
Quintina
Quintirra
Quinyetta
Quionna
Quiria
Quisheena
Quishelle
Quita
Quithisa
Qulanda
Qulantre
Qunices
Quonesha
Quoniece
Quonnisha
Quoshonna
Qurat-Ul-Ain
Quyen
Quyendzi
Quynh
Qvaunda
Qwincia
Qyanisha
Qzuanita

R

Rénee
R. J.
Ra Shae
Ra Shawn
Ra Sheia
Ra Yanda
Ràquel
Ra-Ina
Raadhaa
Raakel
Raamyn
Raba
Rabaa-Lamia
Rabab
Rabecca
Rabecka
Rabeha
Rabia
Rabiyah
Rabya
Rabyah
Racel
Racene
Racha
Rachab
Rachael-Sarah
Rachaele
Rachal
Rachalle
Rachana
Rachel Alexandri
Rachel Marisela
Rachel-Anne
Rachel-Diane
Rachel-Louise
Rachel-Lynn
Rachel-Marie
Rachela
Rachelann
Rachella
Rachita
Rachna
Rachsel
Rachyl
Racine

Rackel
Racquell
Racretia
Radekah
Radford
Radha
Radharan
Radhika
Radie
Radino
Rae Ann
Rae Chelle
Rae Jean
Rae Niece
Rae-Ann
Rae-Anne
Rae-Len
Raea
Raeairra
Raeana
Raeanna
Raeanne
Raeceen
Raechele
Raechell
Raechelle
Raeciana
Raecine
Raeda
Raedeen
Raeden
Raeesa
Raegan
Raeh
Raeisha
Raejean
Raela
Raelee
Raeleen
Raeleesha
Raeleigh
Raeleigha
Raelene
Raelle
Raelyn
Raelynn
Raeme
Raena
Raenah
Raeneice
Raeneisha
Raesha
Raeshelle
Raevathi
Raewyn
Rafaela
Rafella
Rafferty
Raghdaa
Raghdah
Ragina
Ragnhild
Raheena
Rahel
Rahjanni
Rahmia
Rahmina
Rahna
Rahni
Rahsaan
Rahshea
Rahsheda
Rahsheita
Rai
Raia
Raianne
Raichelle
Raileen
Railey
Raima
Raimy
Rainbeau
Rainbeaux
Rainbow
Raine
Rainey
Raini
Rainie
Rainna
Rainy
Rainy Mesa
Raisa
Raisah
Raishada
Raishonn
Raissa
Raiyonte
Raiza
Raizel
Rajaa
Rajal
Rajee
Rajeeyah
Rajena
Rajhans
Rajneesh
Rajni
Rajpreet
Rajveer
Rakecia
Rakeena
Rakeisha
Rakeitta
Rakellie
Rakenya
Rakesha
Rakeshia
Rakisha
Rakole
Raksmay
Raleigh
Ralene
Ralinda
Ralisha
Ralonda
Ralynn
Rama
Raman
Ramana
Ramandip
Ramanjit
Ramanpreet
Ramaya
Ramee
Rameet
Ramesh
Ramey
Ramha
Rami
Ramiah
Ramie
Ramika
Ramina
Ramneek
Ramneet
Ramonda
Ramonique
Ramonita
Ramsey
Ramssel
Ramune
Ramy
Rana
Ranae
Ranan
Ranasha

Ranata
Ranay
Randah
Randal
Randalee
Randan
Randaya
Randchelle
Rande
Randee
Randeep
Randel
Randell
Randelle
Randene
Randereke
Randette
Randi-Lee
Randi-Leigh
Randi-Lyn
Randi-Lynn
Randi-Lynne
Randie
Randii
Randilee
Randilynn
Randle
Randlyn
Random
Randy
Randyl
Ranecia
Raneciavakitta
Ranee
Raneesha
Raneka
Ranell
Ranelle
Ranesha
Raneshia
Ranesna
Rani
Rania
Rania-Mona
Ranice
Raniece
Ranika
Ranisha
Ranita
Raniya
Ranjot
Ranmeet
Ranna
Rannda
Ranny
Ranota
Ranquelle
Ranya
Ranzi
Raona
Raphaela
Raphaella
Raphaelle
Rapheal
Raphine
Raqueal
Raquell
Raquelle
Raqueria
Raquine
Raquisha
Rasamee
Rasanna
Raschél
Raschel
Raschelle
Rashada
Rashae
Rashael
Rashana
Rashanda
Rashani
Rashanta
Rashanudra
Rasharia
Rashaunda
Rashaundra
Rashawn
Rashawna
Rashdah
Rashea
Rashebia
Rasheda
Rashedah
Rasheedàt
Rasheeda
Rasheedah
Rasheema
Rasheena
Rasheeta
Rasheika
Rasheka
Rashel
Rashele
Rashell
Rashelle
Rashi
Rashieka
Rashiema
Rashika
Rashina
Rashll
Rashmi
Rashon
Rashona
Rashonda
Rashunda
Rasika
Rasmi
Rasmydao
Ratanya
Ratasha
Ratia
Ratisha
Ratna
Rattan
Rattyya
Rauchel
Ravae
Ravanjeet
Raveen
Raveena
Ravena
Ravennah
Ravi
Ravijot
Ravin
Ravinder
Ravjeet
Ravneet
Ravnoor
Ravonda
Ravyn
Raweyah
Raya-Gab
Rayah
Rayan
Rayann
Rayanna
Rayanne
Rayce
Raychael
Raychel
Raychelle
Raycine
Raycynthia

Raydin
Raydine
Raye
Rayel
Rayele
Rayelle
Rayena
Rayennon
Rayleen
Raylene
Raylenne
Raylin
Raylona
Rayma
Raymae
Raymesha
Raymie
Raymona
Raynae
Raynande
Rayne
Rayneisha
Raynell
Raynese
Raynetha
Raynisha
Raynolus
Rayonna
Raysa
Rayshada
Rayshanda
Rayshawn
Rayshawnda
Rayshell
Rayshelle
Rayshunda
Rayuana
Rayvaughn
Rayvin
Raywattie
Rayza
Razan
Razia
Rdohla
Re
Re Nia
Rénita
Réshawn
Rea
Reagan
Reah
Ream
Reame
Reana
Reane
Reann
Reannan
Reanne
Reannen
Reannon
Reatha
Reather
Reaundra
Reava
Rebakah
Rebba
Rebbeca
Rebbecca
Rebbecka
Rebbeka
Rebbie
Rébecca
Rebecca Ann
Rebecca-Jane
Rebecca-Lyn
Rebecca-Lynn
Rebeccah
Rebeccea
Rebeccka
Rebecha
Rebecka
Rebeckah
Rebeckia
Rebecky
Rebeha
Rebekha
Rebekka
Rebekkah
Rebekke
Rebel
Rebelle
Rebw
Reca
Rececca
Rechell
Rechelle
Recia
Recita
Recordia
Redawn
Redenna
Redricka
Reeanna
Reebie
Reed
Reegie
Reem
Reema
Reenu
Reesa
Reesey
Reeshonaw
Reetika
Reeva
Reganne
Regba
Regena
Regennia
Regia
Regiena
Reginald
Regine
Reginia
Reginique
Regis
Regla
Rehab
Rehana
Rehann
Rehanon
Reheema
Reibonna
Reid
Reidel
Reidun
Reigan
Reiko
Reilly
Reily
Rein
Reiny
Reiona
Reisha
Reith
Rejina
Reka
Rekeemah
Rekesia
Rekha
Rekia
Rekiah
Rekina
Rekisha
Rekiya
Relichia
Relicia

Rema
Remah
Remee
Remeika
Remeka
Remie
Remonda
Remonna
Remy
Ren
Renada
Renadeau
Renalda
Renarda
Renata-Helena
Renate
Renay
Renaysha
Renda
Rendi
Rene E
René
Renée
Rene-Johanna
Renea
Renecia
Renee Alexandria
Renee-Anne
Renee-Bianca
Renee-Cecile
Renee-Christine
Renee-Claude
Renee-Pierre
Reneen
Reneerose
Reneise
Reneisha
Reneka
Renell
Renelle
Renes
Renesha
Renesia
Renessa
Renetta
Renette
Renia
Renice Layshall
Renilda
Renique
Renise
Renisha
Renitza
Renna
Rennae
Renne
Renneé
Rennel
Rennell
Rennie
Renterial
Renuka
Renyarda
Renyatta
Reo
Reona
Reondda
Reonia
Rephaelle
Requel
Requita
Requitta
Resa
Reshae
Reshana
Reshaunda
Reshaunna
Reshawnda
Reshaye
Resheania
Resheea
Resheka
Reshell
Reshelle
Reshia
Reshina
Reshma
Reshmi
Reshon
Reshonda
Reshonte
Ressa
Ressie
Reta
Retasha
Retha
Retoneya
Revathi
Revati
Revena
Revia
Revida
Rexana
Rexann
Reyan
Reyanna
Reyden
Reyes
Reyme
Reyne
Rezarta
Rezen
Rhachel
Rhami
Rhanda
Rhandall
Rhandi
Rhanion
Rhapsody
Rhawnie
Rheà
Rhéa
Rheabecca
Rhealyn
Rheana
Rheann
Rheanna
Rheannan
Rheanne
Rheannon
Rhegan
Rheine
Rhema
Rhen
Rhenel
Rhenika
Rheta
Rheva
Rhian
Rhiana
Rhianen
Rhianne
Rhiannen
Rhianon
Rhiauna
Rhinnon
Rhodaisjoh
Rholynda
Rhona
Rhonda Chiquita
Rhondelle
Rhondene
Rhondiesha
Rhonesha

Rhonette
Rhoni
Rhonisha
Rhosheda
Rhyan
Rhyanna
Ria
Riah
Riakay
Rian
Riana
Riane
Riann
Rianna
Rianne
Riannon
Rianon
Riayn
Ribbie
Rica
Ricarda
Ricardra
Ricci-Lynn
Ricelda
Richa
Richa Lee
Richanda
Richanne
Richanti
Richard
Richchedda
Richeena
Richel
Richele
Richell
Richeta
Richezza
Richonda
Rici
Ricka
Rickeesia
Rickel
Rickesha
Rickeyah
Rickeyta
Ricki-Jo
Ricki-Lee
Rickia
Rickie
Rickilee
Rickina
Rickita
Rickkeyta
Rickquel
Ricky
Ricoya
Ricquel
Ricquelle
Ricquitayasmine
Ricshema
Ridhi
Rie
Rienda
Rihana
Rihanna
Rihannan
Riina
Riitta
Rika
Rikeisha
Rikell
Rikelle
Riki
Riki-Lyn
Rikia
Rikita
Rikkara
Rikki Lynn
Rikki-Jo
Rikki-Lee
Rikki-Lynn
Rilee
Rileigh
Rilie
Rilla
Rima
Rimple
Rimpy
Rina
Rinada
Rindee
Rindi
Rindy
Rinesha
Rini
Rinkpaul
Rinku
Rio
Rio Whitney
Riona
Riquaya
Riquel
Risa
Risako
Risha
Rishay
Rishona
Rishonda
Ritamae
Ritamarie
Ritney
Ritu
Rituko
Riva
Rivcah
Rivera
Riviane
Rivka
Rivkah
Rivkaw
Rizwana
Ro Shawnda
Roanda
Roanna
Roanne
Roayl
Robab
Robbi
Robbi-Lyn
Robbie
Robbilyn
Robbin
Robbrica
Robbyetta
Robbyn
Robbyn Ros
Robenita
Robernetta
Robert
Robertine
Roberto
Robi
Robina
Robine
Robinn
Robinta
Robyn-Leigh
Robyne
Robynn
Robynne
Rocchina
Rocela
Rochale
Rochel
Rochele
Rochell

Rockelle
Rockia
Rocsana
Rocxann
Rodalyn
Rodeline
Rodeo
Rodericka
Roderika
Rodina
Rodlyne
Rodna
Rodnae
Rodneisha
Rodnesha
Rodnetta
Rodnicka
Rodreicka
Rodricka
Rodrika
Rodshaun
Roen
Roeun
Roganna
Rogena
Roger
Rohana
Roheeda
Rohena
Rohini
Roisin
Rokaiya
Rokeria
Rokeshanik
Rokeshia
Rokiesha
Rola
Rolanda
Rolande
Rolene
Rolisha
Roly
Roma
Romaine
Romanda
Romanelle
Romanique
Romeise
Romeka
Romelle
Romesha
Rometta
Romi
Romie
Romilla
Romina
Romini
Romonia
Romysha
Rona
Ronalda
Ronchell
Rondai
Rondanielle
Rondel
Rondelle
Rondesia
Rondi
Roneceius
Ronecia
Ronee
Roneeka
Roneice
Roneisha
Ronelle
Roneria
Ronesha
Roneshia
Ronessa
Ronetta
Ronette
Roni
Ronica
Ronicca
Ronichia
Ronicia
Roniesha
Ronika
Roniqua
Ronisha
Ronit
Ronita
Ronitta
Ronja
Ronjaunee
Ronkena
Ronna
Ronndelle
Ronneckia
Ronnella
Ronnesa
Ronnesha
Ronnette
Ronneyka
Ronni
Ronnica
Ronnie
Ronnie-Lynn
Ronnise
Ronnisha
Ronnishia
Ronnitra
Ronny
Ronquntia
Ronsheika
Rontavia
Rontica
Rontishia
Rontraya
Ronvegus
Roopa
Roqhelle
Roquanda
Rori
Rortano
Rory
Rosa Lee
Rosa-Lina
Rosabel
Rosaida
Rosalbal
Rosalea
Rosalee
Rosaleen
Rosalena
Rosalia
Rosalin
Rosalina
Rosalinda
Rosaline
Rosalynd
Rosalynn
Rosalynne
Rosamaria
Rosamond
Rosana
Rosangela
Rosann
Rosannah
Rosaria
Rosario
Rosceda
Roschell
Roschelle
Rosciara
Rose Andre

Rose Ann
Rose Marie
Rose Veron
Rose-Ann
Rose-Anna
Rose-Anne
Rose-Lynn
Rose-Mae
Rose-Marie
Rose-Sharon
Rosealenna
Rosealynn
Roseda
Rosee Anne
Roseellen
Roseisela
Rosel
Roselaine
Roselé
Roselee
Roselene
Roselette
Roselica
Roselie
Roselina
Roseline
Rosell
Rosella
Roselle
Rosellen
Rosely
Roselyn
Roselyne
Roselynn
Rosem
Rosemari
Rosemeen
Rosemene
Rosemienta
Rosemonde
Rosena
Rosenda
Rosene
Rosenelle
Roseshar
Rosette
Rosey
Rosezana
Rosezella
Roshae
Roshan
Roshanda
Roshani
Roshanna
Roshanta
Roshaun
Roshaunda
Roshawn
Roshawnda
Roshawnna
Rosheena
Rosheika
Rosheka
Roshele
Roshell
Roshelle
Roshena
Roshenda
Roshenna
Rosheta
Roshni
Roshona
Roshonda
Rosie
Rosilee
Rosina
Rosio
Rosita
Rosli
Roslin
Roslord
Roslyn
Roslynn
Rosonya
Ross
Rossalyn
Rossalynn
Rossana
Rossane
Rosse
Rossetta
Rossie
Rosslyn
Rosy
Roszanna
Roszlynn
Rotasha
Rotem
Roudeline
Rowan
Rowena
Roxan
Roxane
Roxianna
Roxie
Roxie-Lee
Roxie-Sue
Roxolana
Roxy
Roxyanne
Roya
Royal
Royceline
Roychelle
Royelle
Royqesha
Roz
Roza
Rozaida
Rozalyn
Rozalynn
Rozanna
Rozanne
Rozelund
Rozena
Rozetta
Rozina
Rozland
Rrel
Ruan
Rubenna
Ruberta
Rubie
Rubina
Rubinder
Ruby-Jean
Ruby-Jo
Rubyn
Rucha
Ruchelle
Rucille
Rudee
Rudeline
Rudell
Rudelzie
Rudi
Rudie
Rudina
Rudy
Ruem
Ruenda
Rugayyah Cecile
Ruhee
Rukia
Rukina
Rula

Rumdeep
Runaka
Runna
Ruon
Rupa
Rupal
Rupel
Rupinder
Ruqqiya
Ruquya
Ruscelle
Ruselan
Rushell
Rushelle
Rushida
Russellynn
Russet
Russhell
Russhelle
Russi Gabriele
Russnea
Rusti
Rusty
Ruth-Ann
Ruth-Anne
Rutha
Ruthann
Ruthanne
Ruthe
Ruthie
Rutonaya
Ruza
Ruzella
Rya
Ryah
Ryane
Ryanna
Ryanne
Rycca
Rychelle
Rycki-Lynn
Rye
Ryelee
Ryen
Ryette
Rylee
Ryley
Rylie
Rylly
Rylyn
Ryma
Ryndi
Rynesha
Rynn
Rynthia
Ryoko
Ryshanne
Rysheema
Ryshima

S

Sáde
Saacoya
Saadia
Saaqshai
Saara
Saarecka
Saari
Saatu
Saba
Sabah
Sabahat
Saban
Sabaya
Sabbath
Sabeen
Sabel
Sabela
Sabella
Sabena
Saberia
Sabidha
Sabika
Sabill
Sabine
Sabine-Lori
Sabine-Salome
Sabira
Sabre
Sabreena
Sabren
Sabrena
Sabrhina
Sabria
Sabrin
Sabrina-Sally
Sabrinah
Sabrine
Sabrinia
Sabriya
Sabryee
Sabryna
Sabsina
Sachay
Sachét
Sacheen
Sachi
Sachiko
Sacide
Sacora
Sacorya
Sacyrille
Sada
Sadà
Sadaf
Sadarah
Saddaf
Sadé
Sadebeautia
Sadee
Sadef
Sadeka
Sadekie
Sadelasheika
Sadhna
Sadi
Sadia
Sadie-Lynn
Sadra
Saduea
Sady
Sae
Saechelle
Saeedah
Saeko
Saerica
Safa
Safeya
Saffa
Saffire
Saffiyah
Saffron
Safia
Safiah
Safire
Safiyah
Safiyya
Safiyyah
Safya-Sana
Sagal
Sage
Sage-Eli
Sagen
Sagia

Sahah
Sahar
Sahara
Sahardonay
Saharmohamma
Sahba
Sahej
Saheli
Saher-Batool
Sahily
Sahisha
Sahra
Sahsha
Sahvana
Sahvannh
Sahwntaye
Saica
Saida
Saidah
Saige
Saille
Saima
Saina
Saint Julia
Saira
Sairah
Sajedah
Sajida
Sajuliet
Sakara
Sakeena
Sakendra
Sakeria
Sakevia
Sakima
Sakina
Sakinah
Sakira
Sakithiya
Sakkara
Salace
Salandra
Salatha
Salathia
Salee
Saleeha
Saleema
Saleena
Salees
Saleha
Salem
Salema
Salicia
Salim
Salima
Salimah
Salinda
Salisha
Salishya
Salka
Sallee
Salley
Sallie
Sally Ann
Sally-Helene
Sallyann
Sallyanne
Sallyna
Salma
Salny
Salome
Salomi
Salone
Saloni
Salsabil
Salwa
Salyna
Salynn
Samaa
Samaiya
Saman
Samanath
Samanatha
Samandis
Samanitha
Samanithia
Samanta
Samanth
Samantha Desire
Samantha J
Samantha-Claire
Samantha-Jade
Samantha-Jean
Samantha-Joe
Samantha-Jolanta
Samantha-Lynn
Samantha-Rae
Samantha-Sue
Samanthajo
Samanthe
Samanthi
Samanthia
Samar
Samaria
Samarj
Samarol
Samarra
Samaya
Sambath
Sameen
Sameera
Sameerah
Sameese
Samelia
Samella
Sameria
Sametria
Sametrius
Sami
Sami-Jo
Samia
Samielle
Samientha
Samiha
Samihah
Samika
Samil
Samille
Samina
Samira
Samirade
Samirah
Samit
Samitra
Samiya
Samiyah
Samm
Sammanth
Sammantha
Sammar
Sammatha
Sammeka
Sammi
Sammi-Jean
Sammi-Jo
Sammie
Sammijo
Sammille
Sammy
Sammy-Jo
Sammyjo
Samnang
Samnath
Samone
Samonia

Samoria
Samuel
Samya
Samycha
Sanàa
Sana-Shae
Sanaa
Sanah
Sanam
Sanaz
Sancesca
Sancha
Sancharia
Sanchia
Sanda
Sandee
Sandell
Sandia
Sandie
Sandiey
Sandine
Sandip
Sandira
Sandra De Fatima
Sandra Elizabeth
Sandra Ive
Sandra Lee
Sandra-Jo
Sandra-Mac
Sandra-Marie
Sandralynn
Sandrea
Sandree
Sandreia
Sandrenna
Sandria
Sandrica
Sandricka
Sandrika
Sandrina
Sandrine
Sandro
Sandy-Aghavnie
Sandya
Saneen
Sanehjeet
Sanessa
Sang
Sangeeta
Sangeetha
Sangita
Sanha Sony
Sania
Sanica
Sanielle
Sanika
Sanise
Sanisha
Sanita
Sanitareus
Sanitria
Saniyyah
Sankeia
Sankerrya
Sanmathi
Sanna
Sanora
Sanquenette
Sanquese
Sanqunette
Sanserae Des
Santa
Santaniata
Santanna
Santas
Santayia
Santena
Santeria
Santia
Santika
Santina
Santinia
Santoria
Santos
Santoya
Santrell
Santtena
Sanya
Sanyt
Sanzari
Saoirse
Saori
Saory
Saphon
Saphyre
Sapna
Sapphira
Sapphire
Saprina
Saquanda
Saquiba
Saquita
Sara Alice
Sara Ann
Sara Denielle
Sara Elizabeth
Sara Jane
Sara Jean
Sara Rebecca
Sara-Anne
Sara-Ashley
Sara-Dawn
Sara-Dyan
Sara-Eli
Sara-Jane
Sara-Lee
Sara-Lynn
Sara-Mae
Sara-Marie
Sara-Meg
Sara-Niematullah
Sarabeth
Sarabjit
Sarah Ann
Sarah Anne
Sarah Elizabeth
Sarah Jean
Sarah Lyn
Sarah Madeleine
Sarah Marjorie
Sarah Reese
Sarah Ssadat
Sarah Suzanne
Sarah Tiffany
Sarah Williemae
Sarah Yehia
Sarah-Ann
Sarah-Anne
Sarah-Asmahan
Sarah-Dawne
Sarah-Elizabeth
Sarah-Georgia
Sarah-Jade
Sarah-Jane
Sarah-Jayne
Sarah-Jean
Sarah-Jeanne
Sarah-Julie
Sarah-Laine
Sarah-Lee
Sarah-Lisa
Sarah-Lynn
Sarah-Marie
Sarah-Michele
Sarah-Nichol

Sarah-Rose
Sarah-Safwat
Sarah-Sumintra
Saraha
Sarahann
Sarai
Saralee
Saraly
Saralyn
Saralynn
Saranique
Saranna
Sarath
Saravjit
Saraya
Sarazabeen
Sarbjit
Sarde
Sarean
Sareena
Sareesha
Sareeta
Sareka
Sarena
Sarene
Sarenna
Sarenthi
Saresa
Sareta
Sareth
Saretta
Sarette
Sarha
Sariah
Sariann
Sarice
Sarie
Sarika
Sarilla
Sarim
Sarin
Sarissa
Sariyah
Sarkiva
Saroeung
Sarollie
Sarra
Sarrah
Sarrel
Sarri
Sarrie
Sarwat
Sary
Saryahia
Sarynn
Sascha
Sasha-Dawn
Sasha-Lee
Sasha-Sevana
Sashae
Sashah
Sashalai
Sashana
Sashara
Sashel
Sashia
Sashira
Sashsha
Saska
Saskia
Satara
Sataria
Satarra
Satedra
Sateria
Saterra
Saterria
Satha
Sathasiuam
Satin
Satinder
Satonia
Satoria
Satricia
Satu
Satwant
Sau-Wai
Sauanah
Saucha
Saudia
Saudy
Saumininic
Saumya
Sauncherei
Saura
Sausan
Sausha
Savage Julieta
Savaii
Savanah-Ann
Savanha
Savanhan
Savannha
Savauna
Savdah
Savedra
Saveena
Savena
Saveria
Savetri
Savhanna
Savika
Savilla
Savina
Savish
Savita
Savleen
Savory
Sawna
Sawsan
Sawsha
Sawyer
Saxon
Saxxon
Sayaka
Sayda
Saydie
Sayer
Sayla
Sayra
Sayward
Scarlet
Scarlette
Scearia
Schacara
Schaciana
Schae-Ann
Schala
Schaleeshia
Schanel
Schanell
Scharlane
Scharlene
Schaulis
Schaunta
Schauri
Schelby
Schelomite
Scherîe
Scherise
Schevaun
Schikenna
Schina
Schkenna
Schlonda
Schneida

Schneiqueka
Schnella
Schnetta
Schona
Schonie
Schquita
Schrell
Schuyla
Schuylia
Schyler
Scianda
Sciandra
Scion
Scota
Scotia
Scotti
Scottie
Scotty
Sea
Seaana
Seabrin
Seagry
Seaira
Sealii
Sean
Seana
Seandra
Seane
Seanette
Seann
Seanna
Seannalisa
Seantavias
Seanté
Seanteelle
Seantelle
Seara
Searria
Season
Seasons
Seatira
Seattle
Seaward
Sebree
Sebrina
Secelia
Secora
Secord
Secorra
Seda
Seddoni
Sedef
Sedera
Sedika
Sedona
Sedora
Seeley
Seema
Seemab
Seerra
Seethamma
Seham
Seher
Sehren
Sehrezade
Sehrisa
Sehrrin
Sehrvon
Seiarra
Seidi
Seija
Seiko
Seira
Seirra
Seisha
Sejal
Seka
Sela
Selah
Selen
Selene
Selenia
Seleste
Selestia
Selia
Selicca
Selicia
Selin
Selise
Selma
Selua
Selueni
Sely
Selyna
Selyne
Sema
Semaj
Semantha
Sember
Semieal
Semilena
Semjase
Semoia
Sen-Sum
Senait
Senda
Sendiea
Senea
Senecca
Sengareroun
Senise
Senjilynann
Senna
Senobia
Senora
Senovia
Senta
Sentariarl
Sentoria
Sentrella
Seona
Sephora
Sepideh
Sepricia
Seprina
Septembe
September
Sequana
Sequanna
Sequinta
Sequita
Sequoia
Sequorya
Sequoya
Sera
Serafina
Serah
Seraita
Serana
Seraphin
Serean
Seree
Sereena
Seren
Serena-Lynn
Serenda
Serene
Serenity
Serenna
Seretha
Seretta
Sergeline
Serica
Serienna
Serika
Serin

Serinah
Serinna
Serissa
Seritta
Serra
Serrah
Serreh
Serrhia
Serrin
Servia
Sesha
Seshedi
Sessalley
Set
Seta
Setareh
Setera
Seteria
Seton
Seuzeth
Sevan
Sevanah
Sevanh
Sevann
Sevasti
Seveluse
Severine
Sevgun
Seville
Seychelle
Seyka
Sh'vaun
Sha
Sha Lana
Sha Waya
Shàlene
Shàlonna
Shàquria
Shàronda
Shàtarra
Shàvaroughn
Sha-Brielle
Sha-Ritte
Shaadi
Shaaira
Shaaista
Shaakira
Shaalee
Shaanna
Shaara
Shaarkyzzylye
Shabaca
Shabana
Shabeeh
Shabina
Shablanka
Shabnaaz
Shabnam
Shabonia
Shabree
Shabreen
Shabreka
Shacara
Shacari
Shacarra
Shacobi
Shacoby
Shacola
Shacondra
Shacora
Shacorrha
Shacoy
Shacoya
Shacutteyachtre
Shada
Shadae
Shadala
Shadara
Shadaria
Shadarria
Shadaryl
Shadawn
Shaday
Shaddy
Shade
Shadea
Shadeana
Shadeaw
Shadee
Shadeera
Shadella
Shaderra
Shaderric
Shadi
Shadia
Shadiah
Shadie
Shadiya
Shadoe-Ann
Shadon
Shadonna
Shadonya
Shadora
Shadoris
Shadreka
Shadricka
Shadrien
Shadrika
Shae-Lyn
Shaeen
Shaeine
Shaela
Shaelea
Shaelee
Shaeleigh
Shaelene
Shaelie
Shaelin
Shaeline
Shaely
Shaelyn
Shaelynn
Shaelynne
Shaemara
Shaena
Shaenel
Shaentavia
Shaeteela
Shaeya
Shafaq
Shafeeqa
Shafonda
Shafown
Shafu
Shagora
Shaguanda
Shahadah
Shahaleigh
Shahana
Shahar
Shahara
Shaharazad
Shahayla
Shaheen
Shaheena
Shaherose
Shahi
Shahidah
Shahin
Shahina
Shahira
Shahlah
Shahnan
Shahnaz
Shahran
Shahrbonu

Shahzadi
Shaia
Shaida
Shaiday
Shaideria
Shaiereca
Shaila
Shailan
Shaileah
Shailee
Shailey
Shailin
Shailyn
Shailynne
Shain
Shainah
Shainna
Shaira
Shaista
Shaiya
Shaiza
Shajah
Shajna
Shajuan
Shajuana
Shajuanda
Shajuanza
Shaka
Shakala
Shakama
Shakara
Shakarah
Shakari
Shakavian
Shakayla
Shakeanja
Shakebia
Shakeda
Shakedra
Shakeela
Shakeema
Shakeena
Shakeerah
Shakeeta
Shakeeyah
Shakeia
Shakeidra
Shakeila
Shakeima
Shakeira
Shakeita
Shakeitha
Shakeithia
Shakeitriyia
Shakeiva
Shakela
Shakema
Shakena
Shakendr
Shakendra
Shakendria
Shakenna
Shakerah
Shakeria
Shakeriay
Shakesha
Shaketa
Shaketha
Shakethia
Shaketia
Shakeva
Shakevia
Shakevya
Shakeya
Shakeyia
Shakeyla
Shakeyra
Shakiathia
Shakiera
Shakietta
Shakika
Shakila
Shakima
Shakina
Shakinnya
Shakir
Shakirah
Shakirat
Shakirra
Shakitah
Shakiya
Shaklyn
Shakoia
Shakora
Shakoyia
Shakyra
Shala
Shalae
Shalaina
Shalaine
Shalako
Shalalia
Shalamar
Shalana
Shaland
Shalanda
Shalann
Shalauna
Shalaunce
Shalaya
Shalayn
Shalayne
Shaldawn
Shale
Shalea
Shaleah
Shaleana
Shalee
Shaleea
Shaleen
Shaleena
Shaleh
Shalen
Shalena
Shalene
Shalené
Shalepia
Shalesa
Shalese
Shalesha
Shalesia
Shalesta
Shaleta
Shaletha
Shaletta
Shalexis
Shaley
Shalia
Shalicia
Shalika
Shalimar
Shalin
Shalina
Shalini
Shalisa
Shalise
Shalisha
Shalisia
Shalisse
Shalitha
Shaliz
Shallan
Shalleena
Shallete
Shallice
Shallie

Shallingda
Shallo
Shallon
Shallyn
Shalmali
Shalom
Shalome
Shalon
Shalondra
Shalonn
Shalonne
Shalquindra
Shalrie
Shalta
Shalvah
Shalya
Shalyn
Shalyna
Shalynda
Shalynn
Shalys
Shalyse
Shama
Shamae
Shamaine
Shamala
Shamalar
Shamalle
Shamanda
Shamane
Shamani
Shamanika
Shamanique
Shamar
Shamara
Shamarah
Shamari
Shamaria
Shamarla
Shamarra
Shamarri
Shamberli
Shambra
Shambray
Shambre
Shambreka
Shambria
Shamcha
Shameca
Shamecca
Shamecha
Shameeka
Shameika
Shameke
Shamekia
Shamela
Shamelia
Shamella
Shamera
Shamere
Shamerize
Shametra
Shami
Shamia
Shamiah
Shamica
Shamicia
Shamicka
Shamieka
Shamiesha
Shamikia
Shamila
Shamille
Shamin
Shamina
Shaminder
Shamique
Shamir
Shamiran
Shamiria
Shamisha
Shamiska
Shammara
Shammy
Shamon
Shamond
Shamonique
Shamonn
Shamonya
Shamora
Shamorra
Shamorria
Shamorrow
Shamorsha
Shampree
Shamya
Shamyia
Shan
Shan'tel
Shana-Rae
Shanabri
Shanacee
Shanada
Shanael
Shanah
Shanaill
Shanaior
Shanais
Shanal
Shanale
Shanan
Shananee
Shanara
Shanaski
Shanata
Shanatonio
Shanatte
Shanaue
Shanavia
Shanay
Shanaya
Shanda-Lynn
Shandace
Shandalee
Shandalyn
Shandani
Shandara
Shande
Shandease
Shandee
Shandel
Shandell
Shandelle
Shandelyn
Shandesia
Shandice
Shandie
Shandika
Shandoah
Shandon
Shandorra
Shandrea
Shandreka
Shandriah
Shandrie
Shandrieka
Shandrika
Shandryn
Shandy
Shandyn
Shane
Shané
Shanea
Shaneaka
Shaneal
Shaneatra

Shaneatta
Shanece
Shanee
Shaneé
Shaneeka
Shaneen
Shaneese
Shaneia
Shaneika
Shaneil
Shanekia
Shanekra
Shanena
Shanene
Shanequa
Shanerra
Shanese
Shanesha
Shaneshia
Shanessa
Shanetha
Shanetria
Shanetta
Shanette
Shanevya
Shaneya
Shaneyda
Shaneza
Shang
Shania
Shanica
Shanicca
Shanice
Shanicka
Shanicqua
Shanie
Shaniea
Shaniece
Shaniecei
Shanieka
Shaniel
Shaniels
Shanieva
Shanifa
Shanik
Shanike
Shanikia
Shanikka
Shanikqua
Shanikwa
Shanin
Shanina
Shaninder
Shaniqua
Shaniquca
Shanique
Shanisa
Shanissha
Shanisty
Shanitra
Shanivory
Shanka
Shankayes
Shankeeta
Shankia
Shanlantia
Shanlee
Shanlentia
Shanley
Shanlie
Shannél
Shanna Lee
Shanna-Lee
Shannah
Shannasces
Shannda
Shannea
Shanneen
Shannel
Shannell
Shannelle
Shannen
Shannie
Shannika
Shannin
Shanniqua
Shannoa
Shannon Alexandr
Shannon-Leah
Shannon-Lee
Shannon-Lynn
Shannon-Marie
Shannondoah
Shannondoeh
Shanntell
Shannyn
Shanoah
Shanolt
Shanova
Shanovia
Shanqualla
Shanquan
Shanquaneik
Shanqueena
Shanquel
Shanquella
Shanquendra
Shanquetta
Shanquilla
Shanrecka
Shanreka
Shanricka
Shanrika
Shanron
Shantai
Shantal
Shantan
Shantana
Shantanae
Shantanell
Shantani
Shantanickia
Shantanika
Shantanna
Shantara
Shantaria
Shantasia
Shantauia
Shantavia
Shantay
Shantaya
Shantaye
Shanté
Shantea
Shanteal
Shantee
Shanteil
Shanteka
Shantel Harvina
Shantel'-Marie
Shantele
Shantella
Shantera
Shanteria
Shanteron
Shanterria
Shantesa
Shantese
Shanteviya
Shanthikamari
Shanti
Shantia
Shantida
Shantie
Shantieria

Shantikia
Shantil
Shantille
Shantina
Shantira
Shantirea
Shantise
Shantisha
Shantizia
Shantora
Shantoria
Shantoya
Shantoyia
Shantrail
Shantravia
Shantreece
Shantrell
Shanttoria
Shantwanett
Shantwann
Shantyl
Shantyle
Shanucey
Shany
Shanyn
Shaon
Shaona
Shaonda
Shapell
Shaphone
Shappir
Shapree
Shaqella
Shaqia
Shaquadria
Shaquala
Shaqualla
Shaquallia
Shaquan
Shaquana
Shaquand
Shaquanda
Shaquandra
Shaquanera
Shaquani
Shaquanna
Shaquansia
Shaquantia
Shaquavia
Shaquda
Shaqueita
Shaquellia
Shaquese
Shaquetta
Shaquila
Shaquilla
Shaquiondy
Shaquira
Shaquitta
Shaqula
Shaquonda
Shaquoya
Shaqyita
Shar'de
Shar-Dae
Shar-Day
Shara-Lea
Sharada
Sharade
Sharae
Sharaé
Sharah
Sharai
Sharaiah
Sharaine
Sharal
Sharala
Sharalee
Sharalyn
Sharalynn
Sharan
Sharanazar
Sharanda
Sharanjit
Sharasa
Sharau
Sharaunda
Sharay
Sharaya
Shardai
Shardea
Shardee
Shardeia
Shardey
Shardicia
Sharea
Sharease
Sharece
Shareda
Sharedé
Sharedon
Shareean
Shareece
Shareefah
Shareeka
Shareema
Shareen
Shareena
Shareese
Shareeta
Shareka
Sharekia
Sharel
Sharell
Sharella
Sharelle
Sharelyn
Sharen
Sharena
Sharene
Sharesa
Sharese
Sharessa
Sharetha
Shareva
Sharevia
Sharhonda
Shari-Anne
Shari-Lynn
Sharia
Shariah
Shariaha
Sharian
Sharianne
Sharianty
Sharica
Sharice
Sharicka
Sharidan
Sharie
Shariece
Sharieta
Sharifa
Sharifah
Sharika
Sharil
Sharilyn
Sharin
Sharina
Sharinda
Sharine
Sharinika
Sharis
Sharise
Sharisha
Shariss

Sharissa
Sharisse
Sharkila
Sharlaina
Sharlamaine
Sharlane
Sharlee
Sharleen
Sharleine
Sharleis
Sharlena
Sharlet
Sharlett
Sharlie
Sharlisha
Sharlly
Sharlott
Sharlotta
Sharlotte
Sharlyn
Sharlynn
Sharma
Sharmae
Sharmain
Sharmaine
Sharmane
Sharmanta
Sharmanye
Sharmatte
Sharmayne
Sharme
Sharmeca
Sharmeen
Sharmerra
Sharmicee
Sharmika
Sharmila
Sharmin
Sharmiza
Sharmonique
Sharmyra
Sharna
Sharnae
Sharnay
Sharne
Sharnea
Sharnease
Sharnee
Sharneese
Sharnell
Sharnelle
Sharnese
Sharnett
Sharnetta
Sharnise
Sharocco
Sharolyn
Sharon Michelle
Sharon-Nplias
Sharona
Sharonann
Sharondell
Sharonia
Sharonica
Sharonjit
Sharonlee
Sharonna
Sharonnotae
Sharontrell
Sharony
Sharoyal
Sharquita
Sharr-Da
Sharra
Sharrah
Sharrell
Sharren
Sharrese
Sharri
Sharrie
Sharron-Jean
Sharrona
Sharronda
Sharronte
Sharrunia
Sharry
Shartay
Shartez
Shartoya
Sharun
Sharuti
Shary
Sharyl
Sharyl-Lynn
Sharyn
Sharyon
Sharyse
Shasaieh
Shascade
Shasekatanequa
Shasha
Shasha Ra
Shashi
Shashia
Shashonda
Shashonie
Shashonna
Shasonian
Shastavia
Shastina
Shatae
Shataria
Shatarra
Shatasha
Shatashia
Shataura
Shatavia
Shatavius
Shatawn
Shataya
Shatayla
Shatedria
Shateen
Shateira
Shateka
Shatekia
Shatela
Shaterah
Shateria
Shatherian
Shatia
Shatiana
Shatierra
Shatika
Shatila
Shatina
Shatiria
Shatokwa
Shatonia
Shatoniah
Shatonya
Shatora
Shatoria
Shatorria
Shatorya
Shatoshi
Shatoya
Shatoyna
Shatra
Shatreen
Shatreka
Shatrell
Shatrice
Shatrondra
Shatura
Shatyra

Shauda
Shaughna
Shaughnessy
Shaula
Shaumarie
Shaun
Shauna Kaye
Shauna Marie
Shauna-Lee
Shaunaca
Shaunacy
Shaunae
Shaunah
Shauncharae
Shaundala
Shaundel
Shaundra
Shaundrea
Shaundree
Shaundria
Shaundrice
Shaune
Shaunee
Shauneen
Shaunell
Shaunelle
Shaunessy
Shaunetra
Shaunetrious
Shaunette
Shauni
Shaunice
Shaunicy
Shaunie
Shaunika
Shaunisha
Shaunnea
Shaunquala
Shaunta
Shauntae
Shauntavia
Shauntay
Shaunte
Shaunte Rene
Shauntea
Shauntee
Shaunteena
Shauntei
Shauntel
Shauntell
Shauntelle
Shauntia
Shauntier
Shauntiya
Shauntrel
Shauntrell
Shauntrella
Shaunua
Shaunya
Shaurice
Shautae
Shautonja
Shavahna
Shavan
Shavana
Shavanna
Shavanna Virdue
Shavaun
Shaveen
Shavell
Shavonda
Shavondra
Shavone
Shavonn
Shavonna
Shavonni
Shavontae
Shavonte
Shavonté
Shavorae
Shavoun
Shavoya
Shawana
Shawanda
Shawanna
Shawante
Shawday
Shawde
Shawlette
Shawn-Lee
Shawnà
Shawna-Aline
Shawna-Lea
Shawna-Lee
Shawna-Lyn
Shawna-Lynn
Shawna-Marie
Shawna-Nirvana
Shawna-Rose
Shawnacy
Shawnah
Shawnai
Shawnaka
Shawnalee
Shawnassey
Shawnassie-Lynn
Shawndale
Shawndan
Shawndi
Shawndia
Shawndra
Shawndrel
Shawndrell
Shawndylin
Shawne
Shawnee
Shawneena
Shawneequa
Shawneika
Shawnell
Shawnen
Shawnese
Shawnetrae
Shawnett
Shawni
Shawnicces
Shawnicka
Shawnie
Shawnika
Shawnquita
Shawnra
Shawnreka
Shawnta
Shawntae
Shawntakia
Shawntavia
Shawntay
Shawnte
Shawnté
Shawntee
Shawntel
Shawntell
Shawntelle
Shawnteria
Shawntia
Shawntil
Shawntile
Shawntill
Shawntille
Shawntina
Shawntish
Shawntraivia
Shawntrese
Shawntriece
Shawnyell
Shawquice

Shawquita
Shawtay
Shawuoia
Shawvonte
Shawwona
Shaya
Shayda
Shaye
Shayha
Shayia
Shaylagh
Shaylah
Shaylain
Shaylan
Shaylea
Shaylen
Shaylene
Shayley
Shayli
Shaylie
Shaylin
Shaylla
Shaylyn
Shaylynn
Shayma
Shaymaa
Shaynae
Shayne
Shaynee
Shayni
Shayvon
Shazareen
Shazea
Shazeema
Shazeen
Shazeena
Shazia
Shazmin
Shazondra
Shazzmin
Shcara
Shciole
She Ra
Shéjana
Shea-Lee
Sheahna
Sheakita
Shealee
Shealene
Shealtiel
Shealy
Shealyn
Shealynn
Sheamara
Sheana
Sheann
Sheanna
Sheannon
Sheanta
Sheaon
Sheari
Shearll
Shearra
Sheatara
Sheaunna
Sheavon
Sheba
Shebre
Shecky
Shecopi
Shedreka
Sheean
Sheeba
Sheela
Sheena-Lynn
Sheena-Marie
Sheena-Rae
Sheenah
Sheenailla
Sheenan
Sheeneal
Sheenika
Sheenna
Sheera
Sheereen
Sheerie
Sheerra
Sheetal
Sheetara
Shefay
Shehla
Sheida-Myra
Sheighlyn
Sheika
Sheikara
Sheikayvia
Sheikha
Sheikna
Sheila-Dedorah
Sheilah
Sheildell
Sheileen
Sheiletta
Sheilia
Sheillynn
Sheilya
Sheina
Sheirys
Sheka
Shekeena
Shekeia
Shekeisha
Shekena
Shekenia
Sheketa
Shekevia
Shekhana
Shekia
Shekiah
Shekiera
Shekievia
Shekila
Shekilla
Shekima
Shekimah
Shekina
Shekinah
Shekira
Shekirrayah
Shekita
Shekofeh
Shekonna
Shekoufeh-Farrah
Shekufeh
Shelagh
Shelaine
Shelakh
Shelan
Shelanda
Shelayna
Shelayne
Shelbe
Shelbey
Shelbi
Shelbiana
Shelbie
Shelbrina
Shelby-Lynn
Shelcee
Shelda
Sheldena
Sheldon
Sheleah
Sheleatha
Shelecia

Shelee
Sheleen
Sheleena
Shelena
Shelene
Sheley
Sheleza
Sheli
Shelia E
Shelibia
Shelica
Shelicia
Shelina
Shelinda
Shelisa
Shelise
Shelisse
Shelita
Sheliza
Shella
Shellaine
Shellana
Shellany
Shellawenda
Shellby
Shellcy
Shellece
Shellene
Shelley-Ann
Shelley-Anne
Shelley-Lynn
Shelli
Shellian
Shellina
Shellis
Shellomet
Shellsea
Shelly-Anne
Shelly-Lyn
Shellyann
Shelnita
Shelonda
Shelsea
Shelsey
Shelton
Shemaria
Shembril
Shemeca
Shemeeka
Shemeil
Shemeka
Shemekia
Shemekii
Shemel
Shemeque
Shemere
Shemethy
Shemia
Shemica
Shemika
Shemila
Shemir
Shemmer
Shemsije
Shemy
Shemyra
Shenada
Shenae
Shenale
Shenandoah
Shenara
Shenarra
Shenay
Shenda
Shene
Shenea
Sheneda
Shenee
Sheneena
Sheneice
Sheneil
Sheneka
Shenel
Shenela
Shenell
Shenelle
Shenequa
Shenese
Shenetta
Shenica
Shenikah
Shenina
Shenique
Sheniquia
Shenirka
Shenise
Shenita
Shenna
Shenorria
Shentel
Shentelle
Shenul
Sheontee
Sheontra
Sheqita
Shequarius
Shequeit
Shequela
Shequele
Shequenta
Shequete
Shequida
Shequila
Shequita
Shequttia
Sher'ree
Sheraa
Sherae
Sherah
Sherail
Sheraine
Sheralee
Sheralle
Sheralyn
Sheralynne
Sheranda
Sherarose
Sheraton
Sheray
Sheraya
Sherazade
Sherdan
Sherdonna
Sherea
Shereace
Sherece
Shereé
Shereece
Shereen
Shereena
Sherees
Shereese
Shereeza
Sherehan
Shereka
Sherelle
Sherelynn
Sherema
Sheremie
Sherena
Sherene
Sheresa
Sherese
Shereta
Sheretta
Sherette

Sherez
Sherhea
Sherhonda
Sheri-Ann
Sheri-Anne
Sheri-Lee
Sheria
Sheriah
Sherian
Sherianne
Sherica
Sherice
Shericka
Sherida
Sheridan
Sherie
Sheriel
Sheriesa
Sheriffia
Sherilene
Sherill
Sherily
Sherilyn
Sherilynn
Sherilynne
Sherin
Sherina
Sherine
Sherisa
Sherise
Sherise-Marie
Sherissa
Sherisse
Sheritha
Sheritta
Sherka
Sherlesky
Sherley
Sherli
Sherlinda
Sherline
Sherly
Sherlyn
Sherlyne
Shermain
Shermeen
Shermetta
Shermikka
Shermin
Shermise
Shermisha
Shermona
Shermrial
Shernay
Sherneice
Shernel
Shernice
Shernicka
Sheron
Sherona
Sheronda
Sheronica
Sheronna
Sherose
Sherra
Sherrae
Sherrain
Sherral
Sherray
Sherraye
Sherree
Sherreen
Sherrel
Sherrell
Sherrelle
Sherret
Sherrey
Sherrhonda
Sherri-Ann
Sherri-Jayne
Sherri-Lee
Sherri-Lynn
Sherria
Sherriah
Sherriana
Sherrica
Sherricka
Sherrie-Lynn
Sherrie-Lynne
Sherrielee
Sherrika
Sherril
Sherrill
Sherrilyn
Sherrilynn
Sherrina
Sherrish
Sherrita
Sherriva
Sherron
Sherronne
Sherry Ann
Sherry-Ann
Sherry-Anne
Sherry-Jean
Sherry-Lee
Sherry-Lynn
Sherrylynn
Sherryse
Sherstel
Sherstin
Shervahn
Sherveca
Shervonna
Shery
Sheryce
Sherylanne
Sherylly
Sheryy
Shetara
Shetarah
Shetarrah
Sheteria
Sheva
Sheval
Shevani
Shevara
Shevaré
Shevaun
Shevell
Shevelle
Sheveta
Shevie
Shevinia
Shevon
Shevonda
Shevone
Shevonne
Shewandalith
Shey
Sheyama
Sheye
Sheyenne
Sheyla
Sheylyn
Sheyndl
Shi
Shi-Anne
Shiakenia
Shiana
Shianda
Shiane
Shiann
Shianna
Shianne
Shianté

Shibani
Shicara
Shida
Shidiah
Shieesha
Shiela
Shien
Shifana
Shifra
Shihia
Shiho
Shikara
Shikeela
Shikeeta
Shikeshia
Shikeva
Shikha
Shikia
Shikiema
Shikila
Shikira
Shikitha
Shila
Shilah
Shilea
Shileda
Shileen
Shileia
Shilioh
Shilita
Shilla
Shiloh
Shiloh-Marie
Shilow
Shilpa
Shilynn
Shima
Shimaca
Shimara
Shimay
Shimaya
Shimeeka
Shimei
Shimika
Shimikia
Shina
Shinah
Shine
Shineeca
Shineese
Shinelle
Shinequa
Shineta
Shiniqua
Shinita
Shinnel
Shinthuya
Shintula
Shioban
Shiona
Shiquata
Shiquita
Shiquitta
Shirah
Shiral
Shiraye
Shire
Shirece
Shiree
Shireen
Shirelle
Shirhonda
Shiri
Shirin
Shirina
Shirlana
Shirlee
Shirlee-Rae
Shirlena
Shirlene
Shirley El
Shirlina
Shirlnika
Shirlynn
Shirmeka
Shirneka
Shirona
Shirree
Shital
Shivani
Shivaun
Shivawn
Shivon
Shivonne
Shizuka
Shkala
Shkara
Shkeria
Shkitia
Shlaine
Shlea
Shliretta
Shlomit
Shmeika
Shmeka
Shnea
Shneil
Shneka
Shnere
Shnnielle
Shoan
Shobana
Shobha
Shobhna
Shocka
Shocolby
Shokheen
Sholeah
Sholomaine
Sholonda
Shon Dominique
Shonagh
Shonalee
Shonasce
Shondalette
Shondalyn
Shondel
Shondelle
Shondi
Shondia
Shondie
Shondra
Shondreka
Shonee
Shonelle
Shonetevia
Shonetta
Shonette
Shoni
Shonna
Shonneka
Shonnika
Shonree
Shontà
Shonta
Shontae
Shontai
Shontal
Shontalae
Shontara
Shontasia
Shontavia
Shontaviea
Shontay
Shontaya
Shonte

Shonté
Shontecia
Shontedra
Shontee
Shontel
Shontelle
Shonteral
Shonteria
Shontesscia
Shonti
Shontia
Shontina
Shontol
Shontoy
Shontrail
Shontrice
Shopie
Shora
Shorell
Shoresh
Shorisha
Shorlette
Shoshane
Shoshanha
Shoshann
Shoshanna
Shoshannah
Shoshauna
Shote
Shoua
Shounda
Shountàe
Showanda
Showna
Shpetime
Shqipe
Shquila
Shquwanna
Shquyla
Shranika
Shréna
Shree
Shreela
Shreeya
Shreffey
Shreka
Shrell
Shrelle
Shrena
Shreya
Shrivert
Shronda
Shrrie
Shrtavia
Shtara
Shterna
Shuanita
Shubha
Shubreet
Shuda
Shuk
Shuka
Shulamit
Shulanda
Shunderice
Shundrika
Shundrikea
Shunee
Shuneequa
Shunta
Shunté
Shuntel
Shuntia
Shuntravia
Shuree
Shureen
Shurelle
Shuritta
Shurlana
Shushani
Shushawna
Shuteamia
Shvera
Shweta
Shy-Anne
Shy-La
Shyamah
Shyamasundari
Shyan
Shyana
Shyann
Shyanne
Shye
Shyeda
Shyenna
Shyiesha
Shykera
Shykesha
Shyla-Mae
Shylee
Shyleen
Shylia
Shylie
Shylin
Shylisa
Shylla
Shylo
Shylyn
Shylyne
Shymejka
Shymika
Shynetta
Shynice
Shynika
Shyra
Shyrah
Shyrel
Shyrod
Shysheka
Shyteaya
Sian
Siara
Siarah
Siarra
Siavon
Sibeal
Sibel
Siboney
Sibyl
Sicili
Sidanni
Sidney
Sidonia
Sidonie
Sidra
Sidrah
Sieara
Siearra
Siedah
Siena
Sieney
Sienna
Siera-Lynn
Sieria
Siernna
Sierra-Dawn
Sierrah
Sierre
Sifat
Sigal
Signe
Signy
Sigourney
Sigrid
Sigriet
Siham

Sihame
Sikoya
Silena
Silja
Silke
Silkence
Sillenna
Sillvis
Silva
Silvana
Silver
Silvi
Silviane
Silvy
Sima
Simar
Simeonne
Simerjeet
Simerjit
Simha
Simin
Simmerjit
Simmi
Simminie
Simmona
Simmone
Simoane
Simon
Simona
Simonia
Simonne
Simran
Simranjit
Simrat
Simrath
Simren
Simrinjit
Simrita
Simrun

Sina
Sinan
Sinanuu
Sinaria
Sinath
Sincere
Sinda
Sindal
Sindia
Sindie
Sindy
Sinead
Sinnedy
Sinoo
Sinthy
Sintorya
Siobahn
Siobhan Desiree
Siobhana
Siobhann
Siobhon
Siomara
Siovaugn
Siovhan
Sipola
Sirean
Sireen
Sirena
Siri
Sirine
Siris
Sirisha
Sirrah
Sisi
Sisiana
Sissey
Sissy
Sita
Sitarah

Siterria
Sitha
Sithara
Sithru
Siti
Siuleyn
Siumaralys
Siuris
Siv
Siva
Sivan
Size
Sjanita
Sjolin
Skaidrite
Skarlette
Skikina
Skilah
Sky
Skyla
Skylar
Skylee
Skylena
Skyler
Skylynne
Skyra
Slavenka
Slilma
Sloan
Sloane
Smanta
Smantha
Smita
Smithie
Smokey
Snaige
Snehal
Snejina
Snezana

Sniderley
Snoda
Snohti
Snowden
Snowfire
Snwazna
Soaring
Sobhia
Sobia
Socha
Socorro
Soda
Sodany
Sofenya
Sofia-Kady
Sofie
Sofie-Ann
Sofija
Soha
Sohaila
Sohani
Soila
Sojourner
Sokha
Sokhem
Sokhon
Soknetra
Sokontheara
Sokpheary
Sokret
Sokun
Sokunthea
Sokunthirith
Sol
Sola
Solana
Solande
Solange
Solataire

Soleda
Soledad
Soleil
Soleiry
Solena
Solene
Solène
Soley
Solina
Solinda
Solmary
Solmas
Solmaz
Solsha
Solveig
Solvera
Solymar
Somalia
Somaly
Somarlly
Somaya
Somayah
Somer
Somiaya
Sommar
Sommarra
Somneang
Somone
Sompong
Sona
Sonal
Sonalee
Sonatine
Sonci
Sondilyn
Song
Song-Song
Song-Ya
Sonia-Lena
Sonica
Sonida
Sonise
Sonita
Sonja-May
Sonjae
Sonjarenei
Sonjia
Sonnara
Sonnen
Sonnet
Sonnett
Sonni
Sonnie
Sonny
Sonny-Rose
Sonpreet
Sonseeahray
Sonserah
Sonshare
Sonta
Sonyanique
Soonita
Sopari
Sopeany
Sophal
Sophea
Sopheakneary
Sopheary
Sophie-Caroline
Sophie-Christine
Sophors
Sophronia
Sophy
Sora
Soraya
Soriya
Soroh
Sorrell
Sosha
Soshana
Soshia
Sotha
Sothea
Sotiria
Sou
Souad
Soula
Souratda
Sourianna
Sourisa
Southsada
Souzan
Sovathary
Spakethia
Sparkle
Specialee
Spence
Spencer
Spencialya
Speshal
Spirit
Spring
Spyroula
Sreerupa
Srinya
Sripriya
Sriya
Sriyanthi
St Claire
St Mary
Stacci
Stacee
Stacey Ann
Stacey-Ann
Stacey-Gail
Stacey-Lee
Staceyan
Staceyann
Stacie Lou
Stacie-Lynn
Stacie-R
Stacity
Stacy Ann
Stacy Linn
Stacy-Lee
Stacy-Patricia
Stadine
Staesha
Stafanie
Staffany
Staicy
Staisha
Stakelua
Stalicia
Stamatia
Stana
Standricka
Stanetta
Stannie
Star
Star Lynn
Stardreena
Staria
Starisha
Starkeshia
Starlavon
Starle
Starlee
Starleena
Starlena
Starlene
Starlet
Starlette
Starley
Starlight
Starly

Starlyn
Starlynn
Starquisha
Starretta
Starri
Starria
Starrika
Starrlen
Starrsha
Starsha
Starshanna
Starskysha
Startish
Stasey
Stasha
Stashia
Stasia
Stavroula
Stayce
Staycee
Stayci
Staysha
Stazie
Steacy
Steani
Steann
Stecy
Stefan
Stefaney
Stefania-Carmenia
Stefaniane
Stéfanie
Stefanie-Anna-Rose
Stefanija
Stefannie
Stefenie
Steffani
Steffanie
Steffany
Steffi
Steffie
Steffine
Stefi
Stefini
Stefoni
Stehanie
Stellina
Stepahny
Stepanie
Stepfanie
Stepfiterial
Stephaija
Stephaine
Stephanas
Stephane
Stephanee
Stephaney
Stephania
Stephanida
Stephanie Ann
Stephanie Anne
Stephanie Da Silva
Stephanie Marie
Stephanie Michel
Stephanie-Anne
Stephanie-Ashley
Stephanie-Elizabeth
Stephanie-Eve
Stephanie-Gabrielle
Stephanie-Italia
Stephanie-Louise
Stephanie-Lynn
Stephanie-Nicole
Stephann
Stephannie
Stephannie-Colleen
Stephen
Stephene
Stephenis
Stephianie
Stephina
Stephine
Stephinie
Stephyne
Sterfien
Sterling
Stesha
Steshonda
Steva
Stevana
Stevanee
Stevee
Steven
Stevey
Stevie Jo
Stevie Lyn
Stevye
Stina
Stinder
Stoiana
Stoney
Storey
Stori
Storie
Storme
Stormi
Stormie
Stormiee
Story
Su
Su-Lin
Su-San
Suail
Suann
Suanna
Suanne
Subrena
Subria
Subrina
Subrina-Galina
Sucel
Sudie
Sue-Anne
Sueann
Suehaley
Suejira
Suesan
Suetta
Suezanna
Suffa
Suha
Suhai
Suhailla
Suheir
Suira
Sujin
Sukanya
Sukdeep
Sukeenah
Sukeinah
Sukhbir
Sukhdeep
Sukhjinder
Sukhmandip
Sukhmani
Sukhneet
Sukhpreet
Sukhraj

Sukhveer
Suki
Sukina
Sukumarl
Sulema
Sulimar
Suline
Sullivan
Sulma
Sumaira
Sumaiya
Sumandeep
Sumanpal
Sumanpreet
Sumanta
Sumayyah
Sumela-Rose
Sumer
Sumer-Wynn
Sumiah
Suminder
Sumira
Sumiria
Sumita
Sumiya
Sumiyyah
Summaiya
Summar
Summerbreeze
Summerhaze
Summerlee
Summiyyah
Sumnar
Sumphonee
Sumreen
Sun-Young
Sunaina
Sunasha
Sundance
Sunday
Sundee
Sundeep
Sundi
Sundip
Sundrena
Suneet
Sung Yun
Sunghee
Suni
Sunita
Sunitha
Suniti
Sunjoo
Sunkia
Sunne
Sunni
Sunnie
Sunnilei
Sunny-Dawn
Sunshyne
Suntai
Sunya
Superior
Supneet
Supreet
Suprina
Supriya
Suraiyabanu
Surama
Suraya
Surayyah
Surbhi
Suree
Surena
Surenia
Suri
Surielys
Surinder
Surra
Surrania
Surya
Susan Consuelo
Susan Mari
Susan-Pauline
Susanah
Susann
Susen
Sushauna
Sushila
Susselynn
Susson
Sussy
Susy
Sutton
Suva
Suvannah
Suvon
Suweena
Suzan
Suzana
Suzana-Jamal
Suzana-Katarina
Suzane
Suzannah
Suzelle
Suzi
Suzie
Suzy
Suzzane
Suzzette
Svannah
Sverre
Svetlana
Swadi
Swan
Swannetta
Swanteise
Swapna
Swayne
Sweana
Sweet
Sweta
Swetha
Syann
Sybella
Syble
Syboney
Sychelle
Sydania
Sydawn
Sydna
Sydnee
Sydni
Sydnie
Sydnye
Syeda
Syiackcia
Syishia
Syita
Sykia
Sylathia
Sylbreonne
Syleena
Sylena
Sylina
Sylisha
Syliva
Sylva
Sylvanna
Sylvette
Sylvi
Sylvianne
Sylvondria
Sylwia
Symantha
Symara

Symone
Symony
Symphony
Syndey
Syndi
Syndia
Syndle
Syneisha
Synetta
Synnoeve
Synora
Synovia
Syntia
Syntra
Syrah
Syrena
Syrenia
Syrenna
Syretta
Syrina
Syshia
Sytisha
Syvanna
Syvlia-Germaine
Szandra
Sze

T

T
Tîara
T.j.
Ta Lena
Ta Neisha
Ta Ronia
Ta Sha
Tàkeisha
Tàlisha
Tànya
Tàyon
Tabaith
Tabathe
Tabathia
Tabbatha
Tabbetha
Tabbitha
Tabelech
Tabetith
Tabitha-Ashley
Tabithia
Taborah
Tabraella
Tabre
Tabria
Tabrinna
Tabrisha
Tabtha
Tabytha
Tacara
Tacarra
Tacey
Tacha
Tachara
Tachet
Tachia
Tachiana
Tachika
Taci
Tacia
Taciana
Tacie
Tacita-Marie
Tacora
Tacorra
Tacorvia
Tacoya
Tacquila
Tacquira
Tacy
Tacye
Tadra
Taea
Taedra
Taegan
Taeler
Taelor
Taemika
Taeneka
Taesha
Taevia
Tafaria
Taffanay
Taffany
Taffia
Taffy
Taffye
Tafia
Tafisa
Tafoya
Taggarty
Tagie
Tahani
Tahany
Tahari
Taheera
Taheisha
Taheria
Taherrah
Tahigee
Tahina
Tahira
Tahirah
Tahis
Tahisha
Tahlia
Tahmea
Tahnes
Tahni
Tahnie
Tahniesha
Tahniscia
Tahnisha
Tahra
Tahsah
Tai
Taiana
Taicha
Taiche
Taiesha
Taija
Taijàra
Taikenya
Taileisha
Tailisman
Tailyn
Tailynn
Taimhyr
Taimy
Taina
Taira
Tairra
Taisha
Taishainic
Taitiann
Taitianna
Taiva
Taiwana
Taiwanna
Taiylor
Taj
Tajah
Tajawa

[illegible]ia
Tajma
Tajmar
Tajondra
Tajuana
Tajyrea
Takara
Takarra
Takawnza
Takayla
Takeara
Takecia
Takeena
Takeisha
Takeiyah
Takela
Takelia
Takella
Takema
Takemia
Takendra
Takenia
Takenja
Takenya
Takeria
Takesha
Takeshia
Takesia
Takevia
Takevis
Takeya
Takeyia
Takeyla
Takija
Takila
Takilla
Takilya
Takira
Takiria
Takisha
Takishea
Takishia
Takiya
Takiyah
Takkia
Takoya
Takreasha
Takuara
Tal
Tala
Talaina
Talal
Talandra
Talany
Talar
Talaria
Talarria
Talasea
Talauna
Talaya
Talayna
Talea
Taleah
Taleashela
Taleéi
Taleesha
Talei
Taleigha
Taleise
Taleisha
Talena
Talesa
Talesha
Taleshia
Talesia
Taletha
Talethia
Talhmora
Tali
Taliah
Taliatha
Talicia
Taliesha
Talieya
Talihna
Talin
Talina
Talinda
Taline
Talisa
Talisha
Talitha
Talithia
Taliya
Tallenia
Tallese
Tallie
Tallula
Tally
Talnà
Talor
Talsela
Talya
Talyah
Talyn
Talysha
Tam'unique
Tama
Tamaa
Tamah
Tamaiah
Tamaique
Tamaki
Tamala
Tamam
Tamama
Tamanesha
Tamantha
Tamarà
Tamara-Lee
Tamarage
Tamarah
Tamaran
Tamari
Tamaria
Tamarin
Tamarla
Tamarra
Tamarria
Tamarrian
Tamarsha
Tamasyn
Tamatha
Tamber
Tamberli
Tambra
Tambrae
Tambri
Tameca
Tamecia
Tamecka
Tamedra
Tameeka
Tameia
Tameika
Tameira
Tamekia
Tamel
Tamela
Tamelia
Tamer
Tamerai
Tameria
Tameriàs
Tamesha
Tameshia

Tameshkia
Tametha
Tami-Rae
Tamia
Tamiah
Tamica
Tamie
Tamieka
Tamijo
Tamikia
Tamikka
Tamiko
Tamila
Tamilla
Tamille
Tamillia
Tamilya
Tamim
Tamina
Tamira
Tamirra
Tamisha
Tamishia
Tamiya
Tamizan
Tamlin
Tamlyn
Tamma
Tammara
Tammarin
Tammera
Tammerah
Tammisha
Tammra
Tammy-Ann
Tammy-Lee
Tammy-Lynn
Tamnesha
Tamora
Tamoya
Tamra-Ann
Tamrah
Tamsen
Tamsin
Tamsin Mar
Tamura
Tamvi
Tamy
Tamya
Tamyra
Tamzin
Tana-Lee
Tanacae
Tanae
Tanaeah
Tanah
Tanairi
Tanairy
Tanalia
Tanara
Tanas
Tanasha
Tanashia
Tanavia
Tanaya
Tanaz
Tancy
Tanda
Tandalaya
Tandi
Tandis
Tandra
Tandrea
Tandria
Tandy
Tanea
Tanecia
Tanee
Taneé
Taneesha
Taneet
Taneia
Taneka
Tanekia
Tanelle
Tanequa
Taneria
Taneshia
Tanesia
Tanesian
Tanessa
Tanessia
Taneta
Tanetra
Tanetta
Taneya
Tang
Tangameka
Tangania
Tanganika
Tangela
Tangerine
Tangi
Tangie
Tangla
Tangueray
Tanhya
Tanica
Tanieka
Taniel
Taniele
Tanielle
Taniere
Taniese
Taniesha
Tanija
Tanika
Tanikyia
Tanille
Tanina
Taniqua
Taniquia
Tanisa
Tanise
Tanish
Tanishah
Tanishea
Tanishia
Tanita
Tanitra
Taniya
Tanja
Tanjanika
Tanji
Tanjie
Tanjinika
Tankair
Tanna
Tannah
Tanner
Tanneshia
Tannette
Tanneve
Tannia
Tannica
Tanniececia
Tanniesha
Tannise
Tannisha
Tannison
Tannon
Tannus
Tannya
Tannyce
Tanola
Tanosha

Tanoya
Tanquera
Tanqueray
Tanshay
Tansy
Tantashea
Tanvi
Tanvir
Tanya-Diane
Tanya-Fahima
Tanya-Jean
Tanya-Lee
Tanya-Lynn
Tanya-Mae
Tanya-Maryann
Tanya-Rae
Tanya-Stephanie
Tanychia
Tanycia
Tanyekia
Tanyia
Tanyn
Tanys
Tanysha
Tanza
Tanzania
Tanzenia
Tanzi
Tanzshaela
Taqaesha
Taqauaia
Taqiyya
Taquaisha
Taquaja
Taquana
Taquanda
Taquanna
Taquarius
Taquawanda
Taquaysha
Taqueesha
Taquela
Taquella
Taquencia
Taquera
Taqueshia
Taquesta
Taquetla
Taquetta
Taquia
Taquichea
Taquilla
Taquire
Taquisha
Taquitta
Taqunïa
Taquonia
Taquoria
Taquoya
Taqwonda
Tar Anne
Tara Marie
Taràh
Tara-Ann
Tara-Anne
Tara-Brandy
Tara-Dawn
Tara-Lee
Tara-Leigh
Tara-Lyn
Tara-Lynn
Tara-Lynne
Tara-Marie
Tara-Rose
Taradi
Taraea
Tarafanchon
Tarai
Taralee
Tarali
Taralyn
Taran
Taraneh
Taranjeet
Taranjii
Taranjit
Tararora
Tarasa
Tarasha
Taraya
Tarcara
Tarci Lee
Tarea
Tareava
Tarecia
Taree
Tareel
Tareena
Tareka
Tarelle
Tarelsha
Taren
Tarena
Tarese
Taresha
Taress
Taressa
Tarevah
Tareya
Tarez
Tarha
Tari
Taria
Tarika
Tarila
Tarilyn
Tarin
Tarina
Taris
Tarisa
Tarise
Tarisha
Tarissa
Tarita
Tarkecia
Tarlisa
Tarmecia
Tarmeet
Tarmesha
Tarna
Tarneisha
Tarnisha
Tarona
Tarondisha
Taronica
Taronish
Tarpa
Tarquisha
Tarquse
Tarrah
Tarran
Tarranicka
Tarreara
Tarren
Tarrey
Tarrika
Tarrin
Tarron
Tarry
Tarryn
Tarsha
Tarsheka
Tarun
Tarvega
Taryme
Taryn-Amber

Taryn-Mi
Taryne
Tasa
Tasanna
Tasasharenee
Taschell
Tasha-Marie
Tasha-Richel
Tasha-Samboo
Tashada
Tashae
Tashallia
Tashana
Tashanda
Tashani
Tashanika
Tashanna
Tashara
Tashari
Tashauna
Tashawanna
Tashawna
Tashay
Tashayla
Tashe Anne
Tashea
Tasheda
Tasheena
Tasheeni
Tasheera
Tasheia
Tasheka
Tashekia
Tashella
Tasheltraya
Tashena
Tashenna
Tashera
Tasheta
Tashi
Tashiana
Tashika
Tashima
Tashira
Tashjian
Tashka
Tashmeki
Tashna
Tashonda
Tashondra
Tashoya
Tashua
Tashwa
Tashyo
Tashyra
Tasi
Tasiya
Taskeika
Taskilla
Tasleema
Tasleemah
Taslim
Taslima
Tasma
Tasmeer
Tasmin
Tasneem
Tassi
Tassia
Tassiana
Tassie
Taswando
Tatayana
Tate
Tatia
Tatiana-St-Cphanie
Tatiania
Tatianna
Tatica
Tatihana
Tatjana
Tatnay
Tatoya
Tatrina
Tatumn
Tatyana
Tatyanah
Tatyanna
Taubreenia
Taudria
Tauna
Tauné
Tauni
Taunia
Taunisha
Taunya
Taunya-Marie
Tauquilla
Taura
Taurean
Tausha
Tauvia
Tava
Tavah
Tavanisha
Tavarra
Tavasia
Taveena
Tavera
Taverli
Tavia
Tavie
Tavinderpreet
Tavion
Tavita
Tavonda
Tavonna
Tawaka
Tawan
Tawana
Tawana Ifa
Tawanakee
Tawanda
Tawanna
Tawanne
Tawhaucia
Tawna
Tawnee
Tawnesha
Tawney
Tawni
Tawnia
Tawnie
Tawny-Lee
Tawnyell
Tawsha
Tay
Taya
Tayah
Tayana
Taybia
Taybrey
Tayce-Lee
Taye
Tayiah
Tayisha
Tayla
Taylar
Taylea
Taylee
Tayler
Tayleur
Taylin
Tayllor
Taylor-Ann

Taylore
Tayna
Tayra
Taysha
Taysia
Tayva
Tayvonne
Tayyabah
Taz
Tazeen
Tazia
Tazirie
Tazlina
Tazmin
Tchanavian
Tchenavia
Te
Te Lana
Téama
Téare
Técara
Téla
Téleigh
Ténesha
Te-Jhonn
Teàa
Teaairy
Teacora
Teadora
Teaerra
Teagan
Teagen
Teaghen
Teah
Teair
Teaira
Teairra
Teake
Teal
Teala
Teale
Tealia
Tealishia
Teamber
Teana
Teananmarie
Teandra
Teanetta
Teangela
Teann
Teanna
Teany
Teara
Tearanie
Tearassa
Teardra
Tearia
Tearnee
Tearny
Tearra
Tearria
Tearsa
Tearsha D'on
Teasa
Teasha
Teata
Teauana
Tebah
Tebeth
Tebra
Tebresha
Tebria
Tedde
Teddi
Teddra
Teddreiya
Teddy
Tedera
Tee-Jay
Teeairy
Teearia
Teechee
Teedra
Teegan
Teeghan
Teela
Teela-Jose
Teeleetha
Teelia
Teena
Teequa
Teerria
Teesha
Teeya
Tefarrah
Tefaunie
Teffany
Tega
Tegen
Teghan
Tegin
Tegra
Tegwen
Tegwyn
Tehani
Tehawna
Tehealia
Tehila
Tehmi
Tehmina
Tehra
Tehseen
Teia
Teidra
Teihl
Teila
Teilah
Teilichia
Teina
Teineisha
Teira
Teira-Rochelle
Teirra
Teirrie
Teirza
Teisa
Teisha
Tejah
Tejal
Tejan
Tejmattie
Teka
Tekasheena
Tekeeta
Tekeisha
Tekela
Tekelia
Tekeria
Tekeshia
Tekeyia
Tekeysia
Tekila
Tekisha
Tekiva
Tekiya
Tekla
Tekla-Rea
Teknayia
Tekoa
Tekoya
Tekuesa
Tela
Telah
Telanea
Teldra
Telea

Teleisia
Teleita
Telena
Telenica
Teleshia
Telesia
Telicia
Telina
Telisa
Telisha
Telishia
Telita
Telka
Tellisa
Telsa
Telva
Telycia
Temara
Tember
Temeka
Temelia
Temequa
Temerian
Temesha
Temieshia
Temika
Temisha
Temitope
Temkia
Temme
Tempence
Tempest
Tempest-Shahdai
Tempestt
Tempetts
Tempistt
Temprance
Tempres
Tempteste
Tena
Tenae
Tenajis
Tenarra
Tendra
Teneal
Tenechia
Tenecia
Teneil
Teneille
Teneisha
Teneka
Tenena
Tenesa
Tenese
Teneshia
Tenesia
Tenessa
Tenetià
Teneusa
Tenezya
Tengku Elmas
Tenia
Tenice
Tenicia
Tenieka
Tenika
Tenise
Tenishka
Tenleigh
Tenley
Tenly
Tenna
Tenneal
Tenneill
Tenneille
Tennessa
Tennette
Tennia
Tennie
Tennielle
Tennile
Tennisha
Tenya
Tenyka
Tenykia
Teodora
Teona
Teondra
Teonna
Teoria
Teoshia
Tephanie
Teqla
Tequanna
Tequawna
Tequesta
Tequila
Tequilia
Tequilla
Tequirah
Tequisha
Tequonda
Tequra
Tequsta
Terace
Teraco
Terah
Teralee
Terall
Teralyn
Teralynn
Teran
Teranea
Teranee
Teraria
Terashey
Terasina
Tercela
Tercie
Tercina
Terea
Tereasa
Tereatha
Terebia
Terecka
Tereese
Tereka
Terelle
Teren
Terena
Terence
Tereneshia
Teresa-Anne
Teresea
Teresha
Teresia
Teresina
Teresine
Teresita
Teressa
Terest
Teretha
Tereva
Terevia
Terez
Tereza
Tereze
Terhea
Teri-Ann
Teri-Anne
Teri-Lea
Teri-Lee
Teri-Lyn
Teri-Lynn
Teriana
Terianne

Terica
Tericak
Terika
Terike
Terilee
Terilyn
Terilynn
Terin
Terina
Teriquo
Teris
Terisa
Terisha
Teriza
Terkedria
Terkeisha
Termaine
Termieka
Ternisha
Terquinna
Terra-Lyn
Terra-Lynn
Terrace
Terrah
Terralind
Terralyn
Terran
Terranika
Terreba
Terree
Terreisha
Terreka
Terrell
Terren
Terrence
Terrera
Terresa
Terressa
Terri Lynn
Terri-Ann
Terri-Jo
Terri-Lee
Terri-Lyn
Terria
Terrian
Terriana
Terriann
Terrianne
Terrica
Terrice
Terrie
Terrie-Lynn
Terrika
Terrilee
Terrill
Terrilyn
Terrilynn
Terrin
Terrina
Terrionia
Terrisa
Terrisha
Terrissa
Terriyanna
Terrosany
Terruko
Terryca
Terrye
Terryl
Terryll
Terryn
Tershawn
Tershera
Tertia
Terttu
Terun
Teryca
Teryiaka
Teryl
Teryn
Teryna
Terynn
Terza
Tesa
Tesha
Teshaker
Teshana
Teshanna
Teshaun
Teshawna
Teshawnda
Teshay
Teshel
Teshia
Teshownda
Teshura
Tesia
Teslin
Tesna
Tessandra
Tessanie
Tesse
Tessia
Tessica
Tessie
Tessoni
Tesstina
Tetra
Tetriana
Tetuaria
Teuana
Teurshila
Teuta
Teva
Tevicia
Tevin
Tevis
Tewauna
Teyanna
Teyona
Teyuna
Tezcatli
Tezia
Tezlin
Tezra
Thabitha
Thai
Thaina
Thais
Thalia
Thamara
Thametria
Thanh-Linda
Thanh-Tu
Thanh-Vi
Thanhtra
Thanhyen
Thanya
Tharisa
Thashà
Thaviluck
Thayer
Thecla
Theda
Thedorsha
Thedrica
Theindia
Thejuana
Thelkira
Thelma
Thelmalina
Thelmamildreina
Thenesia
Theodisa
Theodora
Theodra

Theohari
Theola
Theondra
Thera
Thera-Lee
Therany
Therea
Thereal
Theresa An
Theresa-Ann
Theresia
Theressa
Theresssa
Therra
Therressa
Thersa
Thespina-Paraskevie
They
Thi-Thuy
Thia
Thidapon
Thidasavanh
Thidiah
Thien
Thien Kim
Thienkim
Thientrang
Thilka
Thirza
Thoa
Thoav
Thomas
Thomasa
Thomasia
Thomasin
Thomasina.
Thomencia
Thomethia
Thomisha
Thomkita
Thomsina
Thong
Thongsanith
Thorri
Thoya
Thrisha
Thu
Thuc
Thuhien
Thun
Thunesha
Thuong
Thurka
Thusnelda
Thuthuy
Thuy
Thuyvi
Thy
Thyshalom
Ti
Ti Anna
Tiérra
Ti-An
Tia Ciarra
Tiaanna
Tiaca
Tiacherise
Tiaesha
Tiahna
Tiaira
Tiairra
Tiaisha
Tiajai
Tiajuana
Tiaka
Tiakeysha
Tialeigh
Tialer
Tiamarie
Tiamayoshia
Tianda
Tiandria
Tianeka
Tianika
Tiann
Tianne
Tianny
Tiante
Tiaon
Tiarah
Tiare
Tiare-Kulia
Tiarra
Tiashauna
Tiatiana
Tiawanna
Tiawna
Tiawni
Tiaya
Tiayahakia
Ticara
Ticbezay
Ticey
Tichia
Tickle
Ticola
Tiéra
Tiea
Tiearra
Tiearria
Tiegan
Tieiaka
Tieisha
Tiela
Tieneasha
Tienna
Tiensha
Tieranni
Tierany
Tierisha
Tierre
Tierrea
Tierria
Tiersa
Tiesha
Tieshka
Tifanee
Tifaney
Tifani
Tifanie
Tifany
Tiffan
Tiffane
Tiffanee
Tiffaney
Tiffani-Lynn
Tiffanie Ann
Tiffannie
Tiffanny
Tiffany Nichole
Tiffany-Ann
Tiffany-Lee
Tiffany-Lynne
Tiffayne
Tiffaynee
Tiffeney
Tiffenie
Tiffeny
Tiffiani
Tiffianie
Tiffiany
Tiffinay
Tiffine
Tiffiney
Tiffini

Tiffinie
Tiffnay
Tiffney
Tiffni
Tiffny
Tiffynie
Tifiney
Tifni
Tigan
Tiger
Tigisti
Tigre
Tiia
Tiira
Tijana
Tijera
Tijuana
Tika
Tikara
Tike
Tikesha
Tiki
Tikima
Tikirra
Tikisha
Tila
Tilah
Tilda
Tilene
Tiletha
Tillery
Tillie
Tillisha
Tillmesha
Tillwonter
Tilly
Tima
Timaka
Timanee
Timara
Timber
Timberlee
Timberly
Timbrell
Timeka
Timera
Timesha
Timi
Timia
Timie
Timika
Timikia
Timindra
Timisha
Timmy
Timna
Timnesha
Timnika
Tin
Tina Marie
Tina-Lee
Tina-Lynn
Tina-Marie
Tinalyn
Tinamarie
Tineal
Tinecia
Tineke
Tineko
Tinena
Tinera
Tinesha
Tineshia
Tinetra
Tinettia
Tinia
Tinice
Tinicquia
Tiniel
Tinisha
Tinnette
Tinnia
Tinny
Tinsia
Tinsley
Tintisha
Tinu
Tiona
Tionda
Tiondrea
Tionna
Tipaleli
Tiphani
Tiphanie
Tiphany
Tipharah
Tiquana
Tiquandra
Tiquesta
Tiquila
Tiqulia
Tira
Tirah
Tirea
Tirena
Tirsa
Tirshka
Tirzah
Tirzha
Tisa
Tisah
Tishana
Tishani
Tishanna
Tishanne
Tishawn
Tishe-Marie
Tisheena
Tishnisa
Tishra
Tishunda
Tishunta
Tisihia
Tisin
Tiswanda
Titana
Titania
Titanna
Titia
Titianna
Titilola
Tiwanna
Tiwena
Tiya
Tiyah
Tiyaira
Tiyana
Tiziana
Tk
Tlayshia
Tnaja
Tnori
To
To-Uyen
Tobey
Tobi
Tobie
Tobie-Jean
Tobishan
Tobva
Toby
Tocara
Tocarra
Toccara
Toccoa
Tocyia

Toddrika
Toe
Tofia
Toilli
Toinetta
Toinisha
Token
Tokesia
Tokoah
Tokoya
Toleda
Tollethia
Toluope
Tolyia
Tomara
Tomasa
Tomasina
Tomberina
Tomea
Tomeca
Tomecha
Tomeckia
Tomeik
Tomeka
Tomekia
Tomesha
Tomi
Tomie
Tomiehsa
Tomiese
Tomika
Tomirain
Tomise
Tomisha
Tomisyn
Tomitra
Tomme
Tommi
Tommi-Jean
Tommia
Tommie
Tommisha
Tommy
Tomorrow
Tona
Tonada
Tonae
Tonaka
Tonda
Tondra
Tondraneicka
Tondrea
Tonee
Toneisha
Toneisheia
Toneka
Tonelle
Tonesha
Toneshia
Tonetta
Tonette
Tonga
Tongela
Toni Ann
Tonia-Marie
Toniann
Tonianne
Tonie
Toniece
Tonielle
Toniesha
Toniette
Tonii
Tonik
Tonika
Tonille
Tonimae
Tonimaree
Tonique
Tonisa
Tonish
Tonisha
Tonishia
Tonitia
Tonja
Tonje
Tonna
Tonneshia
Tonni
Tonnia
Tonnisha
Tonnja
Tony
Tonya-Dawn
Tonyetta
Topacio
Topaz
Topeka
Tora
Toraye
Toree
Torei
Toretha
Torey
Toria
Torian
Toriana
Torianne
Torica
Torie
Torilyn
Torilynn
Torimeaka
Toronda
Torra
Torrey
Torreya
Torri
Torria
Torrilyn
Torrina
Torrita
Torsche
Torsha
Tory-Rose
Torya
Torye
Toscanini
Tosha-Lynn
Toshanti
Toshauna
Toshebia
Tosheena
Tosheria
Toshia
Toshiba
Toshiea
Toshika
Toshiko
Toshima
Toshke
Toterria
Totianna
Tova
Tovah
Tove
Tovia
Towanda
Townsley
Toya
Toyanika
Toyanna
Toyea
Toykia
Toylenn
Toyliah

Toylin
Toyna
Toyneshia
Toyquan
Tracee
Tracell
Tracey-Ann
Tracey-Lynn
Traci Lynn
Traci-Lynne
Tracia
Tracilee
Tracilyn
Tracina
Tracy Anne
Tracy-Ann
Tracy-Lee
Tracy-Lynn
Tradineya
Traeci
Traeir
Traey
Trahmillia
Traice
Trakayla
Tralainna
Tralecia
Tralene
Tralina
Tralinda
Tralonda
Tralynn
Tram
Tramaine
Tramane
Trameika
Trameran
Tramesha
Tramillia
Tramisha
Tran
Tranae
Tranea
Traneice
Traneis
Traneise
Traneisha
Tranell
Traneshia
Trang
Tranice
Tranika
Tranise
Tranissa
Traquella
Traquila
Trarica
Trasha
Trashana
Trashanna
Trashelle
Trashonda
Travia
Travicia
Travilla
Travis
Travonda
Travone
Travonia
Travres
Tray Mika
Traya
Trayce
Trayonna
Tréquis
Tre-Auna
Treana
Treania
Treanna
Treasure
Treaunna
Treausre
Trecia
Treena
Treevonia
Trekeisha
Trekita
Trelanie
Trelisia
Trella
Trellanie
Trellany
Trellyn
Trelody
Tremaine
Tremeka
Tremina
Trena
Trendese
Treneca
Treneice
Trenell
Trenelle
Trenere
Trenetta
Trenice
Trenika
Trenisa
Trenise
Trenisha
Trenita
Trenna
Trentaya
Treonda
Trepany
Trerika
Tresa
Tresca
Treschina
Trescia
Trese
Tresha
Treshana
Treshia
Treshur
Treska
Tresley
Treslie
Tressa Brianne
Tressia
Tressie
Treva
Trevanna
Trevenia
Trevicia
Trevina
Trevonna
Trevor
Trez
Tria
Triana
Trianna
Trica
Tricha
Trichelle
Tricia-Lynn
Tricina
Trickia
Trier
Triffany
Trijidia
Trikey
Trilain
Trilania
Trilby
Trilisa

Trimequilus
Trimesha
Trinda
Trindalyn
Trineane
Trinear
Trinecia
Trinee
Trinera
Trinere
Trinesha
Trineshia
Trinette
Trinh
Trini
Trinia
Trinica
Trinice
Trinidad
Triniece
Trinika
Trinique
Trinisa
Trinita
Trinitie
Trinitte
Trinity
Trionna
Trisa
Trisanne
Trish
Trish-Ann
Trishanna
Trishara
Trishell
Trishelle
Trishia
Trishna
Trisia
Trisihia
Trisina
Trissa
Trissha
Trissillian
Trissy
Tristal
Tristess
Tristia
Tristian
Tristiana
Tristika Shilla
Tristin
Tristina
Tristine
Trivia
Triystan
Trneice
Troi
Troia
Troiana
Tromaneshia
Tronnie
Trophone
Troshara
Troy
Troya
Tru-Shana
Trudessa
Trudi
Trudie
Truessa
Truly
Trundy
Truniece
Truniqua
Trupti
Tryane
Tryanna
Tryna
Trynasity
Trynee
Trysia
Trysta
Trystann
Tsa
Tsadiqua
Tscharner
Tsega
Tsheal
Tshomba
Tsopie
Tsubasa
Tuananh
Tucker
Tuesday
Tuesdey
Tuieba-Basria
Tuinna
Tuituimoeao
Tukesa
Tulinda
Tumba
Tunisha
Tunyator
Tuong
Tuongvi
Tura
Turi
Turkaila
Turkesa
Turner
Turquoise
Tushawn
Tusheena
Tushima
Tuula
Tuyen
Tuyet
Tuyet-Mai
Tuyetnhu
Twaka
Twalla
Twana
Twanda
Twanria
Twant
Twila
Twila-Dawn
Twinesha
Twinky
Twylia
Twylia-Joy
Twylla
Ty
Ty-Nesha
Tya
Tya-Elizabeth
Tyana
Tyanda
Tyann
Tyanna
Tyanne
Tyaonna
Tyara
Tyarra
Tyashia
Tyawna
Tycara
Tyce
Tycee
Tychell
Tychelle
Tyci
Tycoma
Tycora
Tyda

Tyecha
Tyechia
Tyeesha
Tyeice
Tyeisha
Tyeishia
Tyekia
Tyeler
Tyeoka
Tyerra
Tyese
Tyeshia
Tyeysha
Tyfani
Tyfanni
Tyfanny
Tyfany
Tyffani
Tyffanni
Tyffany
Tyffini
Tygh
Tygoria-Eugenie
Tyhema
Tyhina
Tyiece
Tyiesha
Tyine
Tyishia
Tyjuana
Tykaleena
Tykeia
Tykeisha
Tykendra
Tykera
Tykeshia
Tykeza
Tykia
Tykianna
Tykidra
Tykira
Tykisha
Tykorra
Tyla
Tylea
Tyleasha
Tylee
Tylena
Tylene
Tyler-Barbara
Tylia
Tylicia
Tylina
Tyline
Tylise
Tylisha
Tylishia
Tyller
Tylor
Tylynn
Tymarah
Tyme
Tymerial
Tymesha
Tymika
Tymmeka
Tyna
Tynaise
Tynan
Tyne
Tynece
Tyneicia
Tyneil
Tyneisha
Tynesha
Tyneshia
Tynessa
Tynetta
Tynette
Tynicika
Tyniesha
Tynima
Tynisha
Tynita
Tynitra
Tynnetta
Tynorra
Tyona
Tyonna
Typhanie
Tyquanna
Tyquannah
Tyquesia
Tyquilla
Tyraa
Tyrah
Tyran
Tyrashiana
Tyree
Tyreka
Tyrell
Tyrelle
Tyrene
Tyresa
Tyresia
Tyria
Tyrica
Tyricka
Tyrikka
Tyrina
Tyroneisha
Tyronica
Tyrrena
Tyrunza
Tysa
Tysha
Tyshara
Tyshawn
Tyshea
Tysheana
Tysheka
Tyshell
Tyshia
Tyshieka
Tyshyna
Tyson
Tyssa
Tytan
Tyucee
Tywania
Tywanna
Tywathea
Tzivia

U

Uanria
Ubanisha
Uchenna
Udeme
Uesenia
Ugonna
Ukaya
Ulana
Uleasah
Ulinda
Ulise
Ulisses
Ulviye
Ulyssa
Umber
Umta
Una
Unbee
Unica

Unique
Unjanee
Unna
Unnamed
Upkar
Urania
Uremma
Uriah
Urooj
Ursa
Ursala
Urszula
Urva
Usha
Ushika
Uta
Uthona
Uvette
Uyen
Uzezi
Uzma

V

Va-Rhonda
Vaidehi
Vail
Vakeesha
Vakisha
Val-Marie
Vala
Valaine
Valaney
Valantina
Valarae
Valari
Valaria
Valean
Valecia
Valeda
Valee
Valeeka
Valeen
Valeisa
Valen
Valena
Valencia Octavia
Valenica
Valenteva
Valentin
Valera
Valeri
Valérie
Valerie-Anne
Valerie-Rose
Valerine
Valery
Valese
Valeshia
Valeska
Valeta
Valetta
Valezka
Valida
Valien
Valine
Valisa
Valisha
Valissa
Vallan
Vallen
Valleri
Vallerie
Vallery
Vallie
Vallirie
Vallon
Valmira
Valnise
Valona
Valoree
Valori
Valorie
Valtina
Valyn
Valynn
Vamonda
Van
Vana
Vanae
Vanary
Vanassa
Vanda
Vanda-Leigh
Vandana
Vandella
Vandetta
Vandhana
Vandi
Vandoline
Vaneet
Vaneeta
Vanesha
Vaneshia
Vanesia
Vanessa Jeanette
Vanessa Ma
Vanessa-Ann
Vanessa-Lee
Vanessa-Rose
Vanesse
Vanessia
Vanessia Dorthi
Vanessica
Vaneza
Vani
Vania
Vaniece
Vaniessa
Vanika
Vanisa
Vanissa
Vanita
Vanitty
Vanity
Vann
Vanna-Marie
Vannah
Vannahy
Vannaleigh
Vannary
Vannesa
Vanneza
Vanni
Vansessa
Vanshown
Vantasha
Vantha
Vantoria
Vantrece
Vantrice
Vantrisa
Vanya
Varina
Varinda
Varinia
Varjorie
Varnessa
Varonica
Varonika
Varpu
Varsha
Vasanta
Vasanti
Vash-Ti

Vashawn
Vashity
Vashonda
Vashti
Vashtie
Vasiliki
Vasiliky
Vassa
Vassiliki
Vasuki
Vatase
Vatasha
Vauna
Vayola
Vealiese
Veanna
Veda
Vedad
Vedessa
Veeanna
Veena
Veenita
Veeramaneni
Velda
Velen
Velenda
Velia
Velica
Velinda
Vellmari
Vellore
Velma
Velmarys
Velvet
Velynda
Vena
Vencillia
Vendetta
Veneeda
Veneie
Veneigh
Veneise
Veneka
Venera
Venesa
Venesha
Venesher
Venesse
Venessia
Venetia
Venette
Venice
Venicia
Veniece
Veniesa
Venis
Venise
Venisha
Venishia
Venita
Venna
Vennesa
Vennessa
Vennisa
Venus
Veny
Venyda
Vera-Lee
Veranda
Veranne
Verena
Verenice
Verenis
Vereniz
Vergadel
Verhanika
Verica
Verinda
Verinica
Verity
Verlene
Verlie
Verlin
Verlina
Verline
Verlondrea
Verlyn
Vermishia
Verneka
Vernese
Vernesha
Verneshia
Vernessa
Vernetia
Vernetta
Vernette
Vernia
Vernica
Vernicca
Vernice
Vernique
Vernisha
Vernisheia
Vernita
Vernnita
Vernon
Verntoria
Verona
Veronic
Véronic
Veronick
Véronick
Véronik
Veronika
Veronne
Veronnica
Verrissa
Vershonda
Versie
Vertasha
Vertavia
Verteaursha
Veruszhka
Vesenia
Vesinia
Vesna
Vesta
Vesteria
Vi
Vianca
Vianeka
Vianica
Vianna
Vianne
Viatia
Vibhuti
Vicenta
Vichelle
Vichiny
Vicke
Vickey
Vicki-Lyn
Vickilyn
Vickki
Vicktoria
Vicnery
Victasia
Victoria-Anne
Victoria-Cara-Lee
Victoria-Diana
Victoria-Teresa
Victorina
Victory
Vida
Vidamarie

Vidnatu
Vidya
Vielca
Vienette
Vienna
Vienna-Marie
Vienne
Viergela
Vierginie
Vietta
Vijayta
Vika
Viki
Vikiana
Vikie
Vikki
Viktoria
Viky
Vilate
Vilaysone
Vilena
Vilija
Vilma
Vilmaril
Vilmarys
Vina
Vincenza
Vinchontondria
Vincy
Vineet
Vineeta
Vinesha
Vinessa
Vinette
Vinia
Viniece
Vinique
Vinisha
Vinita
Vinitha
Vinnie
Vinora
Vinshelanita
Vintanua
Vinti
Viola
Violeta
Violetta
Violette
Viona
Vira
Virag
Virgen
Virgenia
Virgie
Virgilia
Virgillia
Virginio
Viridiana
Virjeana
Virlisha
Virnell
Vironica
Vishakha
Vision
Vita
Vitalina
Vitaline
Vitamay
Vitoria
Vittoria
Viva
Vivan
Vivecca
Viviane
Vivianna
Vivianne
Vivien
Vivienne
Vivina
Vivion
Vizrel
Vjollca
Vlasta
Vlora
Vn
Vona
Vonceia
Vonche
Voncile
Vonda
Vondeidra
Vondeisa
Vondrea
Voneisha
Voneshia
Vongdao
Vongie
Vonkeshia
Vonmarie
Vonnie
Vonquinette
Vonschell
Vonsha
Vonshae
Vonshala
Vonsheka
Vonshelle
Vonsherie
Vonte
Vontisha
Vontrece
Vontrese
Vontrice
Vontricia
Vontriece
Voreece
Vorner
Voula
Vrinda
Vrolet
Vronica
Vrushali
Vu-Anhtuyet
Vun
Vvelshaundra
Vy
Vyckee
Vyctoria
Vyna

Wa
Wacey
Wadioni
Wadlyne
Wadonna
Wafa
Wai
Wai-Man
Wai-Meng
Waisee
Wajiha
Wajma
Wakena
Wakesha
Wakeshia
Wakesia
Walatta Si
Walderka
Waldine
Waleska
Walheide
Walisha

Walitta
Walkiria
Walmise
Wan Azalia
Wanakee
Wanda Yore
Wandamae
Wandely
Wanema
Wanesa
Waneta
Wanisa
Wanisha
Wanita
Wanite
Waniyetu
Wannoormiz
Wanona
Wantroya
Wao
Waseema
Wassiliane
Watasha
Wattrina
Waukecia
Waunakee
Waunita
Waynel
Waynesha
Waynette
Waynlyn
Wealetta
Wedad
Wednesda
Weiwei
Welcome
Weldianne
Wen-Fai
Wen-Ting
Wendalynn
Wende
Wendee
Wendella
Wendelle
Wendiee
Wentenhawi
Wenzy
Weslene
Wesley
Weslie
Weslyn
Wessal
Westin
Whei
Whelisha
Whisper
Whisteria
Whitani
Whiteney
Whitley
Whitne
Whitné
Whitnee
Whitnei
Whitneigh
Whitney Angeline
Whitney-Dawn
Whitney-Lee
Whitney-Marie
Whitni
Whitny
Whitnye
Whittany
Whitteny
Whittnie
Whyllie
Whytne
Whytney
Whytnie
Wichasta
Widad-Christy
Widdelene
Wideline
Widlene
Widline
Widlyne
Wilaine
Wilda
Wileen
Wiletta
Wilfreda
Wilhamina
Wilhelmi
Wilhelmina
Wiliska
Willa
Willamina
Willanda
Willard
Willene
Willesha
Willetfiotalisa
Willett
William
Willie
Williemae
Williette
Willina
Willisha
Willishia
Willmeisha
Willona
Willow
Wilma
Wilmanie
Wilmara Shay
Wilmayra
Wilmenid
Wilmyne
Wilna
Wilnar
Wilneeda
Wilnise
Wilsoneka
Wilynda
Win
Windee
Windi
Windy
Wineda
Wing
Wing Tung
Winica
Winifred
Winne
Winnella
Winnetta
Winnie
Winnifred
Winona
Winsha
Winshang
Winston
Wintr
Winttana
Wisthiana
Witney
Wonder
Wonita
Wonnita
Woodine
Woodlyne
Worelda
Wossenie
Wray

Wren
Wuallewscka
Wyanita
Wydia
Wyionna
Wykelia
Wykila
Wykita
Wykkina
Wylee
Wymakia
Wymika
Wyn
Wyndee
Wyndy
Wyneshia
Wynette
Wynona
Wynter
Wynterdawn
Wyonna
Wytashanika
Wyvonna

X

Xander
Xandria
Xanne
Xanthe
Xanthia
Xare
Xavia
Xavier
Xaviera
Xeina
Xelyna
Xenia
Xhemile
Xian
Ximen
Ximena
Xina
Xochitl
Xuan
Xuimora
Xymina
Xyomara
Xzabria
Xzacharia
Xzylia

Y

Ya
Ya Keshia
Ya-Jean
Yaasmin
Yaceli
Yacema
Yacheka
Yackelin
Yadili
Yadira
Yadiris
Yadle
Yadreece
Yael
Yaeli
Yaemin
Yafeal
Yaffa
Yafit-Susana
Yahaida
Yahaira
Yahara
Yaharia
Yahira
Yahkaieah
Yahta
Yaicha
Yaima
Yaira
Yaismel
Yaizamarie
Yajaira
Yakeba
Yakeshea
Yakeyna
Yakia
Yakima
Yalaina
Yalanda
Yalando
Yalda
Yalonda
Yalynn
Yamahlie
Yamairy
Yamarie
Yamaris
Yamayra
Yameily
Yamelie
Yameshia
Yamiche
Yamikani
Yamila
Yamile
Yamilet
Yamileth
Yamilett
Yamilis
Yamilla
Yamille
Yamilya
Yamilys
Yaminah
Yamini
Yamira
Yan
Yan-Yan
Yana
Yanae
Yanais
Yanasi
Yancey
Yaneisy
Yaneliz
Yanelle
Yanelly
Yanely
Yanelys
Yaneris
Yaneriy
Yanessa
Yanet
Yaneth
Yanially
Yanicel
Yanick
Yanick Nikita
Yanidza
Yaniela
Yanik
Yanina
Yanira
Yanires
Yanis
Yanisha
Yanitza
Yanixia
Yanna
Yannica

Yannick
Yannina
Yanouche
Yansilya
Yaquita
Yara
Yaraddie
Yaraisanis
Yaraluna
Yarath
Yardlene
Yarelis
Yarelli
Yarely
Yarenis
Yareny
Yarenys
Yarhonda
Yarilin
Yarilynn
Yaritsa
Yaritza
Yarl
Yarleis
Yarlene
Yarnetta
Yaroslava
Yarra
Yasemin
Yashakii
Yashiba
Yashica
Yashika
Yashira
Yashira Ma
Yashmine
Yashoda
Yasimine
Yasmaine
Yasmari
Yasmeen
Yasmina
Yasminda
Yasnai
Yasneli
Yasoda
Yasset
Yasuko
Yasuri
Yasyrys
Yatae
Yaunee
Yavanna
Yavette
Yavonda
Yavonne
Yavotnie
Yawanarai
Yaye
Yazemen
Yazmin
Yazmina
Yazmine
Ybray
Ydalia
Ydaly
Yeacha
Yeala
Yeanelle
Yeasha
Yecheva
Yee
Yee-Ling
Yee-Man
Yehudis
Yeisleny
Yelany
Yeleana
Yelen
Yelena
Yelenne
Yelina
Yelissa
Yen
Yen-Sophia
Yenely
Yenesia
Yenestra
Yeni
Yenih
Yenitza
Yenny
Yentera
Yenzong
Yeoman
Yepsy
Yerinia
Yerresha
Yeseria
Yesmean
Yesmel
Yesmina
Yesnia
Yessena
Yessenia
Yessica
Yessika
Yesung
Yesyka
Yevett
Yeyni
Yharenda
Yhulonda
Yi Mei
Yiannoulla
Yiasha
Yilian
Yiliana
Yineska
Yisel
Yisraela Judith
Yissenia
Yketa
Ylan
Ylana
Ylande
Ylenia
Ylenna
Ylisa
Ymara
Yndie
Ynecia
Yoam
Yoanna
Yocelyn
Yocheved
Yodne
Yodphat
Yoeniza
Yohana
Yohanka
Yoimaira
Yojaira
Yoko
Yola
Yolaika
Yolaine
Yolana
Yoland
Yolanda Marie
Yolande
Yolanwldra
Yolaude
Yolene
Yolibel
Yolina

Yoline
Yolisvette
Yolita
Yollanda
Yolly
Yolonda
Yoma
Yomaira
Yomara
Yomayra
Yona
Yonabien
Yondel
Yontae
Yoome
Yoon-Jung
Yooshika
Yordanos
Yorishia
Yorlanda
Yorlene
Yorshey
Yoscar
Yoselin
Yoselyn
Youlanda
Young
Youri
Youshaima
Youssra
Ysela
Ysgaelle
Yshatia
Yu
Yuan
Yuana
Yuanna
Yudith
Yuen
Yuenna
Yuin-Kay
Yuiza
Yuk
Yuka
Yuki
Yukiko
Yukiya
Yulanda
Yuleisy
Yulesmi
Yuliana
Yulianna
Yulika
Yulisa
Yulonda
Yumberlyn
Yumie
Yumna
Yuna
Yunis
Yunitza
Yurdenia
Yurelli
Yuri
Yuriko
Yurith
Yuroca
Yusa
Yuseimi
Yuset
Yusimy
Yutoyah
Yuuko
Yva
Yvan
Yvania
Yvanna
Yvelise
Yvelyn
Yveon
Yvesrose
Yvett
Yvolaine
Yvon
Yvone
Yvonne-Elisabeth
Yyonny

Z

Zabina
Zaboire
Zabrina
Zabrina-May
Zabrittney
Zacari
Zacceaus
Zacchaea
Zacharie
Zachary
Zachoia
Zackeisha
Zackery
Zadonne
Zadrian
Zafarene
Zaheera
Zahia
Zahida
Zahiyah
Zahra
Zahraa
Zahrah
Zaibis
Zaida
Zain
Zaina
Zainab
Zainap
Zaineb
Zainub
Zaira
Zakaria
Zakaya
Zakeshia
Zakia
Zakiah
Zakir
Zakiya
Zakiyyah
Zale
Zalie
Zalika
Zalina
Zallanea
Zamara Janice
Zamber
Zamora
Zana
Zanani
Zandra
Zandra-Mae
Zandrea
Zandy
Zanella
Zaneta
Zanetta
Zanib
Zanida
Zanikashakeila
Zanishia
Zanna
Zannah
Zannette

Zannon
Zanovia
Zanquandria
Zante
Zantia
Zaquina
Zarabeth
Zarah
Zaranika
Zareda
Zaree
Zareen
Zareena
Zariella
Zarina
Zarnika
Zarria
Zarvondra
Zary
Zasha
Zatee
Zatina
Zatoria
Zavakia
Zavie
Zavonna
Zayba
Zaymara
Zaynab
Zaynah
Zdena
Zea
Zeandra
Zearlisha
Zeboney
Zechari
Zeemin
Zeena
Zeenat
Zeenet
Zeenya
Zehkia
Zehra
Zein
Zeina
Zeinab
Zela
Zelda
Zeldreana
Zelima
Zelleana
Zelyce
Zemrah
Zena
Zenah
Zenaida
Zenea
Zeneida
Zenia
Zenida
Zenita
Zenobia
Zenovia
Zenovique
Zephania
Zephanie
Zephra
Zephria
Zephyer
Zephyr
Zer
Zerlinda
Zerlota
Zerrickia
Zeruiah
Zestina
Zetdi
Zeticia
Zetta
Zeylinet
Zeynep
Zhakeia
Zhaklin
Zhazha
Zhyra
Zia
Zichelle
Zihesa
Zillah
Zilpha
Zina
Zinah
Zinda
Ziniya
Zinnie-Marie
Zinzi
Ziomara
Zipporah
Zipporiah
Zirak
Ziva
Zivanka
Zjani
Zoanna
Zoe Milet
Zoe Yvette
Zoé
Zoetter
Zohnniffer
Zohra
Zohreh
Zoi
Zoie
Zola
Zolene
Zolia
Zondra
Zongkor
Zonia
Zorada
Zoraida
Zoraide
Zorana
Zoreena
Zoya
Zoyara
Zsashaunda
Zsharmia
Zuchitty
Zuigly
Zujey
Zul
Zul Adiene
Zulal
Zulay
Zulaymis
Zuleika
Zuleima
Zulekha
Zulema
Zuleyka
Zullymari
Zulma
Zunilda
Zurelys
Zuri
Zurisha
Zuzu
Zykeisha
Zykia
Zylmaly

• • • • BOYS • • • •

A

À J
A Jay
A'mir
A-Jay
A.
A. (Andrew)
A. Brandon
A. J.
Aaarmondas
Aabid
Aadal
Aadam
Aadames
Aadil
Aaditya
Aahron
Aakash
Aalden
Aalim
Aalok
Aamer
Aamil
Aamir
Aaren
Aareon
Aaric
Aarie
Aarin
Aarol
Aaron Samu
Aaron-Christopher
Aaron-Elmer
Aaron-Michael
Aaronandre
Aarondeep
Aarondonald
Aaronn
Aaror
Aarron
Aart
Aarti
Aaryn
Aashish
Aasit
Aasiya
Aatur
Aazim
Abaasante
Abadis
Abayomi
Abba
Abbah
Abbas
Abbasali
Abbey
Abd
Abdal
Abdalah
Abdalla
Abdallah
Abdalmotalib
Abdeel
Abdel
Abdelazim
Abdelaziz
Abdelhadi
Abdelrahim
Abdelrahman
Abdias
Abdier
Abdirahman
Abdolrahem
Abdoul
Abdual
Abdualhakeem
Abdualla
Abdul Haki
Abdul-Az
Abdul-Azim
Abdul-Rahman
Abdulah
Abdulalrhman
Abdulasad
Abdulazazz
Abdulazeez
Abdulazi
Abdulhadi
Abdulkar
Abdulkareem
Abdullahi
Abdullatif
Abdur
Abdur-Rahaman
Abdurrah
Abdurrahman
Abdurram
Abdurraouf
Abe
Abebaw
Abeed
Abeen
Abel-Rosario
Abelardo
Abele
Abell
Aben
Aberham
Abhay
Abhik
Abhimanyou
Abhinav
Abhiram
Abhishek
Abi Jah
Abid
Abid Allah
Abidali
Abie
Abigail
Abijah
Abimael
Abimbola
Abimelec
Abin
Abir
Abisai
Ablaza
Able
Abnel
Abner
Abra
Abrahim
Abrahm

Abramo
Abrams
Abran
Abrar
Absalon
Absyko
Abubakar
Abul
Abundio
Acacius
Accell
Ace
Acey
Achilles
Acie
Ackeem
Ackim
Actavious
Adair
Adalberto
Adam John
Adam Kristoffer
Adam Oliver
Adam-John
Adam-Kyle
Adam-Michele
Adam-Nicholas
Adam-Warren
Adama
Adamandios
Adamo
Adams
Adan
Adani
Adano
Adante
Adarian
Adarius
Adarsh
Adbeel
Addam
Addason
Adderly
Adderson
Addi
Addie
Addis
Addisson
Addrain
Adebayo
Adebola
Adeeb
Adeel
Adeele
Adeev
Adekola
Adel
Adelbert
Adelfo
Adelkis
Adelmo
Adely
Adem
Aden
Adeniyi
Aderemi
Adesh
Adetokunbo
Adetokynbo
Adetunji
Adewale
Adeyemi
Adgar
Adham
Adhitya
Adhlere
Adi Ikmal
Adib
Adil
Adim
Adin
Adisa
Adison
Aditya
Adlai
Adley
Adlin
Adloph
Admiral
Admon
Adnaan
Adnan
Adolfo
Adolph
Adolphus
Adom
Adon
Adonis
Adonnis
Adonys
Adrain
Adrease
Adres
Adri
Adriaan
Adriam
Adrian-Joseph
Adriane
Adriann
Adrianno
Adriano-Serafino
Adrianus
Adric
Adrik
Adrion
Adron
Adryan
Adryon
Adsana
Adson
Adulphus
Adythia
Aeb
Aengus
Aeolos
Aeric
Aermon
Aeson
Afaese
Afiba
Afif
Aflis
Africo
Afrim
Afsar
Afton
Afzal
Agaazi
Agina
Agostino
Agripino
Agustin
Agyei
Ahamad
Ahamada
Ahamed
Ahaoma
Aharon
Ahasan
Ahdajay
Ahdrae
Ahie
Ahijah
Ahkeen
Ahkieme
Ahmaad

Ahmad Faizal
Ahmad-Falah
Ahmadsyafiiéi
Ahmaud
Ahmir
Ahran
Ahren
Ahron
Ahsun
Aiden
Aik-Shah
Aiksimar
Ailean
Aime
Aimee
Aimen
Aindriv
Ainsley
Aiona
Airamis Jovonte
Airen
Aireus
Airian
Aislinn
Aiyaz
Aj
Aja
Ajai
Ajamarcus
Ajamu
Ajaypaul
Ajaz
Ajenthan
Ajesh
Ajit
Ajmail
Akai
Akash
Akasha
Akeam
Akee
Akeel
Akeen
Akef
Akeylah
Akeyto
Akhenaton
Akhil
Akhilbhai
Akhir
Akhiym
Akhom
Akida-George
Akiel
Akiem
Akif
Akiff
Akihiro
Akil
Akili
Akim
Akima
Akinyemi
Akir
Akira
Akiva
Aklin
Akosa
Akoya
Akram
Akua
Al
Al Salhiem
Al-Amin
Al-Amyn
Al-Nasir
Al-Qadeer
Al-Zah
Ala
Alaa
Alaaddin
Aladdin
Aladean
Aladino
Alaen
Alaia
Alain-Roland
Alainn
Alamjit
Alandis
Alanie
Alanski
Alanson
Alanzo
Alaric
Alasdair
Alastair
Alax
Alayn
Alazavon
Alba
Albaro
Albean
Albee
Albein
Albeno
Alberge
Albert Jr
Albert-Nicholas
Albert-Nissim
Alberto Francisc
Albertson
Albin
Albino
Albrey
Alchea
Alcide
Alcides
Alder
Aldex
Aldin-David-John
Aldrin
Aldwin
Ale Jandro
Aleck
Alecsandar
Aleem
Alejandra
Alek
Alekisanita
Aleks
Aleksandar
Aleksander
Aleksandr
Aleksandras
Aleksey
Aleksi
Aleksis
Aleksy
Alelandro
Alem
Alem Shate
Alen
Aleric
Alero
Alesandro-Silvio
Alessand
Alessandra
Alexandar
Alexander Allan
Alexander Patri
Alexander Philip
Alexander Todd
Alexander-Christopher

Alexander-James
Alexander-Jonathan
Alexander-Miles
Alexander-Rudolf
Alexandor
Alexandr
Alexandra
Alexandras
Aléxandre
Alexandre-O'dell
Alexandro
Alexandros
Alexandru
Alexes
Alexey
Alexi
Alexie
Alexios
Alexius
Alexiz
Alexjandro
Alexqnder
Alexter
Alexxander
Alexys Andres
Alexzander
Alf
Alfedoe
Alfens
Alferd
Alferdo
Alfie
Alfonse
Alfonsia
Alfonza
Alfonzo
Alford
Alfornza
Alfrendo
Alfrido
Algenis
Algenon
Algeren
Algernon
Algie
Algin
Alginavon
Algon
Alharith
Ali Farid
Ali-Reza
Alia
Alian
Aliance
Aliandro
Alicia
Alico
Alicus
Alieu
Alif
Alifa
Alihussein
Alikhan
Alim
Alimer
Alipio
Alireza
Alisdair
Alistair
Alistaire
Alister
Alix
Alixandre
Alixnder
Aljarreau
Aljon
Alkareem
Alkarim
Alla
Allain
Allan Wilfrid
Allan-John-Keith
Allaray
Allax
Allen Mich
Allenby
Allerd Victor
Allessandro
Allex
Allexander
Allie
Allin
Allison
Allister
Allon
Allscott
Ally
Allykhan
Allyn
Alma
Almando
Almario'
Almas
Almassa
Almir
Almo
Almon
Almonzo
Almus
Alois
Alok
Alon
Alondrae
Alonso
Alonté
Alonza
Aloysius
Alpachino
Alpavin
Alpha
Alphanso
Alpheus
Alphons
Alphonsa
Alphonse
Alphonza
Alphonzo
Alphoria
Alpohaeus
Alpriscilo
Alquan
Alquino
Alrico
Alshaun
Alshawnta
Alshay
Alston
Altanes
Altareik
Altaron
Altavis
Altaz
Altonio
Altroy
Altug
Altwan
Aluku
Alva
Alvan
Alvand
Alverce
Alverez
Alvery
Alvez

Alvino
Alvis
Alwahid
Alwin
Alwyn
Alxavier
Aly
Alykhan
Alyn
Alyxander
Alziah
Amad
Amadeaus
Amadeo
Amadeus
Amadio
Amado
Amador
Amadou
Amahd
Amaire
Amalio
Aman
Amanda
Amandio
Amandip
Amando
Amaniel
Amanjit
Amanjot
Amanpreet
Amanveer
Amaobi
Amardeep
Amari
Amarinder
Amario
Amaris
Amarjit
Amarnath
Amarpreet
Amaud
Amaury
Amber
Amberly
Ambez
Amboh
Ambrose
Ambrosio
Amed
Amedeo
Ameen
Ameer
Ameersadruddin
Ameil
Ameir
Amen
Amer
Americus
Amerinder
Amerjot
Ameya
Ami
Amie
Amiel
Amiello
Amihud
Amil
Amin
Aminadab Joa
Amine
Amip
Amira
Amire
Amirhussein
Amishai
Amitabh
Amitabha
Amith
Amiv
Amjad
Amjed
Ammar
Ammer
Ammiel
Amneet
Amod
Amodaos
Amol
Amon
Amorim
Amothy
Ampelio
Amr
Amran
Amreet
Amren
Amrian
Amrinder
Amrit
Amrit-Pal-Singh
Amritpal
Amritpaul
Amro
Amster
Amtr
Amuel
Amun
Amund
Amy
Amzi
An
Ana
Anacleto
Anais
Anand
Ananda
Ananias
Anant
Ananth
Anas
Anastasio
Anastasios
Anastasis
Anathony
Anaya
Anayat
Ancelmo
Ancil
Ancinio
Andamo
Ander
Anders-Erik
Andersen
Anderson
Anderw
Andery
Andi
Andie
Andino
Andis
Andje
Andonn
Andra
Andrae
Andras
Andravious
Andray
Andre-Michel
Andre-Philippe
André-Philippe
Andre-Rafah
Andrecamarate
Andrecito
Andree
Andrei

Andrej
Andrew Da Silva
Andrew Josep
Andrew Joseph
Andrew Mah
Andrew Richard
Andrew Robert
Andrew-Adam
Andrew-Alexander
Andrew-Everett
Andrew-Jan
Andrew-John
Andrew-Jon
Andrew-Mark
Andrew-Mathew
Andrew-Min
Andrew-Zaki
Andrew-Zamaladeen
Andrews
Andrey
Andreyco
Andrez
Andrezej
Andrian
Andriarto
Andrie
Andries
Andrij
Andrija
Andris
Andrius
Andriy
Andron
Andru
Andrue
Andrus
Andrzei
Andrzej
Aneel
Aneesh
Aneidie
Aneil
Aneis
Anel
Aner
Anes
Aness
Anesson
Anetwann
Angat
Angela
Angelito
Angelo
Christoph
Angelo
Clemente
Angelo-Giudeppe
Angelo-James
Angelos
Anglo
Angrej
Angud
Anh
Anh-Huy
Anh-Tuan
Anhban
Aniase
Anicesio
Aniceto
Aniel
Aniello
Anik
Anil
Animesh
Anis
Anish
Anitoly
Anjum
Ankit
Ankur
Ankush
Anly
Anmetrius
Anna
Annais
Annthon
Annunziato
Anoop
Anothony
Anourack
Anousene
Anousone
Anquan
Anquawn
Anree
Anrico
Ansa
Ansar
Ansel
Anselme
Anselmo
Ansis
Ansley
Anslin
Anson Eugene
Ansun
Ansy
Antae
Antaeus
Antanans
Antantly
Antanze
Antarr
Antauis Jermaine
Antavius
Antaw
Antawan
Antawn
Ante
Ante-Juran
Anted
Anteo
Anterial
Anterio
Antez
Anthawn
Anthey
Anthian
Anthino
Anthnony
Anthoney
Anthoni
Anthonie
Anthonio
Anthonu
Anthony Gary
Anthony Ii
Anthony Jr
Anthony-Amerigo
Anthony-David
Anthony-Edouard
Anthony-George
Anthony-Joseph
Anthony-Michael
Anthony-Michele
Anthonydominic
Anthonysha
Anthoy

Anthwan
Anthyoine
Anthyonny
Anti Juan
Antini
Antinio
Antino
Antion
Antionio
Antionne
Antius
Antjuan
Antoin
Antoiné
Antoinette
Antoinio
Antoinne
Antoino
Antone
Antoney
Antoneyo
Antoni
Antonia
Antonie
Antonino
Antonio Jo
Antonio Jr
Antonio-Luca
Antonios
Antonious
Antonius
Antonnio
Antonvan
Antonyia
Antonyio
Antonyo
Antose
Antowine
Antowne
Antowyn
Antrae
Antravious
Antrawn
Antreall
Antrez
Antron
Antrone
Antsyne
Antuan
Antuane
Antulio
Antuquoin
Antwaina
Antwaine
Antwaion
Antwane
Antwann
Antwanne
Antwarn
Antwen
Antwi
Antwian
Antwine
Antwion
Antwoan
Antwoin
Antwoine
Antwon Bernard
Antwone
Antwonn
Antwonne
Antwuan
Antwyon
Anty
Antyon
Antywon
Anu
Anuar
Anubhav
Anubis
Anuj
Anujit
Anup
Anupal
Anurag
Anwan
Anwar
Apolinar
Apollo
Apollos
Apolonio
Apostolo
Apostolos
Appan
Appesh
Appollo
Appolorce
April
Apu
Aqib
Aqkeem
Aquabonf
Aquan
Aquarius
Aquien
Aquil
Aquila
Aquilas
Ara
Ara-yeramia
Aracelio
Araeus
Aral
Aram
Aramia
Aramis
Aramith
Aramys
Aran
Aras
Arash
Aravinda
Arbnor
Arcadio
Arcatric
Arcelious
Arch
Archanel
Archange
Archer
Archibald
Archie-Ray
Arcides
Arcidi
Arcman
Ardalan
Ardavon
Ardell
Arden
Ardin
Ardon
Arduino
Ardziv
Arealious
Areez
Arel
Arelious
Aren
Arend
Argelio
Argenis
Argentria
Argoles
Arhel
Aria
Arian

Ariane
Arias
Arick
Aridius
Arie
Arieh
Ariella
Arien
Aries
Ariez
Arif
Arih
Arij
Arik
Arikan
Arin
Arinda
Arinder
Arion
Aris
Aristides
Aristidis
Aristito
Aristos-Panikos
Aristotelis
Ariya
Ariyel
Arjun
Arjuna
Arjunn
Arkeem
Arkeen
Arkyn
Arlan
Arland
Arlando
Arlandus
Arleigh
Arles
Arley
Arliance
Arlice
Arlie
Arlin
Arlington
Arlo
Arluthur
Arly
Arlyn
Arlynn
Armaan
Armad
Arman
Armanda
Armaude
Armen
Armenta
Armin
Armon
Armond
Armons
Armyin
Arn
Arnaldo
Arne
Arnel
Arnell
Arnesto
Arnett
Arnette
Arnie
Arnny
Arnoldi
Arnoldo
Arnolfo
Arnott
Arnuchar
Arnuchart
Arnulfo
Aronhiaies
Aroniakeha
Aroon
Arouwan
Arpan
Arpit
Arquimedes
Arra
Arran
Arrant
Arri
Arrial
Arrian
Arric
Arrick
Arrington
Arris
Arsalan
Arsenio
Arseny
Arsh
Arsham
Arslan
Arstanza
Art
Artavia
Artavious
Artavis
Artavius
Artelle
Artemio
Artemus
Artene
Artevious
Artez
Arthel
Arthell
Arther
Arthiemarr
Arthonia
Arthur-Santos
Artian
Artie
Artis
Artley
Artreil
Artrell
Artrez
Artumus
Arty
Artyinn
Artym
Arun
Aruns
Arval
Arvell
Arvelle
Arvester
Arvid
Arvie
Arvin
Arvind
Arvinder
Arvis
Arvon
Arvydas
Arya
Aryan
Arzie
Arzzel
As-Samee
Asa
Asaad
Asad
Asadour
Asadul
Asael

Asaf
Asaiah
Asan
Asaph
Ascencio
Ascour
Asdren
Aseef
Asghar
Ash
Ashar
Ashawn
Ashby
Ashford
Ashiq
Ashish
Ashkan
Ashlan
Ashleigh
Ashlen
Ashley Christoph
Ashlif
Ashlin
Ashlone
Ashlynn
Ashmindar
Ashneel
Ashok
Ashoke
Ashor
Ashraf
Ashtin
Ashtyn
Ashur
Ashwin
Asian
Asif
Asim
Asitha
Askia
Aslam
Aslan
Asmar
Asmara
Asmra
Aspen
Assad
Assamid
Assani
Asten
Astin
Aston
Astrel
Asuncion
Aswad
Aswan
Asyad
Ata
Ata-Ul-Salaam
Atallah
Atarian
Atavius
Atef
Athan
Athanase
Athanasios
Athen
Atiba
Atif
Atilano
Atileo
Atim
Atisha
Atit
Atiya
Atlee
Atli
Atrayo
Atrellue
Atryal
Atsa
Atsushi
Atticus
Attilio
Atul
Atwoine
Aubrie
Auburn
Aude
Audi
Audie
Audiel
Audley
Audomano
Audory
Audreaux
Audrew
Audury
Audwin
Audy
Auggie
Augie
Auguste
Augustin
Augustine
Augusto
Aundra
Aundre
Aundré
Aundrea
Aundry
Aunnoy
Auntonio
Aurash
Aurby
Aurele
Aureliano
Aurelio
Aurey
Aurice
Auron
Aurthar
Aurther
Aurthur
Aury
Aury-Meir
Ausborn
Austbrook
Austine
Auston
Austyn
Auther
Authur
Autis
Automn
Autral
Autreau
Autrell
Auttdomm
Autumn
Ava
Avain
Avais
Avaise
Avalon
Avan
Avante
Avanti
Avaranice
Avard
Avaristo
Avary
Aveary
Avedis
Avelardo

Averaam
Averell
Averian
Averic
Averiel
Averill
Avi
Avian
Aviel
Avijshon
Avik
Avimael
Avinash
Avinesh
Avion
Avis
Aviv
Avjit
Avneet
Avneil
Avory
Avraham
Avram
Avrelio
Avriel
Avrohom
Avrom
Avrum
Avry
Awad
Awainine
Awais
Awale
Awtar
Axavina
Axton
Axzavieour
Ayalon
Ayan
Ayanes
Ayaree
Ayaz
Ayazhussein
Aydan
Ayden
Aydin
Ayers-Michael
Ayhab
Ayhan
Ayinde
Aykan
Ayman
Aymeen
Ayobande
Ayren
Ayron
Ayrton
Azad
Azar
Azariah-Hillel
Azarius
Azel
Azfar
Azhar
Azim
Aziqaw
Aziz
Aziz-Eugene
Azlyn
Azon
Azriel
Azul
Azuma
Azumah

B

B.J.
Ba
Baabak
Baaron
Baba
Babak
Babatunde
Baby Boy
Baby Ray
Badal
Baden
Bader
Badir
Bafokeng
Baha
Bahram
Bahron
Bailey
Bailio
Baine
Baird
Baise
Baiza
Bakah
Bakari
Baker
Balchan
Baldemar
Baldomero
Baldwin
Balgene
Baligh
Baline
Balir
Baljit
Baljivan
Baljot
Balkevinjit
Ballard
Balraj
Baltasar
Baltazar
Balthazar
Baltimor
Balvin
Balvinder
Bander
Bandit
Bandon
Bane
Bang
Banjamin-Art
Banjarmi
Banning
Bannister
Bannor
Banny
Banty
Bao
Baptiste
Barak
Barath
Barbara
Barbaro
Barcarie
Barclay
Barcley
Bard
Bardia
Bardiya
Baren
Barent
Barfield
Barheim
Bariah

Barimore
Barinder
Barkell
Barnabas
Barnabus
Barnett
Barney
Baronie
Barre
Barreese
Barret
Barrette
Barrey
Barrick
Barrie
Barrington
Barrion
Barris
Barron
Barronf
Barrymore
Barshion
Barstow
Barteomiej
Barth
Bartholo
Bartholome
Bartholomew
Bartimous
Bartlet
Bartley
Bartlomiej-Dawid
Bartolome
Bartolomeo
Baruch
Bary
Baryn
Barzin
Basant
Baseal
Basel
Bashar
Basheer
Bashir
Bashiyr
Bashkim
Basilio
Basim
Bassam
Bassel
Baughn
Bavarian
Bavin
Baxter
Bayard
Bayden
Baylen
Bayud Dean
Bbarrington
Beaudean
Beaudoin
Beauregard
Beaver
Bebe
Bechir
Beck
Beckett
Bediros
Bedreldeen
Bee
Beecher
Beedabin
Behenzin
Behm
Behn
Behnam
Behnjamin
Behoor
Behzad
Beint-Axile
Bejamin
Bela
Belal
Belfor
Belford
Belinda
Belisaire
Bell-Ami
Bellal
Bello
Beluchi
Belvin
Belvy
Bemjiman
Ben-Aaron
Ben-Asa
Ben-Israel
Ben-yimin
Ben-Zion
Benaiah
Benardo
Benasa
Bender
Bendigo
Bendy
Benedetto
Benedict
Benett
Beng
Benhart
Benicio
Benigno
Benio
Benjaim
Benjaman
Benjamim
Benjamin Bernard
Benjamin Joseph
Benjamin-John
Benjamin-Scott
Benjamine
Benjamyn
Benjemin
Benjermain
Benji
Benjiman
Benjimen
Benjjmen
Benjy
Benmar
Benmont
Benn
Benne
Bennet
Bennington
Benno
Beno
Benoît
Bensen
Bentley
Benuel
Benyamin
Benzie
Ber
Berchel
Berdj
Berdry
Berean
Bereim
Berend
Berenger
Berent
Beresford
Berg

Bergen
Berhane
Beric
Berje
Berkeley
Berkley
Berlin
Berlinsky
Berlitz
Berman
Bernabe
Bernabel
Bernal
Bernaldo
Bernardino
Bernardo
Bernardus
Bernarr
Bernd
Berndt
Bernell
Bernerd
Bernet
Bernhard
Bernhardt
Bernice
Bernie
Berry
Berston
Bertie
Bertin
Berto
Bertram
Bertran
Bertrand
Bertrem
Bertrum
Bertus
Besim
Betino
Beuford
Bevan
Beve
Beverly
Bevin
Bevon
Beynan
Bhapinderpal
Bhasheer
Bhavanjit
Bhavik
Bhavin
Bhavneet
Bhreon
Bhrett
Bhubinder
Bhulinder
Bhupinder
Bhupindex
Bickely
Bidish
Bienuenido
Bienvenido
Bijan
Bijhan
Biko
Bikramjit
Bikrampal
Bila
Bile
Biley
Bilgi
Billal
Bille
Billey
Billie
Billie-Joe
Billijo
Billy Bo
Billy Joe
Billy-Jack
Billy-Joe
Billy-John
Billyjoe
Bily
Bing
Binh
Biniam
Binyamin
Biobele
Birch
Birk
Birmengham
Birney
Biron
Bishop
Bisith
Bivinsky
Bjar
Blade
Blae
Blaed
Blain
Blaire
Blaize
Blakeelijha
Blakely
Blakeney
Blanden
Blane
Blas
Blase
Blayde
Blaze
Bleny
Bleys
Blist
Blu
Blucher
Bluejah
Blunka Jr
Blynn
Blythe
Boanerges
Boaz
Bob-Robert
Bobbeyjo
Bobbi
Bobbie
Bobby-Joe
Boby
Bocephus
Bodee
Boden
Bodey
Bodie
Bodixie
Bodwin
Boe
Boe-Daniel
Boedee
Bogart
Bogdan
Bohdan
Bohdon
Bohumir
Boice
Boiyce
Boleslaw
Bolieslau
Bolivar
Bon
Bona
Bonar
Bonavantura
Bond

Bonell
Boniface
Bonner
Booker
Boone
Booz
Bor-yuan
Bora
Boris
Borja
Borna
Borockis
Borris
Boruch
Borys
Bosco
Bosko
Boss
Boston
Botan
Botelho
Bou
Boudean
Boun
Bounny
Bounthavy
Bourilack
Bovey
Bow-Dee
Bowdrie
Bowdy
Bowen
Bowie
Bowman
Boyce
Boyde
Bozidar-Bobby
Brace
Bracey
Brach
Brack
Bracken
Brackie
Brackus
Brad-Lee
Bradd
Bradden
Bradell
Bradely
Bradey
Bradick
Bradine
Bradlay
Bradleah
Bradleigh
Bradley James
Bradley Timothy
Bradley-Gabriel
Bradley-Wade
Bradnon
Bradoc
Bradson
Bradyn
Brae
Braedan
Braedon
Bragen
Braheem
Braheim
Brahian
Brahiem
Brahima
Brahin
Brahlin
Brahm
Brahman
Brahyn
Braiden
Brain
Brakeem
Braland
Bralen
Bram
Bramdon
Bran
Branan
Brance
Branch
Brand
Branda
Brandaan
Brandall
Brandam
Branddon
Brande
Brandel
Brandell
Brander
Brandi
Brandie
Brandis
Brandley
Brandol
Brandon Jarrod
Brandon Marrio
Brandon-
Brandon-Jay
Brandon-Lee
Brandone
Brandonn
Brandy
Branimir
Branko
Branmichael
Brannan
Branndon
Brannigan
Brannon
Brannyn
Branon
Bransen
Bransin
Branson
Branten-Abdou
Branthon
Brantley
Brantly
Branton
Brantson
Braten
Braton
Braucht
Braughton
Braulio
Braum
Braun
Bray
Brayben
Braydan
Braylon
Brayton
Brea
Breagan
Breandan
Brec
Breck
Breckie
Breen
Brehn
Breken
Breland
Bremen
Bren
Brenan
Brenda
Brenden-Lee

Brendene
Brendin
Brendin-Lee
Brendt
Brendyn
Brene
Brenin
Brenley
Brenly
Brenn
Brenndan
Brennin
Brennon
Brenon
Brent Richard
Brentan
Brenten
Brentis
Brentley
Brentson
Brentten
Brentton
Brentwood
Breohn
Breon
Breontae
Breonte
Breseane
Breshard
Breson
Breton
Brett Nath
Brett-Nathanael
Bretten
Bretton
Brewster
Breyawn
Breyon
Brian Do Carmo
Brian Douglas
Brian Steven
Brian-Christ
Brian-John
Briana
Brianallen
Briane
Brianne
Briant
Briante
Bricen
Briceton
Brick
Bridd
Bridger
Brien
Brience
Brient
Brigdon
Brigg
Briggs
Brigham
Brighton
Brigido
Brigim
Briheem
Briheim
Brijesh
Brik
Brin
Brinsley
Brinson
Brint
Brinton
Briny
Brion
Brisan
Brison
Bristol
Brit
Britain
Briton
Brittain
Brittan
Brittany
Britten
Brittney
Brityce
Broadus
Broam
Brock-T-Anthony
Brocke
Brockett
Brockton
Brodee
Broden
Broderic
Brodey
Brodi
Brodin
Brodreich
Brodrick
Brogan
Brok
Brolin
Bronsun
Brontea
Bronwyn
Brooke
Brooker
Brookin
Brooklynn
Broox
Broque
Broshawn
Brown
Bruce-Allan
Bruceness
Bruckelliott
Brue
Bruno-Anthony
Bruno-Pierre
Bruster
Bryam
Bryan Chris
Bryan Christophe
Bryan Nathaniel
Bryan-Edward
Bryan-young
Bryar
Bryce Lynn
Brycen
Bryceton
Brycon
Brydan
Bryden
Brydon
Brydone
Bryen
Bryent
Bryghton
Bryheem
Bryhim
Brylon
Bryn
Bryne
Brynen
Brynn
Brynyn
Brys
Bryse
Brysel
Brysen
Bryshaun
Brysten

Bryston
Bryt
Bryton
Btzalel
Bubba
Buck
Buckley
Buckner
Bucko
Bucky
Bud
Bud Michael
Budd
Budly
Buel Clifford
Buercy
Buford
Bukola
Bun
Bunroeun
Bunvathana
Burchell
Burdell
Burdette
Burgess
Burke
Burkley
Burl
Burley
Burlin
Burnard
Burnell
Burnett
Burney
Burns
Burrell
Burt
Burton
Busquin

Buster
Butch
Buu
Buzz
Byan
Byes
Bykimm
Byra
Byran
Byron Leonard
Byron-Gustavo
Byrone
Byrum
Byshan

C

C J
C.
C. J.
C. R.
C.J.
Ca Leb
Caberon
Cabin
Cabot
Cacey
Cach
Cachito
Cadarel
Cadell
Caden
Caderal
Cadum
Caedmon
Cael
Caelan
Caeleb

Caeleon
Caelin
Caesar
Cagen
Cagney
Cahle
Cahn
Cai
Caid
Cail
Cailean
Cailen
Cailin
Caillan
Caillin
Cain
Cainan
Caine
Caineth
Cais
Caithrin
Caitlin
Cajun
Cal
Calab
Calahan
Calais
Calan
Calbert
Calcidrick
Calder
Calein
Calen
Calep
Calerbe
Caley
Caliam
Calill
Calin

Calixto
Callahan
Callam
Callan
Calleil
Callen
Callon
Callum
Calob
Calogero
Calolo
Calray
Calrick
Calum
Calven
Calvert
Calvin-Lou
Calvir
Calvyn
Calwyn
Calym
Calyn
Cam
Camar
Camaron
Camber
Cambreil
Cameran
Cameraron
Camerson
Cameyon
Camiel
Camille
Camillo
Camilo
Camiren
Camm
Camon
Campanella

Campbell
Camren
Camy
Cana
Canaan
Candelario
Canden
Candid
Candido
Candonino
Canei
Canel
Caneron
Canggih
Cano
Canon
Cantangalo
Canton
Cantrell
Canyon
Cao
Caolan
Capurs
Car
Cara
Cardale
Cardaro
Cardavian
Cardelius
Cardell
Carder
Cardez
Cardin
Cardo
Cardoza
Careem
Carel
Carell
Carew
Cargil
Cariel
Cariell
Carim
Carius
Carl Alan
Carl Henrie
Carl Henry
Carl Jr
Carl Nicholas
Carl-Heinz
Carlan
Carlando
Carldon
Carlen
Carles
Carless
Carleton
Carlex
Carley
Carlhans
Carlie
Carlif
Carlin-Micheal
Carling
Carlis
Carliss
Carlitos
Carll
Carlos Man
Carls
Carlson
Carlston
Carltez
Carlus
Carlvis
Carlyle
Carman
Carmel
Carmella
Carmichael
Carmiel
Carmon
Carn
Carnelius
Carnell
Carol
Carole
Carols
Caromi
Caronarda
Carooq
Carrado
Carrick
Carricko
Carrie
Carrington
Carrissian
Carroll
Carron
Carrson
Carsley
Carslie
Carsten
Carston
Cartell
Cartez
Carther
Carub
Carvensus
Carver
Carvon
Caryl
Cas
Casca
Casdin
Case
Caseare
Cash
Cashe
Cashmere
Casimir
Cason
Caspar
Cass
Cassandra
Cassell
Cassia
Cassie
Cassius
Cassle
Cast
Casten
Caston
Castro
Catherine
Cathryn
Catlyn
Cato
Caton
Catrell
Caulin
Caunaka
Cavaller
Cavan
Cavell
Caven
Cavin
Cayce
Cayl
Cayle
Caylen
Cayler
Caylin
Caylon
Caylum
Cayse

Caysey
Cazz
Cémone
Ceasar
Cebran
Cecilio
Cecill
Cedar
Cedarian
Cederick
Cedirick
Cedrec
Cédric
Cedrik
Ceejay
Ceenan
Cehunt
Cejay
Celestino
Celica
Celso
Celyn
Cem
Cengiz
Cenk
Centanial
Cephas
Cephus
Cepreano
Cerel
Ceril
Ceritsie
Ceron
Cesare
Cesario
Cetan
Cethan
Cevan
Ceven
Cevin
Ceylon
Chaad
Chabez
Chace
Chachi
Chadam
Chaddrick
Chaddwick
Chade
Chaderick
Chadleigh
Chadler
Chadley
Chadlin
Chadlyn
Chadmen
Chado
Chadric
Chadrick
Chadron
Chadvic
Chadwin
Chadwyck
Chady
Chae
Chaffic
Chafic
Chafick
Chai
Chaice
Chaim
Chaine
Chais
Chaison
Chaka
Chalermchai
Chalie
Chalin
Chalmers
Chalmr
Chalon
Cham
Chamar
Chamarr
Chamroeun
Chams
Chan
Chanbotr
Chanc
Chancelen
Chancellor
Chancey
Chancy
Chand
Chandan
Chandany
Chandara
Chandaravvth
Chandlan
Chandon
Chane
Chaney
Chang
Changler
Chanhee
Chann
Channingtao
Channra
Channy
Chanod
Chanpreet
Chanrathana
Chanse
Chansy
Chant
Chantale
Chante
Chantha
Chanthar
Chanthoeun
Chanthry
Chantra
Chantry
Chants
Chantz
Chanz
Chao
Chapell
Chapin
Chapman
Charah
Charan
Charbel
Charife
Charity
Charityson
Charl
Charle
Charlen
Charles Gracia
Charles-Alexandre
Charles-Eric
Charles-Manrico
Charles-Mohamed
Charles-Paul
Charlesten
Charleston
Charleton
Charley
Charlotin
Charlton
Charly
Charlzell
Charmane

Charng-Rong
Charnice
Charon
Charron
Charvaris
Charvonte
Charvorris
Chas
Chase-Daniel
Chasen
Chasere
Chaseton
Chaseton Lynn
Chasmu
Chasmund
Chason
Chass
Chasten
Chastien
Chastin
Chaston
Chasyn
Chaumncy
Chaunary
Chauncei
Chauncy
Chavais
Chavar
Chavare
Chavaz
Chavien
Chavis
Chavok
Chavotti
Chawki
Chawn
Chay
Chayanne
Chayce
Chaylon
Chayne
Chayse
Chaysen
Chaywavongkot
Chazmin
Chazwic
Chazz
Che
Chéfin
Chedrick
Cheehoon
Cheerag
Chelsea
Chelsey
Chen
Chenaniah
Cheney
Cheng
Chengjou
Cheong
Chequell
Cherie
Cherles
Cherlin
Cheron
Cheroy
Chery
Cheryl
Chesarae
Chesley
Chesney
Chesron
Cheston
Chetan
Chetayen
Chethan
Chett
Chettra
Chevan
Chevas
Chevaz
Cheveck
Chevelle
Cheven
Chevese
Chevi
Chevon
Chevy
Chew
Cheyenne
Cheyn
Cheyne
Cheyney
Chez
Chezrae
Chi
Chianta
Chibuzor
Chicago
Chike
Chilbert
Child
Chimar
Chimere
Chin
Chinedu
Chinedum
Chino
Chinou
Chioco
Chip
Chipman
Chiraag
Chirag
Chirstopher
Chisholm
Chisolm
Chistian
Chistopher
Chith
Chitra
Chiu
Chiu-Ming
Chjace
Chod
Choice
Chom
Choncey
Chonese
Choo-Leong
Choppy
Chouaib
Chourey
Chrasaun
Chravis
Chriag
Chriostpher
Chrisdian
Chrishaun
Chrishawn
Chrisitan
Chrislee
Chrisopher
Chrisotpher
Chrispthur
Chrispus
Chriss
Chrissana
Chrisse Airell
Christ
Christa
Christafer

Christai
Christain
Christan
Christapher
Christar
Christé
Christen
Christensen
Christeopher
Christepher
Christerpher
Christhoper
Christiaan
Christian Kace
Christian-Laurent
Christian-Philip
Christiana
Christie
Christien
Christif
Christifer
Christin
Christine
Christino
Christion
Christipher
Christobal
Christof
Christofer
Christoffer
Christoforos
Christofper
Christoher
Christon
Christopehr
Christoper
Christoph
Christophe-Paul
Christopher Earl
Christopher-Adam
Christopher-Angelo
Christopher-Bruno
Christopher-Corry
Christopher-David
Christopher-Drew
Christopher-Gustavo
Christopher-James
Christopher-Jordan
Christopher-Kevin
Christopher-M
Christopher-Michael
Christopher-Micheal
Christopher-Ryan
Christopher-Scot
Christophere
Christopherr
Christopherson
Christophor
Christorpher
Christos
Christos-Chris
Christos-Mihaly
Christpher
Christphor
Christpor
Christy
Christyan
Chritian
Chrys
Chrysovalanti
Chrystian
Chu
Chuck
Chuckie
Chucky
Chue
Chuefa
Chuefeng
Chukwudi
Chukwuemek
Chukwuemeka
Chun
Chuncy
Chung
Chung-Hey
Chung-yan
Chungo
Chuong
Chuong-John
Churzan
Chyenne
Chyler
Cian
Ciano
Ciaran
Cimani Amani
Cimarron
Cindy
Cinque
Cipriano
Cirilo
Cirk
Ciro
Cirovleal
Cisco
Cissell
Cj
Claeb
Claiborne
Clair
Clais
Clancey
Clancy
Clarance
Clare
Clarentavious
Clary
Clashous
Classy
Claton
Claude-Pascal
Claudel
Claudell
Claudimir
Claudin
Claudinson
Clavonta
Clayborn
Claybourne
Clayburn
Clayne
Clayson
Clayvent
Cleabern
Cleades
Cleanthese
Clearence
Cleason

Cleavland
Cleavon
Cledis
Cleider
Clell
Clemens
Clément
Clemente
Clemie
Clemmie
Clenard
Clent
Clenton
Cleo
Cleon
Cleophas
Cleophis
Cleophues
Cleophus
Cleoson
Cleotis
Clepha
Clerndon
Clete
Cletus
Cleus
Cleve
Cleveland
Clevelend
Clevelynn
Clevie
Cley
Clide
Clidell
Client
Cliff Jr
Cliff-Paul
Cliffard
Cliffton
Cliford
Cliften
Clintay
Clintton
Cliston
Clive
Clivens
Clodee
Clovis
Cloyd
Cloys
Clyant
Clyde-Daniel
Clyford
Clynton
Clyph
Clyvans
Coady
Coale
Coalin
Coatney
Cobe
Cobey
Cobie
Cobret
Coby
Cochise
Coda
Coday
Code
Codee
Codell
Codi
Codiak
Codie
Codrington
Cody-Blu
Cody-J
Cody-Robert
Coedy
Coel
Coenraad
Cogis
Cohan
Cohen
Coidarrel
Cokes
Colan
Colavito
Colbert
Colbey
Colbi
Colden
Cole-Michael
Coleby
Colemann
Colemon
Colen
Coleton
Colewyn
Coley
Colhoze
Colie
Colleak
Colleal
Colleen
Collen
Colleth
Colley
Collie
Collier
Colligan
Collin Jer
Collins
Collis
Collon
Collyn
Colm
Colman
Colon
Colten
Coltier
Coltin
Columbus
Coluqitt
Colyn
Comar
Commodore
Compton
Comrod
Con
Conall
Conan
Conar
Conard
Concetto
Concezio
Concorde
Condredge
Confesor
Cong
Coniah
Conlan
Conlea
Conlee
Conley
Conlyn
Conn
Connally
Connell
Conner
Connie
Connor Aulden
Conon
Conrado
Conrat
Conrey

Conridge
Conroy
Conry
Constadine
Constandine
Constanstine
Constantin
Constantine
Constantino
Constantinos
Contrell
Conway
Conyus
Coolidge
Copie
Cor
Coradaro
Coran
Corant
Corban
Corbett
Corbey
Corby
Corcoran
Cord
Cordae
Cordairo
Cordale
Cordara
Cordarell
Cordareo
Cordarin
Cordario
Cordarius
Cordaro
Cordarrel
Cordarrell
Cordarro
Cordarrol
Cordarryl
Cordaryl
Corday
Corddarro
Cordeal
Cordearo
Cordeiro
Cordel
Cordelle
Cordelro
Cordera
Corderall
Corderro
Corderun
Cordiaro
Cordick
Cordon
Cordswell
Cordy
Core
Coreaa
Corelle
Corey William
Cori
Corian
Coridon
Corie
Corin
Corinthian
Corio
Corkey
Corley
Corliss
Cormac
Cormart
Cornealous
Corneili
Corneilius
Cornel
Corneliaus
Cornelious
Cornelis
Corneliu
Cornellis
Cornellius
Cornett
Corney
Cornie
Corniellus
Corradino
Corrado
Corrdarl
Corrderio
Correnzo
Correy
Corria
Corrie
Corrigan
Corson
Cort
Cortavious
Cortez'
Cortland
Cortnay
Cortne
Corvus
Corwin
Corwinn
Corwyn
Cory Christopher
Coryell
Coryn
Cosby
Cosimo
Cosma
Cosmo
Costandi
Costandinos
Costantinos
Costanzo-Antonio
Costas
Costes
Cotee
Cotey
Cotie
Cotton
Cottreal
Cotty
Cougan
Couger
Coujoe
Coulson
Coulter
Count
Country
Couper
Courey
Cournelius
Courtenay
Courtez
Courtice
Courtlan
Courtlandt
Courtlin
Courtlyn
Courtnay
Courtne
Covelle
Covery
Covey
Covian
Covie
Cowan
Coy Daniel
Coyde

Coyie
Coyle
Coynard
Coyt
Coz
Cragun
Craige
Craigen
Craigery
Craigon
Cran
Crandall
Craven
Crawford
Cray
Crayton
Creadell
Creag
Creaven
Creel
Creeville
Cregg
Creig
Creighto
Creighton
Crendal
Crescencio
Creston
Crew
Criag
Cris
Crispin
Criss
Crist
Cristaph
Cristen
Cristhian
Cristle
Cristoba
Cristobal
Cristofer
Cristoph
Croix
Cronile
Crory
Crosby
Croy
Crushendowe
Cruz
Crystal
Csorrell
Cuauthemoc
Cue
Cuevas
Cuinn
Cullan
Culley
Cully
Culum
Cuong
Cuong-Tuan
Curan
Curdell
Curel
Curits
Curley
Curnell
Curran
Curron
Curry
Curshane
Curtice
Curtis-Patrick
Curtiss
Curtlund
Curtus
Curvin
Cutler
Cutrell
Cvalib
Cw
Cworey
Cy
Cyle
Cyler
Cyley
Cylie
Cylroy
Cymon
Cyra
Cyrel
Cyrell
Cyrelle
Czar

D

D Anthony
D Arco
D Lanta
D Varius
D Wayne
D'andre
D'andrea
D'angelo
D'anthony
D'arcy
D'jay
D'juan
D'markus
D'shaun
D'shawn
D'varrio
D'wayne
D.
Da Jon
Da Rell
Da'juan
Da'meekio
Da'mon
Da-Juan
Da-Ron
Daaron
Dac
Dace
Dache
Dacian
Dacias
Dack
Dacoda
Dacota
Dacster
Dadi
Dadricar
Dadrien
Dae
Dael
Daelan
Daelin
Daemen
Daemon
Daemond
Daenen
Daeon
Daeoo
Daeton
Daevid
Daevon
Daffydd
Dagan
Dagen
Dago
Dagoberto
Dagon
Dah

Daheem
Dahln
Dahn
Dahvéb
Dahvone
Dahyrll
Daichi
Daigoro
Daiib Sabri
Dailin
Daily
Daimean
Daimen
Daimien
Dain
Daine
Dainion
Dainis
Dainon
Dairus
Daiton
Daivid
Dajaun
Dajshon
Dajuan
Dakaota
Dakarai
Dakary
Dakin
Dakoda
Dakotah
Dakotha
Dal
Dalan
Dalas
Dalbir
Dalcio
Dalemetrius
Dalen
Daleron
Dalexi
Daley
Dalfino
Dalian
Dalice
Dalin
Dalione
Daliyl
Daljit
Dallan
Dallen
Dalles
Dallon
Dallyn
Dalmar
Dalmas
Dalmer
Dalon
Dalphanite
Dalpre
Dalvin
Dalvis
Dalwyn
Daly
Dalyn
Dalys
Damail
Damaion
Daman
Damar
Damarcius
Damarco
Damarcus
Damario
Damarius
Damarr
Damascus
Damaso
Damean
Dameion'
Damek
Damen
Dameon
Dameone
Dametri
Damiam
Damiann
Damiano
Damianos
Damie
Damiend
Damietrice
Damin
Damir
Damire
Damitré
Damitriuz
Damiyr
Damoes
Damond
Damone
Damonn
Damonta
Damontez
Damontis
Danaan
Danal
Dananjaya
Danaray
Danaris
Danarius
Danate
Danathan
Danavan
Danavin
Dancorris
Dandrae
Dandras
Dandray
Dandre
Danee
Daneil
Danel
Danen
Dang
Dangelo
Danh
Dani
Danian
Danick
Danieal
Daniekl
Daniel Abram
Daniel Alejandro
Daniel Ant
Daniel Harrison
Daniel Iii
Daniel Lee
Daniel-Andre
Daniel-Andres
Daniel-Blas
Daniel-Christopher
Daniel-J
Daniel-Joseph
Daniel-Joshua
Daniel-Lee
Daniel-Martin
Daniel-Prest
Daniel-Ul-Haque
Daniele-Anthony
Daniell
Danielle
Daniels

Danielson
Danien
Danik
Danikt
Danile
Danilo
Danilou
Danion
Danish
Danjon
Dankeis
Danmar
Danne
Dannial
Dannie
Danniel
Dannielle
Dannil
Dannon
Danny Da Cruz
Danny Lee
Dannye
Danon
Danoris
Danquis
Danson
Dant
Dantae
Dantavious
Danté
Danton
Dantreil
Dantrell
Dantrelle
Dantrez
Dany
Danyale
Danyel
Danyiel
Danyl
Danyle
Danylo
Danzavieran
Danzel
Danzell
Danzick
Daophet
Daphness
Daphnus
Daquan
Daquawn
Daquian
Daqwan
Dar
Dara
Darail
Daralle
Daramius
Daran
Daranarich
Darasy
Darawn
Darbie
Darby
Darcee
Darcel
Darcie
Darcio
Darcy-Claude
Dare
Dareal
Darech
Dareck
Dareek
Darek
Darel
Darelle
Darence
Darendra
Darian
Darian Christoph
Daric
Darick
Darico
Darien
Daries
Darieus
Daril
Dario
Darion
Darione
Darios
Darious
Daris
Darith
Darius Douglas
Darius-Aramis
Dariush
Dariusz
Darl
Darly
Darlymir
Darmonte
Darnall
Darneil
Darnel
Darnelle
Darnnel
Darnyll
Darold
Darone
Daronrick
Daronte
Daroyl
Darral
Darreal
Darrean
Darreio
Darrelle
Darren Jr
Darren-David
Darrian
Darrias
Darrie
Darriel
Darrielle
Darrien
Darrience
Darrieo
Darrion
Darrious
Darris
Darrnell
Darroch
Darrold
Darron
Darrow
Darrus
Darry-Ale
Darryel
Darryk
Darryl James
Darryle
Darryll
Darryn
Darsey
Darshan
Darson
Dartavious
Dartel
Darth
Dartis
Dartrel
Darvell
Darvin

Darvis
Daryck
Daryel
Daryell
Daryle
Daryll
Darylle
Daryn
Darynn
Daryson
Dasaev
Dasan
Dasaun
Dasean
Dashan
Dashawn
Dashiell
Dashielle
Dashnov
Dashun
Dasnu
Dassan
Dassie
Dastin
Dat
Datesh
Dathan
Dathon
Datin
Daton
Datrell
Dauelle
Dauid
Daundra
Daune
Dauntaye
Daunte
Dauntrae
Dauod
Daurell
Daurice
Davan
Davar
Davaris
Davariuss
Davaron
Davarris
Davaugn
Dave Kenny
Daved
Davee
Davel
Daven
Davendra
Davenele
Daverick
Daverous
Daverrell
Davevonn
Davey
Davi
Davian
Daviau
David Alexander
David Benjamin
David Chri
David Elder
David Lee
David Mich
David Prescott
David Sammuel
David-Alexander
David-Er
David-Giang
David-Harry
David-James
David-Lee
David-Martin
David-Raphael
David-Ross
David-Sakhorn
Davide
Davido
Davidson
Davie
Davindra
Davinte
Davion
Davith
Davone
Davonf
Davonn
Davonne
Davonte
Davor
Davoris
Davoud
Davrel
Davron
Davuth
Davvall
Davy
Davyd
Davydeverald
Daw-Owd
Dawan
Dawaun
Dawawn
Dawayne
Dawid
Dawine
Dawishson
Dawit
Dawn
Dawnson
Dawon
Dawoyan
Dawud
Dawvan
Dawyne
Dax
Daxmond
Daxter
Daxton
Dayasingh
Daydren
Daygoro
Dayl
Daylan
Dayle
Daylen
Daylin
Daylon
Daymian
Daymon
Daymond
Dayn
Dayna
Daynon
Dayon
Dayrell
Dayron
Daysa
Daysean
Dayshon
Dayson
Dayvon
Dayyan
Dazman
Dazzmond
De
De Andre
De Andrea
De Angelo
De Ante
De Aundre

De Jon
De Juan
De Marco
De Maris
De Sean
De Vonté
De Wayne
De-Juan
Deaaron
Deacon
Deaengelo
Deaire
Deak
Deale
Dean-Paul
Deandra
Deandrae
Déandre
Deandré
Deandrea
Deane
Déangelo
Deangleo
Deanglo
Deano
Deanothy
Deante
Deanthony
Deantonio
Deanza
Deareo
Dearin
Dearl
Dearloe
Dearmondo
Dearon
Deathony
Deatrick
Deaudra
Deault
Deaundera
Deaundra
Deaundre
Deaundrey
Deaunta
Deavan
Deaven
Deavon
Deavory
Deaz
Deborah
Decanter
Decard
Decaris
Decarise
Decarlo
Decarlos
Decarroll
Decatuer
Decimus
Decio
Declan
Decoltius
Decoreo
Decoriez
Decory
Dederick
Dedric
Dedrick
Dedrix
Dee
Dee-Jay
Deems
Deenerio
Deepan-Saravanan
Deepanjan
Deepinder
Deepraj
Deepu
Deferro
Deginald
Deguan
Dehonis
Deia
Deion
Deiter
Deitrich
Deitrick
Deivan
Deivon
Deivone
Dejan
Dejaun
Dejay
Dejon
Dejoshua
Dejun
Dekan
Deke
Dekeno
Dekorda
Dekota
Dekotes
Dekuan
Dekwan
Del
Delali
Delaljujuan
Delan
Delandon
Delandrius
Delane
Delaney
Delanny
Delano
Delawrence
Delayno
Delbion
Delbis
Deldric
Deldrick
Delessio
Delfino
Delier
Delio
Dell
Dellis
Delma
Delman
Delmar
Delmas
Delme
Delmer
Delmetric
Delmick
Delmore
Delon
Delone
Delone Fra
Delong
Delonny
Delontey
Delorean
Deloren
Deloryan
Delos
Deloy
Deloyd
Delray
Delree
Delreece
Delrick
Delrico
Delrintus
Delromando

Delroy
Delshawn
Delta
Delton
Delvernon
Delveron
Delvoan
Delvon
Delwin
Delwyn
Demani
Demanuel
Demar
Demarcus S
Demare
Demareion
Demariro
Demarius
Demarkes
Demarko
Demarkus
Demarlo
Demaro
Demarquis
Demarr
Demarreio
Demarrio
Demartinez
Demarvis
Demaryea
Demeatric
Demeatrice
Demeatris
Demeco
Demectric
Demeitrius
Demeko
Demel
Demeras
Demere
Demerick
Demeris
Demerite
Demerrio
Demery
Demeterious
Demetre
Demetrea
Demetreius
Demetres
Demetress
Demetreus
Demetri
Demetrias
Demetric
Demetrice
Demetrick
Demetrics
Demetricus
Demetrie
Demetriel
Demetrik
Demetrio
Demetrios
Demetrious
Demetriu
Demetrium
Demetro
Demetrois
Demetruis
Demetrum
Demetrus
Demichael
Demir
Demis
Demitirus
Demitre
Demitreze
Demitri
Demitrias
Demitriu
Demitrius
Demitrus
Demon
Demonds
Demone
Demont
Démont
Demonta
Demonte
Demontez
Demontre
Demoris
Demorris
Demorus
Demps
Dempsey
Demtrius
Demtrus
Demurl
Demyan
Dena
Denali
Denanauth
Denard
Denarice
Denaris
Denarius
Denauld
Denby
Dendell
Dendrick
Deneb
Deneh Cho
Deneil
Denereo
Denham
Denholm
Deni
Deniel
Denin
Denise
Deniz
Denman
Dennario
Dennecko
Dennell
Dennerio
Dennie
Dennis Alex
Dennis-Pimentel
Dennison
Denny-Ross
Deno
Dénon
Denoris
Denorris
Denston
Denten
Dentin
Denton
Dentury
Denuel
Deny
Denys
Denyveaus
Denzel
Denzell
Denzil
Deondravious
Deondray
Deondre
Deondré
Deondrick
Deone
Deonno

Deonta
Deontae
Deonte
Deonté
Deontée
Deonterry
Deontie
Deontre
Deontrea
Deontrez
Deonza
Deorick
Depaul
Deperat
Dequail
Dequain
Dequan
Dequann
Dequaun
Dequinton
Derace
Deraczi
Derak
Derald
Deralle
Deran
Derby
Derecke
Dereious
Derek-Wayne
Dereke
Derel
Derell
Dérell
Deren
Dereon
Derick-James
Dericka
Derico
Derief
Deriek
Derikk
Derilien
Derion
Derios
Derique
Derison
Derk
Derke
Derl
Derland
Dermond
Dermoth
Dernard
Derod
Derone
Deroy
Derrail
Derran
Derreck
Derreke
Derrel
Derren
Derrian
Derric
Derriel
Derrien
Derrijk
Derrik
Derrill
Derrin
Derrious
Derris
Derrius
Derron
Derry
Derryck
Derryn
Derval
Dervel
Dervon
Derwin
Derwyn
Derya
Deryck
Deryk
Deryll
Desean
Deshad
Deshane
Déshant
Deshard
Deshaud
Deshaun
Deshaune
Deshauwn
Deshawan
Deshay
Deshayne
Deshea
Deshin
Deshon
Deshondre
Deshone
Deshonte
Deshun
Desi
Desideri
Desiderio
Desir
Desirae
Desjhaun
Desmofphean
Desmon
Desmund
Desray
Desrick
Dessy
Destin
Destine
Destrey
Destrie
Destry
Desuan
Deter
Deterio
Deton
Detonyo
Detravious
Detrelle
Détri
Detric
Detrick
Detron
Deuel
Deulin
Deundrae
Deune
Deuwayne
Dev
Devain
Devaine
Devall
Devandis
Devane
Devapratim
Devar
Devarian
Devaris
Devarius
Devaro
Devaron
Devaughn
Devein
Deveion
Devel

Devenair
Devendra
Devere
Deverick
Deveron
Deverous
Devery
Deves
Devesh
Devilin
Deville
Devinder
Devine
Devinn
Devirus
Devitt
Devlin
Devlon
Devlyn
Devoderick
Devoen
Devohn
Devone
Devonn
Devonne
Devontae
Devontaine
Devontay
Devore
Devoris
Devorise
Devphn
Devro
Devron
Devry
Devyaun
Devyn
Devyne
Dewaine
Dewan
Deward
Dewayn
Dewell
Dewitt
Dewon
Dewrit
Dewune
Dewwilliam
Dex
Dextar
Dexter-Allen
Dexton
Dextor
Dextrel
Deyssler
Deyton
Deyue
Dezahan
Dezerick
Dezie
Dezmon
Dezmond
Dezyra
Dfonell
Dhameer
Dhane
Dhanvantari
Dhanvir
Dharam
Dheron
Dhiren
Di Mari
Di'angelo
Di'carlos
Diamend
Diamenn
Diamond
Diamont
Diana
Diandre
Diandrea
Diangelo
Dianis
Diante
Dianthony
Diasson
Dibias
Dic-Ln
Dicarrio
Dick
Dickie
Dickson
Dicky
Didier
Didrik
Diedrich
Dieghton
Dien
Dieon
Dierekus
Dieri
Dierros
Dieter
Dieterman
Dietrich
Dieudonne
Dieufran
Dieusirlomme
Dighton
Diivory
Dijon
Dikerson
Dil
Dilan
Dilbert
Diljaan
Dillan
Dillen
Dillin
Dillion
Dilpreet
Dilton
Dimagio
Dimaris
Dimetra
Dimetri
Dimetrius
Dimetrus
Dimitric
Dimitricus
Dimitrie
Dimitris
Dimitrius
Dimitrus
Dimitry
Dimmy
Dimontrie
Dinansky
Dinesh
Dinh
Dinna
Dio
Diodoro
Diogenes
Diondra
Diondre
Dionesios
Dionicio
Dionigi
Dionn
Dionne
Diontae
Dionte
Diontracie
Diontray
Dionysios

Dionysius
Dionysus
Dior
Dip
Dipak
Dipan
Dipen
Dipency
Dipesh
Dirck
Dirie
Diron
Disco
Disma
Disu
Ditaphon
Diuan
Diver
Divito
Diwon
Dixie
Dixon
Diyon
Dj
Djedid
Djidoux
Djilani
Djon
Djuan
Dllayne
Dmarcus
Dmetrius
Dmitri
Dmitrius
Dmonta
Dmytro
Doan
Doan Hung
Doan-Ban
Doane
Dobie
Doc
Dodd
Dodger
Doel
Dohnovan
Dolan
Dolph
Dolphus
Dolton
Dolyn
Domanic
Domar
Domaso
Domenick
Domenique
Domeonie
Domiano
Dominck
Domineck
Dominelle
Domingo
Domingos
Dominic Lee
Dominicke
Dominiek
Dominik
Dominik-Leon
Dominiqu
Dominitric
Dominque
Dominquia
Domion
Domminick
Domnick
Domninick
Domnique
Domonic
Domonic'
Domonick
Domoniqu
Domonique
Don'ya
Don-Erik
Donal
Donat
Donata
Donathan
Donathon
Donato
Donaven
Donavin
Donavon
Donavyn
Donay
Doncarlos
Dondi
Dondiego
Dondrea
Doneal
Doneau
Doneesh
Donel
Donell
Donelle
Donelly
Doney
Dong
Dong-Hee
Dong-Jin
Dong-Kwon
Doni
Donie
Donielle
Doninic
Donivan
Donja
Donlee
Donley
Donminick
Donn
Donna
Donnail
Donnald
Donnate
Donnavan
Donnel
Donnelle
Donnelly
Donniel
Donnubari
Donoven
Donovin
Donquatus
Donray
Donsay
Donsha
Donshae
Donta
Dontai
Dontaivious
Dontallis
Dontao
Dontarius
Dontate
Dontavion
Dontavious
Dontavis
Dontavius
Dontavus
Dontay
Dontaye
Doné
Dontea
Dontee
Dontel

Donteris
Donterrius
Dontez
Dontorien
Dontra
Dontral
Dontrale
Dontray
Dontraz
Dontrell
Dontreze
Dontriel
Donvan
Donveon
Donya
Donyee
Donyell
Donzell
Doobie
Doral
Doran
Dorby
Dorce
Dorell
Doren
Dori
Dorien
Dorin
Dorion
Doris
Dorman
Doron
Dorovan
Dorreall
Dorrel
Dorrell
Dorrelle
Dorrien
Dorris
Dorrsett
Dorsett
Dorsey
Dory
Doss
Doty
Doug
Douglass
Dougles
Dov
Dovid
Dovonn
Dovovan
Dowdle
Dowlin
Doyal
Doyleford
Draemone
Draey
Dragan
Drago
Dragoljub
Dragutin
Drahcir
Draiden
Drajuan
Drakaro
Dramaiya
Dramond
Drangelo
Drannen
Draper
Drashawn
Dravin
Dray
Draydaro
Draypr
Drayson
Drayton
Dreekius
Dremar
Drennen
Dreon
Drescon-Kaleef
Dretwan
Drevon
Drew Christopher
Drexton
Drice
Driu
Drossos
Drrago
Dru
Druan
Drue
Drwain
Dryden
Dshaun
Dshwan
Du'shane
Duain
Duaine
Duana
Duarte
Duayne
Duboise
Duc
Ducamel
Dudley
Dudly
Dugan
Duggan
Duhart
Duilio
Dujuan
Duke
Dul
Dulin
Dum
Dumaka
Duminsley
Dumo
Dumonde
Dung
Duong
Dupre
Dupree
Dura
Durael
Duran
Durance
Durand
Durant
Durc
Durel
Durelle
Durial
Durian
Duriel
Durk
Duron
Duronn
Durontae
Duroy
Durrant
Durreill
Durrel
Durrelle
Durrico
Durron
Durvasa
Durvin
Durward
Durwin
Duryea
Dushan

Dushane
Dushyant
Dustan
Dusten
Dustin Glenn
Dustin-James
Dustine
Duston
Dustten
Dustun
Dutch
Duval
Duvall
Duveuil
Duwan
Duwane
Duwayne
Duy
Duztin
Dvar
Dvonn
Dwain
Dwaine
Dwalyn
Dwan
Dwane
Dwaun
Dwaune
Dwaymon
Dwellas
Dwite
Dwon
Dwuann
Dwyane
Dwyer
Dwyne
Dygo
Dyke
Dyland
Dyllan
Dyllinger
Dyllon
Dylon
Dymar
Dyne
Dyntaniel
Dynza
Dyrail
Dyree
Dyrin
Dyron
Dyshaun
Dyshon
Dyson
Dytadius
Dytaniel
Dytanius
Dyvon
Dywan
Dywane

E

E David
E.
Eaen
Eammon
Eamon
Eamonn
Ean
Earl Sylvester
Earl-Oliver
Earld
Earle
Earlie
Earllonzo
Earlson
Early
Earnie
Earon
Earsel
Earston
Earvin
Eason
Easterm
Easton
Eathean
Eaton
Eb
Ebay
Ebbie
Ebedee
Ebel
Eben
Ebeneezer
Ebenezer
Eberhard
Ebitu
Ebony
Ebow
Ebron
Ebrulik
Ec
Echeva
Eciel
Eclaire
Ecliff
Ector
Ed
Edan
Edaniel
Edd
Eddie Ceyphus
Eddie Nels
Eddrena
Eddrick
Eddybanks
Eddye
Edel
Edelmiro
Edelweiss
Eden
Edenson
Eder
Ederick
Edes
Edgard
Edgardo
Ediberto
Edin
Edis
Edison
Ediudge
Ediun
Ediune
Edjee
Edmar
Edmon
Edmundo
Edner
Edny
Edouard
Edquire
Edrian
Edric
Edrice
Edrick
Edrye
Edson
Eduamel
Eduard
Edvardo
Edvine
Edwardo
Edwards

Edwige
Edwisht
Edwood
Edwyn
Edy
Eerik
Efe
Efehan
Efraim
Efrem
Efren
Efrim
Efron
Efrum
Efstratios
Egeton
Eguel
Ehab
Ehiane
Ehizoje
Ehpa
Ehren
Ehrich
Eicke
Eiman
Ein
Eirain
Eitan
Eivind
Ekain
El-Fellani-A-Mohammed
Eladio
Elain
Elais
Elajawon
Elajuwan
Elan
Eland
Elandro
Elann
Elbert
Elbin
Elbridge
Elbyn
Elchanan
Eldavon
Elden
Elder
Eldra
Eldred
Eldrian
Eldridge
Eldwin
Elease
Eleazar
Eleftherios
Elester
Eletise
Elfantry
Elgan
Elgen
Elgin
Eli-Michael
Elia
Eliaphas
Eliasar
Eliazar
Eliceo
Elidan
Elie
Elier
Elieser
Eliezer
Elifils
Eligher
Eligio
Elih
Elihu
Elijahmir
Elijiah
Elijsha
Elijualwon
Elijuo
Elimelec
Elin
Elint
Elio
Eliot
Eliott
Eliphart
Eliquene
Elisabete
Elisabeth
Elisamuel
Elisay
Elise
Elisee
Eliseo
Elisha Jeremiah
Elishia
Elishua
Eliu
Eliud
Eliut
Elivin
Eliyah
Eliyahu
Eliza
Eliza Kate
Elizabeth
Elizar
Elizardo
Eljen
Eljenon
Eljiata
Elkana
Elkanah
Elkin
Elkins
Ellary
Ellery
Elleston
Ellex
Elliotte
Ellison
Elloirce
Ellsworth
Ellwood
Elma
Elmancie
Elmo
Elmundo
Elno
Eloi
Elon
Élon
Elonzo
Eloy
Elquan
Elrado
Elric
Elroi
Elroy
Elrun
Elshunti
Elston
Elsworth
Eluértice
Eluv
Elven
Elvern
Elvor
Elwayne
Elwin
Elwood

Ely
Emaniel
Emanual
Emanuele
Emareshwa
Emari
Embert
Embery
Emeral
Emergy
Emeri
Emerick
Emerie
Emeril
Emerio
Emesia
Emiel
Emile
Emiliano
Emiliano T
Emilios
Emill
Emille
Emilton
Emily
Emir
Emison
Emitt
Emmaneul
Emmanle
Emmanueal
Emmanuele
Emmanuell
Emmerson
Emmet
Emmit
Emmitt
Emmons
Emmory
Emon
Emrah
Emre
Emreson
Emunah
Enard
Enav
Encarnac
Ender
Eneias
Eni
Enio
Eniola
Ennil
Ennio
Ennque
Enoc
Enoch
Enock
Enok
Enol
Enos
Enosemudia
Enosh
Enric
Enrica
Enrickson
Enrico
Enrico Iv
Enrigue
Enriqué
Enriquez
Enrrique
Ensign
Enstly
Enton
Enver
Enzo
Enzoy
Eo
Eoghan
Eoin
Eon
Epharant
Ephraen
Ephraim
Ephrain
Epifanio
Eralio
Eran
Eranest
Erasmo
Erastious
Erbale
Erbintz
Ercument
Erek
Eren
Erez
Erhard
Eri
Eriberto
Éric
Eric Alexander
Eric Andrew
Eric Lee
Eric Matthew
Eric Vanderbilt
Eric-Albert
Eric-Marcel-Ross
Erica
Erickson
Erico
Ericson
Erie
Eriel
Erien-Issac
Erik Christopher
Erik-Jon
Eriks
Erine
Erinn
Erino
Eriquon
Eris
Erissie
Erland
Erlz
Ermel
Ermin
Ermond
Erneil
Ernesky
Ernestor
Erney
Ernie
Erns
Ernst
Erode
Eroide
Erol
Erold
Eron-Leetel
Errant
Erric
Errick
Errin
Erroll
Erron
Erry
Ersell
Ersin
Erskin
Ertice
Erubiel
Erven
Ervince

Erving
Erving Jr
Erwan
Erwin
Eryc
Eryk
Eryn
Erynn
Esa
Esaias
Esam
Esaw
Escamillio
Esco
Esdras
Eseosares
Esequiel
Eshwar
Esli
Esmel
Esmond
Espie
Essinam
Estabon
Estanislado
Estanle
Estefan
Estel
Estephan
Estevan
Esteven
Estevez
Estin
Estiven
Estrada
Estuardo
Et
Etai
Etavious
Etian
Etienne
Eton
Etston
Ettore
Etwan
Eu Gene
Eual
Euan
Euann
Eucebio
Euel
Eugen
Eugenie
Eugenio
Eugenio-Tosto
Eulalio
Eulan
Eulie
Eulin
Eulogio
Euree
Euri
Eurico
Eusebio
Euseblo
Eusevio
Eustis
Eustratios
Eutimio
Evagelos
Evagglos
Evan-Anthon
Evanald
Evance
Evander
Evangelo
Evangelos
Evann
Evans
Evaristo
Eve
Evedge
Evelio
Evens
Ever
Everardo
Everest
Everet
Everette
Everhett
Everist
Everly
Everol
Evert
Everton
Evian
Evin
Evnel
Evodio
Evon
Evrett
Evyan
Evyatar
Ewan
Ewell
Ewen
Ewiw
Exavier
Exevious
Exor
Exzebelin
Exzequel
Eyan
Eyo
Eyob
Eyon
Ezechiel
Ezeck
Ezeeckel
Ezegozie
Ezeguiel
Ezekeial
Ezekial
Ezell
Ezequiel
Eziakah

F

F Adrian
Faady
Fabayan
Fabeon
Fabiano
Fabien
Fabrice
Fabrizio
Fabronion
Facundo
Faday
Fadhli
Fadi
Fadie
Fadrul Kha
Fady
Fafael-Arman
Fahad
Fahd
Faheem
Fahim
Fahiym
Fahkry
Fahlif
Fahti
Faiad

Fairley
Faisal
Faisel
Faisl
Faithtreon
Faizal
Fajstino
Falone
Fancic
Fanes
Faniel
Fantom
Faraan
Faraaz
Farabi
Farah
Faraz
Faraz-Ul
Fard
Faree
Fareed
Farel
Fares
Farhad
Farhan
Farid
Farin
Faris
Fariz
Farley
Farnando
Faroh
Faron
Farook
Farooq
Farouk
Faroulh
Farrah
Farran
Farrel
Farrell
Farren
Farrin
Farrington
Farris
Farron
Farshad
Faruq
Farzin
Fasel
Fatal
Fatih
Faton
Faustino
Fausto
Favad
Favian
Favis
Favvas
Fayard
Fayaz
Fayyaz
Fayzal
Fazel
Fedele
Federic
Federick
Federico
Fednel
Fedner
Fedrick
Fela
Felando
Felanté
Felder
Felek
Feleti
Feliberto
Felice
Felicia
Feliciano
Felip
Feliz
Fellette
Feloric
Felter
Felton
Femata
Femi
Fendrick
Feng
Fenning
Fennon
Fenton
Feraas
Feranado
Feras
Ferderick
Ferdie
Ferdinand
Ferdinando
Ferenc
Fergus
Ferguson
Ferley
Ferman
Fermin
Fernad
Fernand
Fernandez
Fernando-Claudio
Feron
Feroze
Ferrell
Ferrin
Ferris
Ferron
Fertz
Festa
Feyisa
Fiaz
Fida
Fidel
Fidencio
Field
Fielding
Fields
Fiheem
Filemon
Filex
Filiberto
Filip
Filipe
Filiphi
Filippo
Fillip
Filmore
Filomeno
Finbar
Findlay
Finel
Finlay
Finley
Finn
Finnis
Finus
Fiona
Fiore
Fiore-Michael
Firas
Firmen
Fito
Fitzgerald
Fizal
Flabio

Flamur
Flavien
Flavio
Flavious
Flax
Flem
Fleming
Flemming
Flennord
Flint
Flody
Florenci
Florencio
Florian
Flournoy
Flynn
Flynt
Fode
Folkert
Fondale
Fontadrian
Fontel
Fontell
Fonzell
Forbe
Forbes
Ford
Foro
Fortunato
Foster
Foston
Fotios
Fotu
Fouad
Fouad-Saher
Foy
Fraizer
Franc
France
Frances
Francesc
Francesco-Giuseppe
Franchie
Franchot
Francisco-Fidel
Franciso
Franciszek
Franckendy
Franco
François
Francois-Clovis
Francois-Xavier
Frandy
Franh
Frank Carlo
Frank James
Frank Lee
Franke
Frankin
Franko
Franky
Frano
Franquelin
Franquere
Franscis
Franshun
Fransis
Fransisc
Franson
Frantz
Frantzy
Franz
Franzy
Frasier
Frauncaun
Fraunzell
Frautz
Fravere
Frazer
Frazier
Fred Iii
Fredd
Fredderick
Freddrick
Frédéric
Frederich
Fréderick
Frédérick
Frederik
Frédérik
Frederric
Frederrick
Fredlin
Fredreus
Fredric
Fredrich
Fredrick Jr
Fredricka
Fredrico
Fredrik
Fredson
Fredy
Free
Freedom
Freeman
Freison
Frejdyn
Frences
Frencesc
Frenchie
Frenchy
Frencis
Frensky
Freppel
Frett
Fridlet
Frieson
Frisco
Fritson
Fritts
Frizel
Frizt
Frontroy
Fryderyk
Fryza
Fu
Fuat
Fuk
Fulton
Furana
Furhaud
Furman
Furnandes
Furphy
Furqan
Fusiloa

G

Gaberial
Gabino
Gabner
Gabrail
Gabreil
Gabrian
Gabriel Maroun
Gabriele
Gabriell
Gabry
Gabryn
Gaby
Gaddy
Gadrick
Gaelan

Gaelen
Gaemia
Gaerick
Gaetan
Gaètan
Gaetano
Gaetono
Gagan
Gagandeep
Gage
Gail
Gaius
Gajan
Gajanveer
Gal
Galaib
Galal
Galan
Gale
Galib
Gallagher
Galliard
Galo
Galue
Galvany
Galvin
Gamal
Gamaliel
Gameli
Gamil
Gandell
Ganem
Gannon
Gar
Gar-Kan
Garbhan
Garcia
Gardener
Gardiner
Gardner
Gardy
Gared
Garen
Garencha
Garet
Garey
Garfield
Garhard
Garicin
Garick
Garin
Garinder
Garion
Garis
Garith
Garivin
Garland
Garlen
Garlund
Garlyn
Garman
Garnell
Garner
Garnet
Garnett
Garnie
Garo
Garon
Garran
Garred
Garrell
Garren
Garret William
Garreth
Garrette
Garrey
Garrick
Garrie
Garrik
Garrin
Garrit
Garrith
Garritt
Garrod
Garron
Gartrel
Gartrell
Garvens
Garvin
Garvus
Gary Lee
Gary Mack
Gary-Tuan
Garylee
Garyn
Gasnel
Gaspar
Gaspare
Gassan
Gassem
Gaston
Gates
Gathrel
Gativitis
Gatlin
Gator
Gatta
Gattlin
Gaubert
Gaudencio
Gauntlett
Gaurakisora
Gaurav
Gautam
Gautum
Gavan
Gavell
Gaven
Gavinn
Gavino
Gavoneey
Gavriel
Gayfield
Gaylan
Gayland
Gayle
Gaylen
Gaylloyd
Gaylon
Gaylyn
Gbeku
Gbolahan
Geane
Geary
Geb
Geden
Gedyon
Geff
Geffery
Geffrard
Geffrey
Gehad
Gelani
Gemariah
Gemarley
Gemeil
Gen
Genard
Genario
Genaro
Gener
Generoso
Genesis
Geniale
Gennaro
Geno

Genol
Genoves
Gent
Gentle
Gentry
Geoff
Geoffre
Geoffry
Geordan
Geordann
Geordie
Geordon
George Brandon
George Lee
George-Anthony
Georgeos
Georges
Georgette
Georgie
Georgina
Georgio
Georgios
Geoshawa
Geovan
Geovani
Geovannee
Geovanni
Geovanny
Ger
Gerad
Gerain
Geraldo
Gerale
Geramey
Geran
Gerar
Gérard
Geraro
Geratt
Geraud
Gerben
Gere
Gereald
Gered
Geremia
Geremiah
Geremie
Geremy
Gergo
Gerhard
Gerhart
Geric
Gerimia
Germail
Germain
Germaine
German
Germanie
Germay
Germayn
Germey
Germitrious
Germondi
Gernard
Gerod
Gerodney
Gerold
Gerome
Geron
Geronemo
Geronimo
Gerrad
Gerrael
Gerrald
Gerrard
Gerrardo
Gerre
Gerred
Gerrell
Gerren
Gerret
Gerri
Gerrick
Gerrin
Gerrion
Gerrit-John
Gerritt
Gerrod
Gerron
Gerrysen
Gersao
Gersham
Gershon
Gerson
Gerund
Gervais
Gervis
Geryes
Geurson
Gevins
Gevonta
Geysanh
Geza
Ghabriel
Ghanshyam
Ghassan
Ghee
Ghehori
Ghert
Ghian
Ghiell
Ghino
Ghislain
Gholam
Ghovanny
Ghristos
Ghyslain
Gia
Gia-Minh
Giaco
Giacomno
Giacomo
Gian
Gian Paolo
Gian-Carlo
Gian-Paolo
Giancarlo-Daniel
Giancarlos
Giancarmine
Gianfranco
Gianluca
Gianmichael
Gianni
Gianni-Gerardo
Gianni-Michele
Gianpaolo
Gianpaulo
Gianpiero
Gianvito
Giao
Giavonathan
Gib
Gibb
Gibel
Gibran
Gibrian
Gibson
Gibudale
Gierri
Giffin
Gifford
Gift
Gig
Gil
Gildardo
Giles

Gill
Gillan
Gillermo
Gillis
Gilmer
Gilmore
Gintaras
Gintas
Gioacchino
Giordan
Giordano
Giorgio
Giovanelyarante
Giovani
Giovanni-Antonio
Giovannie
Giovanno
Giovanny
Giovany
Giovonni
Gipson
Girard
Girma
Girradeau
Giscar
Giselle
Gishan
Gislain
Gitti
Giuliano
Giulio
Giuseppi
Giustino
Gjemail
Gjon
Glann
Glendale
Glendle
Glendon
Glenford
Glenmore
Glennis
Glennon
Glenwood
Gleph
Glidden
Gliding
Glover
Gluck
Glyn
Glynden
Glynn
Goce
Godfrey
Godrey
Goebel
Goeffrey
Goerge
Gofery
Golden
Goldy
Gomer
Gomes
Gontrell
Gonzalo
Gonzelas
Gopal
Gopaul
Goran
Gorav
Gorby
Gord
Gordan
Gorden
Gordie
Gordon Jr
Gorge
Gorje
Gosly
Gottfried
Govan
Govid
Govind
Govinda
Gowan
Grable
Grace
Graden
Gradie
Gradon
Graehme
Graem
Grahame
Grahme
Graig
Graison
Graley
Graling
Gram
Gramoz
Grand
Grandiso
Grandon
Granger
Grant-Anthony
Granvel
Granville
Grattan
Gray
Grayden
Graydon
Graylin
Grayling
Graziano
Greagory
Green
Greg Philip
Gregary
Gregery
Greggery
Grégoire
Gregor
Gregore
Gregori
Gregorie
Gregorio
Gregory-Deogratias
Gregory-James
Gregrey
Gregroy
Gregry
Gregson
Greogry
Gressix
Grevaris
Grey
Greye
Greyson
Greyston
Griagal
Griffen
Griffith
Grigory
Gromyko
Grover
Grumecindo
Gryphon
Grzegorz
Guadalup
Guadalupe
Guan
Guante
Guaso
Guberan

Gudrun
Guerby
Guerdy
Gueshomns
Guichard
Guido
Guilherme
Guiliano
Guillard
Guinn
Guiseppe
Guiseppi
Gul
Gulishan
Gumaro
Gunnar
Gunner
Gunther
Guordan
Gur
Gurbir
Gurdeep
Gurdip
Gurinder
Gurjeet
Gurkanwal
Gurkenwal
Gurmakh
Gurmeet
Gurminder
Gurmohan
Gurnam
Gurnick
Gurnie
Gurpal
Gurpartap
Gurpaul
Gurpinder
Gurshan
Gursharn
Gursimran
Gursteven
Gurtej
Guruprit
Gurveer
Gurvinder
Gurvir
Gurwinder
Gus
Guss
Gussie
Gustaaf
Gustaf
Gustav
Gustave
Gustaves
Gustavs
Gustavus
Gustry
Gutchiston
Guthrie
Guty
Guu
Guyon
Guytho
Guyton
Gwinn
Gwyn
Gyasi
Gyo
Gzim

H

Haad
Haadee
Haakin
Haakon
Haamid
Haarun
Haashim
Habacuc
Habib
Hackney
Haddon
Haden
Hadi
Hadleigh
Hadley
Hady
Hae Saul
Haeven
Hafeez
Hafeez-Ul
Hagab
Hagan
Hagen
Hagmane
Hagop
Hai
Hai-yen
Haidyn
Haig
Haim
Hairo
Haisam
Haisley
Haiwan
Hajime
Hak
Hakam
Hakan
Hakeem
Hakiem
Hal
Halburt
Halden
Hale
Haleem
Haley
Halin
Hallan
Hallbert
Hallene
Halley
Halston
Halwinder
Hamal
Hamdeep
Hamed
Hameed
Hamid
Hamilton
Hamin
Hamish
Hamler
Hamlin
Hammam
Hamon
Hamp
Hampton
Hamza
Hamze
Hamzee
Hamzi
Han
Hanan
Hanbin
Hance
Handson
Handy
Haneef
Hanef
Hanh
Hani

Hanif
Hanife
Hankalan
Hannah
Hannibal
Hansel
Hansen
Hansford
Hanson
Hansryan
Hants
Hanwakan
Hanz
Hanzla
Hap
Haraan
Haralambos
Haram
Haramrit
Harbecker
Harber
Harbir
Harby
Harcourt
Hardin
Harding
Hardy
Hari
Hariel
Harilaoe
Harin
Harinder
Haris
Harish
Harjeet
Harjinder
Harjit
Harjot
Harkaran
Harkirat
Harland
Harlen
Harlon
Harman
Harmandeep
Harmander
Harmanjit
Harmeet
Harmen
Harmetis
Harminder
Harmit
Harmon
Harmond
Harmundeep
Harneal
Harneil
Harnick
Haron
Haroon
Haroun
Haroutioun
Harpaul
Harper
Harpinder
Harron
Harsh
Harshjit
Hart
Hartej
Hartford
Hartley
Harun
Harveer
Harvey-Randolph
Harvinder
Harward
Hasaan
Hasain
Hasan
Hasani
Hasanibn
Haseeb
Hashaan
Hashabiah
Hasher
Hashim
Haskel
Hason
Hassen
Hassian
Haston
Hatem
Hatim
Hatsadong
Hau
Haukeye
Hava
Haven
Havenelk
Havery
Havier
Havis
Haward
Hawathia
Hawkeye
Hawkins
Hayato
Hayes
Haylan
Hayne
Hayse
Hayston
Hayward
Haywood
Hazel
Hazem
Hazen
Hazhaar
Hazim
Hearl
Hearold
Heathcliffe
Heathe
Heather
Heaven
Heberson
Hebert
Heberto
Heechan
Heerbod
Heikki
Heinrich
Heinz
Heith
Hekuran
Helaman
Helder
Helder-Francisco
Helibert
Helios
Helmer
Helmut
Helmuth
Hemal
Heman
Hemanth
Hemeak
Hendan
Henderson
Hendrick
Hendricks
Hendricson
Hendrik
Hendrikus
Hendry

Hendy
Henery
Henning
Hennis
Henock
Henok
Henri
Henrico
Henrik
Henrique
Henrry
Henry David
Henry William
Henry-Tran
Hense
Hensley
Herald
Heraldo
Herb
Herberg
Herbertlee
Herby
Hercules
Heribert
Herlan
Herley
Herlin
Herlon
Herman Joa
Hermann
Hermeet
Herminio
Hermino
Hermione
Hermlindo
Hernan
Hernandes
Hernandez
Hernando
Hernani
Hernerce
Hernezdas
Herod
Herode
Heron
Herschel
Hershel
Hershell
Hertrech
Hervens
Hervin
Herwin
Hesam
Hesed
Hesham
Heshima
Hesston
Heston
Heth
Heva
Hewitte
Heyvard
Heyward
Hezekiah
Hicham
Hideo
Hien
Hiep
Hieu
Higue
Hilario
Hilary
Hilbert
Hilberto
Hildo
Hilke
Hill
Hillard
Hillary
Hillel
Hilliard
Hilton
Himesh
Himmet
Hindirk
Hinga
Hinrich
Hipolito
Hira
Hiraldo
Hiran
Hiromi
Hiromitsu
Hisham
Histo
Hitam
Hiten
Hitesh
Hiylke
Hjonathan
Hmzah
Hnaim
Ho
Hoa
Hoai
Hoainam
Hoang
Hoang-Chuong
Hoangthanh
Hobart
Hobbie
Hobby
Hobert
Hobey
Hodges
Hoe
Hoffman
Hoi-Tung
Hoker
Holbeche
Holden
Holdun
Holger
Holland
Holleen
Hollie
Hollis
Holly
Holmes
Holt
Holton
Homar
Homavirak
Homer Lee
Homero
Hommar
Hon
Hondo
Hong
Honojory
Hoover
Horacio
Horatius
Horeb
Horst
Hosam
Hosea
Hossain
Hossam
Hossein
Hosteen
Hoteck
Housten
Houtan
Houtsin
Howie

Hoy
Hoyle
Hoyt
Hrvoje
Hsi
Huan
Hubbard
Hubbert
Hubble
Huck
Huckly
Huddie
Hudes
Hudson
Hudson Clay
Huey
Hughens
Hughes
Hughie
Hugues
Hulme
Hum-Mam
Humam
Humbert
Humphery
Humphrey
Humza
Hunberto
Hung
Hung-Ming
Hunt
Huntley
Hurbert
Hurk
Hurley
Hursel
Husain
Husani
Husein
Husian
Hussain
Hussainhamad
Hussayn-Hassam
Hussein
Hussien
Hussnain
Huston
Hutchinson
Huu
Hyacinthe-Benoit
Hyatt
Hyder
Hyjng-Seok
Hykeem
Hylem
Hyman
Hyme
Hyneef
Hyrere
Hyrum
Hysam
Hyssam
Hyun
Hyunjin

I

Iakov
Ian Nathaniel
Ian-Issac
Ian-Paul
Iannick
Iaren
Iassc
Iau
Ibai
Ibn
Ibrahem
Icarus
Ichael
Ichifa
Idikoro
Idler
Idly
Idrees
Idris
Idriss
Idriys
Idus
Ifeany
Ifeanyi
Ifenwudge
Ifeoluwa
Ifoxa
Iftikar
Iftikhar
Igino
Iglesias
Ignacio
Ignatius
Ignazio
Igor
Ihab
Ihanne
Ihtesham-Ur
Ii
Iii
Iii-Toney
Ijahim
Ijala-Gwindi
Ijaz
Ikaika
Ikarl
Ike
Ikeam
Ikechukwu
Ikee
Ikenna
Ikenori
Ilan
Ilario
Ilayn
Ilbert
Ildefonso
Ilia
Iliad
Ilie
Ilija
Iljahtoa
Illya
Illyas
Ilon
Ilya
Iman
Imani
Imanuel
Imanzi
Imeen
Imen
Imer
Immanuel
Immanuel Christi
Immuneal
Imoh
Imran-Ullah
Imtiaz
Imuahanohano
Imuetinya
Imzan
Inalbert
Inam
Inder
Inder-Pal

Inderbir
Inderjeet
Inderjit
Inderpal
Indervir
Indra
Indrajit
Indrees
Indy
Ineater
Inez
Ingles
Ingram
Injun
Inocenci
Inocente
Inois
Inosente
Ioane
Ioannis
Iqbal
Irais
Iraklis
Iraleigh
Iran
Ire
Iren
Irfaan
Irfaan-Aalim
Irfan
Irfanali
Iric
Irik
Iris
Irish
Irlain
Iron
Iroqouise
Irtiza
Irvington
Irwin
Isa
Isaack
Isaah
Isaak
Isac
Isai
Isaia
Isaiah-John
Isaias
Isaid
Isaih
Isaish
Isala
Isalas
Isamail
Isan
Isdraen
Isham
Ishaq
Ishayaaa
Ishma
Ishmael
Ishmaweel
Ishmeal
Ishmel
Ishmilakeen
Ishwar
Isiac
Isiacc
Isiash
Isidore
Isidoro
Isidro
Isileli
Islam
Isley
Ismail
Ismanuel
Ismeil
Isnell
Isoel
Isokoy
Isom
Isong
Israfel
Isreal
Isrrael
Issa
Issacar
Issakha
Issca
Isser
Issia
Issiac
Issiah
Istvan
Italo
Itthiphol
Iv
Iva
Ivan-Joseph
Ivan-Tomislav
Ivanhoe
Ivano
Ivans
Ivar
Ive
Iven
Ivery
Ives
Ivey
Ivin
Ivins
Ivo
Ivon
Ivonnie
Ivor
Ivory
Ivy
Izaac
Izaak
Izaal
Izaiah
Izaiha
Izak
Izeke
Izette
Izill
Izooba

J

J D
J W
J'on
J'ron
J. D.
J. Michael
J. Wesley
J.C.
J.D.
J.J.
J.T.
Ja
Ja Juan
Ja Lill
Ja Mar
Ja Mel
Ja'darius
Ja'quan
Ja'red
Jaager
Jaan
Jaaron

Jaavon
Jabaar
Jabali
Jaban
Jabare
Jabari
Jabbar
Jabe
Jabez
Jabier
Jabin
Jabir
Jabori
Jabraan
Jabrell
Jabri
Jabriel
Jabrill
Jabulani
Jabus
Jacaras
Jacari
Jacarius
Jacek
Jacen
Jacey
Jachariah
Jachin
Jachob
Jacint
Jacinto
Jack Allen
Jack Peter
Jack-Daniel
Jackeline
Jacki
Jacklyn
Jackub
Jacky
Jaco
Jacob Holland
Jacobb
Jacobi
Jacobis
Jacobo
Jacobo-M
Jacobs
Jacobus
Jacody
Jacolby
Jacori
Jacoun
Jacove
Jacovian
Jacozee
Jacquan
Jacque
Jacqueese
Jacquelienne
Jacqueline
Jacques-Joel
Jacques-Michel
Jacquez
Jacson
Jad
Jada
Jadahn
Jadallah
Jadane
Jadarius
Jadaryl
Jadd
Jaden
Jader
Jadewey
Jadin
Jadon
Jadot
Jae
Jaeden
Jael
Jaen
Jaequer
Jaermal
Jaeson
Jafar
Jafet
Jaffar
Jafrepaul
Jag
Jaganvir
Jagdeep
Jagger
Jagguar
Jagjit
Jagmeet
Jagmit
Jagpal
Jagpaul
Jagroop
Jaguar
Jagvir
Jagwinder
Jahaalid
Jahad
Jahan
Jahaziel
Jahbree
Jahdal
Jahdiel
Jahi
Jahlee
Jahleel
Jahlil
Jahmada
Jahmal
Jahmall
Jahmalle
Jahmar
Jahmel
Jahmiah
Jahmil
Jahmile
Jahn
Jahred
Jahrode
Jahsai
Jahson
Jahvaughn
Jahvine
Jahvon
Jahwaan
Jai
Jai-Lee
Jaiarsh
Jaice
Jaicy
Jaideep
Jaiden
Jaimar
Jaimes
Jaimey
Jaimi
Jaimie
Jaipal
Jaipaul
Jair
Jairam
Jaired
Jairell
Jairett
Jairo
Jairon
Jairus
Jaison
Jajaun

Jajuan
Jak
Jakari
Jake Ryan
Jakevious
Jakie
Jakil
Jakoby
Jakota
Jakub
Jakup
Jalaal
Jalal
Jalani
Jalanni
Jaleel
Jaley
Jalil
Jalon
Jam
Jama
Jamaar
Jamaaravalon
Jamaari
Jamael
Jamahl
Jamahrae
Jamaica
Jamaika
Jamail
Jamain
Jamaine
Jamal-Houston
Jamala
Jamalcolm
Jamale
Jamall
Jamara
Jamarco
Jamarcus
Jamard
Jamared
Jamareiel
Jamari
Jamariel
Jamario
Jamarius
Jamarl
Jamarr
Jamarr'
Jamarvis
Jamason
Jamaul
Jamaunn
Jamaur
Jame
Jamee
Jameel
Jameison
Jamell
Jamen
Jameous
Jamere
Jamerick
Jamerson
James Jr
James Lee
James Leo
James Mich
James Michae
James Mikeaul
James Nicholas
James Robert
James Seth
James-Anthony
James-Daniel
James-Raymond
James-Reuben
James-Russell
Jamese Robert
Jamesian
Jamey
Jameyel
Jami
Jamian
Jamichael
Jamie-Lee
Jamie-Leigh
Jamiel
Jamiell
Jamielle
Jamier
Jamiesen
Jamikal
Jamikle
Jamile
Jamille
Jamin
Jamine
Jamir
Jamirah
Jamirious
Jamis
Jamisen
Jamli
Jammal
Jammel
Jammie
Jammy
Jamnab
Jamod
Jamolise
Jamon
Jamond
Jamone
Jamoren
Jamorreo
Jamorris
Jamoson
Jamse
Jamsett
Jamual
Jamuan
Jamus
Jamyl
Jamyron
Jan Michae
Jan Michael
Jan-Michael
Janal
Janard
Janathan
Jancarlo
Jance
Jancent
Janeil
Janek
Janel
Jangho
Janice
Janick
Janicka
Janielle
Janik
Janile
Janille
Janis
Janmichael
Jann
Janne
Jannot
Janocha
Janorris
Janos
Janse
Jansen

Janset
Janson
Janssen
Janten
Jantzen
Japan
Japeth
Japheth
Japman
Jaquae
Jaquan
Jaquar
Jaque
Jaquin
Jaquoi
Jaquon
Jaqurral
Jaquvaious
Jaqwan
Jarah
Jarame
Jaramia
Jaran
Jaranimo
Jaravis
Jaray
Jarazz
Jarbare
Jarcir
Jardin
Jared Hamilton
Jaredevan
Jaree
Jareek
Jareem
Jareid
Jareil
Jarek
Jarel
Jarelle
Jaremay
Jaremi
Jaremy
Jaret
Jareth
Jaretté
Jarez
Jarhett
Jari
Jarian
Jaric
Jarin
Jarious
Jaris
Jarison
Jarius
Jarlath
Jarmain
Jarmal
Jarman
Jarmar
Jarmarl
Jarmarr
Jarmell
Jarmin
Jarmina
Jarmis
Jarmon
Jarmond
Jarnail
Jarnaldo
Jarnell
Jaro
Jarode
Jarold
Jarom
Jaromiah
Jarone
Jaronniejoe
Jaroslaw
Jarques
Jarquis
Jarrard
Jarratt
Jarrayd
Jarreau
Jarrek
Jarrel
Jarrelle
Jarren
Jarrese
Jarrett Henry
Jarrette
Jarric
Jarrick
Jarrid
Jarriel
Jarriet
Jarrin
Jarrius
Jarrodd
Jarron
Jarrord
Jarrott
Jarrus
Jarry
Jarryl
Jarvae
Jarvanius
Jarvaris
Jarvas
Jarvaska
Jarveal
Jarvey
Jarvice
Jarvie
Jarvin
Jarvorice
Jarvoris
Jarvous
Jaryd
Jaryn
Jasan
Jasbir
Jasdave
Jasdeep
Jase
Jasean
Jaseth
Jashaldo
Jashan
Jashawn
Jashon
Jashua
Jasiel
Jasim
Jasin
Jasinto
Jasjit
Jasjot
Jaskaran
Jaskirat
Jasmain
Jasmany
Jasmeet
Jasmen
Jasmin
Jasmine
Jasmyne
Jasneet
Jason Alexander
Jason-Adam
Jason-Daniel
Jason-Donald
Jason-Fraser
Jason-Hyun

Jason-John
Jason-Michel
Jason-Ormond
Jason-Patrick
Jason-Richard
Jason-Tom
Jasper Tremayne
Jaspreet
Jaspreet-Singh
Jasraj
Jassa
Jasson
Jasten
Jasup
Jasvinder
Jatarrick
Jatavian
Jathan
Jathon
Jatinder
Jaton
Jatonio
Jatorrion
Jatravis
Jatwan
Jauan
Jaumar
Jaumaul
Jaumell
Jaun
Jaunot
Jaunte
Jaurkeen
Jaus
Jaushia
Javad
Javaid
Javanari
Javar
Javares
Javario
Javarius
Javaro
Javaron
Javarous
Javarre
Javarrious
Javarro
Javarte
Javarus
Javas
Javaughn
Javeal
Javed
Javeed
Javeion
Javelin
Javelle
Javen
Javeres
Javiar
Javid
Javielle
Javier-Eduardo
Javiere
Javies
Javin
Javine
Javion
Javis
Javona
Javone
Javoney
Javoni
Javonn
Javonta
Javor
Javoris
Javouris
Jawaan
Jawad
Jawan
Jawann
Jawari
Jawaun
Jawn
Jawon
Jaworski
Jawuan
Jawwad
Jax-David
Jaxom
Jaxon
Jay Cee
Jay-Ile
Jay-Mich
Jay-Micheal
Jayanth
Jaycee
Jaycent
Jayd
Jayde
Jayden
Jaydo
Jaydon
Jaye
Jayesh
Jayk
Jayke
Jayleau
Jaylee
Jaylen
Jaylin
Jaylon
Jaylund
Jaymeson
Jaymie
Jayms
Jayniel
Jaynon
Jaynus
Jayre
Jayron
Jayronn
Jayryl
Jaysen
Jaysin
Jayson-Robert
Jayssen
Jaysson
Jayvin
Jayvion
Jayvis
Jayvon
Jazen
Jazib
Jazmany
Jazmin
Jazper
Jazz
Jazze
Jazzlee
Jazzmen
Jazzmon
Jazztin
Jb
Jc
Je Ronn
Je-Mell
Jéan
Jean Baptist
Jean Carlo
Jean Claude
Jean Louis
Jean Marie
Jean Noel

Jean Patrick
Jean Paul
Jean Phillippe
Jean Yves
Jean-Alain
Jean-Alfred
Jean-Benoit
Jean-Bernard
Jean-Charles
Jean-Christophe
Jean-Cla
Jean-Claude
Jean-D'arc
Jean-David
Jean-Denis
Jean-Emmanuel
Jean-François
Jean-Gabriel
Jean-Guy
Jean-Henri
Jean-Jacques
Jean-Léo
Jean-Louis
Jean-Luc
Jean-Marc
Jean-Marie
Jean-Mathieu
Jean-Maurice
Jean-Olivier
Jean-Patrick
Jean-Paul
Jean-Pavlo
Jean-Perry
Jean-Phillippe
Jean-Pierre
Jean-René
Jean-Rene
Jean-Roger
Jean-Samuel
Jean-Sebastien
Jean-Sébastien
Jean-Simon
Jean-yves
Jeancarlos
Jeanfrancois
Jeangardy
Jeangerald
Jeannah
Jeannie
Jeannot
Jeanot
Jeanty
Jeard
Jearld
Jearmy
Jearrian
Jeb
Jebadia
Jebadiah
Jebahres
Jebi
Jebidiah
Jebrie
Jebson
Jecolby
Jeconiah
Jécory
Jecovei
Jecovic
Jedadiah
Jedaiah
Jedd
Jeddidiah
Jeddler
Jedediha
Jedeiah
Jedi
Jediah
Jedidia
Jeehoo
Jeetendra
Jeetinder
Jefe
Jeferson
Jefery
Jeffar
Jeffe
Jeffeory
Jeffer-Robert
Jefferay
Jeffereoy
Jefferey
Jefferie
Jeffers
Jefferso
Jeffery Stephen
Jeffey
Jefforey
Jeffory
Jeffree
Jeffrery
Jeffrey Da Santa
Jeffrey-Rae
Jeffrie
Jeffy
Jefre
Jefrey
Jefry
Jefte
Jegadeesh
Jehad
Jehan
Jehangir
Jehann
Jehoshua
Jehovani
Jehrardd
Jehri
Jehu
Jel
Jelani
Jellon
Jemaar
Jemael
Jemaine
Jemal
Jemale
Jemario
Jemehyl
Jemel
Jemell
Jemeriah
Jemes
Jemeyle
Jemiah
Jemmy
Jemond
Jémond
Jemone
Jenard
Jenaro
Jenbon
Jency
Jene
Jenel
Jenna
Jennar
Jenner
Jennifer
Jenning Russell
Jennings
Jennoi
Jens
Jensen
Jensy
Jenton

Jentre
Jentrey
Jenym
Jeoffrey
Jeon
Jeordon
Jeovany
Jephrey
Jer-Mon
Jerado
Jerae
Jerahmeel
Jerahmeil
Jerahmy
Jerai
Jerail
Jeraile
Jerakiah
Jerale
Jerall
Jerame
Jeramee
Jeramey
Jerami
Jeramiah
Jeramick
Jeramiha
Jerammie
Jeramy-Gregory
Jeran
Jerard
Jerardo
Jeraude
Jerawn
Jeray
Jere
Jeré
Jeread
Jereamy
Jereb
Jeredd
Jeree
Jereese
Jereken
Jerelle
Jeremaine
Jeremane
Jeremaya
Jeremee
Jeremi
Jeremia
Jeremiah Claude
Jeremiah Maxwel
Jeremial
Jeremias
Jerémie
Jeremii
Jeremoth
Jeremry
Jérémy
Jeremy Donald
Jeremy Kool
Jeremy-Noel
Jeremye
Jeremyu
Jeren
Jereomy
Jeret
Jerett
Jeric
Jericho
Jerick
Jerico
Jerid
Jeriemy
Jeriin
Jerijah
Jerik
Jeril
Jerim
Jerimane
Jerime
Jerimee
Jerimey
Jerimha
Jerimi
Jerimie
Jerimiha
Jerimy
Jerimya
Jerin
Jeriod
Jeris
Jerison
Jeritt
Jermael
Jermail
Jermain
Jermainlee
Jermal
Jermall
Jermand
Jermane
Jermanie
Jermarcus
Jermario
Jermarus
Jermaul
Jermayne
Jerme
Jermee
Jermel
Jermell
Jermere
Jermery
Jermiah
Jermiane
Jermie
Jermiha
Jermile
Jermill
Jermine
Jermonte
Jermy
Jernard
Jero
Jerold
Jerom
Jérôme
Jérome
Jerome Li
Jerome-Robert
Jeromey
Jeromie
Jéron
Jerone
Jeronimo
Jerorus
Jerovani
Jerraile
Jerral
Jerrald
Jerrall
Jerrame
Jerrard
Jerrat
Jerray
Jerred
Jerrel
Jerrelle
Jerremy
Jerren
Jerret
Jerrett
Jerrette
Jerri

Jerrial
Jerric
Jerrick
Jerrid
Jerrie
Jerrill
Jerrin
Jerriott
Jerris
Jerrit
Jerrit Kaisa
Jerritt
Jerrol
Jerrold
Jerroll
Jerrome
Jerromy
Jerron
Jerrot
Jerryll
Jershimon
Jerson
Jervenski
Jervier
Jervis
Jervon
Jervone
Jervonte
Jeryd
Jeryl
Jeryn
Jerzy
Jesam
Jescey
Jesee
Jeshaun
Jeshu
Jeshua
Jesi
Jesiah-David
Jesie
Jesmond
Jesph
Jessé
Jesse Christian
Jesse Thomas
Jesse-Ben
Jesse-Carlin
Jesse-Lee
Jesse-Miles
Jesse-Ray
Jesseb
Jessee
Jessejit
Jessep
Jessey
Jessi
Jessi-Robert
Jessiah
Jessica
Jessie Cleveland
Jessie-Lee
Jessiett
Jessis
Jesson
Jessop
Jesstin
Jesston
Jessup
Jessy-Maurice
Jessye
Jesten
Jestin
Jeston
Jesuel
Jesurun
Jetaime
Jethro
Jetinder
Jetro
Jetson
Jett
Jetter
Jetterric
Jettsen
Jetty
Jeumal
Jevan
Jevar
Jevaun
Jevin
Jevohn
Jevon
Jevonne
Jewell
Jexiel
Jeyre
Jeysel
Jezekiah
Jezreel
Jhamael
Jhan
Jhanick
Jharai
Jhared
Jharell
Jheano
Jhef
Jherell
Jhermie
Jhermirr
Jhetaun
Jhirmaine
Jhomel
Jhonathan
Jhonny
Jhonsoner
Jhran
Jhsi
Ji
Jian
Jian Carlos
Jian-Lok
Jiavodney
Jibrial
Jibril
Jigme
Jignesh
Jihaad
Jihad
Jiles
Jill
Jilson
Jimar
Jimara
Jimarcus
Jimboo
Jimel
Jimelle
Jimenez
Jimerson
Jimitre
Jimmil
Jimmyjo
Jimy
Jin
Jinn
Jio
Jiovani
Jiovanni
Jiovanny
Jireh
Jirisnathaniel
Jiten
Jitendra
Jitesh

Jivan
Jjr
Jm
Jmarce
Jo
Jo Anna
Jo'von
Jo-El
Jo-Jo
Jo-Shua
Joaby
Joachim
Joah
Joahan
Joahua
Joallen
Joam
Joan
Joanathon
Joandi
Joanel
Joanna
Joanne
Joanthan
Joao
Joaquim
Joar
Joary
Joash
Job
Jobanis
Jobe
Jobert
Jobey
Jobie
Joboah
Joby
Jocelin
Jocelyn
Jocindo
Jock
Joco
Jocoby
Jocolby
Jocquet
Jocquin
Jocquinn
Jodah
Jodan
Jodell
Jodey
Jodhan
Jodi
Jodie
Jodiha
Jodin
Jodner
Jodonnis
Joedimarco
Joedy
Jôel
Joel Delorean
Joel-Anthony
Joel-Denis
Joel-Francis
Joell
Joelle
Joelly
Joelun
Joely
Joenathan
Joenns
Joeny
Joeseph
Joestein
Joeval
Joevane
Joevel
Joeydamien
Joeyl
Joffre
Jogues
Johan
Johanan
Johane
Johann
Johann Ant
Johanna
Johannas
Johannes
Johansen
Johanthan
Johatan
Johathan
Johathon
Johaun
Johlen
Johlil
John Abbott
John Anthony
John Carl
John Carlo
John Dale
John David
John Francis
John Hnery
John Jr
John Lukas
John Mark
John Micha
John Michael
John Patri
John Paul
John Raymond
John Robert
John Teague
John Teves
John W.
John Wesley
John-Andrew
John-Anthony
John-Caleb
John-Carlo
John-Charles
John-Clayton
John-Dale
John-Duane
John-Duncan
John-Eric
John-Erling
John-Francis
John-Frederic-Andreas
John-Glen
John-Henry
John-Hovannes
John-Julian
John-Michael
John-Micheal
John-Pau
John-Paul
John-Phillip
John-Ray
John-Rey
John-Ross
John-Stephen
John-Sukhoon
John-Thomas
John-Vincent
John-Wayne
John-William
Johnassie
Johnatan
Johnath
Johnathan Robert

Johnathan-Isaac
Johnathaon
Johnathe
Johnathen
Johnatthan
Johnay
Johndavid
Johne
Johnell
Johnerik
Johney
Johnie
Johnier
Johnkyle
Johnl
Johnlee
Johnluidi
Johnmark
Johnney
Johnni
Johnniathin
Johnnyan
Johnothan
Johnsie
Johnston
Johnsua
Johntae
Johntay
Johnthan
Johny
Johon
Johonson
Johordan
Johory
Johran
Johsimar
Johsua
Johtan
Johusa
Jolan
Jole
Joles
Jolex
Jolly
Jolon
Jolyon
Jomal
Jomannie
Jomar
Jomarion
Jomicah
Jomo
Jon Andrew
Jon Anthony
Jon Austin
Jon Bretrell
Jon David
Jon Derek
Jon Don
Jon Ellis
Jon Erik
Jon Joseph
Jon Michae
Jon Michael
Jon Mikael
Jon Paul
Jon Roth
Jon Steven
Jon-Charles
Jon-Chri
Jon-David
Jon-Erick
Jon-Erik
Jon-Jarge
Jon-Marc
Jon-Mich
Jon-Michael
Jon-Micheal
Jon-Morgan
Jon-Paul
Jonal
Jonal Fred
Jonam
Jonario
Jonatan
Jonatane
Jonate
Jonatha
Jonathan Cody
Jonathan Jerry
Jonathan Scott
Jonathan-Blake
Jonathan-Lee
Jonathan-Reid
Jonathen
Jonathon-Mitchell
Jonattan
Joncey
Joneal
Jonell
Jonerio
Jones
Jonethen
Jong
Joni
Joniel
Jonnatha
Jonnathan
Jonnattan
Jonnell
Jonny
Jonothan
Jonovan
Jonpaul
Jonque
Jonson
Jontae
Jontavious
Jontavis
Jontea
Jonteau
Jontell
Jontez
Jonthan
Jontre
Jontrell
Jonus
Jony
Joon
Joonas
Jor-El
Joram
Joran
Joravar
Jorawar
Joray
Jordache
Jordae
Jordain
Jordan Christoph
Jordan Frederick
Jordan Michael
Jordan-Alexandre
Jordan-John
Jordan-Lee
Jordan-Paul
Jordan-Wade
Jordany
Jordell
Jordenn
Jordi
Jordie
Jordin
Jordon-Michael
Jordyn

Jorel
Jorell
Jorelle
Joren
Jorg
Jorgan
Jorge-Alberto
Jorge-Gabriel
Jorgen
Jorgenicfolas
Jori
Jorian
Jorie
Jorim
Jorin
Jorje
Jorl
Jorrdan
Jorrell
Jortan
Josa
Josaan
Josafat
Josaph
Josch
Jose Angel
Jose Antonio
Jose De Castro
Jose Migue
Jose Rafae
Jose Ramon
Jose Rodrigo
José
Jose-Luis
Josean
Josee
Joseff
Joseito
Joselito
Joseluis
Josemar
Joseph Alexander
Joseph Clifton
Joseph Jr
Joseph Lee
Joseph-Anthony
Joseph-Daniel
Joseph-Francis
Joseph-Matthew
Joseph-Neil
Joseph-Rene
Joseph-Roger-Jonathan
Joseph-Sébastian
Joseph-Shaun
Josephat
Josephe
Josephie
Josey
Josha
Joshau
Joshaua
Joshauh
Joshawa
Joshawah
Joshe
Josheph
Joshiah
Joshil
Joshimar
Joshlyn
Joshou
Joshton
Joshu
Joshua Allan
Joshua Anthony
Joshua Joseph
Joshua Matthew
Joshua Theodore
Joshua Vincent
Joshuaa
Joshue
Joshuea
Joshula
Joshus
Joshusa
Joshuwa
Joshwa
Josiahs
Josian
Josias
Josie
Josieur
Josif
Josip
Joslyn
Josmany
Jospeh
Joss
Josse
Josselyn
Josslyn
Jossy
Jostein
Josten
Jostene
Josue Isma
Josué
Josuel
Josuez
Josuha
Jotham
Jotis
Joubin
Jounathon
Jouni
Jourdan
Jousha
Jouvens
Jovaan
Jovani
Jovanic
Jovann
Jovanni
Jovannie
Jovannis
Jovanny
Jovany
Jovaris
Jovaughn
Jovel
Jovell
Jovenal
Jovenel
Jovey
Jovi
Jovian
Jovoan
Jovon
Jovon'
Jovonn
Jovonne
Jowonn
Joydeep
Joyee
Joyeux
Jozef
Joziah
Jozshua
Jozzepi
Jque
Jr-Scales
Jr.
Jravis
Jray

Juah
Jualandra
Juamon
Juan Alber
Juan Carlos
Juan Felipe
Juan Manuel
Juan Marcos
Juan Pablo
Juan Terris
Juan Tom
Juan-Carlos
Juanassie
Juancarl
Juaniquin
Juanita
Juanky
Juann
Juansamuel
Juaquin
Juaquine
Juaun
Jubal
Jubarry
Jubenil
Jubentino
Judah
Judas
Judazier
Judge
Judney
Judon
Jue
Juel
Juergen
Juewand
Juhyung
Juinting
Jujuan
Julbrine
Jule
Jules
Julia
Juliano
Julie
Juliene
Jullian
July
Julyan
Juma
Jumaane
Jumar
Jumha
Jun
Jun-Long
Junaid
June
Junell
Juniesky
Junior Edgar
Junious
Junius
Junliste
Junmin
Junnie
Junot
Junwen
Junya
Juraile
Jure
Jurell
Jurgen
Jurian
Jurij
Juris
Jurrell
Jusani
Jusdan
Jushua
Jusitn
Juslin
Justain
Justan
Justice
Justim
Justin-Joseph
Justin-Loree-William
Justin-Michael
Justin-Noel
Justin-Phillips
Justin-Shane
Justinalonzo
Justinn
Justino
Justis
Justius
Justn
Justo
Justton
Justun
Justus
Juval
Juvenal
Juvencio
Juvon
Juvone
Juwan
Juwaun
Juwon
Jwalter
Jyaire
Jymal
Jyovanni
Jyromey
Jyron
Jyshon

K

K C
K Dane
K'cee
K. C.
K.C.
Ka
Ka Juanis
Ka-Ho
Ka-Ming
Ka-Tao
Kaan
Kaashif
Kabar
Kabir
Kabran
Kacy
Kadarra
Kadeem
Kaden
Kadir
Kadon
Kadrick
Kadya
Kaecieo
Kaegan
Kael
Kaelan
Kaelen
Kaelin
Kaelyn
Kaem
Kaesy
Kagan
Kagen
Kahabilwa
Kahambrel
Kahari

Kaheer
Kahiem
Kahil
Kahleef
Kahleil
Kahlen
Kahlid
Kahlif
Kahlil
Kahlill
Kahlin
Kahmis
Kahree
Kahseem
Kai-Ching
Kaid
Kaidan
Kaiden
Kaidon
Kaiem
Kaiko
Kail
Kaila
Kailand
Kailen
Kailey
Kailin
Kaime
Kain
Kainan
Kainen
Kaipo
Kairi
Kairo
Kaiser
Kaishif
Kaison
Kaisone
Kaj
Kajetan
Kal
Kalab
Kalahan
Kalam
Kalama
Kalan
Kalani
Kalaum
Kaleaf
Kalee
Kaleef
Kaleem
Kalel
Kalem
Kaleo
Kalet
Kalev
Kaley
Kali
Kalib
Kalieb
Kalief
Kalif
Kalil
Kalim
Kaliph
Kalise
Kallan
Kalled
Kallen
Kallin
Kallum
Kallun
Kallur
Kalman
Kalmin
Kalob
Kalon
Kalonji
Kalop
Kalpesh
Kalsey
Kalub
Kalun
Kalven
Kalyn
Kalynn
Kam
Kamaal
Kamacus
Kamahl
Kamal
Kamalakannan
Kamaldeep
Kamali
Kamalis
Kamalveer
Kamar
Kamardeen
Kamarin
Kamarul Id
Kamau
Kamden
Kamdyn
Kameco
Kamel
Kamen
Kamerdeep
Kamern
Kamil
Kamm
Kammen
Kamon
Kamran
Kamren
Kamron
Kanard
Kanatase
Kandy
Kaneii
Kaney
Kanga
Kangsoo
Kanika
Kanon
Kansas
Kantor
Kantral
Kanwaljit
Kanwar
Kapena
Kapers
Kapil
Kapreé
Kar
Kar-Lon
Karaamat
Karac
Karahn
Karam
Karan
Karandeep
Karanjeet
Karanjit
Karanvir
Karas
Kardin
Kareaan
Karee
Kareeme
Kareen
Karel
Karell
Kareme
Karen
Karey

Kari
Karie
Karington
Kario
Kariym
Karl Abram
Karl-Anton
Karlen
Karlief
Karlin
Karlis
Karlos
Karlton
Karlyle
Karlysle
Karmel
Karmen
Karn
Karndeep
Karneil
Karnell
Karnvir
Karol
Karoly
Karon
Karr
Karrie
Karriem
Karrington
Karrol
Karron
Karry
Karson
Karsten
Karter
Karthik
Kartik
Kartrell
Karun
Karval
Karven
Kary
Kasceem
Kase
Kaseem
Kasen
Kaseym
Kash
Kashay
Kasheen
Kashia
Kashif
Kashmere
Kashmire
Kashney
Kasib
Kasidit
Kasie
Kasim
Kasimir
Kasmen
Kason
Kasonde
Kaspar
Kasra
Kassa
Kassem
Kassidy
Kassim
Kassin
Kassius
Katarius
Katelyn
Katharice
Katherine
Kathleen
Kathryn
Katie
Katlin
Katlyn
Katray
Katrel
Katrell
Katriot
Kattiem
Katzu
Kaukahi
Kaury
Kaushik
Kavakia
Kavaldeep
Kavan
Kaveh
Kaven
Kavi
Kavic
Kaville
Kavin
Kavir
Kavon
Kawai
Kawane
Kawika
Kay
Kayce
Kaycee
Kayeon
Kaylan
Kayleb
Kaylen
Kaylo
Kaylon
Kaylyn
Kayne
Kayon
Kayron
Kayson
Kayvon
Kaz
Kazeem
Kazimierz
Kazimir
Kazman
Kazuo
Kc
Kcey
Kchebe
Keagan
Keair
Keaka
Kealoha
Kean
Keandre
Keane
Keanen
Keanglong
Keannan
Kearney
Keary
Keaten
Keavis
Kedar
Keddrick
Kedes
Kedrian
Kedric
Kedrick
Kedron
Keefe
Keelan
Keeland
Keelen
Keeley
Keelian
Keenebeen
Keenen

Keeno
Keenoah
Keenon
Keeon
Kees
Keese
Keesee
Keeter
Keeth
Keeton
Keetun
Keeven
Keevin
Keevon
Kegan
Keghan
Kegun
Kehl
Kei Lon
Keiffer
Keil
Keilan
Keiland
Keimar
Kein
Keion
Keionne
Keir
Keiran
Keiren
Keiron
Keita
Keith Alan
Keith Amadeus
Keith Hunter
Keith Jerm
Keith-Coty
Keithen
Keithley
Keithon
Keivon
Kejuan
Kelan
Kelbey
Kelby
Kelcy
Keldon
Keldrain
Keldrick
Kele
Kelean
Kelechi
Kelepi
Kelin
Kelis
Kell'n
Kellan
Kellan-Dean
Kelland
Kelle
Keller
Kelley
Kelli
Kellin
Kellon
Kellyn
Kelpesh
Kelse
Kelson
Kelsy
Keltie
Kelton
Keltron
Kelvan
Kelvassicia
Kelvis
Kelvyn
Kelwood
Kelwyn
Kely
Kelynn
Kem
Kemal
Kemar
Kemberlles
Kemish
Kemit
Kemjiro
Kemo
Kemokhambrel
Kemon
Kemp
Kempton
Kemuel
Ken Mei
Ken-Ichiro
Kena
Kenan
Kenard
Kenari
Kenawa
Kenaz
Kencil
Kency
Kendale
Kendali
Kendel
Kenden
Kenderrick
Kendew
Kendley
Kendon
Kendra
Kendrall
Kendrayle
Kendrell
Kendric
Kendron
Kendryl
Kendy
Kendyl
Keneef
Keneth
Keng
Keng-Wui
Keni
Kenise
Kenitchi
Kenith
Kenji
Kenjiro
Kenkinoshamarro
Kenley
Kenn
Kennan
Kennard
Kennardowen
Kennarri
Kennedy
Kenneil
Kennen
Kenneth Conrad
Kenneth La
Kenneth-John
Kennethen
Kenney
Kennie
Kennieth
Kennis
Kennith
Kennol
Kennon
Kennorio
Kennth
Kenny Lynn
Kennyth

Keno
Kenol
Kenon
Kenrick
Kenrik
Kenroy
Kensean
Kensel
Kenshi
Kenshiro
Kensie
Kenson
Kensuke
Kent-Alexand
Kentaro
Kentavis
Kenten
Kenteryl
Kently
Kento
Kentoku
Kentomie
Kentorian
Kentrel
Kentrial
Kentrick
Kentron
Kentwaina
Kentwan
Kenui
Kenuth
Kenward
Kenya
Kenyail
Kenyale
Kenyan
Kenyata
Kenyath
Kenyatta
Kenynn
Kenyoda
Kenyon
Kenzale
Kenzie
Keoki
Keolung
Keondre
Keondric
Keondrick
Keone
Keoni
Keontae
Keontrye
Keony
Keowa
Keran
Kerby
Kerdwin
Kerek
Kerengton
Kerey
Keri
Keric
Kermit
Kernard
Kernwood
Keron
Kerri
Kerrian
Kerrick
Kerrie
Kerringten
Kerrington
Kerron
Kerrun
Kerryn
Kerscheval
Kerstan
Kervans
Kervin
Kerwin
Kesare
Kesava
Kesavan
Kesean
Keshaiv
Keshaun
Keshav
Keshawn
Kesley
Kesly
Kessie
Kesson
Kester
Kestin
Keston
Kestrel
Ketan
Kethkeo
Ketlais
Ketori
Ketsana
Ketter
Keung
Kevarious
Kevas
Kevaughn
Keve
Kévin
Kevin Da Silva
Kevin Michael
Kevin-James
Kevin-Laine
Kevin-Rae
Kevins
Kevion
Kevis
Kevn
Kevon
Kevron
Kevyn
Kex
Key
Keyan
Keyana
Keye
Keyin
Keylan
Keylyn
Keymetrius
Keynon
Keyon
Keyonte
Keyron
Keysto
Keyth
Keyur
Keyvan
Keyven
Kha
Khafre
Khaivien
Khaldoon
Khale
Khaled
Khaleef
Khaleel
Khalfan
Khalfani
Khali
Khalial
Khalif
Khaliff
Khaliq
Khalique
Khaliyl

Kham
Khama
Khamaree
Khambreal
Khambrel
Khambrell
Khambreltraphan
Khamsavay
Khan
Khang
Khanh
Khanya
Kharee
Khari
Kharim
Khary
Khashoggi
Khatlin
Khayree
Khayrudiyn
Khem-Ra
Khemara
Khemmer
Khemra
Khemraj
Khemran
Kheran
Khevis
Khi
Khldoon
Khoa
Khoeun
Khoi
Khomsunt
Khongphe
Khonrad
Khornprase
Khory
Khristian
Khristin
Khristop
Khristopher
Khrum
Khuoc
Khuong
Khuram
Khushdeep
Khushwinder
Khyber
Khylil
Khyree
Khyzeem
Ki
Kial
Kiam
Kian
Kiarie
Kiawa
Kibaya
Kibo
Kida
Kidane
Kieeme
Kielan
Kiely
Kiem
Kienan
Kier
Kieren
Kierian
Kiernan
Kieron
Kierran
Kierre
Kiet
Kieth
Kieu
Kiev
Kievs
Kige
Kijano
Kijuan
Kilani
Kile
Kilee
Kiley
Killian
Kilter
Kim-Wah
Kimani
Kimbal
Kimball
Kimble
Kimbrell
Kimhai
Kimit
Kimlie
Kimmy
Kimon
Kimseng
Kimun
Kimyata
Kin
Kina
Kincaid
Kincheon
Kindeshaun
King
King-Curtis
Kingsley
Kingston
Kinnard
Kinney
Kinnson
Kino
Kinsey
Kinsie
Kinsley
Kinson
Kinsson
Kion
Kip
Kipley
Kipp
Kipton
Kirabu
Kiram
Kiran
Kiranjot
Kiray
Kirce
Kireen
Kiril
Kirill
Kiritpaul
Kirk Douglas
Kirke
Kirkham
Kirkland
Kirkman
Kirkor
Kirkton
Kirkwood
Kironde
Kirpal
Kirshna
Kirsten
Kirstofe
Kirstopher
Kirstyn
Kirt
Kirtis
Kirtley
Kisan
Kishing
Kishon

Kishore
Kisuk
Kit
Kit-Shy
Kittaney
Kiwa
Kiwan
Kiyam
Kiyiem
Kizito
Kjel
Kjell
Klark
Klaus
Klay
Klayton
Kle
Kleber
Kleedis
Klemens
Klifton
Klint
Klinton
Klye
Kname
Knevin
Knoel
Knowledge
Knowlton
Knox
Knut
Knute
Koa
Koal
Kobie
Kobinath
Koby
Kobyn
Koda
Koddyh
Kodey
Kodi
Kodiak
Kodie
Kofeinu
Kofi
Kog
Kohei
Kohl
Koji
Kojo
Kok-Tru
Koki
Kole
Koley
Kolin
Kollin
Kolo
Kolt
Kolton
Komar
Komron
Kong
Kongmeng
Konner
Konnor
Konpheng
Konstadinos
Konstandinos
Konstantin
Konstantine-Peter
Konstantinos
Konstantinos-Kostas
Konstantinos-Panagiotis
Konte
Koob
Koobmeej
Kooly
Koon
Koos
Korak
Koral
Koran
Korban
Korbee
Korben
Korbin
Korby
Kord
Korda
Kordale
Kordd
Kordearl
Kordell
Koreay
Koree
Koreem
Korell
Koreyan
Kori
Korie
Korin
Korlin
Kormel
Kornel
Kornell
Koro
Korrey
Korrie
Korrigan
Korry
Kortez
Kortlin
Kortney
Kosmas
Kosmoe
Kostadinos
Kostadinos-Nikolaos-Kost
Kostandinos
Kostantino
Kostantinos
Kostas
Kotaro
Koty
Kou
Kourtney
Kourtny
Koury
Kouvaris
Kovan
Kovid
Koyin
Koyzell
Kpompoli
Krae
Krag
Kramer
Kraug
Kray
Kreg
Kregg
Kreig
Krestan
Kresten
Kreston
Kriistan
Krisen
Krishen
Krishn
Krishna
Krishneil
Krishner

Kriskumar
Krisopher
Krispian
Krist
Krista
Kristafer
Kristan
Kristapher
Kristen
Krister
Kristien
Kristifor
Kristiian
Kristin
Kristina
Kristjan
Kristo
Kristoferm Michae
Kristoff
Kristoffer-Jon
Kristofo
Kristofor
Kristofor-Beau
Kriston
Kristophe
Kristopher-Cody
Kristophor
Kristor
Kritee
Krosbie-Arlington
Kroy
Krsna
Krun
Krunoslav
Krys
Krystal
Krystian
Krystofer
Krystoffer
Krystopher
Krzysztof
Krzysztof-Lech
Kshawn
Kshidokahan
Kuagn-Hou
Kuang
Kub
Kuhova
Kujtim
Kulin
Kuljeet
Kultar
Kululak
Kulwinder
Kumail
Kumar
Kunaal
Kunal
Kunnal
Kuong
Kupra
Kurie
Kurk
Kurosh
Kurri
Kurry
Kursten
Kurtiz
Kurtley
Kurtlynn
Kurtz
Kush
Kuyle
Kwabena
Kwaku
Kwame
Kwan
Kwansin
Kwaun
Kweku
Kwesi
Kwiana
Kwin
Kwincy
Kwinsha
Kwinten
Kwintin
Kwok
Kwon
Kwong-Kwen
Kwong-yiu
Kwun-yee
Ky
Kya
Kyam
Kyandre
Kydell
Kydi
Kye
Kyeif
Kyel
Kyellan
Kyheem
Kyiel
Kyjuan
Kylan
Kylar
Kyle Micha
Kyle Pierce
Kyle-David
Kyle-John
Kyle-Lee
Kyle-Mathew
Kyle-Patrick
Kylee
Kylen
Kyley
Kylie
Kylief
Kylin
Kylleross
Kyllian
Kylon
Kylor
Kylrin
Kylund
Kyly
Kylynn
Kym
Kymeen
Kynan
Kyol
Kyon
Kyran
Kyree
Kyriakos
Kyrin
Kyrle
Kyron
Kysan
Kywon

L

L C
L'mar
L.J.
La
La Derek
La Jack
La Juan
La Mare
La Ron

La Ruan
La Vance
La Vaughn
La Vell
La'ron
La'von'ta
La-Mar
La-Sean
La-Var
Laartis
Laban
Labar
Labarius
Labib
Labonta
Labrando
Labraunt
Labrawn
Labrone
Labronte
Labros
Labyrinth
Lacardo
Lacatron
Lacey
Lache
Lachlan
Lachlann
Lacy
Ladall
Ladamain
Ladaniel
Ladarian
Ladd
Ladelé
Ladell
Laderrias
Ladexter
Ladextra
Ladislaus
Ladon
Ladonna
Ladrekus
Ladrew
Ladrius
Laeldre
Lafabian
Lafaiete
Lafayett
Lafayette
Lafe
Lafeice
Laferriere
Lafeyette
Lafonzo
Lafrance
Laggarius
Lai
Laif
Laine
Laird
Laith
Lajarvis
Lajavon
Lajoel
Lajos
Lajuan
Lake
Lakelan
Lakendric
Lakendrick
Lakene
Lakhbees
Lakhveer
Lakhvir
Lam
Lamaine
Lamair
Lamarcus
Lamario
Lamaris
Lamark
Lamarque
Lamarr
Lamarre
Lamartez
Lamartine
Lamaskin
Lamaunt
Lambert
Lambros
Lamech
Lamichael
Lamond
Lamondre
Lamone
Lamonte
Lamontie
Lamore
Lamund
Lanar
Lanard
Lancaster
Lance-Alexander
Lancelot
Lancy
Land
Landal
Landan
Landell
Lander
Landers
Landin
Landis
Landiz
Lando
Landre
Landré
Landre-Desire
Landrue
Landry
Landy
Landyn
Laney
Lanfrancof
Lang
Langdon
Langis
Langston
Lanh
Lankford
Lannce
Lanndon
Lannie
Lanoit
Lanorris
Lans
Lansford
Lanson
Lantz
Lanza
Lap
Lapreece
Laprell
Laprintos
Laquan
Laquavis
Laquenton
Laquintas
Laquintiss
Laquinton
Laquon
Lara
Larahn
Laramie
Laran

Laraunce
Laray
Larcarvasus
Lareece
Larel
Laren
Larian
Larico
Larien
Larinzo
Larkeith
Larkin
Larklin
Larmar
Larnel
Larnell
Larod
Larodra
Larome
Larondney
Larondo
Larone
Laronn
Laroy
Laroyce
Larrecus
Larren
Larrence
Larrick
Larris
Larryston
Lars Krist
Larsen
Larson
Larue
Lary
Larzares
Lasalle
Lascell
Lascelles
Lasean
Lashad
Lashajuan
Lashard
Lashaud
Lashawn
Lashon
Lashonne
Lassagesse
Lastar
Laszlo
Laszlo-Jeremy
Lataji
Latari
Latarius
Latarus
Lataurean
Latavius
Lateef
Lateefh
Latez
Latham
Lathan
Lathaniel
Lathen
Latheodore
Lathio
Lathyn
Latif
Latney
Latonya
Latrael
Latral
Latraviaus
Latravious
Latrell
Latrivis
Latron
Lauchlin
Laude
Laughlin
Launce
Launcelot
Laura
Lauran
Laurance
Laureano
Laurel
Lauren
Laurens
Laurent
Laurente
Laurentiu
Laurice
Laurier
Laurin
Lauro
Lautaro
Lauvachack
Lavada
Lavail
Laval
Lavalei
Lavall
Lavalle
Lavalrick
Lavan
Lavander
Lavar
Lavardus
Lavaris
Lavarn
Lavarus
Lavaughan
Lavaughn
Lavee
Lavell
Lavelle
Lavenski
Laver
Lavere
Lavern
Laverne
Laverrick
Lavi
Lavien
Lavince
Lavon
Lavonne
Lavonte
Lavoris
Lavorrus
Lavotte
Lawalter
Lawerance
Lawrance
Lawren
Lawrence William
Lawron
Lawson
Lawton
Lay
Layafette
Layfun
Laymon
Layth
Layton
Lazaiah
Lazar
Lazarito
Lazaros
Lazarrotroshaur
Lazarus
Lazarusie
Lc

Le
Le Mell
Le Neir
Le Ron
Le Roy
Le Torre
Lé André
Le-Roy
Lea
Lealand
Leaman
Leamon
Leanard
Leander
Leandra
Leandre
Leandrew
Leandro
Leandro De Oliveira
Leantonio
Leary
Leathan
Leavi
Lebaron
Lebert
Lebron
Lebryan
Lechas
Lecil
Lecylin
Ledale
Ledford
Ledon
Ledonavon
Ledonshay
Lee Frank
Lee Jay
Lee Michae
Lee Robert
Lee Shaw
Lee Shawn
Lee Shon
Lee Varshay
Lee Zon
Lee-Aeron
Leeallen
Leeam
Leedon
Leeds
Leeland
Leeon
Leeroy
Leevi
Leevon
Leeyuthseila
Lefarris
Lefranc
Lefranz
Lefty
Legarrett
Leger
Legna
Legrant
Legus
Lehi
Lei
Leicester
Leighton
Leintz
Leith
Leivan
Lejjy
Lejoel
Lekeho
Lekeith
Lekendric
Leks
Lelan
Lelann
Lelio
Lemall
Leman
Lemar
Lemarcus
Lemario
Lemmie
Lemond
Lemont
Lemuel
Len
Lena
Lenard
Lenaris
Lenarris
Lendel
Lendon
Lener
Lenford
Leng
Leniel
Lenis
Lennan
Lennard
Lennart
Lennie
Lennon
Lennox
Lenny
Leno
Lenord
Lenorris
Lenroy
Lenson
Lenton
Lenwood
Lenzy
Leobardo
Leobel
Leojoe
Leola
Leolonza
Leomytery
Léon
Leon-Dallas
Leonandy
Leonardis
Leonart
Leoncio
Leondris
Leone
Leonetti
Leoni
Leonidas
Leonides
Leonirez
Leonizio
Leonon
Leontrae
Leopold
Leopoldo
Leopoldo-Maximilian
Leory
Leoterio Da Silva
Leozie
Lequa
Lequan
Lequerio
Lequetin
Lequinn
Lequinton
Lerai
Leraun
Lerenzo

Lerew
Lerico
Lernard
Leron
Lerondo
Lerone
Leroyende
Lerry
Les
Leseth
Leshaun
Leshawn
Leshon
Lesley
Lesly
Lessie
Lestel
Letavian
Leterrio
Letharius
Letif
Letravous
Letrell
Letrone
Letroy
Letterio
Letwan
Leundra
Lev
Levan
Levander
Levaniel
Levar
Levare
Levarr
Levaughn
Levenski
Levi Spencer
Levi-David
Levie
Levil
Levin
Levio
Levis
Leviticus
Levitis
Levon
Levone
Levoris
Levy
Lew
Lewaa
Lewresley
Lex
Lexander
Lexie
Lexin
Leyani
Leyen
Leysi
Leyton
Li
Li-Han
Liang
Liban
Liberatore
Liberio
Liberty
Liborio
Librado
Lief
Liel
Lieno
Lifaite
Lightfoot
Lil Joseph
Lilcliff
Lildevis
Lilgreg
Liltony
Linas
Lincon
Linda
Lindan
Lindel
Lindell
Linden
Lindo
Lindon
Lindy
Linell
Linford
Linh
Linhowe
Linkesh
Linkit
Linn
Linny
Lino
Linster
Linton
Linus
Linvard
Linwood
Linx
Linze
Lional
Lionel-Malcolm
Lionell
Lionso
Lior
Lipara
Lippman
Lisa
Lisco
Lisher
Lisle
Lison
Litommy
Liton
Little
Little John
Lius
Livingston
Livingstone
Livio
Liznadro
Ljubomir
Llewellyn
Lloyd-Victor
Llvarrious
Llyvell
Lnard
Loanell
Loc
Locksley
Locryn
Loern
Logen
Loic
Lois
Lokesh
Lollyd
Loman
Lomar
Lon
Lonard
London
Lone
Lonell
Loneshia
Long
Long-Kim
Loni
Lonie
Lonjino

Lonnelious
Lonnell
Lonniel
Lonny
Lonsdale
Lontay
Lonte
Lonyo
Lonzo
Loon
Lora
Loran
Lorander
Loreen
Lorell
Lorence
Lorenz
Lorenza
Lorin
Lorinc
Loring
Lorinza
Lorinzo
Loris
Lornie
Lorren
Lorrenzo
Loryn
Lotaire
Lotfi
Lothian
Lottie
Louben
Loubens
Loubert
Loubi
Louden
Loudwidge
Louia

Louie
Louigino
Louis Albe
Louis Carlos
Louis-André
Louis-Eric
Louis-Felix
Louis-Francois
Louis-Frederick
Louis-Philippe
Louis-Pierre
Loukas
Loukind
Lounel
Loupierre
Louricaks
Louro
Loutson
Louville
Lovedeep
Lovell
Lovelle
Loveroop
Lovette
Lovey
Lovon
Lovro
Lowan
Lowden
Lowen
Lowery
Lowry
Lowyn
Loxley
Loy
Loyal
Loyd
Loyde
Loye

Lozando
Lu'kee
Luan
Lubz
Luc Ambert
Luc D
Luc-Andre
Luc-Gregory
Luc-Leonard
Lucan
Lucanus
Lucas Chri
Lucas-James
Lucassie
Lucian
Luciano
Lucias
Lucien
Lucinda
Lucino
Lucio
Lucious
Lucius
Luckas
Luckie
Luckson
Lucky
Lucus
Ludwig
Ludwik
Ludwing
Lugan
Luger
Lugusta
Lui
Luibert
Luis Orlan
Luis Steve
Luise

Luiz
Lujack
Luk
Luka
Lukes
Lukus
Lulzim
Lupe
Lupin
Luqman
Luqman Hakim
Lurance
Lurzim
Luta
Lutcher
Lutri
Luwella
Luz
Ly
Lyamn
Lydan
Lydell
Lyden
Lydia
Lydon
Lyell
Lyen
Lyeneil
Lyge
Lykeem
Lyman
Lymon
Lymus
Lyndale
Lyndall
Lyndan
Lyndel
Lyndell
Lynden

Lyndsay
Lynel
Lynell
Lynette
Lynford
Lynn-Thao
Lynnard
Lynne
Lynntrell
Lynnwood
Lynol
Lynwarren
Lynwood
Lynzie
Lyon
Lyonel
Lyvonne
Lzvor

M

M.
Maalik
Maarten
Mac
Mac Kenzie
Macalaster
Macario
Macarthur
Maccabee
Macdonald
Mace
Macean
Macedonius
Maceo
Macer
Macgyver
Machael
Machias
Macio
Macius
Mackay
Macke
Mackensaw
Mackenxo
Mackenzey
Mackenzi
Mackenzly
Mackenzy
Mackey
Mackienzie
Mackinney
Mackinsey
Macklin
Macks
Macksim
Maclain
Maclaine
Maclean
Macleish
Maclovio
Macnaughton
Macon
Macrckendy
Macs
Macsen
Macson
Macthani
Macy
Madalyn
Maddock
Madhusudan
Madian
Madochee
Madrice
Madru
Maea
Maeakafa
Magdiel
Magloire
Magnus
Magoo
Mahaffey
Mahammad
Mahdee
Mahdi
Maheanuu
Mahear
Mahendra
Maher
Mahesh
Mahin
Mahir
Mahlon
Mahmood
Mahmoud
Mahmoud-Reda
Mahmoudabdulred
Maholm
Mahul
Mahyar
Maica
Maikal
Maiko
Maisan
Maison
Maisum
Maitland
Majai
Majed
Majid
Major
Maka
Makael
Makal
Makara
Makel
Makell
Makena
Makendy
Makenric
Makenson
Makenzie
Makin
Makoto
Maksym
Malachia
Malachie
Malachy
Malcham
Malchija
Malcolm Jamal
Malcolm Jamar
Malcom
Malcum
Maleek
Malek
Mali
Malin
Malique
Mallie
Mallik
Mallori
Mallory
Malo
Malok
Malton
Malvin
Malwinder
Mamdooh
Mamdouh
Mamon
Man
Man Cong
Man-Kit

Manan
Manann
Manaure
Manav
Manaway
Manbir
Manco
Manda
Mandel
Mandieep
Mandy
Maneesh
Maneet
Manford
Manfred
Manh
Manhar
Manhhung
Manice
Maninder
Manise
Manish
Manjeet
Manjeev
Manjinder
Manly
Manmeet
Manmit
Manmohan
Mannie
Mannix
Manno
Mannuel
Manny
Manoj
Manolis
Manothong
Manpreet
Manprett
Manprit
Manraj
Manreet
Mansel
Manson
Mansoor
Mansour
Mansur
Manteal
Mantej
Mantia
Manu
Manual
Manuel-Jake
Manuelli
Manuelo
Manuelro
Manuevaha
Manus
Manv
Manveer
Manvel
Manvinder
Manvir
Manwinder
Maor
Maquan
Maquell
Maquez
Maquise
Maqwan
Marady
Marathon
Marbin
Marc Eric
Marc-Alexandre
Marc-Anthony
Marc-Antoine
Marc-Sean
Marcandre
Marcantoine
Marcantonio
Marcarlo
Marcas
Marcedes
Marceles
Marcelin
Marcelino
Marcelis
Marcelius
Marcell
Marcellas
Marcelle
Marcelleous
Marcellin
Marcellous
Marcelluas
Marcellus
Marcelo
March
Marchello
Marchenrie
Marcial
Marciano
Marcien
Marcin
Marcio
Marck
Marckende
Marckenson
Marcko
Marckson
Marckus
Marclo
Marcnell
Marco-Giuseppe
Marcous
Marcquis
Marcsonne
Marcsseau
Marcuis
Marcum
Mardel
Mardochee
Mardrico
Marece
Mareco
Marek
Margaret
Margvine
Maria
Mariah
Mariano
Mariaus
Marice
Maricus
Mariko
Marin
Marino
Marint
Marinus
Mario Jose
Mario-George
Mario-Santino
Marion-Vincent
Mariono
Marios
Maris
Maritza
Marius
Mark Anthony
Mark David
Mark-Anthony
Mark-John
Mark-Joseph
Mark-Julian
Mark-Leonard

Mark-Tonchy
Markaz
Markco
Markcus
Markease
Markee
Markeen
Markees
Markeese
Markei
Markeice
Markeis
Markeith
Markel
Markell
Markelle
Markendy
Markenson
Markerson
Markes
Markese
Markesst
Marketa
Markeunezi
Markey
Markham
Markian
Markice
Markie
Markies
Markiese
Markilo
Markinsey
Markis
Markise
Markist
Marklan
Marklyn
Marko-Franc
Markoneb
Markos
Markose
Markques
Markqueus
Markuee
Markuis
Markuss
Markussie
Markusz
Marky
Marlan
Marland
Marlandis
Marleon
Marley
Marlion
Marlo
Marlom
Marlone
Marlonne
Marlos
Marlow
Marlus
Marlyn
Marnell
Marney
Maron
Maroun
Marous
Marqell
Marqies
Marquan
Marquand
Marque
Marquee
Marquel
Marquell
Marquese
Marquest
Marquet
Marquette
Marquez
Marqui
Marquias
Marquice
Marquie
Marquies
Marquiese
Marquile
Marquin
Marquisa
Marquisee
Marquist
Marquiste
Marqurice
Marqus
Marqwell
Marrian
Marrica
Marricus
Marrio
Marris
Marro
Marsailes
Marsalis
Marsden
Marsean
Marsel
Marselo
Marsha
Marshal
Marshant
Marshawn
Marshel
Marson
Marston
Martalaus
Martavious
Martavis
Martavus
Martee
Martel
Marten
Martez
Martéz
Marti
Martice
Martie
Martiese
Martiez
Martin Lou
Martin Luther
Martin-Ian
Martin-Kazimierz
Martin-Robert
Martine
Martinez
Martiniano Jr
Martino
Martinus
Martiquis
Martis
Martise
Martnezts
Martrel
Martrell
Martrice
Martron
Martyn
Martynas
Marvailes
Marvalous
Marvein
Marvell
Marvelous
Marvens

Marvi
Marvis
Marvllous
Marvyn
Marwan
Marwin
Marx
Marx-Meng
Mary
Marzarius
Marzell
Masaki
Masen
Masico
Masis
Maslot
Masoud
Massena
Massey
Massi
Massimiliano
Massman
Masson
Masud
Mataiasi
Matani
Matchawan
Matchy
Matejs
Mateo
Matere
Mateus
Mathan
Matheau
Matheno
Matheu
Matheus
Mathew-Marcel
Mathias

Mathie
Mathieu-Phillipe
Mathieux
Mathiew
Mathijs
Mathis
Mathu
Matias
Matin
Matlock
Mato-To-
Matrix
Mats
Mattan
Matteo
Mattew
Mattheau
Mattheu
Mattheus
Matthew J
Matthew Jay
Matthew Steven
Matthew Thomas
Matthew Vi
Matthew William
Matthew-Allen
Matthew-Branimir
Matthew-David
Matthew-Linden
Matthew-Luke
Matthew-Mark
Matthew-Maurice
Matthew-Mike
Matthew-Todd
Matthias
Matthieux

Matthiev
Matthiew
Matthue
Matti
Mattias
Mattie
Mattieu
Mattieux
Mattison
Matts
Mattson
Matty
Matuissie
Maturin
Matyas
Mau
Maugro
Maur
Maurance
Maureshia
Maurice Da
Mauriece
Maurikus
Maurio
Maurio Antwoine
Maurise
Maurius
Maurizio
Mauro
Maurrell
Maurtel
Maury
Maverick
Mavin
Mawubi
Mawyn
Maxamillion
Maxe

Maxfield
Maxi
Maxie
Maxim
Maximiano
Maximili
Maximilien
Maximillia
Maximilliam
Maximillian
Maximillion
Maximino
Maxis
Maxmilian
Maxony
Maxwel
Maxwill
Maxx
May
Mayer
Mayfield
Mayko
Maymond
Maynard
Mayur
Mazen
Mazeyar
Mazin
Mazinn
Mazrvel
Mc
Mc Arthur
Mc Donnell
Mc Kenzie
Mc Kinnon
Mcarthur
Mccade
Mccall
Mccarty

Mcclary
Mcclellan
Mcclinin
Mcconnell
Mccoy
Mcdaniel
Mcdonald
Mcdonna
Mcearlon
Mcfarlane
Mcgair
Mcgyver
Mcjune
Mckade
Mckale
Mckean
Mckell
Mckendrie
Mckensey
Mckenson
Mckensson
Mckenzi
Mckenzie
Mckevier
Mckinlee
Mckinley
Mckinnely
Mckinnon
Mckinson
Mclean
Mcshane
Mead
Meade
Meagan
Mean
Meastro
Meco
Medardo
Medgar
Meena
Megal
Megan
Megelle
Meghan
Mehali
Mehdi
Mehmet
Mehran
Mehrayin
Mehraz
Mehrdad
Mehrod
Mehul
Meikeem
Meikel
Meir
Mejdi
Mekal
Mekel
Mekell
Mekhail
Mekram
Mel
Melanie
Melbin
Melbourne
Melby
Meldon
Meldrick
Melec
Melech
Melek
Melesio
Meliek
Melissa
Meliton
Melo
Melony
Melshor
Meltavis
Meltonia
Meltoya
Melville
Melvino
Melvon
Melvyn
Memdela
Mena
Menachem
Menashe
Mendel
Menelaos
Menelik
Meng
Menghini
Menno
Menta
Menyell
Mequel
Mequelin
Meraldo
Merardo
Mercedes
Merchant
Merched
Mercury
Meredith
Merek
Meric
Merick
Merico
Merijn
Meril
Merkel
Merlin
Merlyn
Mero
Merrald
Merrell
Merrick
Merril
Merrill
Merritt
Mershon
Merton
Meru
Mervyn
Meryl
Mesfin
Mesh
Meshcck
Meshech
Meshon
Mesken
Mesmain
Messiah
Messina
Mete
Metin
Metitie
Metrice
Mews
Mhasood
Mhichael
Mhmad
Mi Shawn
Mian
Micael
Micahel
Micaiah
Micajah
Mical
Micha
Michacel-J
Michaèl
Michael Abram

Michael An
Michael Anthony
Michael Da Silva
Michael De Sousa
Michael Henry
Michael Jay
Michael John
Michael Josef
Michael Lynn
Michael Neal
Michael Pa
Michael Paul
Michael Peter
Michael-
Michael-Aaron
Michael-Alan
Michael-Anthony
Michael-Christopher
Michael-James
Michael-John
Michael-Jose
Michael-Joseph
Michael-Jue
Michael-Julien
Michael-Makar
Michael-Vincent
Michaeldavid
Michaele
Michaell
Michaelray
Michaelscott
Michaelthomas
Michah
Michail
Michal
Michale
Michalel
Michaud
Miche
Micheal Fitsgera
Micheal-Lee
Michee
Micheil
Michel-John
Michelange
Michelangelo
Michelet
Michelle
Michiah
Michiel
Micho
Michol
Michon
Michone
Mick
Mickael
Mickeal
Mickel
Mickelle
Mickerson
Micki
Mickle
Mickolai
Micky
Micrus
Micshaw
Middel
Miena
Miequle
Migeel
Migel
Miguel Ant
Miguel-Jose
Miguelangel
Miguelly
Mihail
Mihalis
Mihir
Miika
Mika
Mikaeel
Mikaele
Mikah
Mikail
Mikale
Mikale-Messale
Mikcaela
Mike-Stephen
Mikele
Mikell
Mikellhia
Mikhael
Mikhial
Miki
Mikial
Mikie
Mikil
Mikilo
Mikio
Mikka
Mikkail
Mikkel
Mikko
Mikle
Miklos
Miko
Mikohl
Mikol
Miladin
Milan
Milandeep
Milas
Miledge
Milenko
Milford
Milhem
Milien
Millan
Millard
Milles
Milmus
Milne
Milo
Milon
Milorad
Milson
Miltiathis
Milton Harrison
Milus
Milville
Min
Mina
Mindle
Miner
Minesh
Ming-Sum
Mingo
Minh
Minh Duc
Minhao
Minhduc
Minhhy
Minhkhan
Minhtong
Minto
Minwison
Miqueas
Miquel
Mira
Miracle
Miraj

Mirko
Miro
Miroslav
Miryoong
Mirza
Misael
Mischa
Misha
Mishael
Mishal
Mishaun
Misik
Misineti
Miska
Mister
Misterdamian
Misty
Mitchael
Mitchall
Mitchele
Mitchelle
Mitchem
Mitesh
Mithun
Mitri
Mittin
Mitul
Mixay
Miyacari
Miyuru
Mizell
Mladen
Moataz
Moath
Moazzum
Mobeen
Mobolaji
Moctar
Modale
Modesto
Moeen
Moez
Mofead
Moffat
Mogologanyi
Mohamad
Mohamad Ashraf
Mohamad-Ali
Mohamedali
Mohamid
Mohammad-Rez
Mohammd
Mohammed H
Mohammid
Mohanad
Mohaned
Mohd
Mohd Anas
Mohd Khuza
Mohemmad
Mohit
Mohmad
Mohmad-Fayez-Ali
Mohsin
Mohtanick
Moise
Moise-Gaetan
Moishe
Mokrane
Moktar
Molajuwon
Molden
Moleni
Molitika
Momodu
Monahan
Monarch
Moncarlos
Monchunonzh
Monda
Mondale
Mondarasmey
Mondell
Mondian
Moneeb
Monfort
Mongul
Monica
Monico
Monie
Monir
Monnie
Monquail
Monquisse
Monroe
Monshae
Montae
Montaé
Montague
Montana
Montaque
Montarius
Montaser
Montavess
Montavis
Montay
Montaze
Montee
Monteiz
Montel
Montell
Montello
Montero
Monteze
Montford
Montgomery
Monti
Montiego
Montisze
Montoyae
Montrail
Montrale
Montrall
Montray
Montre
Montreal
Montrel
Montrell
Montrequez
Montrey
Montrez
Moo
Moody
Moore
Mooro
Mordecai
Mordechai
Mordechei
Moreau
Moreese
Morel
Morell
Morexi
Morey
Morgen
Morgon
Moriah
Morian
Moriano
Morie
Morile
Morionté
Morland
Morley

Morlon
Morlyn
Morningstar
Moroni
Morrell
Morresse
Morrison
Morry
Morse
Mortagus
Morton
Mortty
Morvion
Mose
Mosese
Mosiah
Mosie
Moss
Mossab
Mostafa
Mostaffa
Moton
Moua
Mouahmon
Mouhamadou
Mouhamed
Moune
Mounib
Mousa
Moussa
Moustafa
Movina
Moyisse
Mraquise
Mrigender
Mubarak
Mubin
Mubshir-Ahsan
Mudassarkhan
Mudh
Muezzi-Bin
Muhamad
Muhammadali
Muhammed
Muhanad
Muhieldin
Muhsin
Muhuji
Muhye-Uddin
Mukhesh
Mukhtaar
Mukhtar
Muncie
Munden
Muneer
Muneesh
Munish
Munson
Murad
Murali
Muran
Murat
Murat-Togman
Murdush
Murel
Murice
Murney
Murphy
Murrel
Murrell
Murrey
Murtaza
Murvin
Musa
Musaed
Musashi
Mussolini
Mustafah
Mustapha
Muthab
Muther
Muzaffar
Muzahir
Muzammil
Mwaura
My-Son
Mya
Mycal
Mycenzie
Mychael
Mychal
Mychall
Mychalo
Mycheal
Mykael
Mykal
Mykel
Mykolas
Mylan
Mylen
Mylon
Myran
Myreek
Myriana
Myrick
Myrl
Myrone
Mytchel
Myur

N

Na
Náim
Naaman
Naashukwa
Naason
Nabeel
Nabiel
Nabil
Nabil-Ramsey
Nabith
Nabor
Nachiket
Nadab
Nadeem
Nader
Nadim
Nadir
Nadorian
Naeem
Naeoky
Naethan
Nafeese
Nafess
Nafife
Nafis
Nafius
Naftali
Naginder
Naheed
Naheim
Nahemiah
Nahid
Nahshon
Nahum
Naiad
Naif
Naim
Naimul
Nain
Naisa
Naison
Naiym
Naizony

Najahodd
Najam
Najee
Najib
Najjah
Najjam
Nakimah
Nakita
Nakul
Naldo
Nalim
Nalio
Naltwaun
Nam
Namil
Nana
Nandan
Nanik
Naotaka
Naoya
Naphtali
Napoleon
Napthali
Naquiven
Narada
Narciso
Nardel
Naren
Narenda
Narendra
Naresh
Narien
Nariman
Narin
Narith
Narong
Nartavious
Nartavleon
Narudol
Narvel
Naryan
Nasa
Naseef
Naseem
Naseer
Naseri
Nash
Nashaad
Nashon
Nasia
Nasio
Nasir
Nason
Nasrulah
Nasser
Natacha
Natale
Natalie
Natanael
Natasha
Natavis
Natavius
Nate
Nateil
Natham
Nathan Edw
Nathan-Henry
Nathan-Mark
Nathanae
Nathanal
Nathaneal
Nathaneil
Nathanel
Nathaneol
Nathania
Nathaniel-La
Nathanielle
Nathann
Nathanni
Nathanuel
Nathanyel
Nathapon
Natheal
Nathean
Nathel
Nathian
Nathin
Nathinel
Nathniel
Nathon
Nati
Nation
Natívida
Natividad
Natsuto
Natt
Nattapol
Natthan
Natu
Naul
Navada
Navarre
Navarro
Navbinder
Navdeep
Navdeep-Singh
Naveed
Naveen
Navid
Navin
Navjeet
Navjot
Navneet
Navpaul
Navrattan
Nawar
Nawaz
Nayab
Nayan
Naythan
Naython
Nayuk
Nazaire
Nazaret
Nazareth
Nazarie
Nazario
Nazeem
Nazem-Mahmoud
Nazeylyus
Nazier
Nazim
Nazir
Nazrali
Nazrawi
Nazz
Ndung'u
Ndungu
Neacail
Neale
Nectarios
Ned
Nedrick
Nee
Neehar
Neej
Neeka
Neel
Neema
Neer
Neeraj
Nefta
Neftali
Negosh-Ned
Nehemiah

Nehemias
Nehmiah
Neihl
Neilesh
Neilkumar
Neill
Neim
Neiyamia
Nekon
Nelius
Nello
Nelo
Nels
Nelse
Nelsen
Nelson Ant
Nelson De Oliveira
Nelson-Andres
Nemanya
Nemer
Nemi
Nenad
Nephi
Neremie
Nerin
Nero
Nerone
Nerron
Nerses
Nery
Neshan
Nesly
Nesskens
Nester
Nestor
Netavius
Nethanel
Netrho
Nevada
Nevan
Nevarr
Neviah
Nevil
Nevill
Neville
Nevio
Newel
Newell
Newstell
Newton
Nexar
Nezar
Nezekiel Harry
Nga
Ngawang
Nghia
Ngoc
Ngocvan
Ngocvu
Nguyen
Nguyenviet
Nhan
Nhi
Nhut
Nial
Niall
Nian
Niaz
Nicanor
Nicarous
Niccolas
Niccolo
Nichalas
Nichelas
Nichele
Nichlas
Nichlos
Nichola
Nicholaas
Nicholai
Nicholas Anthony
Nicholas John
Nicholas-Alexandre
Nicholasco
Nicholau
Nichole
Nicholes
Nicholi
Nicholis
Nichollas
Nicholos
Nichols
Nicholus
Nichorai
Nichoulas
Nichren
Nickadem
Nickalas
Nickalaus
Nickale
Nickalias
Nickalos
Nickee
Nickel
Nickesh
Nickey
Nickhale
Nickhause
Nickholas
Nicki
Nickie
Nicklas
Nicklous
Nickoda
Nickola
Nickolaos
Nickolau
Nickolaus
Nickoles
Nickolus
Nicky
Niclas
Niclasse
Nico
Nicolaas
Nicolai
Nicolaos
Nicolau
Nicolaus
Nicole
Nicoles
Nicoljay
Nicolo
Nicolos
Nicolus
Nicoly
Nicomedes
Nicson
Nidal
Nieem
Niegel
Niel
Niels
Niesah
Nigel-Keneth
Nigle
Nihad
Nihal
Nii
Nijah
Nijel
Nikalus
Nike

Nikeem
Nikenson
Nikevis
Nikhil
Nikia
Nikiah
Nikili
Nikimo
Nikita
Nikitas
Nikki
Nikki Vince
Nikko
Nikkolas
Niklas
Niklaus
Niko
Nikodem
Nikola
Nikolaas
Nikolah
Nikolai
Nikolaos
Nikolari
Nikolas Leonard
Nikoli
Nikolis
Nikolous
Nikon
Nikos
Nikul
Nikunj
Nilan
Nile
Niles
Nilesh
Nilo
Niloy
Nilpeshkumar
Nils
Nils-Daniel
Nilsbriyan
Nima
Nimesh
Nimish
Nimrit
Nina
Ning
Ninious
Nino
Nioclas
Niraj
Nirakone
Niram
Nirav
Niraw
Nirbhai
Nirel
Nirmalchand
Nirobi
Nishan
Nishant
Nisiah
Nisirr
Nissun
Nitesh
Nitin
Nitron
Niv
Nivaj
Nixon
Nixson
Niyeem
Nizam
Nnamdi
Noal
Noam
Noberto
Noble
Nocent
Nochum
Noe
Noèl
Noël
Noelluis
Nohan
Noko
Nokoni
Noland
Nole
Nolen
Nolie
Nollie
Nolte
Nolyn
Nomikos
Nomman
Noor
Noor-Eddin
Norbert
Norberto
Norcoreyell
Norel
Norie
Noris
Norlan
Norm
Norman Lee
Normand
Normane
Norrel
Norris
Norton
Norvel
Norvil
Norvin
Norward
Nossan
Notel
Noumean
Nouncy
Nouraldeen
Nova
Novel
Noveroop
Noverria
Novius
Nowar
Noyar
Nrsimha
Nthniel
Nu
Nuno
Nunzio
Nuvkaran
Nuwan
Nycholas
Nydean
Nyeem
Nygel
Nykeem
Nykolas
Nylan
Nyle
Nyron
Nzinga

O

O'neal
O'neil
O'ryan
O'shane
O'shea
Oakley

Oarrie
Obadiah
Obadiah Lonnie
Obatoyimbo
Obbie
Obdraniel
Obed
Obed Juan
Obemyer
Obie
Obinna
Obotala
Obou Hénoc
Obra
Obrian
Obrien
Obsner
Ociel
Ocil
Ociris
Octavian
Octavias
Octavio
Octavious
Octavis
Octavius
Octavous
Octavus
Octazious
Octravis
Oda
Odam
Odell
Odema
Odes
Odianosen
Odiles
Odilo
Odin
Odini
Odis
Odley
Odonovan
Ofa
Ohan
Oiral
Oj
Ojay
Ojus
Okechukwu
Okeitha
Okel
Okie
Okunade
Okusitino
Oladapo
Oladele
Olaf
Olajawon
Olajuan
Olajuwan
Olajuwon
Olamide
Olan
Olando
Olangie
Olden
Oldy
Ole
Olegario
Oleh
Olein
Oleksa
Olen
Oles
Olevirio
Olidio
Olin
Olinthus
Oliverus
Olivia
Oljuwoun
Ollie
Olney
Olric
Olufemi
Olugbenga
Olukemi
Olusegun
Oluseun
Oluwarotimi
Olvine
Olyds
Omair
Omar-Farooq
Omaray
Omari
Omarmolito
Omarr
Omeca
Omeed-Reza
Omeil
Omengboji
Omer
Omesh
Omid
Omied
Omiros
Omkar
Omoriodion
Omotayo
Omran
Omroy
Omyry
Onassis
Ondirae
Ondre
Oneal
Oneil
Onel
Onesimo
Onesimus
Oney
Oniel
Onil
Onno
Ontario
Ontonio
Ontreil
Onur
Opton
Ora
Oral
Oran
Orane
Ordan
Ordell
Orelio
Orencio
Orenthal
Orenthanes
Orenzo
Orest
Oreste
Orestes
Orette
Orey
Orfilio
Ori
Oriali
Orian
Oricardo
Oricnneo
Orie
Oriel
Orin

Orion
Orist
Orlan
Orlanda
Orlandus
Orlondo
Orlondon
Ormon
Orneil
Oron
Orondi
Orosman
Orpaz
Orpha
Orpheus
Orr
Orren
Orrett
Orrey
Orrin
Orris
Orscino
Orson
Ortavia
Ortelio
Ortez
Orthell
Ortiz
Ortland
Orvie
Orvil
Orville
Ory
Osahon
Osama Mohammed
Osamah
Osbaldo
Osborne
Osee
Osei-Akoto
Oshai
Oshaun
Oshay
Oshea
Oshiba
Osiel
Osirif
Osiris
Osita
Oskar
Osland
Osman
Osmanantonio
Osmany
Osmar
Osmay
Osmel
Osroe
Ossama
Ostap
Osten
Ostin
Osuardo
Osvadi
Osvalda
Oswald
Oswin
Oteni
Oth-Ni-El
Otha
Othman
Otilio
Otis Williamsfle
Otis-Miles
Otittis
Otoniel
Ottavio
Ottavio-John
Ottis
Otys
Oulay
Ova
Oves
Ovet
Ovidio
Ovtavis
Owais
Owen Manning
Owens
Owuza
Oxone
Ozair
Ozdemir
Ozell
Ozkan
Ozker
Ozzie
Ozzy

P

P.K.
Pable
Pablin
Pablo Lora
Pace
Paciano
Packyleon
Paddrick
Paden
Padraic
Padraig
Padriac
Padric
Padro
Page
Paige
Paiton
Paizley
Pak
Pal
Palash
Paljit
Palmarino
Palmer
Panagiotis
Panagis
Panayioti
Panayiotis
Panayiotis-Peter
Panayoti
Pangus
Pankaj
Panos
Panteli
Pantelis
Paradise
Parag
Param
Paramdip
Paras
Pardeep
Pareet
Parham
Parikshit
Parish
Park
Parkey
Parks
Parley
Parmell
Parmer
Parminder
Parmjit

Parmpal
Parnell
Parris
Parrish
Parron
Parry
Parshwa
Parth
Parthiban
Parveer
Pary
Pascale
Pascual
Paseni
Pashaan
Pasi
Pasquale-Giovanni-Piero
Pasquel
Pastor
Pat
Pate
Patel
Paten
Patluska
Patrale
Patric
Patrice
Patricia
Patricio
Patrick Ad
Patrick Anthony
Patrick Edward
Patrick-Joseph
Patrick-Steven
Patrik
Patrik-David
Patrique
Patrizio
Patryck
Patryk
Patsy
Patteson
Patton
Paublo
Paul Abdal
Paul Alexander
Paul Anthony
Paul Edward
Paul Melvin
Paul Simon
Paul-Andre
Paul-Arthur
Paul-Emile
Paul-Eric
Paul-Jason
Paul-Joseph
Paul-Robert-Daniel
Paula
Pauli
Paulino
Paulius
Pausha
Pavan
Pavandip
Pavle
Pavlos
Pawan
Pawel
Paxston-Lee
Paxton
Payaam
Payam
Payce
Payden
Paydon
Payman
Payne
Pearce
Pearl
Pearse
Pearson
Pebro
Pechsovann
Peder
Pedey
Pedro Martir
Pedrom
Pedrum
Peerless
Pehrson
Pei
Pei-Chung
Peirce
Peirre
Pencivan
Peng
Penisimani
Penna
Per
Per-Erik
Peralte
Percell
Percelle
Perceval
Perchik
Perchristopher
Percules
Percy-James
Peree
Perez
Pereze
Perfecto
Peri
Peris
Peritt
Pernell
Perrie
Perrin
Perris
Perryn
Perseus
Perton
Pervis
Petar
Peter Iii
Peter John
Peter-Emil
Peter-Jacob
Peter-Joseph
Peteranh
Peteris
Peterjames-Omeara
Peterson
Petie
Peto
Petri
Petrie
Petro
Petros
Petrrit
Petrus
Peyton
Phabien
Phalla
Pham
Phanny
Phanor
Phanuel
Phares
Pharo
Pharoah
Phat

Phazna
Phelan
Phelipe
Phelix
Pheng
Phereze
Phey
Phi
Phia
Phichai
Phil
Phila
Philamina
Philander
Philemon
Philile
Philip-Nicholas
Philipe
Philipp
Philippe Michael
Philippe-Aubert
Philippe-Francois
Philips
Phillepe
Phillip Jr Iii
Phillip-
Phillip-Andrew
Phillipe
Phillippe
Phillips
Phillp
Philly
Philmon
Philo
Philp
Phirunna
Phong
Phong Frank
Phong Thanh
Phong-Johnny
Phorrest
Phoummas
Phoung
Phousompasong
Phoutthason
Phoutthaya
Phu
Phuc
Phuoc
Phuong
Phyda
Phyro
Pian
Pier Carlo
Pier-Luc
Pier-Luca
Pierceson
Piere
Piereino
Pierluca
Piero
Pierre-Alain
Pierre-Antoine
Pierre-Charles
Pierre-Marc
Pierre-Olivier
Pierre-Paul
Pierro
Pierson
Pieter
Pike
Pinckney
Pincus
Pinda
Pink
Piotr
Pirtpal
Piseth
Pitersonne
Pitt
Pius
Pjeter
Placido
Plasder
Platino
Pleaze
Pobtsua
Podius
Poindexter
Pola
Polihronis
Polite
Polizois
Pollard
Pollin
Polo
Ponciano
Pondexture
Pongsakorn
Poni
Ponifasio
Pontrael
Poojan
Porfirio
Pornenila
Porsche
Porter
Potolaka
Poul
Poulus
Power
Powion
Prabhjot
Prabhjote
Prabhsimran
Prabhu
Pradeep
Pradel
Praful
Prajesh
Prakash
Praker
Prakit
Pramod
Pranab
Pranay
Pranie
Pranit
Prasad
Prashanth
Prashaun
Prasun
Prathon
Pratik
Praveen
Pravin
Pream
Preben
Preciliano
Precious
Preet
Preetinder
Preetpaul
Pregash
Prem
Prence
Prenceton
Prentice
Prentis
Prerak
Prescott
Presley
Presmir
Pressley
Presten
Prestin

Pretess
Pretice
Pretiss
Previn
Price
Prientkes
Priest
Prilippe
Primo Joseph
Prince Earl
Prince Malachi
Prince Zihar
Princeston
Princeto
Princeton
Princton
Pringle
Printis
Priscilla
Pritesh
Pritpal
Pritpaul
Priyeshkumar
Prnell
Procter
Proctor
Promarty
Promise
Prophet
Prosper
Prudencio
Pruvis
Punkaj
Purav
Purdal
Purnajyoti
Purnell
Putheara

Q

Qadeer
Qadir
Qahir
Qais
Qaisir
Qasim
Qeuntin
Qourtise
Quac
Quadarius
Quadaryl
Quade
Quadeer
Quadell
Quadiem
Quadir
Qualen
Qualin
Quallan
Quame
Quamon
Quan
Quandale
Quanell
Quang
Quanta
Quantas
Quantavi
Quantay
Quantea
Quantelle
Quantez
Quantin
Quantrell
Quaron
Quarry
Quartez
Quasar
Quashawn
Quasim-Ashon
Quaterius
Quave
Quavel
Quavius
Quay
Quay-Jibri
Quddus
Qué
Queira
Quendell
Quenell
Queniton
Quensel
Quenten
Quentez
Quenton
Quentrel
Quenzell
Quest
Questly
Qui
Quiante
Quias
Quicy
Quientin
Quienton
Quillan
Quillon
Quin
Quinard
Quincel
Quincey
Quindale
Quindell
Quinderro
Quinen
Quinica
Quinin
Quinlan
Quinnaland
Quinndale
Quinnell
Quinneton
Quinntal
Quinshun
Quintae
Quintan
Quintann
Quintarious
Quintarius
Quintarvis
Quintavis
Quintel
Quinten
Quintezz
Quintillns
Quintintarell
Quinto
Quintrell
Quinzel
Quinzell
Quion
Quiquin
Quirion
Quise
Quiten
Quitin
Quitman
Qujuan
Quntan
Quntion
Quoc
Quoc-Thanh
Quoc-Trung
Quoc-Vi

Quoc-Viet
Quocdat
Quocthang
Quontez
Quran
Quy
Qwai
Qwenton

R

R B
R.
Ra
Rámond
Ra-Heim
Raad
Raaj
Raashad
Rabah
Rabb
Rabeh
Rabiah
Rabih
Raboham
Rabon
Racarrdo
Race
Racel
Rachad
Rachael
Rachamim
Rachard
Rachaude
Rachel
Rachelle
Rachman
Rachmiel
Radames
Radd
Radell
Radey
Radley
Raed
Raeed
Raegen
Raemond
Raena
Raesean
Raeshad
Rafael Arm
Rafal
Rafaw
Rafe
Rafeal
Rafeé
Rafeeq
Raffael
Raffaele
Raffeal
Rafferty
Raffi
Raffington
Rafi
Rafic
Rafig
Rafiq
Rafique
Rafiqul
Ragen
Raghu
Rahakeem
Raham
Rahdee
Rahdeen
Rahdim
Raheel
Raheen
Raheene
Raheim
Raheman
Rahgnar
Rahiem
Rahiim
Rahin
Rahine
Rahman
Rahmar
Rahmatt
Rahme
Rahmek
Rahmi
Rahmier
Rahmil
Rahmuhl
Rahn
Rahsaan
Rahsaannye Jorda
Rahsan
Rahshad-Sabri
Rahtez
Rahuan
Rai
Raiden
Raihan
Raikang
Raimon
Raimond
Raimonds
Raina
Rainbow
Raine
Rainell
Rainer
Rainey
Rainor
Rainy
Raishard
Raishawn
Raj
Raj Kumar
Raja
Rajae
Rajah
Rajan
Rajarshi
Rajat
Rajbir
Rajdeep
Rajeev
Rajesh
Rajiv
Rajkumar
Rajneel
Rajneesh
Rajohn
Rajon
Rajpal
Rajpreet
Rajsingh
Rajveer
Rajvinder
Rajvir
Rajwinder
Rakan
Rakeem
Rakeen
Rakesh
Rakim
Raleem
Raleigh
Ralex
Ralph-Anthony
Ralphael

Ralphel
Ralston
Ram
Rama
Ramadan
Raman
Ramanan
Ramandeep
Ramanjit
Ramanjot
Ramanus
Ramard
Ramash
Ramblyn
Rambo
Rame
Ramel
Ramell
Rameriz
Ramesh
Ramey
Ramez
Ramfis
Rami
Ramie
Ramieq
Ramil
Ramin
Raminder
Ramirez
Ramiro
Ramneek
Ramneet
Ramo'n
Ramond
Ramone
Ramonte
Ramos
Ramsay
Ramson
Ramuela
Ramy
Ramzee
Ramzey
Ramzi
Ramzy
Ran
Rana
Ranald
Ranard
Ranbir
Rance
Rances
Rand
Randale
Randan
Randdy
Rande
Randeep
Randel
Randelle
Randen
Randi
Randie
Randle
Randol
Randolf
Randolph Jr
Randolth
Random
Randon
Randy Jo
Randy Lanc
Raneir
Ranell
Ranen
Ranferi
Rangle
Rangvald
Ranie
Ranil
Ranique
Ranjeet
Ranjit
Ranjodh
Rankin
Ranndi
Ranolf
Ranon
Ransalear
Ransom
Ranson
Ranulfo
Raol
Raoul
Raphaèl
Raphale
Rapheal
Raphel
Raphese
Raque
Raquib
Rarzell
Ras
Rasaaha
Rasan
Rasand
Rascell
Raschid
Rasem
Rashaadkhimbrel
Rashaan
Rashae
Rashald
Rashan
Rashand
Rashane
Rashann
Rashard
Rashaud
Rashaude
Rashaun
Rashaw
Rashawd
Rashean
Rashede
Rashee
Rasheed
Rasheem
Rasheena
Rasheiem
Rasheme
Rashi
Rashid
Rashidah
Rashied
Rashieda
Rashield
Rashien
Rashiene
Rashif
Rashim
Rashin
Rashod
Rashoda
Rashodd
Rashon
Rashpal
Rashun
Rask
Rasmeybo
Rasmi
Rason
Rasool
Rasson
Rast

Rasul
Ratana
Ratanak
Ratha
Rathana
Rathanak
Rathmany
Rathmony
Rattandeep
Raudel
Rauis
Rauje
Raulin
Raumon
Raun
Raushaid
Raushawn
Rauwshan
Ravdeep
Ravdep
Ravel
Raven
Ravenell
Ravijot
Ravin
Ravinder
Ravindra
Ravneet
Ravon
Ravone
Ravy
Rawle
Rawleigh
Rawley
Rawlin
Rawlins
Rawn
Ray Ii
Ray-Shawn
Rayan
Rayaz
Rayburn
Raychard
Rayco
Raydell
Rayen
Rayfield
Rayford
Rayfus
Rayhan
Rayjon
Raylan
Raylin
Raylon
Rayman
Raymand
Raymaur
Rayment
Raymody
Raymon
Raymond Jr
Raymond'
Raymond-Andrew
Raymondo
Raymone
Raymont
Raymund
Raymundo
Rayn
Raynal
Raynald
Raynaldo
Raynanza
Raynault
Rayne
Raynel
Raynell
Raynold
Raynon
Raynor
Raynord
Rayon
Rayray
Rayshaan
Rayshan
Rayshaun
Rayshawn
Raysheen
Rayshod
Rayshon
Rayshone
Rayshun
Rayshunn
Rayuan
Rayvon
Rayyan
Raza
Raziq
Razmig
Razzi
Rc
Re Shawn
Reaad
Read
Reade
Reaford
Reagan
Real
Reamonn
Reauxdell
Rebecca
Recardo
Recaro
Recha
Recil
Reckie
Reco
Redale
Redden
Redginald
Redmen
Redmond
Redner
Redzep
Ree
Reede
Reegan
Rees
Reeve
Reeves
Refah
Regene
Reggiena
Regiel
Regina
Reginaldo
Reginale
Reginel
Regino
Reglo
Regus
Rehan
Rehman
Reice
Reidar
Reide
Reidmichael
Reif
Reijo
Reik
Reilley
Reilly
Reily
Reimar
Reimond

Reimundo
Rein
Reinald
Reine
Reiner
Reinhart
Reinold
Reishard
Rejean
Réjean
Rekenson
Relandof
Rema
Remario
Remark
Remaro
Remberto
Remeie
Remel
Remingto
Remington
Remington Pierce
Remmie
Remo
Remone
Remus
Remy
Rémy
Remzy
Ren
Rena
Renae
Renal
Renald
Renaldi
Renaldo
Renale
Renan
Renard
Renardo
Renarld
Renato
Renaud
Renauld
Renauldo
Renault
Rendell
Rendle
Rendon
René
Rene Calvin
René-Pier
Rene-Charles
Renee
Renée-Claude
Renel
Renell
Renho
Renier
Renique
Renn
Renny
Reno
Renos
Renould
Renten
Renwick
Renwrick
Renzo
Reo
Reon
Reonal
Rephael
Rernard
Resford
Reshad
Reshade
Reshah
Reshard
Resharrd
Reshat
Reshaud
Reshaun
Reshaw
Reshawn
Reshay
Resheen
Reshey
Resmay
Restar
Resty
Reto
Reuban
Reuben-J
Reubin
Reuel
Reuven
Revelle
Reven
Revenel
Revie
Revis
Rexford
Rexie
Rexton
Rey
Rey Richar
Reyad
Reyes
Reylius
Reymon
Reymundo
Reyn
Reynald
Reynaldo
Reynard
Reynardo
Reynier
Reynol
Reynold
Reynolds
Reyshun
Reyzander
Reza
Rhachad
Rhadshee
Rhafieque
Rhamases
Rhameek
Rhandi
Rhashan
Rhashaun
Rhasod
Rheal
Rhemone
Rhen
Rheubin
Rhian
Rhoads
Rhoan
Rhoderick
Rhodes
Rhodney
Rhomdyl
Rhomias
Rhon
Rhondall
Rhondell
Rhone
Rhyan
Rhydon
Rhymil
Rhyn
Rhys Neven
Ria-Shine

Riad
Riaz
Ric
Rica
Ricado
Ricahrd
Ricaldo
Ricardos
Ricat
Ricca
Ricci
Ricco
Rich
Richalson
Richar
Richard Edward
Richard James
Richard Joseph
Richard Ma
Richard-Alexander
Richard-Mitchell
Richardangelo
Richardo
Richardson
Richenord
Richer
Richerd
Richey
Richie
Richman
Richmon
Richmond
Richshard
Richy
Rick Vincent
Ricke
Rickele
Rickenson
Ricki
Rickinder
Rickney
Ricks
Ricky Raha
Rickylee
Riclais
Rico Demetrius
Ricy
Rider
Ridge
Ridgy
Ried
Rieke
Riel
Rielly
Riess
Rigbert
Rigel
Rigo
Rigoberto
Rik
Rikesh
Riki
Rikinder
Rikki
Riko
Rileigh
Riley Clayton
Rilley
Rilly Ray
Rilye
Rim
Rinald
Rinaldo
Rinesh
Ringo
Rino
Rio
Rion
Riorgan
Riscardo
Rishaad
Rishaal
Rishad
Rishan
Rishard
Rishaun
Rishawn
Rishi
Risson
Risto
Ritalanda
Ritash
Ritch
Ritchard
Ritchie
Riteau
Ritesh
Rith
Rito
Rittner
Riyad
Riyaz
Riyazmohammad
Rj
Rmar
Ro'tez
Roan
Roary
Rob
Robae
Robart
Robb
Robben
Robbert
Robbi
Robbin
Robe
Robel
Roben
Robenson
Roberd
Robert A
Robert Douglas
Robert Eldon
Robert Jr
Robert Lee
Robert Mifchael
Robert Octavia
Robert Paul
Robert Quinton
Robert Ray
Robert Tho
Robert Tyson
Robert-Andre
Robert-Gerard
Robert-James
Robert-Lee
Robert-Richard
Robert-William
Roberto-Nicola
Robertson
Robertwillia
Robhy
Robiard
Robie
Robin John
Robinder
Robinjeet
Robinn
Robins
Robinson
Robson
Robude
Roby
Robyn

Rocco-Nicholas
Rocedric
Roch
Rochana
Rochenel
Rock
Rockencherry
Rockford
Rockie
Rockland
Rockle
Rocklege
Rockne
Rockwell
Rocrast
Rod
Rodapheny
Rodd
Roddrae
Roddrick
Roddy
Rodelin
Rodell
Roderic
Roderik
Rodgers
Rodgrick
Rodgy
Rodlet
Rodlin
Rodman
Rodmond
Rodnell
Rodney Wittingto
Rodni
Rodnie
Rodnne
Rodrequius
Rodrequois
Rodrey
Rodric
Rodrickie
Rodride
Rodrigue
Rodriguez
Rodrikos
Rodriquez
Rodrrick
Rodrugue
Rodshawn
Rodtana
Rodulfo
Rodverl
Rody
Roel
Rogan
Rogdry
Rogel
Rogelio
Rogerck
Rogerick
Rogerio
Rogerlio
Rogers
Rogzel
Rohan
Rohin
Rohit
Roi
Roja
Rojarick
Rojay
Rojelio
Rokellekashayne
Rokerry
Roko
Rokus
Rolan
Rolanda
Rolando Ii
Rolf
Rolfe
Rolin
Rolito
Rolkes
Rolland
Rollin
Rolly
Rolvestre
Rolvin
Roma
Romain
Romalice
Romando
Romane
Romano
Romar
Rome
Romeash
Romel
Romell
Romenzo
Romeo
Roméo
Romeo Edward
Romer
Romero
Romido Rodrigo
Rominder
Romis
Romke
Romman
Rommel
Rommie
Rommy
Romney
Romolo
Romond
Romone
Romoney
Romono
Romulo
Romulus
Romy
Ronak
Ronal
Ronald-Rasheed
Ronaldo
Ronale
Ronan
Ronanthony
Ronard
Ronathan
Rondale
Rondall
Rondeal
Rondell
Ronderick
Rondey
Rondie
Rondrell
Rondretti
Rondric
Rondrick
Rondriquez
Rondy
Roneet
Roneil
Ronel
Ronell
Ronelle
Ronere
Ronerick
Roni
Ronie

Ronier
Ronjon
Ronjot
Ronkino
Ronn
Ronnel
Ronnell
Ronney
Ronnold
Ronrico
Ronshea
Ronshon
Ronson
Rontae
Rontarius
Ronte
Ronté
Ronterius
Ronterryeous
Rontez
Rontravis
Rony
Ronyell
Ronza
Ronzial
Roodney
Rooney
Roongrote
Rooseveth
Roosman
Roqklynn
Roque
Rorey
Rorny
Rorric
Rorthana
Roryon
Rorysford
Rosalio
Rosando
Rosario
Rosby
Roschoe
Rosendo
Rosevelt
Roshad
Roshan
Roshankumar
Roshanty
Roshard
Roshawn
Roshay
Roshe
Rosheen
Roshene
Rosland
Rosman
Rosny
Rosolino
Rossco
Rossell
Rossi
Rossia
Rossington
Rosston
Rosten
Rostin
Roston
Rosvel
Rosze
Roszell
Rotario
Rotem
Rothana
Rotimi
Rouba
Roudoloshire
Roudy
Roue
Rourke
Rovinder
Rovon
Rowan
Rowdey
Rowdy
Rowe
Rowell
Rowen
Rowland
Roxas
Roxy
Roy Cordell
Roy Joseph
Royace
Royal
Royale
Royd
Roydell
Royden
Royjoe
Roylee
Roylin
Roylonn
Royse
Royston
Roytavis
Rsiryjah
Ru
Ruan
Ruari
Ruary
Rubens
Rubenson
Rubin
Ruby
Rubyia
Rucel
Ruddie
Ruddledge
Ruddy
Rudelle
Rudi
Rudolf
Rudolphus
Rudra
Rudy Izhar
Rudyard
Rueal
Rueben
Ruedi
Ruel
Rueshea
Ruffis
Rufino
Rui
Ruland
Rulon
Rulx
Rumaan
Rumaldo
Rumenique
Rundeep
Ruodrik
Ruolz
Rupayan
Rupert
Ruperth
Ruperto
Rupinder
Rurik
Rusfleu
Rush
Rushi
Rushil
Russ
Russelle

Rustin
Rustom
Ruston
Rustyn
Ruth
Ruwan
Ruy
Ry
Ryal
Ryan Christopher
Ryan Craig
Ryan Jay
Ryan Kirk
Ryan-Allen
Ryan-Blair
Ryan-James
Ryane
Ryanjit
Ryann
Rychard
Rydel
Rydell
Ryder
Rye
Ryedrekis
Ryel
Ryen
Ryin
Ryjean
Ryke
Rykeith
Ryker
Rykk
Ryland
Rylar
Rylee
Ryley
Rylie
Rylin
Rylund
Ryman
Rymeik
Ryna
Ryne Joseph
Ryo
Ryoh
Ryon
Ryosuke
Ryota
Ryotaro
Ryshawn
Rysheed
Ryson
Ryuan
Ryun

S

Sa Sha Ron
Saad
Saadiq
Saagar
Saager
Saahil
Saaidullah
Saamy
Saaron
Saba
Sabas
Sabastian
Sabastien
Sabatino
Saben
Saber
Sabin
Sabino
Sabir
Sabre
Sabrea
Sabree
Sabron
Sacha
Sachin
Sackim
Sadale
Sadarius
Sadat
Sadayo
Sade
Sadela
Sadem
Saderick
Sadiq
Sadique
Sadrarick
Sae
Saeed
Saeed-Joe
Saehirk
Sael
Safa
Safraz
Sagar
Sage
Sagrado
Sahand
Sahba
Sahel
Sahil
Sahir
Sahle
Sahmaun
Saia
Said
Saied
Saif
Saige
Saimon
Sainsmy
Saintales
Saintfluer
Sajid
Sajjad
Sajmir
Sakal
Sakkuna
Sakorey
Saksinnarung
Sal
Salaahud
Saladeen
Salah
Salah-Eldeen
Salahadeen
Salahudin
Salaim
Salamonie
Salar
Salazar
Saleem
Saleh
Salem
Salil
Salim
Salio
Saliym
Salmaine
Salman
Salmino
Salomon
Salvadore
Salvator
Samael
Saman

Samanth
Samantha
Samanthony
Samar
Samath
Samauel
Samaul
Sambath
Sambo
Sambok
Samedy
Sameeh
Sameer
Sameh
Samer
Sametrius
Sameul
Samey
Samho
Sami
Samie
Samiel
Samier
Samil
Saminder
Saminderjit
Samiron
Samit
Samiuela
Sammail
Sammee
Sammie
Sammuel
Samnang
Samnoeun
Samoadarries
Samone
Samora
Sampath
Sampher
Sampson
Samroeun
Samual
Samuel Jr
Samuel-James
Samuela
Samule
Samwise
Samy
San
Sanak
Sanchaz
Sanchez
Sand
Sandan
Sander
Sanders
Sandev
Sandip
Sandonnie
Sandor
Sandra
Sandro
Sandro-Xavier
Sands
Sandu
Sanford
Sang
Sangeet
Sanjan
Sanjay
Sanjeet
Sanjeev
Sanjiv
Sankalp
Sankendrik
Sankesh
Sanna
Sanson
Santana
Santanna
Sante
Santelle
Santinne
Santino
Santo
Santokh
Santon
Santonio
Santos
Santosh
Sao
Sapan
Saqib
Saquan
Sara
Sarah
Sarantos
Sarath
Saravanan
Saravong
Sareivudh
Saren
Sarfaraz
Sarhadon
Sarhan
Sarit
Sarith
Sarkis
Saro
Saroeum
Saroeuth
Saronda
Sarron
Sartaj
Sarvjit
Sascha
Saschel
Sat
Satchel
Sateki
Satharit
Sathavaram
Sathea
Sathya
Satinder
Satish
Satnam
Satoeun
Satori
Satoru
Satoshi
Satsantokh
Satveer
Satvinder
Satvir
Satyan
Saud
Saulmon
Saulo
Saum
Saumel
Saumya
Saundro
Saurabh
Saurav
Saurod
Sausha
Sauveur
Savas
Saverio
Saverla
Savier
Savikar
Savin
Savinien

Savino
Savius
Savoeun
Savory
Savoth
Savouth
Savvas
Sawn
Sawyer
Saxon
Sayd
Saye
Sayed
Sayid
Sayjel
Sayre
Sayres
Sayyad
Sayyed
Schaan
Schadrac
Schaefer
Schaffer
Schaun
Schayler
Scheinderley
Schelvin
Schemel
Schneider
Schneur
Schnieder
Schylar
Schyler
Scobie
Scorpeo
Scorpio
Scotie
Scottey
Scotti
Scottie
Scottland
Scotty-James
Scoye
Scy
Scye
Se
Sea-yeen
Seabury
Seagle
Seah
S'ean
Sean Anthony
Sean Christopher
Sean Conway
Sean Micha
Sean Michael
Sean Pierre
Sean-Arthur
Sean-Francois
Sean-Michael
Sean-Pat
Sean-Patrick
Sean-Paul
Sean-Thomas
Seandell
Seandor
Seane
Seann
Seantez
Seanthan
Seanvon
Searle
Seaver
Sebasiano
Sebastia
Sebastian-Edward
Sebastian-Robert
Sebastiano
Sebastien-Georges
Sebastin
Sebastion
Sebbie
Sebon
Sebring
Secil
Secondino
Sedad
Sedale
Seddon
Seddrick
Sedecki
Sedell
Sederick
Sedney
Sedric
Sedrick
See
Sefesi
Sefton
Segen
Sei
Seibie
Seif
Seifuddin
Seika
Seina
Seira
Seivlye
Sejdalija
Sekel
Sekiyo
Selah
Selcres
Selden
Seldon
Selford
Selim
Selley
Selmar
Selwyn
Semaj
Semerrill
Semi
Semil
Semisi
Sen
Senay
Seneca
Sengming
Senh
Sennin
Senopha
Sentalle
Sentrell
Seon
Seong
Seong-Soo
Sepasetiano
Sepehr
Sequin
Serafim
Serafin
Seraphin
Sereno
Sergei
Serginio
Sergio Matthew
Sergion
Serigo
Serjio
Servando
Sesar
Set

Sethan
Sethe
Setriakor
Settimio
Seumas
Seung
Seung-yule
Sevag
Seve
Sevé
Severan
Severian
Severiano
Severin
Severn
Severo
Sevien
Seville
Sevric
Sevrin
Seyed
Seyed-Amir
Seyed-Hossai
Seymour
Seza
Sh-Ron
Shaadi
Shaan
Shabazz
Shabir
Shacore
Shadd
Shaddon
Shaddy
Shade
Shadee
Shadeed
Shaden
Shadey
Shadi
Shadie
Shadrach
Shadrack
Shadrick
Shadron
Shadwick
Shady
Shae
Shael
Shafaet
Shafarr
Shafeth
Shaffer
Shafik
Shafin
Shah
Shahab
Shahaboddine
Shaharul
Shahe
Shahee
Shaheed
Shaheen
Shahif
Shahin
Shahir
Shahmir
Shahrokh
Shahryar
Shahzad
Shai
Shaikan
Shain
Shaine
Shakee
Shakir
Shakoor
Shalal
Shalamar
Shalin
Shallman
Shallon
Shalom
Shalon
Shalor
Shamaia
Shamaine
Shaman
Shamar
Shamari
Shamario
Shamarr
Shamarra
Shamaul
Shameer
Shamel
Shamell
Shamez
Shamik
Shamine
Shamir
Shamit
Shammarr
Shamon
Shamone
Shamontate
Shamorcus
Shamowl
Shamsuddin
Shamus
Shamyr
Shan
Shana
Shanae
Shanard
Shanawaz
Shandon
Shandore
Shandro
Shandy
Shane-Alan
Shane-Andrew
Shang
Shang-Lun
Shani
Shanil
Shanilde
Shankar
Shanler
Shannan
Shannen
Shannen-Doh
Shanon
Shant
Shantae
Shantanu
Shantelle
Shanti
Shantie
Shanton
Shanty
Shaon
Shaphen
Shaquai
Shaquina
Shaquon
Shar-Ron
Sharard
Sharbel
Shard
Sharee
Shareed
Shareef
Shareef-Hakeem
Sharef
Shareff

Shariff
Sharis
Shariyar
Shariyf
Sharlay
Sharlette
Sharmarke
Sharn
Sharoad
Sharod
Sharoddarone
Sharon
Sharone
Sharonn
Sharrod
Sharron
Sharvez
Sharyif
Shatara
Shatravins
Shaughn
Shaun Daniel
Shaun-Louis
Shauna
Shaunavan
Shaundarius
Shaundelle
Shaunden
Shaundre
Shaune
Shauniece
Shaunn
Shauterrious
Shavalis
Shaveen
Shavil
Shavon
Shavonski
Shaw
Shawe
Shawen
Shawlathe
Shawmund
Shawn Mich
Shawn-Matthew
Shawn-Philip
Shawndall
Shawndeep
Shawndell
Shawnden
Shawne
Shawnee
Shawnie
Shawnkarl
Shawnn
Shawnta
Shawntae
Shawntell
Shawnton
Shawon
Shay
Shayan
Shaye
Shayland
Shaylen
Shaylon
Shayn
Shaynan
Shaynen
Shayon
Shdell
She-Ming
Shea-Andre
Sheaha
Shean
Shederick
Shedrach
Shedrick
Sheehan
Sheen-yeong
Sheeraz
Shehab
Shehmir
Shehram
Shehzad
Sheiban
Sheiff
Sheik
Sheila
Shekhar
Shelbre
Shelden
Sheldon-Abraham
Sheldonn
Sheldron
Shelley
Shellton
Shelte
Shelton
Shelvin
Shelvis
Shemaiah
Shemiah
Shenard
Sherad
Sheradon
Sherard
Sheraz
Sheream
Sherebiah
Shereif
Sherette
Sheri
Sheridan
Sherief
Sherif
Sheriff
Sheriffolawale
Sherley
Sherlon
Shermahri
Shermaine
Shermarl
Sherod
Sheroidrahsaan
Sherome
Sherone
Sherperd
Sherrad
Sherrard
Sherrard Jermell
Sherriff
Sherrita
Sherrod
Sherrodd
Shervin
Sherwaine
Sherwin
Sheumais
Sheungfai
Shevon
Shey
Sheyland
Shezad
Shi
Shigemitsu
Shihab
Shikeith
Shilan
Shiley
Shilif
Shilo
Shiloh
Shilom
Shimicheal

Shimon
Shimshon
Shin
Shing
Shingai
Shingo
Shiran
Shiraz
Shiree
Shirel
Shiron
Shirrell
Shiu
Shiv
Shiva
Shivan
Shiy
Shkeel
Shlomo
Shminder
Shmuel
Shneiur
Shneur
Sho
Shodd
Shoeb
Shomar
Shomari
Shomberg
Shon
Shondale
Shondel
Shonntay
Shontae
Shontarious
Shorey
Shorikus
Shouan
Shougo
Shouhei
Shoun
Shreyes
Shridhar
Shripal
Shuhei
Shumacher
Shumann
Shundell
Shungu
Shurajit
Shvawn
Shwan
Shy
Shyam
Shyhem
Shykee
Shykeem
Shyle
Shylor
Shymar
Shyree
Shytwin
Si
Siam
Siamak
Sian
Sias
Sibre
Sid
Sida
Siddell
Siddhant
Siddik
Siddiq
Sidey
Sidharth
Sidhartha
Sidhdharth
Sidney-James
Siek
Siera
Sierra
Sigfredo
Sigifred
Sigmund
Sigurdor
Sijin
Sikander
Sikel
Silias
Silis
Silne
Silvain
Silvan
Silvanus
Silverio
Silvestr
Silvio
Sim
Simbat
Simcha
Simerdeep
Simmeion
Simmie
Simmon
Simon-Alexandre
Simon-Andre
Simon-Mieczyslaw
Simon-Olivier
Simon-Pierre
Simonas
Simone
Simran
Simranjit
Simranpal
Simren
Simuel
Simyon
Sin
Sina
Sinan
Sinclair
Sindley
Singh
Singleton
Sinisa
Sinny
Sinuhe
Siona
Sione
Sioneone
Siosiua
Sir
Sir Brock
Sir Dwayne
Sir Francis
Sir George
Sir Juan
Sir William
Sir-Jonathan
Siraaj
Sirage
Siraj
Sirajaldin
Sirak
Siranthony
Sirish
Sirnard
Sirpatrick
Sirten
Sirvalier Joaqui
Sishir
Sitar
Sittiphong

Siu
Siva
Siville
Sixtus
Siyavash
Sjohn
Sjon
Skeeter
Ski
Skiffington
Skip
Skipper
Sky
Sky Lee
Skye
Skyelar
Skyeler
Skyhawk
Skylee
Skylor
Skylour
Slade
Slan
Slater
Sloan
Sloane
Slobodan-John
Smith
Snary
Snider
Snowden
So Phha Ry
Soakai
Soane
Sochan
Socorro
Soctt
Soda
Sodrel
Soeum
Sohaib
Sohail
Sohan
Sohayl
Soheib
Soja
Sokbunara
Sokcheata
Sokha
Sokhar
Sokhen
Sokhon
Sokleng
Sokpath
Sokratis
Sokty
Sol
Solahudeen
Solim
Soll
Solmon
Soloman
Somaark
Somali
Somchai
Someari
Sommoeun
Somnang
Son
Sona
Sonam
Sonawahese
Sonel
Sonephet
Song
Sonlam
Sonnel
Sonnie
Sonvi
Sony
Soo
Soo-Hon
Soon
Sophana
Sophane
Sophanna
Sophax
Sophay
Sopheak
Sopheakdara
Sopheap
Sophen
Sophia
Sophol-Song
Sophon
Sorann
Sorel
Soren
Sorie Anthony
Sorin
Sornara
Sorrell
Sosito
Soteer
Sotero
Sothana
Sothea
Sotirios
Sotiris
Sotorios
Souhail
Soukthiran
Souleh
Souren
Souriya
Sousakhone
Souvanh
Sovaland
Sovanda
Sovann
Sovanna
Sovannara
Soventin
Sovida
Sovuth
Sowande
Soweto
Spanish
Spanser
Sparkie
Spence
Spencre
Spero
Spiridon
Spiros
Sprague
Spyros
Srec'ko
Srinivas
Srinivasa
Stabler
Stachel
Stacius
Stafford
Stafford-Roy
Stamatis
Stan
Stancy
Standley
Stanford
Stanislas
Stanivan
Stanleydesousa
Stanly
Stann
Stanphanie

Stanson
Stantell
Stanton
Staphano
Star
Star Light
Starbuck
Staret
Starlevon
Starling
Starlon
Starwin
Stas
Stasiu
Stathis
Stavan
Stavise
Stavros
Steave
Steavon
Stebenson
Stedman
Steech
Steed
Steel
Steele
Steeve
Steeven
Stefane
Stefanos
Stefanson
Stefaun
Stefawn
Stefen
Steffan
Steffin
Steffon
Stefford
Stefin
Stefon
Stefone
Stein
Steiner
Steiven
Stelio
Stelios
Stellan
Stellard
Stelth
Stem
Sten
Stendley
Stenvens
Stepfon
Stephan-Alfred
Stephan-Andrew
Stephanas
Stéphane
Stephane-Laurent
Stephane-Rodol
Stephanie
Stephano
Stephanos
Stephen Derek
Stephen Joseph
Stephen Laurent
Stephen Paul
Stepheno
Stephens
Stephenson
Stephfan
Stephin
Stephone
Stepven
Stepven-Thong
Stergos
Sterle
Sterling James
Sterlyn
Steryling
Steth
Stetsen
Stetson
Stevan
Stevario
Stevean
Stevem
Steven Andrew
Steven-Christopher
Steven-Jeffrey
Steven-Michael
Steven-Paul
Steven-Robert
Stevenarc
Stevenle
Stevens
Stevens Ru
Stevenson
Stevie Lee
Stevin
Stevn
Stevon
Steward
Sthephane
Sthervinson
Stielf
Stig
Stile
Stilianos
Stimson
Stipan
Stirley
Stirling
Stiven
Stjepan
Stjepan-Steve
Stoddard
Stokely
Stokes
Stone
Stoney
Stony
Storm
Stormi
Stormy
Story
Strahan
Stratton
Stravious
String
Struggler
Stryker
Sttolkin
Stuarrt
Sturgis
Su
Subhir
Subin
Sudeep
Sue
Suette
Sufyaan
Sufyan
Sugmad
Sugunan
Suguru
Suhail
Sujal
Sukh
Sukha
Sukhbir
Sukhdeep
Sukhjit
Sukhmander

Sukhmeet
Sukhprit
Sukhraj
Sukhtej
Sulabm
Sulaiman
Sulaman
Sulaye
Sulaymaan
Sulayman
Suleman
Sullivan
Sultaan
Sultan
Sumaan-Ashraf
Sumeer
Sumeet
Sumesh
Sumir
Sumit
Summet
Summit
Sumner
Sun
Sun-May
Sundip
Suneil
Sung
Sung Kyung
Sungmin
Sunil
Sunish
Sunit
Sunny
Sunra
Sunthara
Suntiara
Sunvir
Suparsh
Suraj
Surbir
Surdarrious
Suresh
Surisack
Surjit
Surush
Susacki
Susan
Susano
Sushant
Suthya
Sutton
Sutyabhushan
Suudimon
Suvit
Suvon
Suzanna
Svarn
Svavar
Svea
Svein
Sven
Swaggart
Swain
Swanson
Sy
Syam
Sycil
Syda
Sydney
Syeed
Syeem
Sykinah
Sylas
Sylvan
Sylvanus
Sylverster
Sylves
Sylvestre
Sylvio
Symon
Symone
Synepherine
Syntyron
Syree
Syriane
Sythan
Szaja
Sze-yu

T

T C
T J
T Jae
T.
T.J.
Ta Von
Taahron
Taari
Taaryon
Taase
Taavo
Taayo
Tab
Tabari
Tabarus
Tabber
Taber
Taber Travis
Tabin
Tabious
Tabitha
Tabor
Taboras
Tabraz
Tabreeze
Tacari
Tacaris
Tacorrick
Tacory
Tacovi
Tacoy
Tadarias
Tadarvis
Tadashi
Tadd
Tadd John
Taddius
Tade
Tadeas
Tadeusz
Tadgeman
Tadious
Taegan
Taen
Taeron
Tafarere
Tafari
Tafarie
Taft
Tafton
Tag
Tage
Taggart
Taggert
Taha
Taharqua
Taheer
Tahir
Tahkai
Tahner
Tahron
Tahsaun
Tahsin

Taifang
Taiki
Taimak
Taimark
Taio
Taion
Taire
Tairus
Taiser
Tait
Taite
Taiwan
Taj
Taj-Michael
Tajeldin
Taji
Tajiddin
Tajinder
Tajuan
Tájuan
Tajudeen
Tajwan
Tak
Takafumi
Takao
Takashi
Takayuki
Takeaki
Takeef
Takeel
Takeyo
Takius
Takuma
Takuto
Tal
Talain
Talbot
Talbott
Talen
Talesun
Talha
Talia
Talib
Talib Din
Talib-Deen
Taliesin
Talimoni
Talin
Tallas
Talley
Tallin
Tallis
Tallon
Talmadge
Talmage
Talmont
Talond
Talwinder
Tam
Tama
Tamaki
Tamal
Tamar
Tamarcus
Tamario
Tamaris
Tamarius
Tamarr
Tamas
Tamauri
Tamekia
Tamer
Tamime
Tamir
Tamisha
Tammer
Tamoi
Tamoor
Tan
Tanar
Tandon
Tandre
Tanella
Tanery
Tanesha
Taneshia
Taniela
Tanika
Tanios
Tanis
Tanislao
Tanjit
Tanna
Tannor
Tanoa
Tanorris
Tanuel
Tanvir
Tanyr
Tanzer
Tanzi
Tao
Tapan
Taquan
Taquarious
Tarance
Taranpal
Taras
Tardkham
Tareck
Tareek
Tareiquis
Tarek
Tarell
Tarelle
Tarence
Tarick
Tarik
Tarius
Tariz
Tarl
Tarndeep
Tarnorris
Taro
Tarold
Taron
Tarone
Taronish
Tarquin
Tarquine
Tarrance
Tarrel
Tarrell
Tarren
Tarrence
Tarreq
Tarri
Tarris
Tarrod
Tarry
Tars
Tarthell
Tarun
Tarvaris
Tarvarres
Tarvis
Tarvon
Tarvoris
Taryl
Taryn
Tasha
Tashambe
Tashee
Tasheed
Tashi
Tashon

Tasmin
Tasmine
Tation
Tatizes
Tatsuki
Tatum
Taubars
Taufik
Tauheen
Tauni
Tauris
Taurmel
Taurus
Taustin
Tavane
Tavar
Tavaras
Tavari
Tavarian
Tavarius
Tavarri
Tavarris
Tavars
Tavarse
Tavarus
Tavden
Taveress
Tavias
Tavier
Tavin
Tavious
Tavis
Tavish
Tavius
Tavon
Tavores
Tavoris
Tavorius
Tavorris
Tavous
Tavuris
Taw
Tawaun
Tawine
Tawn
Tawone
Tawrence
Tay
Tayari
Taygen
Tayler
Taylon
Tayne
Tayon
Tayquere
Tayron
Taywan
Taz
Tazwell
Tc
Teagan
Teague
Teagun
Teair
Teairez
Teak
Teancum
Teandrea
Teanlorg
Tearance
Tearrance
Techalin
Tecko
Tecum
Tedd
Teddie
Teddirk
Tedmund
Tedric
Tedrick
Tedrin
Tedroy
Tedson
Tee
Tee Tee
Teedray
Teedron
Teejay
Teel
Teele
Teemu
Teeton
Teeyon
Tefari
Tegan
Tegrity
Teilo
Teirone
Tej
Tejas
Tejinder
Teko
Telacy
Telem
Telesfor
Tell
Tellan
Telle
Teller
Tellez
Tellis
Telly
Telvin
Telwin
Temarcus
Temez
Temitope
Temmy
Tempest
Tendayi
Tenille
Tenkera
Tennesy
Tenneyson
Tenniel
Tennison
Tennor
Tennyson
Tenorris
Tenqualus
Teodoro
Teon
Teory
Teovaldo
Terail
Teran
Terandel
Terbares
Tercel
Tereance
Tereik
Terel
Terelle
Terez
Teric
Terick
Terin
Terio
Terios
Termaine
Termane
Termayne
Termon
Teron
Terone
Terrace

Terrail
Terrain
Terral
Terrale
Terrall
Terran
Terraye
Terreal
Terrelle
Terren
Terrez
Terri
Terrian
Terrick
Terrie
Terriel
Terriell
Terrik
Terril
Terrill
Terrin
Terrington
Terrious
Terris
Terrod
Terrol
Terron
Terrone
Terry-Michael
Terryl
Terrynce
Terryon
Tersen
Terumi
Tervarius
Terver
Tery
Teryl
Teryn
Tesleem
Tess
Tessa
Tethsia
Tetric
Tevadavid
Tevaris
Tevarus
Tevin
Tevis
Tevita
Tevlin
Tevon
Tevoris
Tewfic
Tex
Texder
Teyler
Teyrnon
Teziatrius
Tezzie
Thaao
Thad
Thaddaeus
Thaddeau
Thaddeaus
Thaddiaus
Thaddius
Thadeaou
Thadeous
Thadeus
Thadieus
Thadious
Thadius
Thadler
Thadus
Thageesan
Thai
Thaidene
Thain
Thaine
Thaiva
Thamar
Thame
Thames
Thamonn
Than
Thanasi
Thanasis
Thane
Thang
Thanh
Thanh-Giau
Thanh-Hai
Thanh-Long
Thanhda
Thanhtrieudavid
Thaniel
Thara
Tharemy
Tharon
Thason
Thatcher
Thaxton
Thayer
Thayne
The
Thea
Theadore
Theapolis
Theara
Thearn
Theary
Thehandre
Theirry
Thekema
Themis
Themistoklis
Themon
Theoardra
Theodin
Theodis
Theodist
Theodon
Theodoor
Theodoric
Theodoro
Theodoros
Theodoulos
Theodric
Theodroe
Theodros
Theoharis
Theoma
Theon
Theophane
Theophelius
Theophile
Theophille
Theophilos
Theophilus
Theopolis
Theory
Theotis
Theran
Theren
Theresa
Therim
Therin
Therman
Therron
Theshan
Thesis
Thesmond
Thessalonians
Thessalonis
Theus

Theyvanderarajah
Thiago
Thien
Thien An
Thien-An
Thierda
Thierry
Thieu
Thilasak
Thimothy
Thinh
Thoeun
Thoi
Thoi-Thien
Thom
Thomas Jam
Thomas Leigh
Thomas-C
Thomas-George
Thomas-Gordon
Thomasjames
Thomes
Thompson
Thomy
Thong
Thony
Thor
Thoralf
Thorian
Thornson
Thornton
Thorsten
Thoryn
Thoun
Thoung
Threece
Thristian
Thriston
Thristov
Thruman
Thuan
Thuan-Tom
Thuong
Thurman
Thurmond
Thurston
Thuy
Thyshawn
Ti
Tiago
Tiano
Tiara
Tiarnan
Tiarrol
Tiaz
Tiberio
Tibius
Tibor
Tiburcio
Tich
Tiddy
Tidora
Tie Rre
Tiebara
Tien
Tier
Tierell
Tierre
Tieruse
Tiesen
Tiffany
Tigh
Tighe
Tigy
Tiheem
Tihsheem
Tijan
Tiji
Tijowaun
Tikki
Tikori
Tikoyo
Tiler
Tillman
Tillmon
Tillous
Tilson
Tilton
Timaris
Timathy
Timekin
Timio
Timithy
Timmathy
Timmie
Timmoty
Timmthy
Timo
Timon
Timonthy
Timote
Timothey
Timothie
Timothy James
Timothy-James
Timothy-John
Timothy-Kwong
Timothy-Matthew
Timothy-Michael
Timur
Tin
Tina
Tinnius
Tino
Tion
Tiplin
Tipton
Tiquan
Tiracuis
Tirard
Tiras
Tirell
Tirqueon
Tirrell
Tishaud
Tisign
Tison
Tiszon
Titas
Titis Chris
Tito
Tivon
Tj
Tjayda
Tmars
To
Toan
Tobby
Tobe
Tobey
Tobi
Tobiah
Tobie
Tobin
Tobyn
Tod
Todd Michael
Todd Rick
Todd Ricks
Toddrell
Toddy
Toinie
Tojyn
Toker
Tolani

Tolis
Tom Jr
Tomah
Tomah-Tahee
Tomais
Tomarkcus
Tomarqus
Tomasz
Tome
Tomer
Tomes
Tomez
Tomi
Tomie
Tomislav
Tomlin
Tommaso
Tommi
Tommie Iii
Tommy "t"
Tomo
Tomod
Tomoki
Tomone
Tomonthy
Tomothie
Tomy
Tomy-Lee
Toney
Tong
Tonga
Toni
Tonio
Tonira
Tonnie
Tonny
Tono
Tony Jay
Tony-Col
Tony-Kit-Wah
Tonyminh
Toon
Top
Tor
Toran
Torance
Toravian
Toray
Torben
Tore
Torean
Toreen
Toreence
Toreey
Torell
Toren
Torey
Torgus
Tori
Torian
Toric
Torieono
Torin
Torisen
Torlf
Tormaigh
Toroice
Torr
Torrance
Torre
Torrean
Torrell
Torren
Torreon
Torres
Torrevio
Torri
Torrian
Torrie
Torrin
Torris
Torry
Torsten
Torvarius
Torynce
Tosh
Toshif
Toshua
Tou
Toufic
Toufie
Tousant
Toussaint
Toven
Tovin
Towan
Towand
Townsend
Townshend
Toy
Toyce
Toze
Tozh
Tra
Trabian
Tracey
Trad
Tradale
Tradarryl
Trae
Traeden
Trahern
Trai
Traivus
Tramaike
Tramain
Tramaine
Tramayne
Tramel
Tramiel
Tramone
Tramontee
Trampes
Tran
Tranard
Trance
Trandle
Trandon
Trang
Trans
Tranterrain
Trapper
Tratavis
Travais
Travale
Travance
Travanti
Travard
Travaress
Travaris
Travarius
Travarus
Travaughn
Travaun
Travelis
Travell
Travelle
Traveous
Traver
Traverez
Travers
Traves
Traveus
Travian
Travice
Travien

Travious
Travis Jabar
Travis John
Travis Terry
Travis-Anthony
Travis-James
Traviss
Travon
Travontae
Travor
Travoris
Travorus
Travus
Tray
Traylin
Traynard
Trayon
Trayshawn
Treat
Treavor
Trebor
Trechard
Tredel
Tredrell
Treigh
Trelaine
Trell
Tremain
Tremell
Tremieko
Tren
Trenard
Trendon
Trendun
Trenedy
Trenis
Trennard
Trentan
Trente
Trenten
Trentin
Trentis
Trenttonio
Treon
Trepper
Tress
Trestan
Treston
Trev
Trevais
Trevan
Trevar
Trevares
Trevaris
Trevarus
Trevaughn
Trevel
Trevell
Trevelle
Treven
Trevian
Trevin
Trevino
Trevis
Trevnor
Trevon
Trevonn
Trevor John
Trevor-Andrew
Trevoris
Trevorus
Trey John
Treymane
Treyonte
Treyson
Treyvor
Tri
Tri Kenny
Trigg
Trimaine
Trimeka
Trinh
Trinh-Hai
Trinidad
Trinidy
Trinition
Trinity
Trintahn
Trinton
Trione
Trisan
Trishawn
Tristan-Elvis
Tristan-Ulric
Tristano
Tristen
Tristian
Tristin
Triston
Tristram
Triz
Trodney
Trofim
Troi
Trokon
Tromaine
Tron
Trong
Tronodd
Troop
Trovis
Troy Alan
Troycie
Troye
Troyrantae
Troyton
Truan
Trueman
Truett
Truitt
Truly
Trumaine
Truman
Trung
Trung-Quoc
Trussler
Trustan
Trustin
Trustrum
Truyen
Tryistan
Trystan
Trysten
Trystian
Tryston
Tschuccarri
Tse-Heng
Tse-Mian
Tsering
Tsomwe
Tsung
Tsvaris
Tu
Tuan-Thach
Tuarence
Tuarus
Tubal
Tuboris
Tucson
Tudor
Tufa
Tufik
Tug
Tukulolo
Tullio
Tulugak

Tumsaa
Tumua
Tunde Ra
Tung
Tung-Jing
Tunou
Tura
Turance
Turboreesee
Tureese
Turell
Turhan
Turi
Turin
Turmel
Turner
Turone
Turquoise
Turrell
Turrind
Turwin
Tushar
Tuvia
Tuyen
Tvanm
Twan
Tway
Twayne
Twuan
Ty Christopher
Ty'juan
Ty-Jorel
Tyaaron
Tyaun
Tyce
Tycel
Tycory
Tydamien
Tydel
Tyee
Tyeis
Tyel
Tyerone
Tyesn
Tyeson
Tyevan
Tyger
Tyhim
Tyjuan
Tyke
Tykeem
Tykwan
Tylan
Tylar
Tyle
Tylee
Tyleigh
Tyler-John
Tyler-Mathew
Tyler-Michael
Tylere
Tylil
Tyller
Tylon
Tylor-John
Tymeik
Tymek
Tymithy
Tymorris
Tymothee
Tymothi
Tymothy
Tynan
Tynario
Tynell
Tyone
Typhil
Tyquan
Tyquann
Tyquis
Tyra
Tyrae
Tyrael
Tyrail
Tyral
Tyrall
Tyran
Tyrane
Tyray
Tyre
Tyrea
Tyreas
Tyrease
Tyrece
Tyreck
Tyreé
Tyreece
Tyreef
Tyreek
Tyreel
Tyreen
Tyreese
Tyreice
Tyreik
Tyrek
Tyreke
Tyrelle
Tyren
Tyrenzo
Tyres
Tyrese
Tyric
Tyrice
Tyriece
Tyriek
Tyrik
Tyrill
Tyrin
Tyriq
Tyrique
Tyriske
Tyrod
Tyrome
Tyrone Jam
Tyrone Jr
Tyrone-Delon
Tyrone-Nigel
Tyroney
Tyronn
Tyronna
Tyronne
Tyroun
Tyrrel
Tyrrell
Tyrren
Tyrus
Tyruss
Tysen
Tyshan
Tyshaun
Tyshawn
Tyshinn
Tyshon
Tysie
Tysne
Tyson-Jamar
Tysone
Tythan
Tytus
Tyus
Tyvarrus
Tywan
Tyward
Tywon
Tywone
Tyyon

Tyzchell
Tze
Tze-yound
Tzvi

U

Ubadah
Ubaldo
Uberto
Uchechukwu
Uddhava
Udell
Udomdej
Uhuru
Ukiah
Ulie
Ulises
Ulishes
Ulric
Ulrich
Ulrick
Ultan
Ulyses
Ulysse
Umar
Umar-Shareef
Umayr
Umberto
Umer
Umut
Unark
Undra
Undrea
Undrially
Unice
Unnamed
Untavius
Uptej
Urayoan
Urban
Urbano
Urbanus
Urell
Uri
Uric
Urie
Uriel
Urijah
Uris
Urocca
Ursus
Urvence
Usama
Usman
Usmanulaziz
Utah
Utal
Uwais
Uwemedimo
Uzair

V

Vac-Wood
Vache
Vachel
Vadim
Vadis
Vahid
Vahndrell
Vai
Vailios
Vair
Vairavamurthy
Vaivelata
Valdemar
Valdez
Valencio
Valenté
Valentin
Valentine
Valentino
Valeriano
Valery
Vallen
Valmiki
Valtez
Valtonio
Vamsi
Vanard
Vanark
Vandad
Vandel
Vaneet
Vanessa
Vang
Vangelis
Vanh
Vanier
Vanjois'
Vann
Vannak
Vannara
Vannarath
Vannarith
Vanness
Vanno
Vanray
Vanross
Vanshawn
Vansky
Vansom
Vante
Vanthoeun
Vantonio
Vantonn
Vantrae
Vantrell
Vantrise
Varant
Varie
Varinder
Varlondea
Varmar
Varnell
Varnoil
Varron
Vartevar
Varun
Vasant
Vaselios
Vashae
Vashan
Vashawn
Vashon
Vasil
Vasile
Vasilije
Vasilios
Vasilis
Vasillios
Vasily
Vasjah
Vasshawn
Vasu
Vatche
Vatelli
Vaughan
Vaun
Vaurus
Vavega
Vayka
Vea

Veairrus
Vecas
Vechethtra
Vedhas
Veeraj
Vegas
Veino
Velai
Veli-Matti
Vellis
Veloy
Velton
Ven
Venancio
Vence
Vencente
Vendell
Venitez
Venkatesan
Venne
Venny
Venton
Verdell
Verdieu
Vereak
Verlin
Verlondon
Vermar
Vermont
Vern
Verna
Vernal
Vernard
Verndell
Vernell
Verner
Vernest
Vernet
Vernie
Vernine
Vernis
Vernol
Vernon Phill
Versharl
Vertice
Vertreees
Vesone
Vexay
Vhohn
Vi
Viaks
Vic
Vicent
Vicheth
Vicken
Vickenson
Vickers
Vickram
Vickramjeet
Vickrum
Vicky
Victa
Victer
Victor Jr
Victoria
Victoriano
Victorin
Vidal
Vidas
Videsh
Vidoje
Viet
Viet-Dung
Vietnam
Vignesh
Vigyan
Vijeshanand
Vikarm
Vikas
Vikram
Vikrant
Vikranth
Vikrum
Viktor
Viktors
Vilaivanh
Vilay
Vilfranc
Viljoen
Ville
Vilma
Vilner
Vimal
Vinay
Vincan
Vincent De Paul
Vincente
Vincentq
Vincenzo-Pasquale
Vincient
Vine
Vineal
Vinh
Vinh-Khang
Vinicio
Vinieth
Vinkevus
Vinnie
Vinnis
Vinoth
Vinson
Viponjit
Virack
Virath
Virel
Viresh
Virgial
Virgilio
Visarion
Visente
Vishaal
Vishal
Vishnuprakash
Vishon
Vishvajit
Vital
Vitor
Vitorio
Vitsanu
Vittal
Vittorio
Vivek
Vivekinan
Vladimire
Vladjimir
Vlair
Voinea
Vojislav
Vojtek
Volan
Volci
Vollie
Volome
Volrick
Voltaire
Von
Vonchae
Vondae
Vondre
Vong
Vonray
Vontago
Vontarius
Vontaviurs
Vontel

Vontess
Vontez
Vonzeal
Vorapon
Voughn
Voung
Vrajesh
Vreeland
Vrej
Vu
Vuk
Vuong
Vuthy
Vy
Vybus
Vyron
Vytas

W

W C
W Md Rayma
W Timothy
Waad
Wabon
Wacey
Wachi
Waco
Wadie
Wadly
Wadner
Wael
Waford
Wagas
Wahab
Waheed
Wahid
Wai
Wai-yan
Waide
Waine
Waisen
Waite
Waitman
Waiton
Waiying
Waiyip
Wajnick
Wake
Wakeem
Wakefield
Walberto
Walcov
Waldale
Waldemar
Walden
Waldermar
Waldo
Waldron
Waldson
Waldy
Waled
Waleed
Wales
Wali
Walid
Walie
Walker
Wallen
Wallen Jr
Wally
Walner
Walnes
Walnick
Walon
Walph
Walsh
Walt
Waltey
Waltoguy
Walton
Waly
Walzer
Wan
Wang-Kei
Wangdu
Wankimson
Wanniver
Wanye
Waqas
Waqass
Ward
Warde
Wardell
Waris
Warith
Warnell
Warner
Warrenson
Wasay
Waseam-Ziad
Waseem
Wasim
Wassillie
Wassim
Wasyl
Wathson
Watson
Waverly
Wayde
Waydell
Wayland
Waylen
Waylin
Wayman
Waymon
Wayne-Paul
Waynell
Waynemond
Wazinberg
Wd
Webb
Webber
Webner
Webster
Wecker
Weedny
Weesam
Wegie
Wei
Weichurn
Weidner
Welch
Weldon
Welfredo
Wellington
Wells
Welton
Wenceslao
Wendale
Wendall
Wendel
Wendy
Wenford
Weng
Wenjye
Wenzel
Wenzell
Werlay
Werner
Wes
Wesam
Weslee
Wesley-Aaron
Wesleyan

Weslie
Wesly
Wesner
Wess
Wessam
Wessex
Wessley
West
Westbrook
Westen
Westin
Westly
Weylin
Whaqui
Whatley
Wheeler
Whiddon
Whit
Whitaker Martin
Whitsome
Whitt
Whittier
Whittney
Whyet
Wick
Widely
Widny
Wiebe
Wifredo
Wil
Wilben
Wilber
Wilbin
Wilbur
Wilburn
Wilburt
Wilcley
Wilcy
Wildalson
Wildy
Wiley
Wilferd
Wilford
Wilfrid
Wilfride
Wilfried
Wilgienson
Wilgims
Wilhelm
Wiliame
Wilkie
Wilkin
Wilkins
Willaim
Willam
Willberto
Wille
Willeam
Willem
Willey
Willi
Willia
William Clarence
William Donald
William Iii
William Jaynes
William Keith
William Richard
William-Jay
William-John
William-Joseph
William-May
William-Samu
Williams
Williamson
Willice
Willie Fred
Willie Jam
Willie Japhus
Willonte
Wills
Willtavious
Willus
Willy
Willyam
Wilman
Wilmer
Wilmer Ole
Wilmont
Wilmot
Wilner
Wilnick
Wilsean
Wilton
Win
Wince
Wincer
Windel
Windell
Winder
Windham
Windsor
Windy
Winfred
Winfried
Wing
Wing-Chiu
Wing-Kit
Winluck
Winslow
Winson
Winter
Winterford
Winton
Winvincent
Wisam
Wiselet
Wisley
Wisner
Wisny
Wison
Witzchok
Wizner
Wlaa
Wladislav
Wladislaw
Wolf
Wolff
Wolfgang
Wolgans
Won
Wonderful
Wonleys
Woo Nam
Wooddy
Woodford
Woodley
Woodriff
Woodrow
Woodsen
Woody
Worrin
Worry
Worsester
Worsley
Worth
Wouter
Wray
Wren
Wriley
Wt
Wulfric
Wunlee
Wydale
Wydeen

Wydell
Wykeim
Wykheem
Wylie
Wyman
Wyndell
Wynn
Wynne
Wynten
Wynton

X

Xaaming
Xackery
Xaiver
Xande
Xanious
Xanivan
Xavian
Xavon
Xedrick
Xerxes
Xevair
Xian
Xivilai
Xizavier
Xochil
Xou
Xren
Xristopher
Xuan
Xuan-Zhan
Xub
Xuong
Xykeva
Xzaiveous
Xzaiver
Xzavaier
Xzaver
Xzavian
Xzavier
Xzavion
Xzerreon

Y

Y'shua
Yaacov
Yaakov
Yacoub-youssef
Yadnoe
Yadrick
Yahmon
Yahya
Yair
Yairon
Yakeen
Yakov
Yale
Yalier
Yamad
Yamael
Yamato
Yamene
Yamil
Yan
Yancey
Yanci
Yancy
Yandel
Yanell
Yang
Yanic
Yanick
Yanik
Yaniv
Yann
Yanni
Yannick
Yanno
Yantley
Yany
Yao
Yaohuy
Yaphet
Yaque
Yarema
Yarmes
Yarnell
Yaron
Yarred
Yarvell
Yaseen
Yaser
Yasha
Yashar
Yashpal
Yashua
Yasin
Yasmanny
Yasnel
Yasser
Yasunori
Yasuyuki
Yaudet
Yavari
Yavel
Yavuz
Yazmany
Ydelio
Ydelso
Yeager
Yechezkel
Yechiel
Yeeleng
Yeghish
Yehuda
Yeimah
Yelemis
Yeng
Yens
Yeoryios
Yerasimos
Yerseth
Yesson
Yeuan
Yeysson
Yhwhyowc
Yi
Yi-Xi
Yick
Yil
Yileng
Yimin
Ying
Yioryo
Yisachar
Yishai
Yisrael
Yisroel
Yitony
Yitzak
Yitzchak
Yitzchok
Yitzhak
Yiu
Yki
Ylallo
Yle
Yoan
Yochanan
Yoefi
Yoehun

Yoel
Yogesh
Yogin
Yohan
Yohance
Yohane
Yohann
Yohannes
Yohn
Yolando
Yom
Yomni
Yonas
Yonatan
Yonathan
Yonaton
Yonattan
Yonel
Yones
Yonesse
Yonito
Yonnik
Yoon-Ho
Yoonjae
Yordan
Yorel
Yorick
York
Yorkie
Yorlan
Yorr
Yosef
Yoseph
Yoshihito
Yoshiki
Yoshiyuki
Yoshua
Yosmani
Yosuel

Yosuke
Yosvany
Youlaine
Young
Youngdawn
Youri
Yousaf
Youseef
Yousef
Yousif
Youssel
Yousuf
Yovani
Yovanny
Yovany
Yoyie
Ysmael
Ysoir
Yu
Yuá-Vtu
Yudavraj
Yue
Yue-Cheng
Yues
Yufes
Yui
Yuil
Yuki
Yul
Yule
Yumonpierre
Yun-Sang
Yun-yue
Yung-Chung
Yupeng
Yuri
Yurij
Yurri
Yury

Yusab
Yusef
Yusnier
Yusuel
Yusuke
Yuta
Yutaka
Yuuki
Yuvraj
Yuzo
Yuzo-John
Yvan
Yvelan
Yvens
Yves-Andreas
Yves-Stephane
Yvon

Z

Zabdiel
Zabem
Zabulan
Zac
Zacaras
Zacariah
Zacarias
Zacarious
Zacary
Zacc
Zaccari
Zaccary
Zacchaeus
Zacchea
Zacchurchalom
Zaccury
Zacerry James
Zach

Zacha
Zachard
Zachare
Zacharey
Zachari
Zacharias
Zacharry
Zacharty-Todd
Zachary Le
Zachaury
Zacherey
Zacheria
Zacheriah
Zacherie
Zacherius
Zachirias
Zachory
Zachre
Zachrey
Zachri
Zachry
Zachury
Zack
Zackari
Zackaria
Zackariah
Zackarie
Zackery Scott
Zackie
Zackorie
Zackory
Zackree
Zackrey
Zackry
Zackterrus
Zacory
Zacyre
Zaden
Zadiel

Zado
Zafar
Zaffar
Zafir
Zafri
Zahair
Zaheed
Zaheer
Zaheeruddin
Zahi
Zahid
Zahir
Zaid
Zain
Zain-Ul
Zaire
Zak
Zakarai
Zakareeyah
Zakari
Zakaria
Zakariya
Zakary
Zake
Zakery
Zaki
Zakir
Zakkai
Zakqary
Zakree
Zakri
Zakry
Zamal
Zaman
Zameer
Zamin
Zamir
Zan
Zandrae
Zandy
Zani
Zanross
Zantavius
Zaquan
Zarick
Zarif
Zarin
Zarkeus
Zarley
Zaronn
Zarrick
Zarry
Zasim
Zataurean
Zaveion
Zaven
Zavian
Zavier
Zavin
Zavior
Zaybien
Zayne
Zayviyus
Zbar
Zeb
Zebadee
Zebadiah
Zebedee
Zebediah
Zebulen
Zebulon
Zebulun
Zebulyn
Zecharia
Zed
Zedekiah
Zedidiah
Zedrick
Zeem
Zeeshan
Zeevy
Zeferino
Zeffrey
Zeggeree
Zehann
Zeke
Zeljko
Zello
Zelmay
Zelos
Zemarr
Zemiley
Zen
Zenan
Zenas
Zengani
Zennen
Zennon
Zeno
Zenon
Zentil
Zenus
Zenzo
Zephan
Zephania
Zephaniah
Zephram
Zephran
Zeppelin
Zeren
Zerius
Zerrick
Zeshan
Zeshawn
Zeth
Zeth Alan
Zettie
Zettis
Zeus
Zev
Zeyauollah
Zgille
Zhachori
Zhi
Zhi-yang
Zhipeng
Zhivago
Zhoadi
Ziaad
Ziad
Ziare
Zigfrids
Zigmund
Zikee
Zikeem
Zimier
Zino
Zintis
Zion
Zirjan
Zishan
Zissis
Ziyad
Zjarard
Zjok
Zjygk
Znathani
Zodi
Zoel
Zohaib
Zoheb
Zoilo
Zoltan
Zolten
Zoneck
Zoran

Zorian
Zsolt
Zuair
Zuber
Zubin
Zuh-Jyh
Zul
Zulfiqar
Zulfiqar-Ali
Zulhilmi
Zuriel
Zvonimir
Zy
Zyad
Zyan
Zymri
Zytavius

Sources

The compilation of this book was a much larger task than originally anticipated. Thanks to the excellent response of the governments of the states of the United States and provinces of Canada, we received twice as much data as expected. We sincerely thank all these contributors for their help. A detailed list of the sources of information appears below. In all cases, the data used were the most up-to-date available at the time of compilation. Data were made available by the following provinces and states.

United States

Alabama Department of Public Health, Bureau of Vital Statistics, 1986 popular names

Alaska Department of Health and Social Services, Division of Public Health, complete 1986 data

California Department of Health Services, Health Data and Statistics Branch, 1986 top 20 names

Colorado Department of Health, Health Statistics Section, complete 1986 data

Connecticut Department of Health Services, Data Processing, complete 1986 data

Florida Department of Health and Rehabilitative Services, Office of Vital Statistics, complete 1986 data

Georgia Department of Human Resources, Vital Records Services, 1986, 100 most popular names

Idaho Department of Health and Welfare, Division of Health, Biostatistical Services, 1986 popular names

Kentucky Department of Health Services, Office of Vital Statistics, complete 1986 data

Louisiana Department of Health & Human Resources, Vital Records Section, 1986 popular names

Massachusetts Department of Public Health, Division of Health Statistics and Research, complete 1986 data

Missouri Department of Health, State Center for Health Statistics, complete 1986 data

Montana Department of Health and Environmental Sciences, Vital Records and Statistics Bureau, 1986 top 50 names

Nebraska Department of Health, Health Data and Statistical Research, complete 1986 data

New Mexico Vital Statistics Bureau, 1986 top 20 names

New York Department of Health, Office of Public Health, 1986 most popular names

Pennsylvania Department of Health, Division of Health Statistics and Research, (virtually) complete 1986 data

South Dakota Department of Health, Center for Health Policy and Statistics, complete 1986 data

Utah Department of Health, Bureau of Vital Records, complete 1986 data

Vermont Department of Health, Vital Records Section, complete 1986 data

Wisconsin Department of Health and Social Services, Center for Health Statistics and State Registrar of Vital Statistics, 1986 top 50 names

Canada

Alberta Department of Social Services and Community Health, Vital Statistics Branch, complete 1985 data

British Columbia Ministry of Health, Division of Vital Statistics, complete 1986 data

Ontario Ministry of Consumer and Commercial Relations, Office of the Registrar General, complete 1986 data

Saskatchewan Department of Health, Vital Statistics Branch, complete 1986 data

Manitoba Community Services, Vital Statistics, 1986 popular names

New Brunswick Department of Health and Community Services, Vital Statistics, complete 1986 data

Newfoundland Department of Health, Vital Statistics Division, complete 1983 data

The provinces of Nova Scotia, Prince Edward Island and Quebec were willing but unable to supply data at this time.

Bibliography

Ames, Winthrop. *What Shall We Name the Baby?* New York: Pocket Books, 1963.

Bains, Mohinder Singh. Punjabi Language School, Edmonton, Alberta, Canada. Personal correspondence, 1989.

Browder, Sue. *The New Age Baby Name Book.* New York: Workman, 1974.

Dunkling, Leslie Alan. *The Guinness Book of Names.* Guinness, 1986.

Dunkling, Leslie and William Gosling. *The Facts on File Dictionary of First Names.* New York: Facts on File, 1983.

Kolatch, Alfred J. *The Jonathan David Dictionary of First Names.* New York: Penguin Books, 1980.

Kolatch, Alfred J. *Today's Best Baby Names.* New York: Putnam, 1986.

Lansky, Bruce. *The Best Baby Name Book in the Whole Wide World.* Deephaven, Minnesota: Meadowbrook, 1984.

Lawson, Dr. Edwin D. Professor of Psychology, College at Fredonia, State University of New York. Board of Editors, NAMES. Personal correspondence, 1989.

Le, Rev. Thanh Trung. President, Nguon Sang Heritage Language School Association, Edmonton, Alberta, Canada. Personal correspondence, 1989.

McCue, Marion J. *How to Pick the Right Name for Your Baby.* New York: Grosset & Dunlap, 1977.

Sanduga, Dean. Arab Link, Edmonton, Alberta, Canada. Personal correspondence, 1989.

Stewart, George R. *American Given Names.* New York: Oxford, 1979.